THE BLOOD OF HEROES

ALSO BY JAMES DONOVAN

A Terrible Glory:
Custer and the Little Bighorn—the Last Great Battle
of the American West

Custer and the Little Bighorn:
The Man, the Mystery, the Myth

THE BLOOD OF HEROES

The 13-Day Struggle for the Alamo —
and the Sacrifice That Forged a Nation

JAMES DONOVAN

Little, Brown and Company
New York   Boston   London

Little, Brown and Company
Hachette Book Group
237 Park Avenue, New York, NY 10017
www.hachettebookgroup.com

First Edition: May 2012

Little, Brown and Company is a division of Hachette Book Group, Inc., and is celebrating its 175th anniversary in 2012. The Little, Brown name and logo are trademarks of Hachette Book Group, Inc.

The publisher is not responsible for websites (or their content) that are not owned by the publisher.

The Hachette Speakers Bureau provides a wide range of authors for speaking events. To find out more, go to www.hachettespeakers bureau.com or call (866) 376-6591.

Endpaper illustraton by Marty Brazil

Maps by Jeffrey L. Ward

Library of Congress Cataloging-in-Publication Data
Donovan, James
    The blood of heroes : the 13-day struggle for the Alamo—and the sacrifice that forged a nation / James Donovan.—1st ed.
        p. cm.
    Includes bibliographical references and index.
    ISBN 978-0-316-05374-7
    1. Alamo (San Antoneo, Tex.)—Siege, 1836.   I. Title.
    F390.D66 2012
    976.4'03—dc23   2011050067

10 9 8 7 6 5 4 3 2 1

RRD-C

Printed in the United States of America

TO THE MEMORY OF MY FATHER,
JAMES MICHAEL DONOVAN JR. —
HE WAS A GOOD MAN

- TEXAS -
During the Revolution
1835–1836

CHIHUAHUA

Pecos River

Rio Grande

Colorado River

Frio River

Medina River

San Antonio de Béxar

Presidio del Rio Grande
Guerrero

Nueces River

COAHUILA

EL CAMINO REAL

MEXICO

Laredo

TAMAULIPAS

Revilla

Rio Grande

Monclova

Camargo

Reynosa

NUEVO LEÓN

Monterrey

0 Miles   50   100
0 Kilometers   100

Saltillo

© 2012 Jeffrey L. Ward

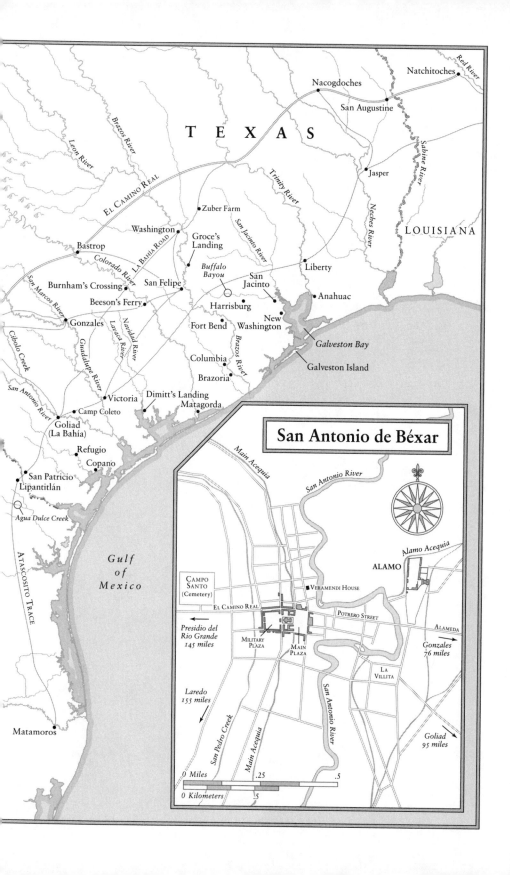

CONTENTS

CONTENTS

THE BLOOD OF HEROES

PROLOGUE

Just past nine o'clock, sometime after darkness had fallen and before the near-full moon rose, a fleet mare slipped out the south gate of the battered old mission. Riding bareback, using only a bridle—every ounce counted now if he was to outrun General Ramírez y Sesma's lancers—the rider leaped over the moat, spurred his horse to a full gallop, leaned low to hug her neck, and held on for dear life as man and mount thundered through the Plaza de Valero amid scattered musket fire, hoofbeats echoing against the fortress walls. He headed southeast, along the San Antonio River, toward Goliad—or Fort Defiance, as Colonel James Fannin had dubbed the presidio there.

Fannin and his four hundred men were at least two full days' ride away. If the colonel could be persuaded to lead his force to Béxar, it might be four or five days before they arrived. That might be too late. But perhaps they were on the march already.

The Mexican army besieging the fort for the past twelve days outnumbered the small garrison ten to one. Their artillery had bombarded the Alamo almost constantly, though not one Texian or Tejano defender had been killed. But around five that afternoon, the earsplitting barrage had stopped.

James Allen's swift horse and his own slight frame had been two important reasons the post commander, Lieutenant Colonel William Barret Travis, had chosen the twenty-one-year-old college student from Missouri to deliver another desperate plea for assistance from the run-down fort.

That Saturday, March 5, 1836, had dawned cool and clear — clear enough to reveal that the Mexican lines surrounding the fortress had moved closer again the previous night, the eleventh since the Texian forces had retreated into the compound at the approach of Santa Anna's army; an artillery battery now stood just two hundred yards from the north wall. The red flag hoisted above Béxar that first day had made clear the fate of any rebel, Anglo or Mexican, taken alive while fighting for Texas independence: death.

Over the previous twelve days, almost a dozen couriers had made it through the Mexican lines and reached the two closest Texian communities east of Béxar — Gonzales, seventy-five miles away, and Goliad, ninety-five miles downriver, where Fannin and his volunteers held the presidio there. Travis's requests for food, clothing, ammunition, ordnance, and, most important, reinforcements, had gone unanswered, at least as far as the garrison knew, save for thirty-two brave souls sent from the town of Gonzales five days earlier. Other than that, nothing — no word from the provisional governor and council in San Felipe, eighty miles beyond Gonzales, or from Fannin . . . only a message two days earlier from Travis's warm friend Major Robert "Three-Legged Willie" Williamson, stationed in Gonzales, who entreated them to hold out and who promised to send aid soon.

Travis's two-hundred-odd men were exhausted and bedraggled from twelve days of almost constant bombardment and little sleep. They had done all they could to fortify the old mission, but the stone and adobe walls had been erected as protection against Indian attacks, not artillery. Though the enemy's largest fieldpiece was only an eight-pounder, the incessant shelling had taken its toll on the walls, particularly the weak northeastern section, which had begun to crumble. Worse, the compound was far too large to be ably manned by so few defenders. With Fannin's four hundred, they might have a chance, but an all-out attack seemed imminent—probably even before the rest of Santa Anna's army, comprising thousands more men, reached Béxar. As it was, the Mexican entrenchments were moving closer every night.

As the rider disappeared into the darkness, the Mexican troops lay back down to sleep, or tried to. Tomorrow, and its bloodshed, would come soon enough.

ONE

The Hotspur

He hungered and thirsted for fame—not the kind of fame which satisfies the ambition of the duelist and desperado, but the exalted fame which crowns the doer of great deeds in a good cause.

JONATHAN KUYKENDALL

On a cold day early in February 1836, a well-dressed young man on a horse trotted along the road—little more than a well-worn cart path, really—from the small town of Gonzales westward to San Antonio de Béxar. He was twenty-six, and he had already written his autobiography. He exuded self-assurance, and ambition burned in his breast, but he could be brusque, and perhaps because of that, the men under his command respected him, but did not warm to him. The rebel Texian army had no money for arms and ammunition, much less clothing for its few hundred soldiers, and the uniform he had ordered had not been delivered yet. Thus, despite his newly appointed rank of lieutenant colonel of cavalry in the regular army, he wore the fine clothes of a gentleman.

His civilian dress was no indication of a lack of courage. He had proven his mettle several times in the past few years— at the port village of Anahuac, staked to the ground with Mexican riflemen aiming at him; then three years later, leading a group of militia to seize the garrison there; and at the siege of Béxar this past fall, in the thick of things with his company of mounted scouts.

His name was William Barret Travis, and he did not want to return to Béxar. A few weeks before, his good friend Henry Smith had been elected governor by the Consultation, the meeting of representatives of most of the Texas settlements that was convened to discuss the increasing friction with Mexico and organize a provisional government to handle matters. The Consultation had been held in the town of San Felipe, the center of the Anglo colonies, where Travis resided. At Travis's own suggestion, Smith appointed him lieutenant colonel and commander of cavalry, then charged him with raising a legion of dragoons—one hundred armed horsemen—to reinforce the depleted garrison at Béxar. All signs pointed to a large Mexican army on the march to Texas to quash the nascent rebellion in the troublesome colony.

Almost three weeks of recruiting had yielded only thirty-five men, and several of those had deserted the unit on the road. With a legion, a man could make a mark; a third of that number, not so easily. Travis himself had to provision, equip, and sometimes supply mounts for his volunteers, and the job kept him fully occupied. His personal affairs and business concerns suffered, particularly his successful law practice, though the recent acquisition of a partner had helped the latter somewhat. But the unceasing work took its toll. On January 28, soon after leaving San Felipe, dog-tired and disillusioned, Travis had written to Smith from Burnham's Crossing on the

Colorado River, just thirty miles west on the Béxar road, and asked to be allowed to return:

> I shall however go on & do my duty, if I am sacrificed, unless I receive new orders to counter march. Our affairs are gloomy indeed—The people are cold & indifferent—They are worn down & exhausted with the war, and in consequence of dissentions between contending & rival chieftains, they have lost all confidence in their own Govt. & officers. You have no idea of the exhausted state of the country....I have strained every nerve—I have used my personal credit & have slept neither day nor night, since I recd orders to march—and with all this exertion, I have barely been able to get horses & equipment for the few men I have.

He was still at Burnham's Crossing the next day, gathering supplies and preparing to move out toward Gonzales, when he wrote Smith again. This time he asked to resign.

> Not having been able to raise 100 volunteers agreeably to your orders, & there being so few regular troops altogether, I beg that your Excellency will recall the order for me to go on to Béxar.... The fact is there is no necessity for my services to command so few men. They may now go on to San Antonio under command of Capt. Forsythe....I hope your Excellency will take my situation into consideration and relieve me from the orders which I have hitherto received, so far as they compel me to command in person the men who are now on the way to Béxar. Otherwise I shall feel it due to myself to resign my commission.

Travis was a revolutionary, of the most extreme type. He had already demonstrated, more than once, his willingness to sacrifice his life for the cause of freedom for Texas. Just a few months earlier, it was his leadership during the assault on Anahuac that had galvanized the rebellion. His War Party held political sway, the revolution was in full swing, and the colonists now over-whelmingly favored independence. Whatever might happen next, William Barret Travis had already made his mark. But the new commander of cavalry was not a happy man as he rode west.

This dissatisfaction would have been hidden from the men he commanded. By nature, Travis kept his own counsel. Not even the detailed diary he maintained, in which he listed (in Spanish, to be discreet) his many romantic conquests, told all, though it did reveal his innate stubbornness. After failing to ford a surging creek on a visit to one inamorata, he had writ-ten, "This is the first time that I have given up."

He possessed other qualities that shaped him every bit as powerfully. He was intelligent and good with words, both spo-ken and written. A born romantic, he had been raised on Sir Walter Scott's Waverley novels and Jane Porter's *The Scottish Chiefs*, a glorified account of Scotland's fight for freedom. Like Samuel Adams in the American Revolution sixty years before, he was an effective and energetic firebrand, and no man in Texas could claim more credit for the present uprising. The grand gesture, the dramatic phrase, appealed to Travis, and he made good use of it. He was also a man who not five years earlier had deserted his wife and family, who had slunk virtu-ally penniless out of Alabama to escape debtors' prison. He was living proof of the widely held belief that a man could remake himself in Texas. And like many of the men of the American Revolution, or any other revolution, he was fortu-nate in that his ambition did not interfere with his patriotism.

* * *

WILLIAM BARRET TRAVIS HAD COME into the world August 1, 1809, in Edgefield, South Carolina, the first of ten children born to Mark Travis, a farmer, and his wife, Jemima. His father moved his large family to Alabama when William was eight. His was a family with deep American roots: Travises (or Traverses) had emigrated from England to the colonies almost two hundred years before William Barret's birth.

Near the small town of Sparta, Alabama, young Travis attended a better school than most rural areas could boast of, then finished his education with a few years at a local academy that stressed classical learning. During these years he developed a passion for reading that would never flag.

The boy with reddish-brown hair and blue eyes grew into a tall, handsome man. Not long after finishing his studies, during a brief stint as a teacher, Travis fell in love with one of his students, the lovely Rosanna Cato. They married in October 1828—he was barely nineteen, she was sixteen—and moved into a small house in the town of Claiborne, Alabama. Nine months and thirteen days later they were blessed with a son, Charles Edward.

Travis's ambitions could not be contained by a classroom, however. Several months before he married he cast about for a more lucrative profession. He soon found it, and made the acquaintance of James Dellet, one of the best attorneys in the area, who agreed to take him on. After a year of intense study, Travis passed the state bar. He began practicing in February 1829; he was not yet twenty. He also became involved in other activities. He was appointed adjutant of the local militia regiment, and joined the Masonic order. But a plethora of attorneys in the area made work for a new one hard to come by, and his earnings were meager. The cost of maintaining a household consisting of a young wife, an infant, and three slaves on loan from his parents was more than he could afford.

So the enterprising Travis bought a printing press and began a newspaper, publishing and editing it himself. He even took on outside printing jobs to pay his mounting bills, but those jobs soon dried up, and the newspaper failed early in 1831.

That same year he abandoned his pregnant wife and son. The reasons bandied about were varied: Travis suspected Rosanna of infidelity; he killed a man, perhaps the object of her indiscretions; he lost a heated political dispute. These and other explanations circulated for decades afterward. In fact, Travis would later write in his autobiography that "my wife and I had a feud which resulted in our separation" — but he assured his wife that he would return for them or send for them as soon as he could. But the main reason he left was the least glamorous one: debt. A judgment for several unpaid bills was brought against him in court, and he faced a possible prison term. And while Travis may have genuinely planned to send for his family, or return at some point, as he told his wife, he would do neither.

Instead, Travis left for the Mexican province of Texas, the destination for many a desperate man running from the law, creditors, or any number of other troubles or mistakes — even from himself. GTT, for "gone to Texas," was a familiar catchphrase in the Southeast, often seen scrawled on an empty shack after its inhabitant had packed up and left, usually in the middle of the night. Land in Texas could be had for a pittance. Word was that a man could make a new beginning there, even forge a new life, free from lawmen or creditors once he crossed the Sabine River, separating Mexico from the United States.

Though a law the previous year had made immigration from the United States illegal, it did little to stem a steady tide of newcomers to Texas. In the spring of 1831, Travis crossed the Sabine and made his way to the heart of Anglo settlement in Texas — San Felipe, the bustling town of about fifty log houses and stores in Stephen Austin's colony, the earliest and the largest of the chartered settlements granted by Mexico. There he introduced himself to the slight, soft-spoken Austin, and met Frank Johnson, the local *alcalde*, an official whose duties combined those of mayor, marshal, and judge. In May, just a few weeks after his arrival, Travis made a down payment of ten dollars for a title to land — the standard 4,428 acres (one league) due a single man, as he listed himself. He would never settle on it, but he was a landowner, at least, and commanded all the respect due to one. His new life had officially begun.

But since San Felipe had its share of enterprising young attorneys, he soon moved sixty miles east to Anahuac, on the northeastern end of Galveston Bay near the mouth of the Trinity River. Located on a bluff near the water, the sparse settlement comprised a couple dozen small log houses and shops, and served as the customs port of entry into Texas. That meant paperwork and negotiation, and Travis soon found legal employment. He began learning the official language, Spanish, and the laws of Mexico. Before he left San Felipe, he had asked Austin to recommend him to the U.S. Senate in a bid to become the American consul for the Galveston coastal area. Austin had agreed to do so, and though in his letter of recommendation he admitted that his knowledge of Travis was limited, he mentioned that Travis was well thought of by other respectable citizens. Though Travis never pursued the post, Austin's letter indicates how quickly Travis was accepted into the community, and how impressive other men found him. In Anahuac, he shortly made a name for himself as a capable attorney — and enough money to begin looking for more land in the area. He also became known as an activist in local politics. For more than a decade, the Anglo colonists had gotten along fine without any help from Mexico. But the Mexican government's increasing intrusion into their lives in the way of import duties and taxes, and curtailment of rights they had become accustomed to as Americans—such as an efficient local judicial system—was not appreciated by the settlers. Rebellion was simmering, and Travis eagerly jumped into the cauldron.

His baptism by fire came in the spring of 1832. Late in the previous year a Mexican garrison and customs house had been installed on the northeastern edge of Galveston Bay. Colonel John (Juan) Davis Bradburn was sent there to enforce the collection of duties and help control the increased smuggling of goods, slaves, and illegal immigrants through the area. He named the settlement Anahuac—which means "place by the water" in the Aztec language. Bradburn's seventy-five soldiers built a barracks and office a half mile south of town and settled in, and with the arrival of a customs collector, began to uphold the law. Colonists had enjoyed a seven-year exemption from tariff duties, and they resented the resumption of charges—though according to the agreements negotiated by the *empresarios,* or land agents, the exemption period had expired in November 1830.

Bradburn, a Virginia-born mercenary, had served in the same militia unit as frontiersman and land speculator James Bowie during the War of 1812. Soon after, he fought for Mexico's independence and was rewarded with a colonelcy. At first the Anahuac community greeted him warmly, hoping for leniency from a fellow American. But Bradburn had become a Mexican citizen, and a staunch patriot, and their feelings cooled as he made clear his enthusiasm for his work—indeed, he had been promised a promotion for a job well done.

The April 6, 1830, ban on immigration had placed the still-in-process legal titles of many long-established settlers in jeopardy — many *empresario* contracts were in danger of suspension, and others in colonies with few inhabitants would be canceled. When the tactless Bradburn refused to allow the Mexican authorities to issue settlers' titles, tension was further increased. Colonists held meetings down the coast in Brazoria, and sent a delegation to protest the continual collection of tariffs, to no avail. The fact that Bradburn's soldiers — some of whom were conscripted convicts — terrorized the citizenry without reprisal, by means of drunken insults, fights, and at least one reported rape, only raised the temperature. A showdown was inevitable.

The men in Anahuac organized a militia company, ostensibly for protection against Indians, electing as their captain attorney Patrick Jack, who shared an office with his friend William Barret Travis. Jack was arrested for accepting the position, since a militia was in violation of Mexican law, but was soon released. Meanwhile, the owner of two runaway slaves had hired Travis to recover the men; Bradburn had given them sanctuary and used them as laborers on his barracks, and he refused to yield them despite repeated prodding from Travis. When a mysterious cloaked figure delivered letters to a Mexican sentry that announced a militia marching on Anahuac for the purpose of taking the blacks by force, a nettled Bradburn suspected a hoax, with Travis behind it. On May 17, he sent a dozen soldiers to the attorneys' office to take Travis into custody for questioning. When Jack barged into Bradburn's office demanding his friend's release, he, too, was arrested. Fifteen other purported troublemakers would eventually join the pair as Bradburn attempted intimidation.

Travis and Jack were first placed in the guardhouse, then moved to an empty brick kiln. No formal charges were filed, though Bradburn announced a military trial for the prisoners to be held in Matamoros, three hundred miles away in the

Mexican state of Tamaulipas. These developments further enraged the Anglo colonists, who sometimes failed to remember that they were no longer in the United States and that their civil rights were no longer protected by the U.S. Constitution. "They all go about with their constitution in their pocket, demanding their rights," wrote one Mexican general after an 1828 tour of Texas. Soon, about 160 settlers from Austin's colony organized and marched toward Anahuac. Led by Frank Johnson, the vocal leader of the independence movement, and Robert "Three-Legged Willie" Williamson, the handsome, fun-loving San Felipe attorney whose wooden leg never seemed to impede his movements, the group reached the town on June 10 and approached the garrison.

Bradburn ordered the two prisoners bound and staked to the ground. Guards were posted around them, their rifles pointed at the pair. The colonel threatened the prisoners with death if the colonists opened fire. Travis, his hands tied over his knees, shouted at Johnson's group to ignore his personal safety and attack the fort in the name of a higher duty. He would die like a man, he told them.

Both sides stood down. The colonists left after issuing a warning to Bradburn threatening action if any harm should come to the two attorneys. Over the next few days there were skirmishes, including a small battle at Velasco, seventy miles down the coast, and a near siege of Anahuac. Finally Bradburn's superior arrived from Nacogdoches and negotiated a truce, removing the colonel from command. Travis and Jack were released on July 2, after seven weeks of imprisonment. Bradburn, fearful for his life, stole out of town and made his way east to New Orleans.

Stephen Austin was eventually able to persuade the authorities that the fracas merely indicated the colonists' hatred of Bradburn, not a desire to rebel against their adopted homeland. But Travis and his compatriots were feted as heroes of the emerging Texian cause—whether it be independence, statehood, or just the civil rights every American immigrant expected.

Perhaps in an effort to capitalize on his newfound fame, in August Travis moved inland, west to San Felipe and its five-hundred-odd inhabitants. He had been an unknown when he arrived there a year earlier; now he hoped his celebrity and experience would bring in enough business to support him. His gamble paid off. Though there were still several capable attorneys in the area, this time he found all kinds of work, from land dealings and slavery transactions to wills and colonization cases and criminal defense. He soon developed a thriving practice, earning enough to rent a house for a year and buy another house and a hundred acres east of town for investment purposes. He also sent a man back to Alabama to pay his debts there. Travis continued to buy even more land, and eventually owned so much that he was able to donate five hundred acres on the Brazos River to an enterprise attempting to introduce a steamboat into the interior waterways of Texas. He employed a French gardener, and rented or bought a few slaves, among them a woman named Matilda and a twenty-year-old man named Joe, who hailed from Kentucky—"five feet ten or eleven inches high, very black, and good countenance," according to a friend of Travis's.

He also developed a busy social life, and engaged in the usual pursuits of a single man in such a place: gambling, Masonic meetings, stag parties, horse races, and the occasional dance or ball. He liked to dress well. As his income increased so did his wardrobe, and he became fastidious about washing his clothes (not a particularly common affectation in his part of the world at the time). He enjoyed buying gifts for others, particularly children, and frequently contributed to charitable causes. He continued his voracious reading, mostly history and historical novels—whatever he could buy or borrow in the small frontier town. He never was much of a drinker beyond the occasional social libation, but he began to play at faro and other card games, losing a bit more than he won. And he cut quite a swath through the small group of single women in the area, some of them proper, but more of them prostitutes.

Late in 1833 he met a young woman named Rebecca Cummings, a few years older than he, who helped her brother John run an inn on Mill Creek about seven miles north of San Felipe. He continued to see other women (and occasionally bed them) while courting her, but he spent more and more time at Mill Creek, and not just for the superior food and comfortable lodging. Soon he fell in love with Rebecca, and gave up other assignations. He eventually told her about Rosanna, having changed his mind about returning to his wife and family in Alabama, if that had truly been his intention at all. By mid-April 1834, Rebecca agreed to marry him once his divorce was finalized in Alabama. Rosanna had acquiesced to an official end to the marriage and agreed to grant Travis custody of Charles Edward, a concession Travis lost no time acting upon. Within a month, he had met with her in Brazoria and returned to San Felipe with his four-year-old son. Though the Alabama legislature still needed to legally dissolve the marriage, and that could take some time, he was confident that it would happen, particularly since Rosanna had also found someone else, a man who wanted to wed her.

San Felipe was not only the headquarters of Austin's colony; it was truly the center of Anglo Texas. Everyone important eventually came through the town, and politics was the lingua franca at every tavern. After the Anahuac disturbance, Travis had remained uninvolved in such discussions for a time, but he was soon swept up into the political maelstrom. For the moment, those favoring peace held sway in most of Texas. Disenchantment with the Mexican government was growing, however, and San Felipe was the beating heart of the revolutionary spirit.

For a while relations remained peaceful. In February 1834, Travis accepted a position as secretary of the San Felipe *ayuntamiento* (city council), and worked closely with his friend Robert Williamson, the new *alcalde*. The job put him in the middle of things, politically speaking, and increased his influence. He also began mixing with other members of the fledgling War Party, young hotspurs dissatisfied with the thought of Texas as a Mexican state. For these War Dogs, as they were called, independence was the only answer—and if that meant war, so be it, and the sooner the better.

In June 1833, Austin had been sent to Mexico to deliver the colonists' proposal for statehood. He would not return to Texas again until September 1835, almost two years after his arrest and imprisonment for treason. By that time, events outside his control would be set in motion, events that would decide the future of Texas, and Travis would find himself in the thick of them. Once again, the flash point was Anahuac.

Since the 1832 disturbance, customs collection in the area had been neglected. In the spring of 1835 the cash-strapped Mexican government sent another customs officer to Anahuac, with another company of troops to assist him in carrying out his duties. There followed the inevitable clashes between soldiers and citizens, who felt that the taxes were unfairly levied. When a friend of Travis's, an Anahuac merchant named Andrew Briscoe, was jailed for suspicion of smuggling—or perhaps for embarrassing the new customs officer, it was not quite clear which—the news spread through the colonies. At a secret War Party meeting held in San Felipe, a plot was hatched to free Briscoe from jail — and Anahuac from military rule. Travis was not only at its center, he was elected to lead the ambitious attempt. The two dozen volunteers for the expedition elected Travis commander. Their password slogan, likely his suggestion, was "victory or death."

Down the coast from Anahuac, they chartered a sloop, mounted a six-pound cannon, and sailed into Galveston Bay. Late in the afternoon of June 27, they reached Anahuac and fired a cannon shot to announce their presence. The rebels rowed ashore in two small boats, then sent a demand for surrender to the officer in charge, Captain Antonio Tenorio. At some risk to his life, Travis met with Tenorio and insisted on an immediate capitulation. After a period of discussion, the Mexican garrison of forty-four men surrendered, and were paroled after pledging to leave Texas.

A few days later, Travis returned to San Felipe to find himself castigated for his actions. The Peace Party still prevailed, and the majority of Texian colonists were fearful of reprisals, with good reason: a federalist uprising in the Mexican state of Zacatecas in May had been brutally crushed by General Antonio López de Santa Anna, the recently elected president, and the news of his punitive actions there was both fresh and frightening. Several Texian communities issued resolutions condemning the Anahuac action and pledging their loyalty to the Mexican government, Travis being prominently — and pejoratively — mentioned in more than one. His Mexican counterpart, Captain Tenorio, rode to San Felipe and was received as a hero.

Travis, angry and dismayed, published a notice in a newspaper asking the public to withhold judgment, an announcement that satisfied no one. Then he wrote to the military commander in Béxar, Colonel Domingo de Ugartechea, suggesting they open a correspondence that would allow Travis to explain his actions. He received no reply. Instead, the Mexican authorities issued orders in August for the arrest of Travis, Robert Williamson, Frank Johnson, and several other agitators. Santa Anna himself issued the orders.

Most of the Anglo colonists were not happy with Travis's actions. They had worked long and hard for what they had, and any trouble with Mexico might cause them to lose everything. But if Travis was a hothead, he was their hothead. The thought of several of their most prominent citizens being seized and put on military trial, and perhaps executed, was intolerable, and the local authorities refused to carry out the arrest orders. More meetings were held in Anglo communities throughout the province. Another convention, this one referred to as a Consultation, was called for October 15 in Gonzales, the center of *empresario* Green DeWitt's colony to the west of San Felipe, and the call went out for delegates from every settlement in Texas.

Travis hoped to attend as a delegate. He spent a good deal of his time writing letters to influential friends and acquaintances, stirring them to the banner of rebellion. "We shall give them hell if they come here," he wrote in late August 1835, upon hearing the news that two hundred *soldados* (soldiers) would be garrisoned in San Felipe within a few weeks:

> Keep a bright lookout. Secure all the powder and lead. Remember that war is not to be waged without means. Let us be men and Texas will triumph.... If we are encroached upon, let us resist until our bodies & our property lie in one common ruin, ere we submit to tyranny.

Travis even advised Austin, who arrived in San Felipe in mid-September, on the delegate elections and the upcoming convention. But before the Consultation could convene, the war that Travis had advocated so enthusiastically broke out in earnest. In the village of Gonzales, colonists resisted attempts by Mexican troops to confiscate a single unmounted cannon tube. It was hardly a battle—hardly even a skirmish—yet the shots fired there finally ignited Texian passions in a way that Travis's mere words had so far failed to do.

THAT WAS IN OCTOBER. It had brought Travis the rebellion he had longed for. And then, in the chilly first days of 1836, his orders to reinforce Béxar.

Now, early in February 1836, at the age of twenty-six, Travis, like some romantic hero of yore, commanded a cavalry legion (or what passed for one). Three months after entering the service as a lieutenant, he had been unanimously elected lieutenant colonel—and that after his recommendations for a corps of cavalry had been accepted and then implemented with only a few changes. His name was known in every household in Texas, and respected in most of them: public opinion had changed drastically over the previous few months, and few colonists still supported the status quo. Travis was present at the dawn of a new country, instrumental in its birth and fighting for its existence against a despot, much as his two grandfathers, both of them veterans of the American Revolution, had done sixty years before. Anything seemed possible: greatness, riches, even immortality. Just the previous August he had written to a friend, echoing Thomas Paine: "Huzza for Texas! Huzza for Liberty, and the rights of man!...God grant that all Texas may stand as firm as Harrisburg in the 'hour that will try men's souls.'...I feel the triumph we have gained and I glory in it. Let Texas stand firm and be true to herself and we will have nothing to fear."

He had led his command from San Felipe west to Beeson's Ferry on the Colorado River, where they had stopped for a few days to scour the countryside for more necessities. They came up with some provisions, a horse, saddles, bridles — some charged to the government, some to Travis's personal credit. He managed to recruit one volunteer, but the new man hardly made up for those whom Travis had lost. By the time the legion arrived at Burnham's Crossing, twenty miles upstream, a few days later, nine others had deserted the group, a dispiriting turn of events. Then Travis had written the two letters to Smith, asking for new orders in the first and offering his resignation in the second. He lingered on the Colorado, hoping for a quick reply from Smith, but none came. He traveled west toward Gonzales, and somewhere on the road decided to go on ahead alone to Béxar. The men were in good hands under his second in command, Captain John Forsyth, a New Yorker who had relocated to Kentucky after the death of his wife in 1828. Forsyth had raised a company of volunteers when war in Texas broke out, and joined Travis's mounted spies at Béxar; soon after the battle he received a commission as a captain in the Texian cavalry. He had spent every penny he had helping Travis with expenses. His commitment was not in doubt, nor was his competence; Travis could confidently leave him in charge.

Indeed, he had already done so once — for entirely personal reasons. Before Travis left the Colorado River area, he had made a special trip to spend some time with his son, then six, at the home of David Ayres, a friend of Travis's upriver in Montville. Charles had only recently begun boarding there; he would soon begin attending the school that was scheduled to open on February 1. Before Travis had to leave, the boy whispered in his father's ear, asking for fifty cents to buy a bottle of molasses to make candy. Travis handed him the four bits, so Charles and the other children would have their candy that evening—a pleasant thought for Travis while riding away.

TRAVIS'S LEGION WAS HARDLY WORTHY of the name, a source of some embarrassment. Which was not to say there were not good men behind him: William Garnett, the young Baptist preacher from Virginia; the small, redheaded jockey from Arkansas, Henry Warnell, who always had a chaw of tobacco in his cheek (his wife had died in childbirth, and Warnell had left his infant son, John, with friends to seek his fortune in Texas); and his personal aide, Charles Despallier, the young Louisiana Creole whose brother, Blas, counted James Bowie as a good friend. Still, Travis hoped an express from Henry Smith or Sam Houston was on the way from San Felipe that would relieve him of his current orders. Until then he would do his duty. His country—for he did think of Texas, the land he had lived in for less than five years, as his country—needed him.

He passed the first of the markers on the crude road—the numeral 1 emblazoned on a stake beside the trail, signifying one mile from Béxar. A few minutes later he reached the empty thirty-foot-high watchtower and the other old, abandoned Spanish army structures on Powder House Hill, where he could look down the gently sloping road into the tranquil and lush San Antonio River valley. A half mile away was the battered town of Béxar, still recovering from the previous winter's siege and battle, and the high bell tower of the Church of San Fernando looming over the town's pale stone buildings.

Even closer, on the east side of the shallow San Antonio River, was the dilapidated mission turned fortress called the Alamo.

TWO

"O! He Has Gone to Texas"

A vast howling Wilderness of wild things, wild cattle wild Horses wild Beasts and Birds, and wild Men savages hostile in the extreme...

JAMES HATCH, *Lest We Forget the Heroes of the Alamo*

The very earliest explorers—Spanish conquistadors such as Hernán Cortés, Francisco Pizarro, and Francisco Vásquez de Coronado—marched deep into the heart of the wilderness in search of gold and other precious minerals. The kingdom of Gran Quivira, where everyone ate from dishes and bowls of gold...the Seven Hills of the Aijados, where gold was even more plentiful...the Sierra de la Plata, or the Silver Mountain—all these had lured men seeking fortunes. But these searchers found no gold or silver, and the land they called Tejas, or Texas, an Indian word meaning "friend," was ignored for a century and a half. Early in the eighteenth century, Catholic missionaries ventured north from New Spain in search of souls to save. Soldiers accompanied them for protection against the Indians, who liked their souls just as they were.

The men who followed the priests, almost without exception, came for the land.

BY THE MID-1600s, the Spanish claimed all the territory from the Pacific to the Gulf of Mexico and more beyond—from California to the Florida peninsula. (France, Spain's chief rival in North America, claimed Louisiana, the Mississippi Valley, and Canada.) Since Cortés had conquered the Aztec empire in 1521, Mexico City had become the center of Spain's empire in the New World. The wealth of the Aztecs, and that of the Incas of Peru, had funded Spanish wars and further voyages of exploration. But after two major expeditions in the mid-1500s—Coronado's epic trek across much of the American Southwest, and Hernando de Soto's journey through the Southeast, neither of them finding the fabled cities of gold or any wealth at all—Spain abandoned any further exploration into the far northern frontier of its colonies.

In 1690, the church-controlled Spanish authorities decided to establish missions near the Rio Grande to Christianize the natives there, not just for altruistic reasons but also for political reasons, to help guard New Spain's borders. Nacogdoches, in the far eastern reaches, was established in 1716, then a few others in the area followed, each with a presidio to house a company of soldiers. Two years later, in 1718, came the mission of San Antonio de Valero, situated in a picturesque valley watered by a small river. Other missions and presidios followed.

By the early 1800s, after the French and Indian War, the American Revolution, the French Revolution, and the subsequent political maneuvering, much of the region's ownership had changed hands—sometimes more than once. The British had claimed much of the Floridas over the previous century, and in 1763 Spain ceded that province to them in exchange for Cuba. Twenty years later, England returned Florida to Spain, which had also added Louisiana to its empire a year earlier. Despite its extensive holdings in the New World, there remained only a few Spanish settlements east of the Mississippi.

Three years after Spain returned Louisiana to France in 1800, a cash-strapped Napoleon sold Louisiana to the fledgling United States, doubling that young nation's territory. Though the phrase "manifest destiny" would not be coined until 1845, its doctrine of God-approved expansion across the continent had already taken hold. The Louisiana Purchase, it seemed, had only whetted the young republic's appetite. President Thomas Jefferson claimed Texas as part of the deal, and in 1806 sent troops to explore the limits of lower Louisiana much as he had sent Lewis and Clark to follow the Missouri west to the Pacific two years earlier. (The prescient Jefferson was convinced of the region's value: fourteen years later, he would write to President James Monroe, "The province of Techas will be the richest state of our Union, without any exception.") Spanish troops were sent to block them, and the two columns met in east Texas; war was averted when the opposing army commanders wisely agreed to a twenty-mile-wide Neutral Ground between Louisiana and Texas, which was allowed to stand by their respective governments. The dispute was finally solved in 1819, when Spain ceded the Neutral Ground to the United States for $5 million and the American renunciation of any claims on Texas they might have held from the Louisiana Purchase.

But it would not be long before the United States made overtures to Spain about the availability of Texas. Though no deal was struck, Spain was now fully alerted to the intentions of its hungry neighbor to the north. Texas was emerging as an increasingly important buffer zone, both against rapacious European powers and the intransigent aboriginals who fiercely resisted encroachment on their homelands. The Spanish government countered with attempts to bring Mexican settlers into the area to populate the territory and tame the wilderness— but found few takers.

Then, in December 1820, a risk-taking fifty-eight-year-old American named Moses Austin arrived in sleepy Béxar, the capital of the province, with a plan of colonization: he would bring three hundred American families to Texas to do what New Spain could not.

Austin had some experience with this. Two decades earlier, he had, with the permission of the Spanish authorities, established a lead-mining operation and colony in northern Louisiana; the venture was successful, and made Austin a rich man. But the War of 1812 had drained his manpower and forced him to substitute slave power; he spent too much money feeding and housing them, driving him into deep debt and reducing his fortune to nothing. When his business failed in March 1820, he was jailed for nonpayment of debts and his lead works auctioned for a fraction of their worth. He was released from prison to find himself virtually penniless. A lesser man would have fallen into the poorhouse and obscurity, but the resilient Austin had already come up with another colonization scheme, again in a Spanish territory.

He thought his plan would be irresistible to Spanish authorities eager for industrious settlers in their far northern province. Austin would publicize the opportunity and procure the immigrants, taking care to accept only those who could prove their responsibility and good citizenship. He knew the Panic of 1819 had resulted in many Americans losing their land, and many more unable to afford the land they wanted and needed. In a predominantly agrarian society, land was as necessary to liberty—true liberty, meaning the freedom to work for oneself—as anything on a piece of paper.

Austin would handle all sales of land. Settlers would swear to become dutiful citizens of New Spain, their fealty to include the practice—or at least the outward assumption—of Catholicism, Mexico's national religion. For a nominal fee, which would cover Austin's administrative costs—about a tenth of the price of government land in the United States—they would receive full and legal title to generous territorial grants, and exemption from taxes and import tariffs for seven years. In return, New Spain's new citizens would develop the country through the cultivation of sugar, corn, and cotton, and strengthen Spanish claims of possession; Americans were already crossing the Sabine River into the eastern portion of Texas, but these colonists would enter on Mexican terms, and swear allegiance to New Spain. For his part, Austin would be compensated by large land grants, which he could then sell for profit—if he was successful.

Similar colonization plans had been proposed before: in 1813, royal permission had been granted to an American named Richard Raynal Keene to import settlers into the province, but political upheavals had waylaid that enterprise. Now the Mexican governor, wary of anything American, refused to listen to Austin's proposal and ordered him to leave immediately. That same afternoon, disappointed and resigned to defeat, he prepared to depart on the long trek home. But as he walked across the main plaza of Béxar, he ran into a slight acquaintance—a Dutchman he had met twenty-three years previously in a Tennessee tavern when he was canvassing for Louisiana colonists. The man was now calling himself Baron de Bastrop for added prestige, and serving as second *alcalde* of Béxar. Austin told him his story, and persuaded Bastrop of the viability of his own colonization plans. The "baron"—like

Austin, an opportunist—was cash-strapped at the moment, but he saw a chance to make some money by aiding Austin. He was not without influence with the authorities, and he agreed to intercede. He obtained another audience with the governor, and a few days later he and Austin explained the proposal, no doubt emphasizing its advantages to New Spain. This time, the governor approved, and forwarded the petition to the proper authorities.

A jubilant Austin returned home to Missouri, confident his plan would be approved. Many months on the road had worn him thin, though, and the cold, wet journey across the desolate territory of east Texas induced pneumonia. By the time he reached home he was in bad shape. He never fully recovered. Five days after his reunion with his family, he received word that his petition had been approved. He threw himself into preparations for his return to Texas, eating and sleeping little. He died a few months later. His wife later wrote that before his last breath, he gasped out his dying wish: that his son Stephen would "prosecute the enterprise he had commenced."

Stephen Fuller Austin was not by nature the risk taker his father was. But he was endowed with a unique combination of qualities essential to his new position of immigration agent/administrator—*empresario*—of a country within a country. He possessed intelligence, integrity, levelheadedness, and tact, and his frail physique belied a quiet determination that would be necessary for the many trials ahead. He had just finished a legal education when he was informed of his father's death—and of his final request. Moses Austin had been imploring Stephen to join in the enterprise, and he had been considering it. Now, with the approval and the financial backing of his legal mentor, he accepted his new fate and headed west—only to find that Mexico had recently won its independence, making his father's deal null and void and requiring Austin to travel to Mexico City, where he spent eleven months, until he finally won the new government's approval. By 1825, despite several obstacles — among them a failed crop, repeated Indian attacks, and a cargo ship that ran aground, destroying all the supplies on board — Austin settled the three hundred families he had promised under contract to bring to Texas (297, actually). After enduring more than its share of growing pains, his colony began to thrive.

A new law enacted that year permitted individual Mexican states to form their own colonization policies, and some two dozen other *empresarios* — all but a few of them Anglos — soon followed Austin's lead, receiving extensive land grants covering almost the entire territory. None of them was as successful as Austin, but over the next decade they brought in thousands of colonists. Thousands of others streamed into Texas without permission, and many of them — in a time-honored American tradition reaching back two hundred years — set down stakes wherever they found unoccupied land. By 1835, Texas claimed some thirty-five thousand residents, all but a few thousand of them Americans, most from the southern states of Tennessee, Kentucky, and Missouri. Not all shared the high moral character of Austin's original Old Three Hundred, as they came to be known. Some were fugitives from the law, or from family or creditors. Others moved to Texas intent on shady pursuits, such as smuggling or speculating in land or slavery.

They all found a land abundant in the things that mattered to an agrarian society. Though there was no river approaching the size of the Mississippi, a half dozen or so waterways, rather evenly spaced and somewhat navigable, coursed through most of the central, eastern, and southern parts of the province and drained into the Gulf of Mexico. Rolling prairies ideal for grazing or farming made up much of the terrain, and the climate was healthy and the temperatures moderate. "It's fine rich land, high and healthy and free from mosquitoes and in short it is the richest, most beautiful country I ever beheld, fine lumber for every purpose and plenty of it," wrote one colonist to his wife back in the United States. Another settler with fewer specifics but more poetry declared to a friend back east: "Every poor man in your country that fails to come to Texas and inherit the goodly country does not only stand in his own light he does injustis to his posterity hear is the land that flows with milk and honey come all of you and posses it."

And possess it they did. By the mid-1830s, there were more than a dozen settlements stretching from the Sabine River on the east to Béxar, three hundred miles to the west, all in the southern half of the province and all but three of them Anglo in origin. Most structures were crude wooden houses, with just a few mercantile establishments. But surrounding them in every direction were thousands of farmers and their families, industriously working their land and slowly building new and better lives for themselves. As word of the rich new land spread via letters and advertisements and returning travelers, immigration rose sharply.

It was not all milk and honey. The land itself could be unforgiving; a drought leading to a bad crop, or a dangerous "norther" (a sudden drop in temperature accompanied by a frigid winter wind that would come slicing down from the north), could spell the difference between meager prosperity and bare survival—or even death. "A vast howling Wilderness of wild things, wild cattle wild Horses wild Beasts and Birds, and wild Men savages hostile in the extreme," was the way one early immigrant described Texas.

Wild horses, beasts, and birds could be advantageous to a frontiersman, but "wild Men savages" often spelled trouble. Some of the tens of thousands of Indians in Texas in the 1820s—the Wacos, the Tawakonis, and others—had grudgingly accepted the presence of the white invaders. But others resisted fiercely. Neither the cannibalistic Karankawas along the coast, nor the Apaches in the far west around Béxar and south of there, could boast sufficient numbers to mount large-scale attacks. But a much more populous tribe to the north posed a far more serious threat: the Comanches, the People of the Horse.

Like many other Great Plains peoples, the Comanches took to the horse and gun—both introduced by Europeans—with relish. Before these innovations, the short, stocky Comanches, an offshoot of the Shoshone tribe, were a semisedentary population of hunters on the edge of the Rocky Mountains. By the early nineteenth century, they had become the finest horsemen on the continent, roaming the southern plains as far as the Rio Grande and beyond in search of the great herds of buffalo, their staff of life—and in search of more horses, as well as captive women and children to replenish their numbers. They had driven the less populous Apaches out of the south Texas area and terrorized the Spanish inhabitants for a century. For the most part, they remained north of El Camino Real, the "Royal Road" of the Spanish empire that belied its name: a simple cart path that arced from the Rio Grande through Béxar all the way to Nacogdoches in east Texas and beyond.

If the Comanches had been better organized and their resistance better planned, colonization in Texas would have been impossible against ten thousand motivated horse soldiers. One measure of the Comanches' ferocity could be found in their elite warrior society, the Lobos (Wolves), who were not allowed to retreat from the scene of a battle, not even when they were vastly outnumbered—each brave had pledged to die rather than surrender his ground, even if the other warriors were in full retreat. But the Comanches possessed no form of government, roaming the country in nomadic bands that had little contact with each other. The immigrants, on the other hand, as their own numbers increased, turned to collective action for strength. Some organized militias to defend themselves against the Indians. More often, "ranging companies"—the precursors of the Texas Rangers—would venture far from home in search of Indians. These sweeps proved effective, and some smaller bands and tribes negotiated truces or gave the Anglo settlements a wide berth. The Comanches continued their raids on outlying or vulnerable farms or settlements, though some would trade with white men for goods they needed.

After a decade of *empresario*-induced immigration, settlers had little to complain about aside from intermittent Indian attacks. They were slowly but steadily taming the Texas wilderness, and some were doing more than just surviving. Farms throughout the territory were producing enough crops to feed families and take to market for sale or barter. Near the coast, extensive river-bottom plantations were springing up to take advantage of a highly profitable cash crop: cotton. These large enterprises required plenty of manpower, and that meant, for optimum results, slave power.

Slavery had recently been made illegal in Mexico, and that included Texas. (Never mind that Mexico had its own "peculiar institution"—its peonage system—in which dirt-poor peasants toiled on huge haciendas with little chance of earning freedom. They were burdened with massive debt, and, like southern slaves, endured hopeless conditions such as corporal punishment and severe penalties for escape. The sale of these human beings resembled slavery to a discomfiting degree.) But this abolition was roundly ignored by Texians, as they called themselves, most of whom had come from southern slave states, and it was not long before they figured a way to get around it legally: a slave owner would force his chattels to enter into contracts as indentured servants, whose length of service—usually ninety-nine years—and pitiful rate of compensation made it impossible for them to earn their freedom. Even without such pretense of legality, slaves were openly bought and sold, and advertised in the colonists' newspapers. The Mexican authorities made no effort to police these widespread violations. Though slave-owning colonists were in the minority, by the mid-1830s slaves would make up a tenth of the Texas population.

In this and other matters, the distant Mexican government interfered little with the affairs of their new citizens, and for the most part this laissez-faire approach was appreciated by the colonists. True, there was little in the way of government services or infrastructure, such as good roads, public schools, a just and efficient court system, and other necessities that Americans were accustomed to. But while each *empresario* acted as a one-man government, settling disputes and organizing militia and issuing rules and laws when necessary, the level of freedom enjoyed was extraordinarily high. No effort was made to enforce the Catholic religion, conscript soldiers, or levy taxes, even after the seven-year grace period had elapsed. The colonists were left alone to handle virtually every aspect of their lives. For most of them, the situation was more than tolerable.

But events several hundred miles to the south would change everything.

AFTER THE MEXICANS HAD OVERTHROWN their Spanish oppressors, they adopted a republican form of government in 1824 that was in some ways more liberal and federalistic than that of the United States. Battered by the country's weak economy and inexperience with democracy, Mexico went through several leaders and coups d'état in the ensuing years, until one leader, the conservative Anastasio Bustamante, executed his predecessor. When his centralist party, desirous of curtailing states' rights, extending privileges to the military and the Church, and effecting a regime headquartered in Mexico City, came to power in the early 1830s, things began to change—especially with respect to the nation's most distant territory. Mexico regarded its neighbor to the north with great suspicion, convinced that the United States hungered after Texas. (In fact, the U.S. government had made several overtures about buying the area, and had tendered several offers for it, from the Adams administration onward.) Spurred by a detailed report that vividly described a plethora of industrious, thriving Anglos eager to re-create their United States on Mexican soil, the new regime decided to take action. A law passed in April 1830 provided for military occupation of Texas, in the form of garrisons in the larger municipalities, and called for customs houses to be erected in several towns, which would act as ports of entry and would collect duties on imports. Worst of all, any further American immigration was prohibited.

The diplomatic Stephen Austin managed to obtain a temporary exemption from the immigration ban, but as troops—largely unschooled peasants pressed from the fields—began to march into Texas, the colonists' dissatisfaction with the new regime continued to escalate. And with thousands of Americans each year illegally entering Texas across the Red River to the north and the Sabine to the east—many of them rough elements and squatters who felt less loyalty to Mexico than those who had received land grants—rumors of an American invasion, whether government-sponsored or fostered through independent filibustering schemes, increased, and Mexican distrust and jealousy kept pace.

After another round of political maneuvers in Mexico City, an ambitious military hero of the revolution named Antonio López de Santa Anna—a tall, charismatic criollo hailed as the savior of Tampico, the coastal city where he had driven off an invading Spanish force—swept into power in late 1832. Since he fought on the federalist side, with those favoring the liberal constitution of 1824 and stronger states' rights, Texians eager for separate statehood hailed the general's victory and looked forward to his support. Bored with the actual work of running a country, and aware that the capital was a hotbed of centralists, the new president retired to his extensive hacienda in Jalapa, in the state of Veracruz, and left his liberal vice president, a former physician and professor named Valentín Gómez Farías, in Mexico City to run the country. But he kept his finger to the wind.

A change in its direction was not long in coming. Farías initiated several expansive reforms, most of which reduced the power of the Church and the military, but resistance from those two institutions and the landed gentry pushed Mexico deeper into political chaos and potential civil war. Representatives of those three classes made the journey to Santa Anna's hacienda to implore him to help. The new system was not working, they told him, and stronger leadership was required. Fortunately for them, Santa Anna's only loyalty was to his own ambition.

In April 1834, fifteen months after his retirement, Santa Anna made a triumphant return to Mexico City and seized the reins of power from his vice president. Making short work of the liberal constitution of 1824, he assumed near-dictatorial powers, dissolved the country's Congress, and canceled Farías's republican legislation. Mexico, Santa Anna decided, was not ready for democracy. "A hundred years to come my people will not be fit for liberty," he told the former American minister to Mexico. "They do not know what it is, unenlightened as they are, and under the influence of a Catholic clergy, a despotism is the proper government for them."

When he called for greatly reducing the independent state militias and declared that state governors and legislatures would be controlled by the central government, almost half the country's nineteen states expressed their dissatisfaction in some way, several in outright revolt. Those states farthest from Mexico City protested most.

The liberal-leaning city of Zacatecas, home to several rich silver mines, refused to disband its large, well-trained militia. Santa Anna decided to act quickly to crush the uprising there first. He knew the region well, having spent years as a young cadet with General Joaquín de Arredondo hunting down insurgents and Indians throughout the area.

In April 1835, he led a four-thousand-man army out of Mexico City north to Zacatecas. Three weeks later, before dawn on May 11, he met the city's four thousand militiamen on the outskirts of the mountain city. They were well armed and supplied, but undertrained and badly led, and their commander, former Zacatecas governor Francisco García, lacked military experience. The apparently evenly matched contest proved to be no contest at all. The centralist artillery and infantry successively battered and overwhelmed the *cívicos,* and when the latter turned and ran, the government cavalry turned the right flank and swooped down on the survivors from the rear. After two hours, the battle was over. The centralists incurred only a hundred casualties; the Zacatecan militia lost as many as twelve hundred citizens. "The field of battle presents a most horrifying picture," exulted Santa Anna after the carnage, in a letter to Mexico City.

Santa Anna's *soldados* were rewarded with a period of forty-eight hours in which to sack Zacatecas, and they responded enthusiastically in a riot of destruction, rape, pillage, and murder. Foreigners, especially the British and Americans, were paid particular attention, and many were killed. The city would not recover for years. The victorious commander returned to Mexico City in a triumphal tour that wound through several cities, whose inhabitants turned out to celebrate him with parades and parties.

When news of the Zacatecas butchery reached Texas, Anglo colonists took note, and some settlements organized Committees of Safety and militia companies. They knew that Santa Anna would likely attend to them next. He had visited punishment and death without mercy on his own people. They were in no doubt as to what he would do to those born on foreign soil.

Soon after his return to Mexico City, the "Hero of the Fatherland" met with an Anglo political prisoner. At the April 1833 Consultation, Texian delegates had drafted a constitution for statehood, and Stephen Austin had been chosen to deliver it to the Mexican authorities. He arrived in Mexico City a few months later and presented the petition to acting president Farías, who ignored Austin for several months. A disgusted Austin wrote a letter in October to the Béxar *ayuntamiento* recommending that they organize a state government without permission. The letter contained several incendiary statements, including "The country is lost if its inhabitants do not take its affairs into their own hands." Soon after, Austin succeeded in persuading the government to repeal the April 1830 immigration ban, and gained several other concessions — though statehood was put on hold.

In January 1834, on his journey home, Austin was arrested at Saltillo on suspicion of attempting to incite insurrection in Texas: his October letter had fallen into the wrong hands and been sent to Farías in Mexico City. The man who had preached and lived allegiance to his adopted country for so long was transported to the capital in irons and jailed in the century-old Prison of the Inquisition. He was denied a trial, and kept in solitary confinement for three months. The authorities moved him to another jail, and then another. He was finally freed eleven months later, on December 25, under a general amnesty for political prisoners. But he was not allowed to leave the city until June. He reached the port city of Veracruz in July 1835 and prepared to sail for New Orleans.

But the weary *empresario* ran into trouble leaving the country — a not-so-simple matter of the wrong papers. To gain permission to leave, he called on Mexico's president, the general again relaxing at his hacienda just outside Veracruz. The hero of Tampico, and now Zacatecas, the self-styled Napoleon of the West, cleared up the problem, and told Austin he would visit Texas the following March — as a friend. Austin took his leave, but was unconvinced. "His visit is uncertain — his friendship more so," Austin wrote of his meeting with Santa Anna. His suspicions would prove to be well founded.

THREE

"The Celebrated Desperado"

He seemed to be a roving man.

Captain William Y. Lacy

O n the warm, clear morning of September 19, 1827, two groups of well-dressed men made their way by small boat, by horse, and then by foot to a peninsular sandbar on the Mississippi side of the Mississippi River, just above Natchez. A duel had been arranged between Samuel Wells and Dr. Thomas Maddox. There was bad blood between the two, and between several other members of this unusual excursion party, most of them prominent gentlemen from Rapides Parish in Louisiana.

Samuel Wells had brought with him one brother, two cousins, and two other friends, one of whom was thirty-year-old James Bowie.

Ten men and several servants accompanied Dr. Maddox, including Major Norris Wright, the former sheriff of Rapides Parish — a small man but a crack shot with a pistol who had slain more than one enemy in a duel. A year earlier, Wright and Bowie had crossed paths at an Alexandria, Louisiana, hotel card game, and a long-simmering enmity between the two—likely a mix of politics and personal animus—erupted. Bowie, having heard that Wright had been slandering him, confronted the major; in response, Wright had fired a pistol at point-blank range. Somehow, the bullet—perhaps deflected by a pocketknife or a silver dollar—only bruised the target's left side, and the tall, thickly muscled Bowie pounced on the smaller man and had to be dragged off before he strangled him.

The single-shot flintlock pistols of the day were unreliable and took time to reload, and might "snap," or misfire, for one reason or another. After the altercation, Bowie decided to carry a large hunting knife in a leather scabbard for protection, as a regular part of his dress. He would not be found defenseless again.

Most of the men this September day were armed with one or two pistols. At least a couple in the Maddox party carried shotguns, another a hunting rifle, and two others wielded sword blades concealed in canes. Five doctors in both groups were present to minister to any wounded.

Previous incidents in the long-simmering feud included political arguments, unpaid loans, personal insults, a sword-cane stabbing, shootings, and, inevitably, an insult to a woman's name. Several other dueling challenges had gone unanswered; this one would decide, in an instant, whose side would claim the greater honor.

The location on the Mississippi side of the river had been chosen because dueling was illegal in Louisiana. The sandbar was heavily wooded, save for an open area in the center, where only an occasional piece of driftwood jutted out from the bare sand. For decades men had fought duels here—a Mississippi governor for one, the military man Winfield Scott for another—and some had died here.

Now, under a bright sun, with the loud murmur of the river in the background, Bowie and the Wells faction stood less than a hundred yards from the field of honor, in a grove of willows above the beach. The Maddox party gathered a few hundred yards away at the opposite end of the sandbar.

Just after the appointed time of noon, the two duelists, Wells and Maddox, took their places eight paces apart in the sand, their pistols at their sides. On the count of three they raised their weapons and fired. Neither scored a hit. Another round was fired—the code duello required at least two exchanges of fire—and neither man's aim was any better. Some of the onlookers, and certainly the two principals, breathed a sigh of relief, hoping for an amicable settlement. Neither Wells nor Maddox held any special animosity for the other, but had simply been caught up in the rigid code of honor peculiar to the American South. Now that honor had been upheld on each side, the two shook hands, and Maddox suggested they all celebrate with a glass of wine—his friends had brought some. They turned and walked across the sandbar in the direction of the Maddox party.

Had some blood been spilled, that might have been the end of it.

Both groups of observers emerged from the willows and made their way toward the principals. The Wells faction was much closer, and they hurried across the sand at an angle, arriving first to confront the duelists—that Wells and Maddox had settled did not mean everyone else had. One of Samuel Wells's cousins, the volatile Samuel Cuny, confronted Colonel Robert Crain, of the Maddox party. "We might as well settle our troubles here and now," he said, and began to draw his pistol. Trying to prevent bloodshed, Cuny's brother stepped in front of him, and Wells grabbed his shoulders. Crain stepped back, but when James Bowie moved toward him, he let loose with one of his two pistols.

The ball missed Bowie, who fired a second later, yelling, "Crain, you have shot at me, and I will kill you." Crain turned and retreated a few steps, jumping across some gullies in the sand. By this time Cuny had freed himself and moved toward Crain, who fired his other pistol at him, hitting him in the thigh. Cuny fell backward to the sand, blood pumping from his injury; the ball had severed his femoral artery. He would die from severe hemorrhage within minutes.

Bowie drew his knife and charged Crain, who turned and threw his spent pistol at Bowie, knocking him off his feet. As Bowie stood up, Maddox grabbed him, but Bowie threw him off. Norris Wright and two of his cohorts, the Blanchard brothers, ran up. Bowie veered off to a thick driftwood tree stump sticking six feet out of the ground and took cover behind it. Wright strode forward and drew his pistol.

"You damned rascal," yelled Bowie. "Don't you shoot." Someone scampered over and handed him a pistol and Bowie and Wright fired at each other, both missing. Wright leveled another pistol at Bowie and pulled the trigger; the ball slammed into Bowie's chest, traveled through his lung, and exited out his back. Bowie staggered, then plowed through the sand toward Wright before a shot from one of the Blanchard brothers passed through his thigh, and he finally fell to the ground.

Wright and one of the Blanchards unsheathed their sword canes and fell upon the downed Bowie. They stabbed him several times, but Bowie fended off some blows with his knife and free arm, though one stroke tore into his free hand. Another found his breastbone, which bent the blade.

Somehow Bowie found the strength to sit up and grab Wright's cravat. Wright reared back, pulling Bowie to his feet. Bowie put all his remaining strength into one thrust with his big knife into Wright's chest, then he twisted the blade. Wright collapsed, dying, onto Bowie, pinning him to the ground.

Blanchard stabbed again at Bowie, but then Thomas Wells shot him in the arm, allowing Bowie to reach up and slice Blanchard in the side. Blanchard retreated, the melee ended, and the Sandbar Fight quickly passed into legend.

Bowie, the recipient of several deep stab wounds, at least two lead balls, and one accurately hurled pistol to his head, was "not expected to recover," claimed one newspaper. But it would take more than that to kill Jim Bowie.

The Sandbar Fight was reported in newspapers across the country, including the young nation's most widely read news-weekly, *Niles' Weekly Register,* published in Washington, D.C. Bowie's superhuman feats of personal combat in the free-for-all made his reputation as perhaps the most feared fighter in the South and on the frontier. Years later, he would tell a Presbyterian minister he happened to be traveling with of the fracas and of his encounter with Wright. "It did my very soul good," he said, "to wrench it through his heart, and kill such a mean puppy, who would stab a man already down." Courteous to strangers, loyal to friends, and chivalrous to women, James Bowie was unforgiving of any man who became an enemy.

BOWIE WAS BORN IN 1796 in southern Kentucky, the son of Rezin Bowie, of Scottish descent, and the Welsh-blooded Elvira "Elve" Jones, an iron-willed young volunteer nurse during the Revolutionary War. She cared for Rezin after he sustained an injury while fighting the British with Colonel Francis Marion, married him soon after, and bore him several sons and daughters. In 1800, the family moved to Spanish-owned Missouri, on the Mississippi. When James was six, Rezin moved his family again, this time downriver to the bayou in Louisiana, some thirty miles west of Natchez. A few years later, in 1809, the Bowie patriarch pulled up stakes one more time, to another bayou eighty miles south, near Opelousas, where the family prospered in the timber-cutting business.

By that time the Bowie children were reaching adulthood, or nearing it. James and his brother Rezin Jr., almost three years older, were inseparable: always outdoors, hunting, fishing, roaming the countryside, roping and capturing wild deer and horses, even riding alligators and catching bears, except when Elve Bowie—an "exceedingly pious woman," according to the oldest Bowie brother, John—kept them inside to teach them the basics of the three Rs—"reading, writing, and 'rithmetic," as they were colloquially referred to. Whenever possible she would bring a circuit rider in to preach to her brood. As an adult, James would fill out to a muscular 180 pounds and six feet, with chestnut brown hair and dark gray-blue eyes set deep in a fair-complected face that women found attractive. His eyes were calm and penetrating until he was angered—when, it was said, they resembled a tiger's.

In January 1815, with the British preparing an expedition against New Orleans, eighteen-year-old James and his brother Rezin mustered in Opelousas. Their military regiment marched toward the Crescent City, but the Battle of New Orleans concluded on January 8, before they arrived. In that clash, Andrew Jackson defeated the British, and peace between the two nations was made days later.

Young James had little money and few belongings other than his wits and his brawn, but he and his brothers had been raised to be enterprising. Over the next few years, while working in the family timber-cutting business, he slowly acquired free open land or inexpensive tracts for little money down. By the time he was twenty-three, he owned several slaves and a good bit of land. He was also gaining a reputation as a fearless backwoodsman, one whom few men dared to insult. When that happened, the Bowie blood came up, and he would often take matters into his own hands—literally. "It was his habit to settle all difficulties without regard to time or place," remembered one friend, "and it was the same whether he met one or many."

Bowie and his brothers moved into a more profitable business in 1819. The African slave trade had been abolished nine years earlier, but the burgeoning plantation culture in the Deep South and west of the Mississippi created a lucrative market for smuggled slaves. Those captured by the authorities were sold at auction. Like a few other states, Louisiana gave half the auction proceeds to the parties who turned in the slaves or provided information leading to their seizure.

The resourceful Bowie brothers—they all stuck close together, particularly James and Rezin—quickly learned the ropes. They did much business with the man who dominated slave smuggling in the area, Jean Laffite—who, along with Andrew Jackson, was credited with saving New Orleans from the British. The Bowies added a brilliant twist to the scam: after they turned in the "found" slaves to the authorities, they would outbid other buyers at auction. Pocketing their reward of half the proceeds, they would in effect pay only half the final price and receive clear title to their chattels to boot.

Two years of this netted the brothers Bowie a small fortune, but their scheme was a delicate one, with a finite profit potential, and they got out before officials became too suspicious of the brothers' knack for finding their source of bounty. Next up for the Bowies was an even more lucrative business: land speculation on a grand scale.

In itself, the buying of uninhabited land, sometimes on credit or on easy terms, reselling it at a higher price, and then paying off the original note—thus making a tidy profit with little capital ventured—was not illegal. Many men were involved in similar schemes in the young country's new territories, and Arkansas and Louisiana were rife with opportunity: they had changed hands more than once, and the confusing lack of clear title and multiple sovereignties created a muddled and wide-open market for fraud and forgery. Over the next decade, the Bowies jumped in feetfirst, none more enthusiastically than the brother some now referred to as Big Jim Bowie. Before the end of the decade, he engineered more than one hundred forged land claims and titles comprising eighty thousand acres in Arkansas and almost as many in Louisiana — enough to make him the largest landowner in the region if and when the claims were patented and thus legitimized.

But the Bowies' massive land schemes caught the attention of the U.S. attorney general, who instigated a thorough investigation that canceled almost all the fraudulent transactions — the audacity, method, and scale of which led these and similar claims to be known as Bowie claims. The attorney general also threatened legal action and possible criminal charges. Though neither of the brothers would ever be officially charged, and though the widespread knowledge of the scams did not prevent the election of Rezin Bowie to the Louisiana legislature three times, brother James had worn out his welcome.

But Big Jim had already set his sights westward, on an area even more wide open and promising: Texas, whose abundant land and rumored silver deposits seemed ripe for the Bowie touch.

He had made his first trip to the Mexican province in 1828, riding first to Stephen F. Austin's San Felipe, where he talked of building a much-needed cotton mill, then westward 150 miles to San Antonio de Béxar. There he introduced himself to the town's leading citizen, Don Juan Martín de Veramendi, soon to be vice governor of Texas — and his lovely daughter, sixteen-year-old Ursula. He made a few more trips over the next few years, and became much better acquainted with Texas and Ursula. By early 1831, he moved there for good. He became a Mexican citizen, fluent in Spanish, and the tentative owner of almost a million acres of land, largely through the engineered — but legal — purchase of more than a dozen eleven-league grant leases, available only to Mexican citizens.

That was also the year Bowie engineered another advantageous acquisition. In April, he married Ursula Veramendi in Béxar's Church of San Fernando. The groom was thirty-five, his bride nineteen, but it appeared to be a love match for both. Bowie was now related to one of the most powerful families in the Mexican state of Coahuila y Tejas.

After living in a few different rented houses, in early 1832 the couple moved into the modest Veramendi mansion in town. Over the next few years Bowie spent more time on the road than he did at home, working in various mercantile activities and nursing his land grants along toward confirmation, always after a bigger score. He had heard stories of the fabled silver mines in the San Saba hills to the northwest, and in November 1831, accompanied by his brother Rezin and nine other men, traveled one hundred miles to the area of the mines. He took with him a thirteen-year-old boy named Carlos Espalier, a mulatto orphan that he and Ursula had informally adopted into their home.

Six weeks after leaving, the party was attacked by a band of 124 Indians. Over the course of ten hours, besieged in a grove of trees behind a makeshift breastwork of saddles, packs, and rocks, the men withstood a furious series of assaults. When the Indians finally left the area, one of Bowie's men lay dead and three others were wounded. They estimated thirty Indians killed and forty injured, and even if these numbers were exaggerated, the losses Bowie's men inflicted were impressive. A small band of Texians in a crude fort had withstood odds better than ten to one.

As word spread of the battle, James Bowie's reputation as a fighter and a leader of men increased. He was a man to be reckoned with, one who could impose his will on a situation, no matter how dire. If the Sandbar Fight had made him famous, this clash made him a Texian to whom others looked for direction and leadership.

OVER THE NEXT FEW YEARS, Bowie seemed always to be on the move. His peregrinations encompassed business dealings in Saltillo, the state capital; far-ranging expeditions into the wilderness in search of hostile Indians—and gold and silver; and on to San Felipe, Brazoria, and other points farther east, such as New Orleans. And of course, he made trips back to his kin in Louisiana, where he found most of his holdings gone. In addition, an 1833 U.S. Supreme Court ruling would negate the Bowie claims in Arkansas, further depleting his assets.

As events in his new country edged it closer toward outright rebellion, Bowie followed suit. After the Travis-instigated takeover at Anahuac in the spring of 1832, similar disturbances erupted at Nacogdoches and the port city of Matamoros. In July, when Stephen Austin needed a man he could count on, he asked Bowie to ride with all due haste to Nacogdoches to defuse a volatile situation involving, again, a confrontation between a fed-up citizenry and a Mexican garrison: the military commander there had demanded that the locals surrender their arms. Their refusal to do so was predictable and justified, since they would have been left with no defense against Indians. Bowie arrived in town one day too late to prevent a skirmish between the two hundred soldiers and three hundred Texians, but when the Mexicans evacuated that night, Bowie took control. He chose twenty men to accompany him in pursuit of the garrison troops. After some clever tactical maneuvering, he returned the next day with two hundred prisoners, who were escorted to Béxar and eventually returned to Mexico.

Bowie spent little time with his young bride, but she bore him two children, who died soon after birth. When an outbreak of cholera spread across the Mississippi Valley and then farther west into Texas, he was bedridden in Natchez with a bout of malaria. He was still recuperating early in November when he received news of Ursula's death in Monclova, where her family had fled from the cholera. Ursula, her mother, her father, and her adopted brother all died from the disease within days of reaching the city. The Bowies had been married for only two and a half years.

The news almost destroyed the weakened Bowie, and although he made a complete recovery, at least physically, more than one man would detect tears in his eyes when his late wife's name was mentioned. When he was able, he left Natchez and returned to Béxar in early 1834. After a monthslong expedition into far north Texas, in June he traveled to Monclova, the new capital of Coahuila y Tejas, where he eventually amassed—legally, though aided by a few corrupt politicians—more than half a million acres of Texas land. If the Mexican immigration laws loosened up, Bowie could make a fortune in sales to immigrants, even without the eleven-league leases. He spent almost a year in Monclova, wheeling and dealing with several other speculators.

When Santa Anna, now virtually a dictator, got wind of the massive land grabs effected by Bowie and other speculators, he had their claims annulled, and Bowie and several others were arrested in late May 1835 and taken to Mata-moros. A couple of weeks later Bowie and his friend Blas Des-pallier escaped when their captors relaxed their guard. They made their way overland to Texas, eventually reaching Nacog-doches in October.

Bowie's treatment at the hands of the Mexican authorities—and, undoubtedly, the loss of his potential fortune—pushed him further toward those clamoring for war and indepen-dence. Santa Anna's decision to reopen the customs houses in Texas and enforce the collection of import duties had been unpopular with a populace increasingly at odds with their Mexican hosts. After Travis seized the Anahuac garrison, Texian settlements large and small began to organize local militias in preparation for a major confrontation that appeared increasingly inevitable. Within days of Bowie's arrival in Nacogdoches, a hundred men gathered in the town square and elected Bowie "colonel" of their hastily formed militia, an hon-orary rank often bestowed upon a leader of a group of armed men in the South—and a recognition of a man's leadership, charisma, and popularity, qualities Bowie possessed in spades.

He and his men marched to a warehouse the Mexicans used as an armory and broke in, arming themselves with muskets. Nothing came of it; the majority of the locals seemed less than excited about the idea of armed revolt. But a week or so later, Bowie learned of the whereabouts of dispatches directed to the Mexican consul in New Orleans. He engineered the pack-et's seizure, then read the letters aloud before a town meeting in the Nacogdoches public square. Besides arrest orders for Travis and his cohorts, the dispatch discussed the possibility of a military occupation of Texas—news that pushed the enraged townsmen closer to action.

By late summer Bowie was on the road again, this time eastward, to his old stomping grounds in Louisiana. After several weeks spent visiting friends and talking up investment schemes, he returned to east Texas by early October with some associates. He had been there barely a week or two, tying up loose business ends, when the news arrived of an outbreak of hostilities in Gonzales, and a Texian army mobilizing for action. That was all Jim Bowie needed. He and his companions saddled up and rode west.

FOUR

"The Burly Is Begun"

Nothing but the certainty of hard fighting, and that shortly, could have kept us together so long.

BURR DUVAL

The settlers of *empresario* Green DeWitt's colony, immediately west of Austin's colony, and DeWitt's only town, Gonzales, were an especially hardy breed. They had to be, for as the westernmost Anglo settlement in the province, DeWitt's colony made a tempting target for predatory Indian tribes such as the Tawakonis, the Wacos, and the largest and fiercest, the Comanches. And because it was the settlement farthest from the coast, its store of supplies, both essential and nonessential, was sparse. But the land in the grant, stretching northwest along the Guadalupe River, was as fine and fertile as any in Texas. "It is a remarkably healthy and pleasant country, well watered... with valuable streams for mills and a forest of pine timber," observed an early visitor. "All the hills and dales, woods, and prairies, abound with buffalo, deer and turkey and occasionally black cattle for milk and work, and mustangs for riding."

The town of Gonzales had been laid out a decade earlier, on the west bank of the Guadalupe River, about seventy-six miles east of Béxar and eighty miles west of San Felipe. The first few years of its existence were tenuous ones. There were frequent Indian attacks, and most of the colony's early settlers came in from their fields at the end of the day and remained overnight with their families in the small fort near the river constructed for just that purpose. But a decade of steady immigration and enterprise had transformed Gonzales, and though Indians were still a constant threat, flocking to the fort was no longer a nightly ritual. By 1835 the village comprised more than thirty structures, including two small hotels, a kitchen, two blacksmith shops, a few mercantile establishments, and the requisite grogshop or two—one, named Luna, was just a few yards behind a small kitchen and restaurant owned by erstwhile moonshiner Adam Zumwalt, known as Red Adam. Most were only crude one-story log buildings, but Gonzales was beginning to look like a town. A large schoolhouse was under construction, and there was even a hat factory opened by New Yorker George Kimble and his business partner, Almeron Dickinson, a blacksmith from Tennessee whose comely young wife, Susanna, had recently given birth to a daughter they named Angelina. The hats were made of wool and rabbit fur—"not very handsome, but serviceable," remembered one DeWitt colonist.

There were other signs of civilization. Early the previous summer, the town's first ball had been held in the small inn owned by Thomas Miller, considered the richest man in town. Folks came from forty miles around, many of them displaying admission cards that read: ADMIT MR. _____ AND SWEETHEART TO BALL AT MILLER HOTEL. Women wore fancy white dresses for the first time in years. In the large dining area serving as the ballroom, candles on boards stuck in the walls cast a warm glow as George Washington "Wash" Cottle and Dr. John Tinsley fiddled away, Cottle calling the sets of Virginia reels, cotillions, and other dances and singing:

> We'll dance all night
> Till broad daylight
> And go home with the gals in the morning.

Everyone, young and old, danced. The floor was so crowded that the dancers had to take the floor in two shifts. The ball went on until eight the next morning. Everyone left saying they'd had the time of their lives.

Until the fall of 1835, DeWitt colonists had condemned previous revolutionary acts of the pro-independence War Dog party. Their *ayuntamiento* had refused to attend the 1832 convention for fear that the citizens might be associated with the independence movement. They had even passed a resolution of loyalty to Mexico in July. Their sentiments began to change in September, though, after twenty-five Mexican soldiers brazenly appropriated Zumwalt's store to quarter for the night; for no apparent reason, a Mexican soldier used his musket to bloody the head of colonist Jesse McCoy—recently elected second lieutenant of the Gonzales militia—as the young Tennessean attempted to make his way into Zumwalt's storeroom. That act, combined with news of Santa Anna's dictatorial takeover and brutal subjugation of the rebellious state of Zacatecas in May—news that was gleaned from occasional newspaper accounts and a steady stream of stories from riders along the Béxar–San Felipe road—considerably jaundiced the colonists' views.

Thus, in late September, when a Mexican corporal and five soldiers rode from Béxar to Gonzales with an empty oxcart and appeared at the river's edge opposite town, requesting the return of their cannon, the townspeople were not as eager as they might have been to hand it over. The gun in question

was only a six-pounder, and was crudely mounted on a makeshift wooden caisson. Green DeWitt had requested it in 1831
to help defend his town against Indian attacks. It was an old
piece of artillery, showing visible damage and evidence of
crude repairs, and was good for little more than a loud noise
and a large belch of smoke—the better, it was hoped, to scare
off the Indians. But the Texians knew that the authorities in
Béxar had no need of it; there were several larger cannon at
the Alamo, the old Franciscan mission east of town now home
to a presidial unit charged primarily with protecting the locals
against Comanche raids.

Their position was made known when the corporal and his
men were disarmed by a dozen townsmen and taken prisoner,
then paroled back to Béxar. The townspeople quickly called
a meeting at which they discussed the ramifications of their
actions. They knew more soldiers, many more, would return,
and soon. But they voted to continue their resistance; only
three citizens were in favor of returning the six-pounder. The
colonists began to prepare for the ensuing troubles, and most
of those on the west side of the Guadalupe moved across the
river into town, or into the woods or upriver to hide.

A few days later Colonel Domingo de Ugartechea, the military commander in Béxar, sent one hundred dragoons under
Lieutenant Francisco de Castañeda to secure the piece. The
lieutenant had been stationed at Béxar for more than a dozen
years, and had commanded the Alamo presidial company for
fourteen months—he owned two small houses on the northwest corner of the old mission, where he lived with his wife
and family. But he had never been ordered to commandeer a
cannon. Besides, he was a federalist himself. Nevertheless, he
led his troop out of the compound and toward the small Anglo
settlement two good days' ride east.

Though about a hundred colonists and their families lived

in the area, only eighteen were on hand when the lieutenant arrived at the banks of the rain-swollen Guadalupe on September 29. They had hidden all the canoes and the ferryboat on the east side of the river. When Castañeda yelled across the river and demanded the cannon, the Texians, to gain time, told him the *alcalde* was not at home, but would return the next evening. The *presidiales* fell back and bivouacked a half mile from the river.

While this small force prevented Castañeda and his men from crossing the Guadalupe and entering town, express riders galloped north and east, requesting reinforcements. Militiamen from Bastrop (which had been renamed Mina in 1834; its name would officially become Bastrop again in 1837), located on the upper Colorado River, along with militiamen from San Felipe, Washington, and other settlements on the Brazos, quickly organized and rode to Gonzales. When the colonists had initially confronted the small group of soldiers who had come for the cannon, they had sent the soldiers back to Béxar with a message intended to confuse the Mexican commanders about the situation. This had bought some precious time, and now more such delaying action by the town's leaders gained them another day. By September 30, a hundred men had gathered in the settlement, most of them congregating at Winslow Turner's double log hotel; the next day, there were 168 men. Green DeWitt's daughter Naomi offered up her wedding dress for a proper flag—a white banner bearing the words COME AND TAKE IT above the outline of an unmounted cannon.

Castañeda moved his company upriver in search of a crossing. That night, to the howling of a distant wolf pack, the Texians crossed the Guadalupe with the six-pounder, now mounted on a pair of oxcart wheels. They decided to take the offensive. At four the next morning, in a dense fog, a skirmish broke out when the Mexican pickets fired on the Texian advance guard. After a parley that produced nothing, James C. Neill, a Bastrop man who had served under Andrew Jackson against the Creek Indians, fired the first cannon shot of the resistance. The Texians opened fire and charged. The Mexicans, who had been instructed to retire if the opposing force was superior, wheeled around and fled, having already lost one soldier.

Over the next week, men continued to arrive in Gonzales, until about three hundred colonists, embracing a dozen or so militia companies from various settlements, were gathered there. Turner's two-story hotel continued to serve as the rallying point. Each company elected its own captain, but none recognized a commander in chief. There was no consensus of opinion regarding Mexico: "Some were for independence; some for the constitution of 1824; and some for anything, just so it was a row," remembered one volunteer. The one thing they agreed on was the need to march to Béxar and finish the job. General Martín Perfecto de Cós, commander of the Eastern Interior Provinces, was probably there by now, with seven hundred troops or so. The son of a doctor, Cós was a small, elegant man—he wore gold earrings and traveled with gold candlesticks—and a longtime supporter of Santa Anna. Most believed he would march to Gonzales to take care of the problem himself. But save for their effective cavalry and the recently arrived Morelos Battalion, a regular army unit of two hundred veteran infantrymen, the Texians were unimpressed with the Mexicans' show of force. Many troops sent to the northern border states were convicts given the thorny choice of prison or Texas, and the Mexican army in general was underfed, underpaid, undersupplied, and unmotivated to fight a war few of them understood.

It was vital to whip Cós before he received reinforcements. The officers sent a rider with an express message to Stephen Austin in San Felipe, imploring him to come lead the Army of the People, as they now called themselves. Just a few weeks earlier, Austin had been told that Mexican troops would march into the colonies and take care of the rabble-rousers whether things calmed down or not. That had prompted him to write a broadside on September 19 that was circulated throughout Texas, in which he said, "Nothing was to be gained by further conciliatory measures.... War is our only resource." In private letters he had expressed his feelings even more strongly. "The country has a cause; and a just and glorious cause to defend," he wrote a friend on October 5. "From this time forward those who are <u>not</u> for the cause ought to be treated as enemies — there is no middle ground." Mexico's most loyal colonist had finally concluded that independence was the only answer.

The forty-year-old *empresario* was in poor health, and his military experience consisted of seven uneventful weeks in the Missouri militia and a few raids he had led against the Indians; he knew his limitations better than anyone. But he was the one man all the colonists respected, and upon his arrival in Gonzales on October 11, he was unanimously elected commanding general of the Texian forces. The ragtag army, including nearly every able-bodied man in DeWitt's colony, began a slow march westward the next day, following the rudimentary road laid out several years earlier by Byrd Lockhart, the colony surveyor. (For his considerable efforts in clearing a path from Béxar to San Felipe wide enough for an oxcart, Lockhart had asked for and received four choice leagues of land.)

Most of the three hundred men were landowning farmers, with a few merchants and mechanics, as skilled craftsmen were called, mixed in. A handful of them owned slaves; the rest were too poor for such luxuries. The majority of them had wives and families at home. Few of them had professional military training, but many had served with small militia units against Indians or in earlier skirmishes against Mexican garrisons. Not every man had a gun—and some of their weapons were held together with "buckskin string and spit," remembered one volunteer—but those who did were proficient with them, whether they carried a Kentucky long rifle accurate at more than two hundred yards, less accurate but sturdy muskets, or short-barreled shotguns for close action. Some carried flintlock pistols, and almost every man wore a large knife in a sheath attached to his belt. A leather shot pouch suspended by a broad strap that went over the shoulder held rifle balls, bullet molds, "bullet patchin'," gun wipes, and an extra flint or two; attached to this pouch was a powder horn.

The group bore little resemblance to an army—at least not to "the army of my childhood dreams," remembered Noah Smithwick, a blacksmith. "Buckskin breeches were the nearest approach to a uniform, and there was wide diversity even there, some being new and soft and yellow, while others, from long familiarity with rain and grease and dirt, had become hard and black and shiny. . . . Boots being an unknown quantity, some wore shoes and some moccasins." Some sported broad-brimmed sombreros, others military headgear or top hats, or the occasional coonskin cap with the tail hanging down behind. Most wore hunting shirts or jackets with homespun blouses underneath, though an occasional buffalo robe could be seen. They rode large American horses and small Spanish ponies, half-broke mustangs and methodical mules. Few had canteens; most carried a Spanish gourd or two full of water.

DeWitt's colony had contributed more than its share of personnel: left behind were only a dozen men, most of them invalids, and hundreds of women and children. Altogether, Austin's Army of the People was a disparate and rowdy lot, with only one thing in common, at least as they saw it: the desire and willingness to fight for their freedom from a tyrant's oppression. Their chance would not be long in coming.

FIVE

The Army of the People

All are united, our frontier is attacked & who says now that we shall not fight? Let us go at it heart & hand—stand up like men & have nothing to fear.

WILLIAM BARRET TRAVIS

The rebels followed Byrd Lockhart's blazed trail westward. Through the forests, large trees bore carved numerals denoting the number of miles from Béxar, and wooden posts did the same on the prairie, where the men kept an especially close watch—no one wanted to get caught in the open by the Mexican lancers, whose reputation as well-trained warriors preceded them.

The Texians were an army of irregular riflemen, and it was to their advantage to keep to the woods. About fifteen miles west of Gonzales they camped on Sandies Creek, near John Castleman's place, the farthest outpost of Anglo settlement. The desolate location required constant vigilance against roving Indian parties, and each evening Castleman's family retreated into their house, enclosed by strong palisades. A cold rain rendered the army's bivouac highly uncomfortable, since few men had brought tents or shelters.

Another day or two through miles of sandy soil and forests of mesquite and oak brought the army to Cibolo Creek, twenty miles from the provincial capital. The steadily flowing waters, combined with a shallow ford at a bend where the road crossed the creek, made it a popular *paraje,* or resting stop. They remained there a few days while more reinforcements arrived, then moved to the Salado River, just three or four miles from Béxar. Overhead, Halley's Comet was visible in the night sky, and the men argued over whether it was a good omen or bad. When the news arrived that, on October 10, a group of Texians had taken control of the Presidio La Bahía near Goliad and its fifty-four Mexican troops, every man knew what that meant: the last Mexican soldiers in Texas lay ahead of them.

One of the new arrivals was James Bowie, recently returned to Texas from another visit to Louisiana and Mississippi. He rode into camp with a group of friends and followers and immediately sent a courier into town conveying his compliments to the people of Béxar. Stephen Austin, grateful for Bowie's veteran presence, gave him command of a large company and sent him toward the string of missions stretching a few miles downriver below the town, to reconnoiter and forage for corn or other stores for the hungry command. Bowie's connections in Béxar proved invaluable, and he supplied Austin with much-needed intelligence—for instance, that Cós's army numbered six hundred men at most.

William Barret Travis was there also. He had joined a militia company in San Felipe just before the Gonzales incident, but a bout of influenza had prevented him from riding there immediately. When he finally arrived in Gonzales it was as an elected lieutenant. He was also a delegate to the Consultation, now rescheduled to meet in San Felipe on November 1, but he and several other representatives decided to remain with the army and march to Béxar.

Another valuable addition was twenty-eight-year-old Juan Seguín, whose father, Erasmo, was a good friend of Stephen Austin's and a former Béxar *alcalde*. Erasmo Seguín was one of the town's most prominent citizens, and he had raised his children in a cultured, liberal atmosphere; both men were staunch federalists, and Juan had recently returned from skirmishing with centralist troops near Monclova. The Seguín family owned one of the largest ranches in the area, a nine-thousand-acre tract thirty miles downriver, where Erasmo had built a fortified compound known as Casa Blanca. General Cós, upon his arrival in Béxar, and upon learning of Juan's siding with the rebels, had booted the elderly Erasmo out of town without a horse. He walked the thirty miles downriver to his ranch.

The handsome young Seguín brought with him a company of thirty-seven other mounted Tejanos. Many of them were recruited from the ranches on the lower San Antonio River, though at least fourteen were deserters from the Alamo presidial garrison. From the town of Victoria to the southeast, *alcalde* Plácido Benavides arrived with another twenty-six Tejano volunteers, and at least forty more from the ranches south of Béxar rode into camp over the next several days led by Seguín's brother-in-law, Salvador Flores. A total of 135 Mexican Texians would sign up, all declaring themselves loyal to the Mexican constitution of 1824. They would provide valuable scouting and foraging services, and also serve as fighters, in the months to come.

San Antonio de Béxar lay in a valley of rolling prairie land between two parallel streams: San Pedro Creek on the west and the San Antonio River on the east. The area surrounding these waterways, nestled between low hills on either side and favored with large oaks and pecans, had attracted men for thousands of years, perhaps more; its beauty was such that many proclaimed it the prettiest spot in Texas. Between them was a town of some sixteen hundred souls, only a few of them Anglos — though many *bexareños* had fled their dwellings for the ranches along the river to the south. Thick-walled stone and mortar buildings crowded the broad dirt streets around the two squares, the Plaza de las Islas (Main Plaza), nearer to the river, and the Plaza de Armas (Military Plaza), to the west; between them stood the Church of San Fernando and its bell tower. Beyond the few blocks of downtown began a spread of log houses and even cruder habitations, the mud-and-stick shacks called *jacales*. Above and below Béxar, fields of corn were watered by *acequias,* man-made irrigation ditches that flowed through and around the town. A few miles to the west lay a range of limestone hills.

To the east, across the sixty-foot-wide river lined with cypresses, *acequias* also flowed on either side of the former mission originally named San Antonio de Valero but now called the Alamo, after a presidial company once garrisoned there from Alamo de Parras, Mexico. Built more than a hundred years before, the crumbling compound had been one of five missions in the area; the ruins of the other four lay along the river to the south. Beginning with the Alamo in 1793, all had been secularized when the numbers of Indian converts had dwindled. The compound had been a military post for more than thirty years. A thick adobe wall surrounded most of the Alamo's buildings. Several hundred of Cós's men were there, fortifying the makeshift redoubt with several artillery pieces, a few of the larger ones being placed in the roofless church. The front of the structure had been piled high with dirt and rubble, and a crude ramp enabled cannon to be dragged to the top, albeit with great difficulty.

The fortifications in town were even more impressive. Log and earth barricades, some of them twelve feet high, blocked the main streets and reinforced the doors to several of the larger buildings, and nine cannon on swivels protected the town squares and the roads leading to them. At the entrance of every street, a ditch was dug ten feet wide and five feet deep. Over this was a breastwork of upright posts built with portholes for muskets and a large one in the center for cannon.

On October 27, while the Texians were still camped on the Salado, five miles outside of town, Austin authorized Travis, the owner of several fine horses, to raise a cavalry command of fifty or so volunteers, each to be armed with a double-barreled shotgun and a brace of pistols. Travis wasted no time in doing so, and the next morning, his horsemen were in the saddle and on the road toward Béxar. They had just crossed the San Antonio River when they heard gunfire up ahead.

The day before, Austin had sent Bowie and James Fannin—an ambitious young Georgia slave trader who had attended West Point for two years before moving his family to Velasco in 1834—to the mission closest to Béxar, Concepción, to lead a scouting party in search of an acceptable bivouac for the army. Juan Seguín accompanied them as guide. They were to return by dark. The detail of ninety-two men reached the abandoned mission, and the river a quarter mile beyond, just about noon. They promptly engaged in a skirmish with a small force of Mexican cavalry, which galloped back to town. Bowie decided the position was too good to risk losing, regardless of Austin's orders to return by nightfall. He carefully placed his men near a bend in the river just west of the mission, on a broad river bottom six feet below the rolling prairie, and settled in for the night.

Early the next morning a dense fog covered the ground. A Texian picket saw a Mexican cavalry scout, took a shot at him, and rifle and musket fire promptly erupted from both sides. General Cós had learned of the detachment and sent out four hundred men to cut off and destroy it; they quickly surrounded the outnumbered Texians. The colonists were backed up to a body of water that, while preventing an attack from the rear, made retrograde movement difficult and invited attack on the flanks.

Fortunately for Bowie and his men, the Mexicans neglected such tactics and made a direct assault. As they did so, Bowie shifted his two wings to a more favorable position. As Mexican infantry and artillery advanced across the prairie, he shouted to his men, "Keep under cover, boys, and reserve your fire; we haven't a man to spare." A scatterload of canister (a tin cylinder filled with lead or iron balls) from two Mexican cannon ripped through the trees above the Texians, and pecans rained down on the ground. Some men ate them in between the Mexican infantry charges, which their accurate long-rifle fire repelled. After the third charge, Bowie ordered his men up and over the riverbank and into the enemy lines. They captured one of the cannon, turned it around, and blasted a load of canister into the Mexicans, who retreated to Béxar. The triumph was small but significant. The rebels had suffered only two casualties, one wounded and one dead. The Mexican losses were fifty, with at least twenty killed.

The clash at Concepción—another instance of Bowie directing a severely outmanned contingent to victory—immediately raised the spirits of the Texians. The battle also demonstrated the effectiveness of well-aimed rifle fire against a larger attacking force, even one supported by cavalry and artillery.

Austin's rebels rushed to the sound of the guns from their camp six miles south at Mission San Francisco de la Espada, the last in the chain of abandoned missions. He was initially eager to pursue the Mexicans into Béxar with a full-fledged assault. But after Bowie and other leaders objected, pointing to the town's fortifications, its many artillery pieces, and Cós's ample and well-trained force, he pulled his troops back. A few days later, after further consultation with his officers, Austin's army settled down for a siege. The Mexicans were low on supplies, and in this case discretion, not valor, seemed the wiser path. Austin took his men to a position almost a mile north of town, near an abandoned sugar mill, leaving Bowie and Fannin at Concepción.

On November 1, a few days after the Concepción battle, Austin put the question to a council of his officers: Attack or siege? The majority voted against storming Béxar, and the army settled into siege mode. The next five weeks tested the mettle and determination of the Army of the People in more ways than one.

In San Felipe, meanwhile, the Consultation laid the groundwork for a working government by establishing a provisional authority, the General Council, and electing a governor — while at the same time voting 33–14 against a declaration of independence from Mexico and in favor of the Mexican constitution of 1824. Officially, at least for now, Texas considered itself a state of Mexico, separate from Coahuila — and its citizens considered themselves loyal to their adopted country. But they were virtually without funds, provisions, or a regular army, though they unanimously elected a commander in chief of the nonexistent forces: Sam Houston, the former governor of Tennessee and apparently the only man in San Felipe interested in the job.

A hero of the War of 1812 and one-time protégé of Andrew Jackson, the hard-drinking, charismatic Houston had resigned his governorship after a disastrous six-week marriage apparently doomed from the start: she had loved another, and was pressed into the socially advantageous union by her family.

He went to live with his friends in the Cherokee Nation for three years, where his 6-feet-2-inch frame and fondness for the bottle earned him the Indian name Big Drunk; more than once his common-law Cherokee wife, Tiana Rogers, had to fetch Houston and throw him over his horse to get him home. He had partially vindicated himself, though, with a triumphant appearance in Washington, D.C. While in town as head of a Cherokee delegation, he caned a congressman who had insulted him on the House floor; put on trial, he defended himself with a fiery speech that convinced the legislative body to issue him only a slight reprimand. His stirring oratory was reprinted far and wide, and thrust him back into the national spotlight. In 1832 he moved to Nacogdoches, where he started a law practice. In December of that year, while in San Felipe on business, he met Jim Bowie, and the two shared a Christmas dinner there. Bowie also escorted Houston to Béxar, where he introduced him to the town's upper-crust citizens, such as the Veramendis, Bowie's in-laws.

Rumors had circulated for years that Houston was in Texas to procure the territory for his former mentor, President Jackson—Old Hickory's desire to possess the area was well known, and he had authorized more than one botched attempt to purchase the Mexican province. (He was not alone: over the previous decade, his presidential predecessors had made three proposals to the Mexican government for the purchase of all or part of Texas.) Houston, a striking figure in his greasy buckskins and colorful Mexican blanket, had recently been elected the Nacogdoches delegate to the Consultation. He advocated American annexation in private, and it appears he was indeed scouting the territory for Jackson—at least after his initial plan, to buy up the remaining land of an entire colony, fell through when another *empresario* beat him to it.

There were those who distrusted Houston's motives, and

disapproved of his rambunctious and sometimes scandalous ways—he could outdrink and outswear any man he met, and his fiery temper made him almost as many enemies as friends. But there were few men who could match his military experience and towering presence, so he was given command of a 1,120-man army that had yet to officially sign up a single soldier. Besides commanding them, Houston was also charged with raising all military forces, regular, auxiliary, or otherwise—an imposing task in itself, even without the handicap of having no staff. Indeed, the aversion of old settlers and new volunteers to the rigors and restrictions of the regular army would result in few recruitments—at the height of the hostilities four months later, they would total a hundred men at most. But volunteers by the hundreds responded to the proclamation he boldly issued on October 8—a month before he was appointed commander in chief—calling for help of a more informal nature:

> Volunteers are invited to our standard. Liberal
> bounties of land will be given to all who will join our
> ranks with a good rifle and one hundred rounds of
> ammunition.... The morning of glory is dawning upon
> us. The work of liberty has begun. Our actions are to
> become a part of the history of mankind.

Lofty sentiments aside, there was no lack of problems for Austin's army. The weather was turning nasty—the first norther blew into the area at the end of October, and another dropped temperatures a week later. Food, gunpowder, and other basics were in short supply. Discipline was virtually nonexistent: copies of the standard texts of the day—Scott's *Infantry Tactics,* von Steuben's *Regulations for the Order and Discipline of the Troops of the United States,* and Cooper and Macomb's *Cooper's Volunteer's Manual*—were requisitioned by the General Council in late November, though they would never arrive. "There was little time for military tactics," recalled one volunteer, "but it was necessary that we learn to act in concert, the most important maneuver being to fire by platoons and fall back to reload." If they mastered that maneuver and had a chance to display it, no one ever remembered later. The Army of the People was, at this point, little more than a well-intentioned mob. Indeed, these American-born Texians had a habit of insisting on elections rather than merely obeying their elected superiors, who as a result often had to word their orders in the form of requests. "Everyone acted as he pleased and the officers were so far obeyed, as suited the whims and caprices of the men," recalled a member of the New Orleans Greys, two companies of which were raised, outfitted, armed, and sent to Texas by businessmen in the Crescent City upon news of the outbreak of hostilities. (All 118 of the newcomers wore gray clothing bought there just before leaving, usually including a snug-fitting waist-length jacket with a high collar, possibly military surplus from the War of 1812; many also wore soft, long-visored sealskin hunting caps.) Another Grey recalled that after breakfast, "we then broke into small groups if there was nothing to fear from the Indians or large groups of the enemy and galloped away as we pleased." For entertainment, some men eager for action made their way to an artillery entrenchment thrown up south of camp, about a thousand yards from town, where they would take turns blasting cannon shots at the Alamo and place bets on their accuracy. Other militiamen amused themselves by chasing down the brass cannonballs that the Mexicans in the fort shot at the Texian camp.

Others, once their terms of volunteer service expired, drifted off steadily; one night an entire company melted away after dark. Many left to return home—they had marched to

Béxar to fight, not sit around idly and indefinitely while the Mexican garrison was starved out. Word had spread that a large cannon had landed at Velasco, and when a man wished to leave, he would declare that he "was going after that cannon." Some remained only when the General Council announced that those who stayed until the fall of the town would receive twenty dollars a month.

While Travis's mounted force, augmented by Captain Seguín's vaqueros, scoured the countryside and burned much of the grass on the road south to the Rio Grande to hinder the advance of any other troops from Mexico, the rest of the eight-hundred-man force conducted itself much less militarily. Drunkenness was so common that Austin, in consternation, sent a plainly worded message to the General Council: "In the name of Almighty God, send no more ardent spirits to this camp—if any is on the road, turn it around or have the head knocked out." Drunks wandered through the campsite, firing their guns randomly, wasting ammunition, while others spent much of their day gambling and cockfighting. One man murdered another and was strung up from a pecan tree the next day. Winter was setting in, and most of the men were without warm clothing. When it rained, the army in its ramshackle camp of tents and huts was especially miserable, and the unsanitary conditions and lack of proper doctoring or medical supplies resulted in much sickness, no doubt exacerbated by the camp's proximity to a field where cattle were slaughtered. (After visiting the camp, Houston expressed worry that an epidemic might break out.) Great flocks of vultures grazed among the hundreds of carcasses, heads, and skins, most of them picked clean. Even a few wolves and coyotes roamed there, for the most part undisturbed. In a very real sense, it was not clear which side was under siege and which was better off.

The boredom was relieved only by an occasional brushup,

such as the skirmish that came to be known as the Grass Fight. An enemy column of one hundred cavalry and as many mules was sighted south of town on the morning of November 26, and a rumor spread that the pack train conveyed silver intended to pay the Mexican garrison. Bowie was dispatched to reconnoiter. He recruited several of the best marksmen and galloped out of camp, quickly followed by most of the volunteers, eager to share in the booty. About a mile outside Béxar, Bowie's force charged into the mule train. After a flurry of exchanged gunfire, the Mexican dragoons abandoned the mules and made for safety. The Texians pursued them to within three hundred yards of town. Cós sent a column of reinforcements, who persuaded the men to turn back. Instead of silver, the mule packs contained freshly cut grass for the garrison's starving cavalry mounts.

A further blow to the army's hopes came in mid-November, when the General Council relieved Stephen Austin of command in order to send him to the United States to garner support for Texas. Austin, so frail and weak that he needed to be helped onto his horse, had requested the move: "I believe that my wornout constitution is not adapted to a military command, neither have I ever pretended to be a military man." Before he left, on November 22, Austin ordered an assault on Béxar to begin the next day at dawn. The weather was damp and very cold, and late that night, his two divisional commanders informed him that the majority of the men were reluctant to participate. Stunned, Austin called off the attack. He left for San Felipe two days later. His men, aware of his devotion to the Texian cause, shook hands with him in silence.

Elected general in Austin's stead was Edward Burleson, a veteran Indian fighter from Bastrop. As a fourteen-year-old private in his father's company during the War of 1812, Burleson had shot a Creek chief, and he had fought many other

Indians since arriving in Texas in 1830. He was known to be fearless in battle. His father, James, now sixty years old, had also joined the Texian army, and had participated in the Grass Fight.

A week later the army had dwindled to about seven hundred men, and seemed close to dissolution. Money was scarce, supplies were running out, and the perseverance necessary to maintain a months-long siege had all but evaporated. Most of the Texian colonists had returned home, replaced by fresh arrivals from east Texas and beyond, the first of the volunteers from the United States, most of them young single men responding to news of the Texian revolt and eager to join the fight for freedom—and free land. Upon receiving intelligence of the Mexicans' weakened state and meager provisions, Burleson issued another attack order on December 1. When his officers reported, yet again, of the unwillingness of officers and men, Burleson canceled the assault. Two days later he announced that the siege would be abandoned. What was left of the army would retreat to the east side of the Guadalupe, to Gonzales or Goliad, there to wait out the winter. The revolution, if it was to continue, would have to wait until spring.

Hundreds of men left, and the rest prepared to break camp. Some of the volunteers, particularly the New Orleans Greys, had been eager for action, and expressed their discontent. Discord spread, until it appeared as if the disorderly troops might fight among themselves and ignore the enemy below the river.

Then, late one afternoon, a Mexican officer rode out of town and surrendered to the rebels. When he spoke of the poor morale of the Mexican troops, the argument for an attack was renewed. A leader was needed, someone to champion an attack, to rally the men before they all left. Into the midst of this confusion of packing, leaving, and vociferous discussion rode the man who would do just that.

SIX

The Battle of Béxar

I am of opinion it Will be a Serious one unless we are aided a mediatly Send us help and we never will quit the field until we can Enjoy our Constituanal rites.

EDWARD BURLESON

Ben Milam had already packed several lifetimes into his forty-seven years. He was a longtime Texian, sometime *empresario,* and full-time adventurer. Though barely literate, he could claim as much military experience as anyone in camp. He had fought in the War of 1812, engaged a few years later in a filibustering expedition into Mexico with the notorious James Long, battled Karankawa cannibals near the coast, and in 1821 served as a colonel in the army of the new Republic of Mexico for a time. When Agustín de Iturbide had assumed the imperial crown, Milam had resigned his commission, declaring that "he would never serve a king." By order of that monarch, he had been pursued, arrested, and imprisoned for a short time, until the republicans took over in March 1823. He had received a large land grant above DeWitt's in 1826,

though six years later he had only introduced fifty-two families into his colony, and his license was not renewed. At one
time he held claim to twenty-two Mexican mines. Such a life
held little room for a woman, and the only one he had ever
been engaged to had given up waiting for Milam and married
someone else.

But his many ventures had proven unsuccessful, and by
1835 he owned little more than one eleven-league grant. For
his various offenses, he had seen the inside of more than one
Mexican prison. He had only just escaped from one in
Monterrey—a friend arranged a horse and provisions—and
made his way hundreds of miles to Texas, somehow reaching
Goliad just in time to join the action there. His clothes in tat-
ters, he had donned items taken from the Mexican garrison
there, but the pants and sleeves were at least six inches too
short on Milam, who was slightly above average in height. A
few days later, when he rode into the camp at Gonzales, Austin
had made him commander of a mounted spy company.

The former Kentuckian's right knee was seriously arthritic
and his lower back gave him trouble, but he was still well
muscled and energetic. Just returned from a long scout toward
the Rio Grande, he became furious upon hearing of the plans
to fall back to winter quarters. He found General Burleson's
adjutant, the short-tempered Frank Johnson, and filled his ear.
Johnson, a longtime resident of Texas and an independence
firebrand from the beginning, was persuaded, and the two
marched to Burleson's tent and laid out their plan. Burleson
listened and agreed—he had not wanted to call off the previous attack, and told Milam that if he could muster enough
volunteers, they could proceed with an assault the next day.
Milam walked outside to find hundreds of expectant men.
Word had spread that something was up.

One friend of Milam's remembered his "commanding

appearance and fine address," and Milam drew upon both of those traits now. He took off his slouch hat, waved it above his head, and called out loud and clear, "Who will go with old Ben Milam into San Antonio?"

Scores of volunteers gathered near the tent yelled, "I will!" and "We will!"

Milam stepped across a path that ran in front of the tent — one man later claimed he drew a line in the dirt — and shouted, "Well, if you're going with me, get on this side of the road!"

The men roared in approval and rushed to fall in line with Milam. By the time they were accounted for, they numbered more than three hundred, including every able-bodied New Orleans Grey. In true democratic fashion, and to no one's surprise, they chose Milam to lead them. A few captains made speeches against the venture, and some of the men begged their friends not to throw away their lives so foolishly. But after a time was set for early the next morning, the volunteers prepared for the assault. Others continued to mount their horses and head for home.

Bowie had left in late November, most likely fed up with Austin's indecisiveness and the chaotic mess known as the Army of the People. Austin's command style had been less than dynamic: his weakly worded orders almost begged to be ignored, and Bowie had taken full advantage — "Contents duly considered," Bowie had replied to one of Austin's written directives. After duly considering Austin's "orders," he usually did as he thought best.

Bowie had departed, albeit on orders, to oversee the work fortifying Goliad, ninety-five miles down the San Antonio River, which would serve as winter quarters for the Texian forces. Travis left also, about the same time. He had achieved recognition for striking, with just a dozen horsemen, a large herd of Mexican mounts fifty miles south of Béxar. He led a dawn attack straight into the Mexican camp and took the *soldado* escort unit prisoner without a shot fired. When Austin learned of the three hundred captured horses, he praised his young cavalry captain. Travis returned to San Felipe at the end of November and was commended by the General Council there, and news of his fine work appeared in the town newspaper.

Burleson would supervise the operation from camp, where the remaining two hundred or so men would constitute a reserve. Few of them gave the assault force much of a chance against the well-fortified Mexican army.

On the north side of Béxar, half the distance to town, the assault force assembled at three a.m. Only two hundred men, fifteen small companies, showed up—the remainder apparently heeded the attempts to discourage them, including predictions that they would be butchered. A norther was blowing in, knocking down tents and makeshift huts, and the weather had helped persuade others to remain in their warm bedding. Milam's stalwarts wrapped their woolen blankets about them, shivering, as they waited for the signal. The moon was full and still high in the western sky.

At five o'clock that morning, December 5, a blast split the cool air as a cannonball crashed into the north wall of the Alamo. It was a diversion: earlier, chief artillerist Captain James Neill, who had fired the first cannon shot at Gonzales, had snuck a gun and its crew across the San Antonio River closer to the fort. The roar of the piece was answered by bugles, drums, and artillery fire, as well as the satisfying sight of a horde of Mexican infantrymen moving toward the mission, lit by the flare of rockets set off as alarms. The ruse had worked perfectly.

When Neill's cannon boomed, Milam's men dropped their blankets and scampered as quietly as possible the quarter mile south through the barren cornfields and into town—down two parallel streets toward the two northern corners of Main Plaza, with Milam at the head of one column and Frank Johnson leading the other. Two local men guided Johnson's unit: Samuel Maverick, an enterprising young man from Virginia who had only recently arrived in Béxar, and Erastus "Deaf" Smith, a New York native and scout extraordinaire—despite being hard of hearing—who lived south of town with his Tejana wife and four children. Guiding Milam's division was John W. Smith, a local carpenter and translator (nicknamed El Colorado for his red hair), and Hendrick Arnold, a free man of color and Deaf Smith's son-in-law. Johnson's men skirted a campfire of sentries, then ran into a single vedette as they reached town: Smith quickly shot him dead. But other pickets spread the alarm, and the Mexican artillery opened fire with volleys of grapeshot and canister on the *norteamericanos* in the narrow dirt streets.

Less than a hundred yards from the well-fortified Main Plaza and its seven cannon, the Texians hugged the walls. They broke down the thick wooden doors of a few stone and adobe houses and jumped inside. Several of the buildings were residences occupied by families that had elected to stay in town, and some of the terrified inhabitants ran into the streets in their nightclothes. Other structures were warehouses and businesses where Mexican troops had been quartered, and in these the Texians found themselves in deadly combat involving pistols and Bowie knives, though some *soldados* swiftly dived out the few small windows.

Now both armies were well entrenched, sometimes just yards from each other behind three-foot-thick walls. What followed was a house-to-house and often hand-to-hand struggle that would ultimately last for five grueling days, each one cloudy and frigid. Mexican Brown Bess muskets using weak gunpowder charges were no match for the Texians' accurate

Kentucky long rifles and double-barreled shotguns. But the Mexican forces had the advantage of position. Each house, each garden, and sometimes each room became a fiercely contested battleground, a fort to be taken with great effort and at great peril. Since the strategically placed cannon made the main streets virtual shooting galleries, some Texians took it into their heads to move forward by climbing to the rooftops of the one-story houses, taking cover behind the low parapets around each roof. But the blue-coated *soldados* had beaten them to it, and a dozen or so sharpshooters armed with Baker rifles in the bell tower of the church looming over the plaza found rebel targets and forced them off. To complicate matters, the gusty wind blew the powder out of the Texian rifle pans. A few of the assault parties were forced to hack holes in the ceilings and drop down ten or twelve feet into the houses, some of which contained *soldados*. The Texians battered the outside wall of one building until it fell onto the occupants inside. The rubble nearly buried some women and their families, although, bizarrely, one small *bexareño* emerged into a yard and told the rebels that there would be a fandango held there that night.

From his camp almost half a mile north of Béxar, Burleson kept his cavalry patrolling the outskirts of the town to prevent enemy forces from leaving or entering. Most of the horsemen were Juan Seguín's rancheros, who also foraged local ranches for beeves and grain, though about forty of them had given up their mounts to join Milam's assault force. The mounted patrols prevented Cós from sending in some of his presidial units as reinforcements.

The fighting eased up after sundown. A supply party appeared with water, milk, munitions, and barbecued beef. Burleson made his way into town and conferred with the assault leaders, who had finally established communication with each other by digging a trench between the two positions. The resistance had been stronger than they had expected—stories of untrained, convict-heavy Mexican army battalions, and the Texians' successful skirmishes of the previous two months, had led to overconfidence—and they had suffered eleven casualties, one dead and ten wounded, who were taken back to camp to the makeshift hospital of Drs. Samuel Stivers and Amos Pollard, a staunch abolitionist from Massachusetts. But they refused to give up the territory they had fought so hard to win, and decided to continue the assault. Burleson also brought the news that some of the men who had left the previous day had returned. Milam and his fighters spent the evening cleaning their arms and filling sandbags for protection, then they wrapped themselves in their blankets and slept a few hours.

The next day was colder than the first. General Cós ordered his artillery, both around the plazas and in the Alamo, to open an effective crossfire at dawn. The rebels dug more trenches to facilitate the safer movement of men and artillery. Both sides fought with tenacity and courage. Much of the combat this day was also hand-to-hand, especially after firing from a Texian artillery piece sent the church-tower snipers scattering. Muskets and rifles gave way to pistols, Bowie knives, and bayonets. Progress was slow and tedious, often accompanied by the screaming of women and children. With crowbars, axes, and crude wooden battering rams ten feet long, the rebels would bash holes in the thick walls that made one house look like a "pigeon nursery from whence flame and lead poured out as fast as the men could load and fire," one Texian recalled. Sometimes the Mexicans would do the same while the attackers reloaded. When the opening was large enough, Milam's men made their way through and into the house, which might be occupied by *soldados*. Some fought back. Others surrendered and were released on a pledge not to return to Béxar, though not all honored the parole. Occasionally, while occupying either side of a house wall, the two sides would argue the causes and prospects of the battle and the civil war.

By sunset the Texians had moved forward another half block or so. The men were chilly, exhausted, and filthy, and the mortar dust settling on them conferred a ghostly appearance. But they hunkered down that night in the stone buildings, some of them building small fires to ward off the chill.

When the sun rose on the third day of the assault, it revealed a new threat on the Texians' left flank: to the west, across the river near the old mission, the Mexicans had erected a redoubt that was now full of infantry. Behind them, four cannon just outside the fort's entrance supported them. But the volunteers' accurate rifle fire quickly put the *soldados* and the artillerymen to flight. Before the day was over the Mexicans would draw the cannon within the walls by means of lassos.

Inside the town another problem presented itself. The defenders had fortified a house directly in the path of Johnson's division, and the heavy small arms and artillery fire from it made progress impossible. Only when a six-pounder was wheeled up from the Texian lines outside town and a barrage of cannonballs unloaded did the Mexicans abandon the stronghold. When a Texian officer ordered the cannon into the open street facing the enemy breastworks, two of the gun's crew were shot dead and three others wounded. The second lieutenant manning the gun, a Virginian named William Carey, continued to load and fire it with two other men. He barely escaped death when a musket ball passed through his hat and creased his skull. Carey was made first lieutenant soon after, when the man he replaced was cashiered for cowardice.

That afternoon, Milam led a final push toward Main Plaza, then made his way through the rubble to confer with Johnson at the large Veramendi house, called by some of the men the Bowie house since it had been owned by the latter's former father-in-law. Milam suggested a daring plan to capture General Cós, who was issuing commands from a house south of the plazas. Dressed in a white blanket coat, Milam stepped into the courtyard about one p.m. with a small field glass to get a better look at the Mexican command post, and to determine the best route there. A second later he fell to the ground, a bullet through his right temple, and died instantly. A Texian pointed toward the river less than a hundred yards away, where a puff of smoke had appeared in a cypress along the opposite bank. Several men took aim and fired, and a body dropped to the riverbank and rolled into the river. After the battle the Texians would learn the name of the sniper: Felix de la Garza, reputedly one of the best shots in the Mexican army.

The stunned Texians buried their captain in one of the trenches they had dug in the yard, along the east wall, and spent the rest of the day wondering who would replace Milam's strong leadership and calm under fire. His loss "put a considerable damper on the army," remembered one attacker. Rumors of a large Mexican reinforcement nearing town were rampant. That evening the Texian officers selected Frank Johnson to oversee the assault. He knew Milam's plan well and had no desire to change it. About ten o'clock that night, in a chilling drizzle, four companies of volunteers attacked and seized a stone house just north of the church.

The fourth day was more of the same — bracing cold, stiff resistance, and every foot advanced bought in blood and sweat. In the afternoon a furious artillery barrage pinned down a company of rebels behind some flimsy *jacales* and an adobe wall. When a well-aimed load of grapeshot tore down even that poor protection, one infuriated Texian, a tall, red-headed scout named Henry Karnes, who had ventured into

Texas as a trapper and decided to stay, yelled for cover and dashed across a street through heavy fire to a stone house bristling with Mexican muskets at every window and on the rooftop. The twenty-three-year-old Tennessean carried a crowbar in one hand and his rifle in the other. He hit the door and began to pry it open while his comrades loosed a steady fire on the soldiers on the roof. By the time he broke the door open and burst into the house, most of the men were right behind him. The bulk of the *soldados,* taken aback by such madness, skedaddled. The rest were taken prisoner.

Both sides were exhausted after four grueling days of almost constant struggle. One of the two Texian columns had been reduced by half, to forty-nine men, and they were almost out of ammunition, with little gunpowder left. A frigid rain the next morning resulted in less gunfire on both sides due to damp powder, and eased the stench of dead animals rotting in the streets. But the rebels pushed on, past blackened tree stumps and smoldering ash heaps and piles of rubble, until they were just yards from Main Plaza, Cós's final line of defense in the town and the most fortified.

At midmorning a roar of voices, the ringing of the church bells, and martial music from the Mexican band in the Alamo signaled what the Texians had been dreading: the arrival of four hundred reinforcements from Zacatecas and San Luis Potosí, escorted by Colonel Domingo de Ugartechea and a 250-strong contingent of experienced troops drawn from every branch of the military — cavalry, infantry, and artillery. They marched through the streets of Béxar, across the wooden footbridge spanning the river, and into the Alamo, accompanied by sixty *soldaderas* — soldiers' women — and their children, as was the custom in the Mexican army.

Though they were many in number, the new arrivals were far from fresh: in the last twenty-four hours, none of them had eaten more than a piece of hardtack due to the constant rain. Many had lost their shoes and sandals in the mud. They had force-marched from Saltillo (which, a short time earlier, had been renamed Leona Vicario after a heroine of the revolution, though both names were still used), almost four hundred miles away, through burned prairies and cold rains, fifty-five days straight, and had gone the sixty miles to Béxar without a break. They were bone-tired.

With them rode Captain José Juan Sánchez, proud scion of a family that had distinguished itself militarily from the thirteenth century onward in Spain and the New World. A quarter century earlier, Sánchez had been a classmate of Santa Anna's in officers' training, and then an early champion of Mexican independence, earning the rank of captain in his teens. Now he was the adjutant inspector of the northern Mexican states of Nuevo León and Tamaulipas, ordered to Béxar to observe and serve where needed. His salary was not enough to support his wife, Ana, and their six children, and he wanted a better-paying job. He reported to Cós later that morning, then began his inspection duties.

A newly confident Cós raised a black flag over the fort, the sign that no quarter would be given to the enemy. But most of the new soldiers were raw recruits, including numerous convicts in leg chains. These untrained and exhausted felons, many of whom could not even load their rifles, were in no shape to join the fray, and instead of bolstering the command, they made the situation worse, particularly since food supplies were already alarmingly low and they had brought little with them. Without their help, Ugartechea's reinforcement was effectively a wash: the escorting troops only replaced two hundred of the best-mounted *presidiales* who had deserted the night before and galloped off toward the Rio Grande.

Meanwhile, the rebels continued their assault on Main Plaza, and Cós transferred his command post across the river and into the Alamo. That afternoon, he devised a desperate strike against the enemy camp a half mile above the fort. Two columns, one of cavalry and one of infantry, approached the Texian position from opposite sides in a classic pincer movement. But the gun crews of James Neill were ready and waiting. When the Mexicans came within range, the Texians let loose a storm of canister shot. The attackers turned and retreated into the Alamo.

Inside the town, the fighting continued past midnight, when the last fortified house defending Main Plaza was taken by a force of rebels, most of them Greys. Under a nearly full moon, about thirty Texians crawled low along house walls to avoid musket fire from the windows inches above them—so close that their whiskers and hair were burned by the blaze of the guns overhead—then rushed the square. They immediately encountered two six-pounders aimed directly at them. The Texians tried to spike the cannon, but as they did so the plaza filled with troops. A Mexican officer gave the order to fix bayonets and led a group of *soldados* in a charge into the rebels. The rebels took refuge in a stone structure called the Priest's House, at the northeast corner of the square, after forcing out its defenders and sending twenty women and children into safer rooms. The Mexicans rallied around three cannon—two of them six-pounders just fifteen paces from the house—and pounded the building incessantly. As they did so, Captain Sánchez directed a howitzer bombardment from the atrium of the church.

By now, the rest of the Texian forces had lost contact with the Greys in the Priest's House, and reported that they had all probably been killed. The news reached Burleson in the Texian camp right after he was informed of Ugartechea's reinforcements. He summoned Johnson and suggested a withdrawal from town. They had only one powder keg left, and many of the men carried just a few rounds in their pouches. Under the circumstances, retreat appeared to be the wisest option.

But simple escape would not be so easy. The men inside the Priest's House were enduring a furious bombardment. They threw any furniture they could find against the doors and windows, but cannonballs continued to blast through. The Greys' leader turned to his men and gave them a choice: retreat, surrender, or die. The Greys were exhausted and short on powder, but to a man they told him, "Die or do." They would remain where they were and sell their lives as dearly as possible.

About one in the morning, Cós decided to consolidate his forces. He ordered the remaining infantry troops in Béxar to start moving across the river. What was left of the elite Morelos Battalion acted as a rear guard near Main Plaza as the sick and the wounded and all remaining arms and munitions were transported to the Alamo. Cós continued to discuss his options with his officers, who had rejected his suggestion that they counterattack.

As the night wore on, conditions worsened for the Mexicans. Provisions were almost gone, even basics such as water and firewood, and there were now more than 1,100 men to feed. Hundreds of horses were starving; some were eating the cloaks of the troops and even gnawing on wooden cannon parts. The garrison's morale had plummeted after the two hundred *presidiales* had deserted, and now panic set in. The unshackled convicts insulted and even attacked their officers, and frightened women and children spread confusion as they ran about the fort. Word spread that the defense had become a total rout, and cries of "We are lost" were heard everywhere.

As the crowd lurched into chaos, Cós tried to calm the troops, but his voice was drowned in the tumult. In the darkness he was trampled and injured, and though he finally restored a semblance of order, he had to retire to a bed. They could hold out for a few days, he knew, but unless they broke out, the final result seemed inevitable.

At six a.m. the general summoned Captain Sánchez, who had grabbed his musket and joined the fighting near Main Plaza with the Morelos Battalion. Cós sent him back across the river to approach the enemy and obtain the best terms of capitulation possible. As the captain made his way to the plaza, he met the Morelos commander, Colonel Nicolás Condelle, who with seventy of his men was still guarding the retreat under the battalion banner. Earlier, in the heat of battle, the colonel had told Sánchez that they would die there if necessary. Now, when Sánchez told him of his mission, Condelle objected: "The Morelos Battalion has never surrendered," he said. Some of his subalterns agreed, and even threatened Sánchez with their muskets—one fired and missed. The captain shouted that he had his orders. Condelle gave in, and permitted him to proceed. Sánchez raised a truce flag at the main square about seven a.m., and was soon surrounded by jabbering colonists.

When the grime-covered rebels in the Priest's House cautiously emerged in the early morning light after the gunfire had stopped, they saw the truce flag, and a white banner flying above the mission across the river. Somehow every Texian in the house had survived, though one Grey had been badly wounded. They escorted Sánchez to Colonel Johnson, who sent for Burleson.

The negotiations lasted until two the next morning, when they finally hammered out a generous eighteen-point agreement—though its magnanimity was viewed by some of the rebels as a "child's bargain." The officers would receive paroles to return to the interior of Mexico, and the army would leave within six days. They gave their word that they would not oppose the reestablishment of the constitution of 1824 or reenter Texas under arms. The Texians allowed them to keep their personal guns and ten bullets a man, and even supplied a small cannon for protection against Indians; the rest of the artillery pieces, about twenty, would stay. Meanwhile, the Mexican troops would remain in the Alamo, and the rebels in town across the river. But by the afternoon of the next day, soldiers of both armies were mingling, some playing cards together, particularly the men of the local Alamo and Béxar garrisons. That evening, the rebels celebrated their victory with a fandango. The Mexican tricolor again flew over the Church of San Fernando.

On December 14, Cós marched south toward Laredo with a thousand men, including Captain Sánchez and the weary conscripts who had just completed the same arduous 150-mile route six days before. Cós had suffered 150 casualties, most of them men in the Morelos Battalion, against five Texian deaths. More than thirty seriously wounded *soldados* remained behind at Military Plaza, with one doctor to minister to them. With the column rode Lieutenant Francisco de Castañeda and four members of the Alamo company—his men and those of the Béxar garrison were given the option of staying in town with their families, and these four were the only ones who had not taken advantage of the offer. Most of the *presidiales* were unmounted. Behind them the Mexican army left a small arsenal—about twenty cannon, eleven thousand musket cartridges, more than three hundred functional muskets, much powder and cannon shot—and, of more immediate value, almost two hundred blankets that would be fully appreciated by the chilled Texians. Many of the volunteers moved into the Alamo, where they sought out the best-sheltered corners for protection against the cold; a group of nine Greys claimed the church as their quarters. Thieves had stripped the roofless structure of all ornaments, but outside, the four sandstone saints in alcoves on either side of the door remained. Women from the town still crossed the river to kneel before them and pray.

The next day, Edward Burleson left Béxar for his farm in Bastrop, accompanied by his aged father, who had taken sick after the Grass Fight. Many of the remaining settlers, eager to return to their farms, followed, taking their carts and wagons with them. All but a dozen or so Gonzales men walked or rode back to DeWitt's colony. Most of the colonists were only a few days' ride from home; with any luck, they would make it in time for Christmas dinner. Their families needed them: Indians had been taking advantage of their absence to step up their raiding, and soon it would be time for plowing. Besides, there was no need for them in Béxar, and it was cold, and few of the men wore winter clothing. Juan Seguín's company of mounted Tejanos disbanded, and Seguín rejoined his wife, María Gertrudis, and his four young children. Other *bexareños* began to trickle into their battered town from the ranches along the river.

Many of the rambunctious young volunteers from the United States signed on for a new adventure that promised plenty of plunder and action — an expedition south to Matamoros, on the south bank of the mouth of the Rio Grande, deep within the Mexican state of Tamaulipas. The prosperous port city of six thousand allegedly harbored many federalist sympathizers; together they might spark a widespread uprising in northern Mexico against the centralists. Just as alluring were its rumored riches: $100,000 per month in revenue, which could help fund the Texian revolution. The General Council had tentatively supported the idea, and Colonel Johnson and Dr. James Grant, a wealthy Scotsman and former *empresario* who owned a large hacienda in northern Mexico, appointed themselves leaders of the expedition. On December 30, after appropriating most of the provisions and ammunition recently sent by the General Council from Gonzales, Grant led two hundred volunteers down the road along the San Antonio River toward Goliad while Johnson rode to San Felipe to obtain authorization for the expedition.

As word of the victory spread eastward to the colonies, Texians rejoiced in the fact that there were now no Mexican troops in the province. That an undisciplined group of backwoods militiamen could defeat a European-style army almost twice its size called forth echoes of a similar rebellion a half century before, and references to "the sons of '76" were frequent. The news was celebrated outside Texas as well: in New Orleans, rehearsals began in mid-December for a play to open on January 1 entitled *The Fall of San Antonio, or Texas Victorious,* which featured Ben Milam's inspiring call to duty and his death—and threw in an Indian war dance as well. In far-off New York, on the first day of the new year, another drama, *The Triumph of Texas,* opened at the Bowery Theatre.

Most Texians assumed the war was over, that the Mexican government would leave Texas alone, or that other Mexican states would join the revolt and overthrow Santa Anna. Only a few thought otherwise. Sam Houston was one of them, and he called for Texians to rally and join the regular army. Nobody listened to him. Newspapers as far away as New York reported what was widely believed: "No other expedition can be fitted out by Mexicans against Texas until spring; and then the army of the Patriots will be sufficiently strong to repel them."

On November 24, the day he left, Stephen Austin had told his men that he had received word of an army of ten thousand Mexican *soldados* preparing to march into Texas and put down the insurrection, much as they had in Zacatecas—that is to say, in a most unpleasant manner. Now, a month later, word began reaching Béxar and then the Anglo settlements to the east that an army was indeed on its way north, its leader none other than the despot himself. It seemed that Santa Anna, the former federalist who considered himself the Napoleon of the West, had definite plans for these traitors to their adopted homeland. In taking Béxar, a Mexican stronghold for a century, the ungrateful rebels had humiliated their mother country. Now it was imperative that he retake and hold the town, not only to establish a supply base from which to attack the Anglo colonies but also for another, more compelling reason: revenge.

SEVEN

"A Mere Corral and Nothing More"

The men in my command have been in the field for four months, they are almost naked, and this day they were to receive pay for the first month of their enlistment, and almost every one of them speaks of going home.

LIEUTENANT COLONEL JAMES C. NEILL

The triumphant Army of the People, or at least what remained of it in Béxar, was dressed in rags.

By the end of December, Edward Burleson and Frank Johnson had departed the battered town, leaving newly promoted Lieutenant Colonel James Neill in charge of the hundred-man garrison. Neill came from a long line of soldiers—the blood of ancient Irish warrior chieftains dating back to the fourth century ran through his veins. His father and his grandfather had both fought in the Revolutionary War. After commanding an infantry company under Andrew Jackson at the Battle of Horseshoe Bend, Neill had been commissioned a colonel in the Alabama militia. He had also served two terms as a state congressman there before a statewide drought laid waste to his farm and compelled him to take his wife, daughter, and two sons to Texas in 1831, where he had settled in Austin's colony. The forty-seven-year-old Neill was an experienced leader of men, a good soldier who followed orders, and was well respected by his comrades. "Nature has given him a giant frame and a mind incapable of despondency," remembered a friend. But the following six weeks would test his equanimity. He faced serious problems with this command, and it did not take long for the situation to raise his ire.

Neill had little enough to command in any case. A mass exodus had left him with few men and even sparser resources. Most of the Texian settlers had left for their homes to the east. The remainder, almost all of them young immigrants from the United States hungry for action, had preemptively set off with Dr. James Grant on the Matamoros adventure—a plan for which Colonel Johnson was belatedly seeking approval in San Felipe.

The volunteers under Grant had taken most of the horses, food, ammunition, clothing, blankets, and medical supplies from the garrison, and had impressed additional livestock from the locals. An outraged Neill immediately began to fire off letters to Sam Houston and Governor Henry Smith imploring them for help, and claiming that the garrison would be unable to defend itself against the imminent Mexican attack— a line of argument more likely to sway them than appeals regarding his unit's near destitution, which was his primary concern at that moment.

Neill kept quarters in town, as did about half the soldiers. The others moved into the Alamo. Those residing in the old Spanish mission were commanded by William Carey, the thirty-year-old Virginian who had arrived in Austin's colony just two months before rushing to Gonzales to join the volunteer army. He had been elected captain by the fifty-six men in his artillery corps — his Invincibles, he called them — after his several displays of bravery during the battle of Béxar.

The one hundred men left in Béxar soon dwindled to eighty, including two dozen New Orleans Greys, almost all of whom were reassigned to an infantry unit. Most of the eighty were volunteers, each with that infuriating and predictable volunteer's disdain for orders and military hierarchy. Morale soon became a major problem, and early in January, Neill and Carey twice called the men out on general parade to deliver morale-boosting speeches. Those helped — if only for a while. The soldiers had not been given their wages, though they had volunteered to remain in Béxar with the understanding that they were to be paid monthly, and most of them were still dressed in their now-threadbare summer clothes. They had signed on for a four-month hitch, to serve until regular army units showed up to take over. But after only a month, with no money, monotonous meals, and miserable conditions, the patriotism had worn off for some, and men had begun leaving.

Those who remained staved off boredom as any army does: with women, gambling, games, and alcohol — mostly corn liquor, which was occasionally supplemented by the Mexican libations of choice, tequila and mescal. The more literate of the volunteers from "the States" wrote the occasional letter home and entrusted it to the next man leaving for the east. In the evenings, the soldiers dropped in on fandangos to dance, drink, and debauch all night. Though impoverished and stripped of much of its resources — virtually every structure bore innumerable scars from artillery barrages and rifle and musket fire, and fragrant carcasses of livestock caught in the crossfire lay everywhere — the town and its resilient residents had returned to a semblance of normalcy.

By day the men made themselves a little more useful, after a desultory fashion. They slept, wandered the dirt streets, admiring the pretty señoritas, and occasionally pitched in to help fortify the Alamo under the direction of attorney Green "Ben" Jameson, recently appointed engineer to the post. The previous December, General Cós had moved most of the cannon there; now the rebels dragged the remaining few tubes into the mission and destroyed the fortifications in Béxar, per Johnson's orders. One work party spent time digging a well in the mission's courtyard. John W. Smith, the Béxar carpenter and jack-of-all-trades who had guided Milam's columns into town, was appointed public storekeeper to the garrison, and inventoried the captured Mexican guns and ammo and property in accordance with General Houston's orders.

Jameson proved himself invaluable. He and Neill had helped reestablish the functions of government and assured the town leaders that the rebel army would back their civil authority, which encouraged their cooperation when it came to supplies, or at least such supplies as the impoverished area could afford. Houston had also demanded an inventory of needed materials for repairing the fortifications, and toward that end Jameson had drawn up extensive plans to repair and strengthen the crumbling compound. Cós had made some significant additions to the mission during his time there, but after more than fifty days of sporadic rebel bombardment the compound was in need of serious reconstruction. Jameson had spent much time examining Fortress Alamo, as he called it, noting Cós's fortifications, and was not impressed. But he was confident he could improve them significantly.

Though Jameson was not a trained engineer—until joining the volunteer army he had acted as sales agent in the coastal town of Brazoria for the Galveston Bay and Texas Land Company, and had taken on numerous lawyering tasks—he had clearly found some schooling in the subject somewhere. He had also, apparently, found his calling. He produced a detailed plan that included, among many ideas, "a pass from the present fortress to a contemplated drawbridge across a contemplated ditch inside a contemplated half moon battery.... A part of said ditch, as well as a trap door across said ditch, which is contemplated to be raised by a tackle from inside the half-moon battery." Not all his designs would be implemented, but they were ambitious, and impressive to all who heard them.

Most of the rebuilding was done by officers, and made more difficult due to the scarcity of tools; the officers also stood guard and patrolled every night—on foot, since mounts were scarce after Grant left. The volunteers' ongoing resistance to orders still posed a problem; in addition, the severe lack of clothes and the meager diet—all they had to eat was beef and corn—took its toll on morale.

Eventually the last of the cannon were carted across the river and up through the main gate. Most of the tubes were wheeled onto platforms built along the mission perimeter, while others were positioned at windows and embrasures cut through the walls. A few were placed to fire directly over the wall—*en barbette*—which increased their field of fire but made their gunners easy targets. A couple of days after Cós's departure, a large iron-barreled eighteen-pounder had arrived from Captain Philip Dimitt at Dimitt's Landing (a coastal village founded by him), east of the town of Goliad. Jameson and his crew managed to hoist it onto a wooden platform erected over dirt and rubble from the collapsed roof of a one-story house at the northwest corner of the mission compound, and it now commanded the town to the west and the countryside to the north. They had only a few eighteen-pound balls at the time, but loads of *langrage,* bags of bits and pieces of iron—cut horseshoes, nails, and such—which could be deadly at close range, as could canister shot. The tube could also be adapted to fire slightly smaller balls if necessary.

Besides the ongoing problem of supplies, clothing, and ammunition—they were still short on good powder, although the inferior Mexican variety was abundant—Neill had other headaches. Food remained scarce, and rumors had been circulating that a large party of Comanches was near, and was readying an attack. And since Grant's Matamoros expedition had left them with almost no horses for reconnaissance, they had no definite idea of the whereabouts of the Mexican army. The Texians were sure that Santa Anna's spies were in Béxar, but they had had no luck catching them. So far, the intelligence advantage seemed all with the enemy.

On January 6, word reached town that there were a thousand troops on the march from Laredo on the Rio Grande. Rumors of a similar sort had been circulating for more than a month. Neill sent a long report that day to the General Council in San Felipe. "We Know not what day, or hour, an enemy of 1,000 in number may be down upon us," he wrote, "and as we have no supplies or provisions within the fortress we could be starved out in 4 days by anything like a close siege." He criticized the actions of Johnson and Grant, praised the valor of his troops over the previous ten weeks, and pleaded for more men, provisions, medical supplies, and his garrison's pay—"If there has been a dollar here I have no knowledge of it."

On January 8, a Comanche appeared in town, the bearer of bad tidings. "His nation is in an attitude of hostilities toward us," an understated Neill wrote to the General Council. The last thing the Texians needed was hundreds of Comanche warriors assaulting them. Fortunately, the Indian leaders were willing to discuss the situation, and quite possibly a treaty, but it needed to be done soon. Through the first half of January, though, Neill received no reply at all from anyone.

It would be a while before Neill and the Béxar garrison would find out why no answer was forthcoming. Besides the simple fact that the provisional authority had no money and no source of revenue, relying almost solely on donations and loans—Stephen Austin and the two other Texian ambassadors were in the United States doing all they could to drum up support in cash and manpower—there was a more serious problem. The government was quickly degenerating into a chaotic mess. Tellingly, it had failed to take advantage of the respite from military activity afforded by the victory at Béxar on December 10. The Texian leaders had been presented with an opportunity to address the immediate problems they faced, particularly that of provisioning the army. Instead, they had done almost nothing.

Upon receiving Neill's expresses from Houston's headquarters at Washington, a small village thirty miles upriver from San Felipe, Henry Smith forwarded them to the General Council with a letter excoriating the council for its actions. Smith was severely lacking in diplomatic skills but acutely aware of the danger of dithering while a large army was marching into Texas, a habit polished to perfection by the General Council. Smith and the General Council also differed on other matters large and small—most important, whether Texas was a Mexican state (the council's position) or an independent nation, which was Smith's position. As a consequence, their relationship was rocky. Then it got worse.

In his letter, he called the General Council members scoundrels, Judases, and wolves, and the Matamoros expedition predatory. He tried to suspend the council members; they in turn voted to impeach him. Smith refused to countenance their actions and continued to exercise the powers of his office—or at least he attempted to, given the weakened state of his support, for he was essentially powerless. The two factions spent more time blasting each other with charges and countercharges than applying themselves to the task at hand. Several General

Council members left San Felipe in disgust, and when a two-thirds quorum then failed to be reached, those remaining appointed a new governor and a small advisory committee to act for the General Council until a constitutional convention could convene almost two months later, on March 1.

THOUGH NEILL LACKED THE HORSES necessary for ranging reconnaissance patrols, Béxar was not entirely in the dark. Juan Seguín had sent mounted spies as far south as the Rio Grande. Even before they returned, rumors of Santa Anna's approach sent tremors through the town. Twenty-three years earlier, an avenging Mexican army had reached Béxar and defeated a large force of rebel *norteamericanos* and Tejanos. Two days after the decisive Battle of the Medina, General Arredondo's triumphant army had swarmed through the town in a fever of pillage and murder. Béxar had never completely recovered. Many of its residents retained vivid memories of the nightmarish occupation, and had no wish to repeat it. Now families began leaving town in droves. Several volunteers left with them, and by late January the garrison was reduced to seventy-five men fit for duty.

Other *bexareños* remained in town, at least for the moment. The two Navarro sisters, twenty-four-year-old Juana and nineteen-year-old Gertrudis, had been raised by their uncle Governor Juan Martín Veramendi and his wife, Josefa, and Juana had been adopted by them. She and her stepsister, Ursula, had been very close, and she was fond of her brother-in-law, James Bowie, who addressed her as Sister. The Navarro family was one of the most prominent in town. The sisters' father, Angel, the town's political chief, was loyal to Santa Anna, while their uncle José Navarro was a supporter of Texian independence and busy in San Felipe politics. Juana's first husband had died, leaving her with a young son, Alejo, and just weeks earlier she had wedded Dr. Horace Alsbury, a Texian who had taken part in the siege and battle of Béxar and who was still attached to the garrison. Alsbury, one of Stephen F. Austin's Old Three Hundred—the first group of settlers in his land grant—hailed from Kentucky. He and his new wife had taken her sister, Gertrudis, into their home.

Another soldier was also fortunate enough to enjoy the company of his family. One night in early November, artillery lieutenant Almeron Dickinson's dark-haired young wife, Susanna, had been asleep at their home in Gonzales when a group of renegade volunteers from Louisiana passing through the village broke into her house—as they had broken into every other house in town. She and her year-old daughter, Angelina, had escaped serious injury, but when the news reached Dickinson he rode east as soon as he could and brought them to Béxar. She left behind three feather beds, her fifty-piece china set, and most of their household goods—even their cows and oxen. In Béxar they boarded at the home of Ramón Músquiz, the town's former political chief and still a staunch centralist, on the northeast corner of Main Plaza. Despite her husband's allegiances, Mrs. Músquiz took a shine to Susanna and her blue-eyed daughter.

These few remaining residents were among the exceptions, however. Béxar, for the most part, was voting with its feet.

When Neill saw the families leaving town, he sent expresses to Sam Houston, in Goliad, and the governor and General Council in San Felipe. To the provisional government he once again pleaded his case. "Unless we are reinforced and victualled, we must become easy prey to the enemy," he wrote, and in disgust ended with: "I shall not make again application for aid, considering it superfluous but wait the result of either receiving aid or an attack before it should arrive, in which case

I will do the best I can with the small force I have." His letter to Houston was even more desperate:

> The men in my command have been in the field for four months, they are almost naked, and this day they were to receive pay for the first month of their enlistment, and almost every one of them speaks of going home, and not less then twenty will leave tomorrow, and leave here only about 80 men under my command, and there are at Laredo Three Thousand men under the command of General Rameriz, and two other generals and it appears by a letter received here last night, one thousand of them are destined for this place and two thousand for Matamoros, we are in a torpid defenseless situation, we have not and cannot get from all the citizens here Horses enough since Johnson and Grant left, to send out a patrol or spy company.... I hope we shall be reinforced in 8 days or we shall be overrun by the enemy, but if I have only one Hundred men, I will fight one thousand as long as I can; and then not surrender —

The government for the most part ceased to function, though each group continued to issue competing and sometimes conflicting orders. The four-man advisory committee sometimes dwindled to two members, but still issued occasional recommendations to the governor; some were implemented, some were not. Just when Texas most needed guidance and organization, infighting between its political leaders had rendered its governing body ineffectual and unfocused. The military, most in need of attention at this time, split into ever-smaller units instead of concentrating its forces. And the government proved incapable of supplying the most basic needs of an army, even one as small as this. Texas slowly fell into a state of chaos and apathy that was apparent to all. "That our government is bad," San Felipe's *Telegraph and Texas Register* editorialized, "all acknowledge, and no one will deny."

On January 19, the arrival of a small reinforcement cheered Neill's bedraggled garrison. It was only a force of about thirty volunteers, but the man leading them could inspire even the most apathetic soldier.

James Bowie had been the first choice of Houston and Smith to lead the Matamoros expedition—back when those two had been enthusiastic about it, and before they realized its many weaknesses—and Houston had issued orders to that effect on December 17. But Bowie, as usual, was on the move, and it took more than a week for the directive to reach him. Bowie rode to San Felipe, and on December 28 appeared before the General Council and outlined his plan for the expedition; the next day the council's military affairs committee passed a resolution supporting the appointment. But before a decision could be made by the General Council as a whole, a comedy of orders ensued. When Frank Johnson arrived in San Felipe on January 3 to report that he had already sent James Grant with volunteers toward Matamoros, the council dropped Bowie and authorized Johnson to assume command of the operation. Johnson bowed out three days later over the council's refusal to approve his officer recommendations, which led to James Fannin's appointment as expedition commander the next day—this despite the fact that he was an officer in the regular army and thus required to take his orders from his commanding officer, General Houston, who had ordered him to Matagorda, on the coast, to begin enlisting and training recruits.

When Johnson changed his mind the following day, he was reinstated, though Fannin was not relieved of command. That made three leaders of the excursion—four if the actual leader in the field, Grant, was included, particularly since he declared himself the acting commander in chief of the federal army. The General Council's failure to muster a quorum and its corresponding lack of authority further muddied the question of command. For his part, Houston was informed of none of these developments, some of them directly undermining his authority. Such was the near-total dysfunction that characterized the Texian cause.

The legitimacy of the Matamoros expedition and its leaders was further undermined when Fannin issued a proclamation to his men that "the troops should be paid out of the first spoils taken from the enemy." Houston was aghast when he read it. The statement, he told Smith, "divests the campaign of any character save that of a piratical or predatory war," rather than characterizing it as one in defense of principles and civil and political rights. What, he wondered, would be the reaction of the civilized world? And the proclamation would surely have an adverse effect on the heretofore friendly residents of Matamoros, whose possessions were no doubt the spoils referred to.

Meanwhile, Bowie—acting on direct orders from his good friend Houston—left to meet Grant and the volunteers at Goliad, determined to take control of the expedition. He reached the small town on the lower San Antonio River on January 11 to find Grant organizing his forces with complete disregard for Bowie's orders from Houston. That same day, the General Council issued a statement that it did not recognize Bowie as an officer in the Texian army, further sabotaging his authority to lead the expedition. Since Bowie, in truth, had no formal commission—his rank of colonel was only an honorary one, bestowed upon his election as leader of the Nacogdoches militia the previous year—there was little he could do but wait for Houston to show up and sort things out if possible.

Houston arrived on January 14 and proceeded delicately. Since he had no official say over the volunteer army, any control he had over its officers was based on his charisma, their familiarity with him, and their loyalty to him or to Smith. Houston attempted to dissuade volunteers from embarking on what increasingly appeared to be a foolhardy venture, citing the serious lack of supplies and the difficulties of attacking a well-fortified city of twelve thousand after a two-hundred-mile journey. A few days later, when Grant led his men to the town of Refugio, twenty-five miles to the south, Houston accompanied the expedition.

Houston had been an effective orator during his political career, and he used all his powers now in speeches and asides to large and small groups of volunteers. By the time he left for San Felipe on January 28, he had managed to talk most of the men out of participating, though Grant and Johnson, who joined the army at Refugio, seemed determined to continue, and rode ahead to San Patricio, a small town on the Nueces River, then the southern border of Texas. The remainder of the volunteers decided to remain in Refugio, and when James Fannin arrived with two hundred more men, they threw their lot in with him.

While awaiting supplies, Fannin received word on February 7 that General José Urrea had reinforced Matamoros with six hundred men. Fannin switched plans and took his men to Goliad to regarrison the presidio there, despite word from Johnson that if Fannin marched to Matamoros immediately, he would be joined by an army of eight hundred unhappy Mexican troops from the border state of Tamaulipas.

The chaos continued. Only sixty-five men had followed Grant and Johnson out of Refugio. They rode south to San Patricio, where they headquartered and spent the next few weeks rounding up horses in the area for the army of volunteers they still expected. Near the end of February, Grant rode south on a foraging expedition with twenty-six men while Johnson and thirty-four volunteers remained in town. In the cold and rainy predawn hours of February 27, Johnson's detachment was surprised by a forward unit of the Mexican invasion column moving up the coast into Texas under Urrea, Santa Anna's best commander. Only Johnson and four others escaped alive. Three days later and twenty-five miles south, at Agua Dulce Creek, Urrea ambushed Grant's company and killed all but a few. The Scotsman might well have escaped, but he rode back to aid his trapped comrades and fell with them. That was the end of the ill-fated Matamoros expedition.

By then, Houston had received Neill's missive regarding the deplorable conditions at Béxar, and the news that a thousand Mexican soldiers were on the march to the town. He had long wanted to send a capable commander there with reinforcements. His options at the time were weak, since few of the men or their officers recognized his authority. In desperation, he asked Bowie to raise a company of volunteers and go to Neill's aid. Bowie agreed to Houston's request — as always, he was ready and willing to ride to the place where the action was likeliest. Besides, Béxar was a home of sorts, albeit one somewhat haunted by memories of his young wife, Ursula, and the Veramendi house, where they had lived for a while.

"He met my request with his usual promptitude and manliness," Houston wrote later, adding, "There is no man on whose forecast, prudence, and valor, I place a higher estimate." On January 17, Houston wrote to Governor Smith:

> Colonel Bowie will leave here in a few hours for
> Bexar, with a detachment of from thirty to fifty men.
> Capt. Patton's company, it is believed, are there now. I
> have ordered the fortifications of Bexar demolished,

and if you should think well of it, I will remove the cannon and other munitions of war to Gonzales and Copano, blow up the Alamo, and abandon the place, as it will be impossible to keep up the Station with volunteers. The sooner I can be authorized the better it will be for the country.

Copano, a small town on the Texas coast about thirty-five miles south of Goliad, was vital to supplying that post as well as Béxar. To Houston, the thought of detachments of his meager army holed up in forts eventually to be besieged by a Mexican force numbering in the thousands was intolerable. He much preferred the strategy of repairing eastward to Gonzales — on the other side of the ample Guadalupe River, where the terrain favored his irregulars — rather than defending his territory on the more open plains, where the well-drilled Mexican *soldados* and lancers owned the advantage. But Houston had no official control over volunteers, so such orders had to come from the governor and the General Council. Due to the fractured government's relentless squabbling, Houston would not receive the authorization he craved. Worse, his authority as commander in chief would be undermined.

In the meantime, he understood the dangers faced by the force at Béxar, and was doing what he could to bolster the garrison there. Besides the reinforcements of Bowie and those of Captain William Patton, one of Houston's recent appointments, he had sent an express to Captain Dimitt on the coast, asking him to raise a hundred men and march to the Alamo as soon as possible.

Bowie finally gathered a company of about thirty men — at the low end of Houston's cautious estimate — mostly from Captain John Chenoweth's Invincibles, and rode hard up the Béxar road, ninety-five miles north along the San Antonio

River. He arrived in town on January 19, two days later, to find the garrison in bad shape, and still sorely lacking just about everything, from clothing and shoes to medical supplies and money. On the positive side, morale and discipline had recently improved, the news of one thousand Mexican soldiers on the march to Béxar proving to be a great motivator.

With Bowie was James Bonham, a tall, darkly attractive lawyer from South Carolina recently arrived in Texas. He and William Travis had been neighbors as boys in the farm country of Edgefield County, separated by just a couple of years in age and five miles in distance, and they had attended the same country schools. Whether they were acquainted at the time is unknown, though they may have encountered each other in the classroom or on the playground. Regardless, they definitely ran into each other in San Felipe in the fall of 1835.

Bonham's blood fairly dripped rebellion: both his grandfathers and his father had fought in the Revolutionary War, and his overactive passion for the then-current nullification and secession movements had gotten him expelled from South Carolina College in his senior year. After passing the bar in 1830, he had been named colonel in command of an artillery company in Charleston. He was also a favorite of the ladies, who admired him for his courtroom caning of an opposing lawyer who, Bonham claimed, had insulted his female client. After Bonham was sentenced to ninety days for contempt of court, his female fans brought him flowers and food during his stay in jail. In Mobile, in the fall of 1835, he helped organize a Texas volunteer group dubbed the Mobile Greys. Soon after arriving in Texas in November, he wrote to Houston volunteering his services without compensation: "I shall receive nothing," he insisted, "either in the form of service pay, or lands, or rations." Though he had announced plans to open a law office in Brazoria, he proceeded to Béxar and arrived a few days after Cós's surrender. He accompanied the rest of the Greys when they left with Grant for Goliad, but remained loyal to Smith and Houston. After Houston gave him a commission as second lieutenant in the cavalry, he had decided to return with Bowie to the Alamo, where Travis and his cavalry legion had been ordered. Bonham was also a friend of James Fannin, who had recommended him highly, as had Houston: "His influence in the army is great," Houston had written to Lieutenant Governor James Robinson before the General Council split, "more so than some who '*would be generals*'"—a thinly veiled put-down of Fannin.

Captain William Patton, Houston's other reinforcer, had arrived from Velasco at the end of January leading eleven volunteers. With Bowie's company, the garrison now numbered about 115 men, including thirty-four wounded and sick.

Near the end of the month, Neill finally began to receive messages from what was left of the provisional government: a resolution from the General Council empowering him to hire Tejanos to gather cattle and other supplies—pointless, since these were virtually nonexistent in the area. Nothing in the way of money, provisions, or clothing arrived. On January 27, a disgusted Neill sent curtly worded replies expressing his disappointment to both Smith and the council.

That same day a Tejano arrived directly from the Rio Grande with detailed intelligence of a Mexican army marching into Texas, a force he described down to the number of wagons and mules and the identity of the brigade's commander—General Joaquín Ramírez y Sesma, who had led the cavalry in the battle at Zacatecas. The only bright spot was news of Travis's imminent arrival; his mounted company would be put to good use in the field.

All the while, Dr. Amos Pollard, serving as chief medical practitioner, did what he could to ease the suffering of the nearly three dozen sick and wounded. Most were billeted in the second floor of the old *convento* building in the Alamo compound. Included in his rounds were visits to the thirty or so Mexican wounded from the Béxar battle, who were lodged in the barracks in Military Plaza and scattered in residences around town. Pollard's ministrations were limited by a severe shortage of medicines. The arrival with Patton's small company of Dr. John Sutherland, a forty-two-year-old widower from Virginia, alleviated the problem somewhat. Though Sutherland was a practitioner of the popular but peculiar Thomsonian, or botanic, system — which relied on steaming, sweating, and purging, aided by infusions of roots and herbs, to expel the cause of a sickness — he carried some conventional medicines with him. Between the two of them they managed to alleviate the suffering of their patients, and even cured a few.

The men were incensed upon hearing from an express rider that a loan of $500, donated by a citizen of Alabama for the sole use of the Béxar garrison, had been appropriated by the General Council. They also learned of the council's impeaching Henry Smith, "the legitimate officer of the government" in their eyes. On January 26, a week after Bowie's arrival, they called a meeting to craft and approve a proclamation to the council expressing their support for Smith and condemning the council's actions as "anarchical assumptions of power to which we will not submit":

> Resolved, . . . That the conduct of the president and
> members of the Executive Council in relation to the
> FIVE HUNDRED DOLLAR LOAN, for the liquidation
> of the claims of the soldiers of Bexar, is in the highest
> degree criminal and unjust. Yet under treatment however
> liberal and ungrateful, we can not be driven from the
> Post of Honor and the sacred cause of freedom.

Just for good measure, they also expressed their contempt for anyone connected to the Matamoros expedition.

It was a strongly worded statement of principle and intent. The Béxar garrison was not only standing fast against the advancing Mexican army, they were defying their own Texian government — or at least its current leaders.

A month earlier, Neill, an experienced artilleryman, had boasted that they could defend the broken-down fort against the entire Mexican army with two hundred men. But weeks of neglect from above had weakened his resolution, and Houston's orders as delivered by Bowie, to remove all the artillery to Gonzales or Copano, made more and more sense — particularly in light of the recent news that there were sixteen hundred Mexican soldiers on the Rio Grande headed for Béxar, with three thousand more under the command of Santa Anna not far behind. The idea of holding out against such numbers appeared foolhardy. By the time Bowie arrived, Neill was fully ready to take his command to Copano to join the forces there. But there were neither the necessary teams nor available carts to carry the pieces — some were siege guns, without carriages — so that idea had to be scotched. And Bowie's presence, and his aura of confidence, changed things.

Bowie had been instructed to destroy the fortifications in town. Houston wanted to abandon the post completely. But as Bowie and Neill examined the improvements and repairs to the Alamo, which Jameson was supervising, and heard the would-be engineer's ambitious plans to further fortify it, a peculiar thing happened. The old mission, and the twenty or so cannon there, began to work their spell.

It was an age of artillery. Napoleon, the most brilliant military genius of the time, had been an artilleryman — "Great battles are won with artillery," he had asserted. More than two decades earlier, the Corsican had won a series of great battles with his trailblazing use of large, mobile batteries, and his triumphs had been extensively reported and analyzed; everyone in the Western world with an interest in the military was familiar with his innovative strategy. As Neill and Bowie watched Jameson position the tubes in the Alamo, the conclusion seemed inevitable: to yield such an impressive collection of cannon seemed a shame. To forget the fundamental wisdom of artillery defense, to underestimate the stubborn punch provided by fortified artillery, would be foolhardy. Had not the Ottomans in the walled port city of Acre, in the Holy Land, withstood Napoleon's army for two months in 1799 with only mud-and-stone walls and plenty of large cannon until reinforcements had arrived?

Another factor was the citizenry of Béxar. Most of them, particularly the more influential among them, had cooperated with the Texians. Some of the Tejano merchants had generously given their entire stocks of goods, groceries, and beeves for the use of the garrison, and Neill estimated that 80 percent of those remaining would join the rebel cause if reinforcements arrived soon. Besides, Bowie felt sympathy for the people of the town that had once been his own. Santa Anna was likely to treat the *bexareños* as Arredondo had in 1813, and as he had treated the Zacatecans in June: with murder, rape, and pillage of rebels and innocents alike. On February 2, Bowie wrote Smith: "The citizens of Bexar have behaved well...[and] deserve our protection and the public safety demands our lives rather than to evacuate the post to the enemy." Bowie was clear about the stakes as he saw them:

The salvation of Texas depends in great measure in keeping Bejar out of the hands of the enemy. It serves as the frontier picquet guard and if it were in the possession of Santa Anna there is no strong hold from which to repell him in his march towards the Sabine.... Colonel Neill and myself have come to the solemn resolution that we will rather die in these ditches than give up this post to the enemy.

Bowie was not requesting permission. He and Neill, and whichever men elected to follow their lead, would remain in Béxar. "Our force is very small...the returns this day to the Comdt. is only one hundred and twenty officers & men," Bowie finished. "It would be a waste of men to put our brave little band against thousands," he wrote. Indeed, it would be suicide. But, Bowie explained, they would hold the line at Béxar if need be. If they did not fight Santa Anna here, the Mexican army would drive into the colonies—including Bastrop, just a few days' march up El Camino Real, where Neill lived with his family. His grown sons, Samuel and George, could fend for themselves— the previous summer, they had participated with their father and ninety other Texians in a grueling six-week Indian expedition, and had just signed up with Robert Williamson's newly formed ranging company. But that left his wife, Harriett, and their teen-age daughter alone at home. For Neill and Bowie alike, the defense of Béxar was personal as well as patriotic.

DESPITE THE ADDITION OF THE volunteers under Bowie and Patton, the post was woefully undermanned, and the situation soon became worse as more than a dozen men prepared to leave over the following week or two upon receiving their discharges; to their minds, a couple of months was more than enough time to serve without pay, provisions, or proper cloth-ing. Others took a few days' leave to explore the area for the land bounties they would receive, further thinning the garrison's ranks. Some would return. Some would not.

For months rumors had been circulating of hundreds or even thousands of Americans marching to Texas to fight for their cousins' cause, and when they arrived, the men could leave—at least those with homes. When the call for volunteers had been made in December to keep possession of Béxar, it was assumed that they would stay only until enough regulars arrived to man the post; many of the men had only expected to remain a month. The recent news of a Mexican army marching into Texas made the need for regular troops even more imperative. Yet significant reinforcements remained but a deflated hope.

Not that those who stayed were taken lightly by their leaders. "All I can say of the soldiers here is complimentary to both their courage and their patience," Bowie wrote. Only a few had ever served as regulars, but most had faced Mexican troops. Many of them had fought at Concepción, endured the fifty-five days of the siege on Béxar, and participated in skirmishes almost daily. If supplied, they would "fight better than fresh men," observed Jameson in a letter to Houston.

Beyond their lack of training and their mixed experience was a quality that Bowie could not have missed—one that certainly played a significant part in his decision, supported by Neill, to pit this "brave little band" against Santa Anna's army. These men, volunteers and regulars alike, shared a flinty attitude that heartened their officer corps. These men had not run off with Grant and Johnson on their will-o'-the-wisp expedition, nor had they left, as some had, after the long weeks of neglect at the hands of their government. They had stayed. And they would keep on staying.

The voice of one defender spoke the mood of all: "If we

succeed, the Country is ours. It is immense in extent, and fertile in its soil and will amply reward all our toil. If we fail, death in the cause of liberty and humanity is not cause for shuddering. Our rifles are by our side, and choice guns they are, we know what awaits us, and are prepared to meet it." Regulars would surely arrive, and shortly. But if they were on their own, so be it.

EIGHT

The Napoleon of the West

If I were God, I would wish to be more.

GENERAL SANTA ANNA

Antonio de Padua María Severino López de Santa Anna y Pérez de Lebrón, known to most simply as Santa Anna, would be elected president of Mexico a total of eleven times over a period of twenty-two years. His chief appetites were cockfighting, gambling, women, the trappings of luxury, and the acclaim of the Mexican people. To that end, he liked nothing in the world better than riding through the streets of Mexico City to a hero's welcome after rescuing his beloved young nation yet again. And now he wanted nothing more than to crush the Anglo colonists in the remote northern province of Texas who had rebelled against their new country — no, he did want more than that: only the execution of every last one of the traitors would satisfy him.

Santa Anna was born February 21, 1794, in the mountain city of Jalapa, in the coastal province of Veracruz, one of seven children. His parents were criollos — people of Spanish descent born in Mexico—and solidly middle-class. The elder Santa Anna earned a good living as a mortgage broker, and occasionally served in minor government positions, which provided enough income to send his son Antonio to school. The boy displayed a lively intelligence, but he cared little for schoolwork, and never learned to speak or read any language but his own. He was branded a troublemaker, and when he was in his teens his parents opted to apprentice him to a merchant firm in the nearby port city of Veracruz. Antonio quickly realized he did not want to be a shopkeeper. Instead, in 1810, at the age of sixteen, he joined the colonial Spanish army as an underage infantry cadet. Nine weeks later, the Mexican War of Independence began.

After transferring to the cavalry, where he chased rebels and Indians, he made lieutenant at the age of eighteen. Young Santa Anna had found his calling. A year later, in 1813, he marched hundreds of miles with General Joaquín de Arredondo and an eighteen-hundred-man royalist force across the arid desolation of northern Mexico. Their destination: that charming town of San Antonio de Béxar, scene of an uprising against colonial rule led by a mixed group of Mexican revolutionaries and Anglo filibusters who had defeated a Spanish army and boldly proclaimed themselves the Republican Army of the North. Arredondo, the commandant of Mexico's Eastern Interior Provinces, had become brutally efficient over the last few years at suppressing revolts.

Young Santa Anna—at 5 feet 10 inches, tall for a Mexican of the time—was handsome, save for his slightly bulbous nose, and had a saturnine expression that women found appealing. He fell in love with Texas and wrote of "the beauty of its country," one that "surpasses all distinction." On a sweltering August day, the royalist troops faced a force of fourteen hundred insurgents in the four-hour Battle of the Medina, twenty miles south of town, and emerged victorious, killing six hundred rebels and suffering only fifty-five dead and 178 wounded. One hundred prisoners, including many Americans, were put to death, and on the way to Béxar two hundred more were captured, most of whom were shot. Others were hunted down as far east as the Trinity River, almost 250 miles away. In all, an estimated thirteen hundred republican rebels lost their lives.

Arredondo conducted executions for several days. The heads of those he had killed were placed in iron cages and left on display in Military Plaza for most of the year. The victors occupied the town for two months, executing sympathizers, humiliating women, and enjoying the pleasures and plunder due a conquering army. Arredondo cited Lieutenant Santa Anna for bravery.

The junior officer would never forget his first major battle, a complete triumph, which further solidified his emotional attachment to Texas—along with a robust contempt for the Anglo barbarians from the north. Under Arredondo, he also learned the best way to crush a rebellion: destroy every enemy, whether through battle or execution.

Over the next several years Santa Anna spent much of his time pursuing outlaws, Indians, and insurgents. He received several citations and eventual promotion to the rank of lieutenant colonel. In the beginning stages of the War of Independence, Santa Anna fought against the rebels. But a few months before independence from Spain was achieved in September 1821, he declared his loyalty to Agustín de Iturbide, the royalist officer turned rebel and the future emperor of Mexico, and in return was made a full colonel. After victories at Córdoba and his hometown of Jalapa, he led the rebel troops who drove the Spanish out of the city of Veracruz. Iturbide rewarded him with the rank of brigadier general and the post of commandant of the province of Veracruz, where he used his position to acquire extensive landholdings, including a large estate just outside Jalapa.

Santa Anna was a born opportunist, and over the next few years his allegiance changed with Mexico's constantly shifting winds of fortune. In 1822, he aligned himself with a group of military leaders working to oust Iturbide, eliminate the monarchy, and transform Mexico into a republic. The plan succeeded—Iturbide abdicated, was exiled to Italy, then attempted to slip back into the country, only to be caught and executed by a firing squad—and the result was the liberal constitution of 1824, which emphasized civil rights and a federalist system of government. Santa Anna soon retired and spent the next few years at his hacienda, Manga de Clavo. In 1825 he married a lovely eighteen-year-old with a large dowry. He would father several children by her, and more by other women. (He was notoriously unfaithful: four women would claim to have borne him a total of seven illegitimate offspring.)

In 1828, out of retirement and serving as governor of Veracruz, he, along with other generals, staged a coup that ousted the sitting president, Manuel Gómez Pedraza, and established the liberal-minded Vicente Guerrero in office. Santa Anna resumed his duties as governor. Then, in the summer of 1829, twenty-seven hundred Spanish troops landed on the eastern coast of Mexico near Tampico, three hundred miles up the coast from Veracruz. Here was a situation begging for boldness, and Santa Anna obliged. Without authorization, he mobilized a militia of two thousand men and set sail for Tampico, where he defeated the Spaniards after a few weeks of sporadic fighting. He led his troops to Mexico City, where he received unanimous adulation as the Hero of Tampico. Later that year, the vice president, Anastasio Bustamante, led a conservative coup that unseated and executed Guerrero. The unpopular Bustamante was ousted in 1832, and in April 1833,

Santa Anna was elected president of Mexico on a platform of peace, prosperity, and "an end to hatreds." He was hailed as a federalist hero throughout the country — even the colonists in the far-off province of Texas passed resolutions expressing their approval of "the firm and manly resistance made by the highly talented and distinguished chieftain" and pledged their "lives and fortunes on the support of the distinguished leader who is now so gallantly fighting in defense of civil liberty." Failing to attend his own inauguration, he retired to his hacienda in Jalapa and left the tedium of administration to his vice president, Valentín Gómez Farías.

But Farías's democratic federalist reforms, particularly laws curtailing the power of the Church and the army, turned those institutions, and the conservative upper class, against him. Santa Anna, sensing a change in the political weather, gained the backing of those groups and switched sides. In April 1834 he returned to Mexico City and deposed Farías, then dissolved the Congress and began canceling Farías's reforms in favor of a strong centralist government. In Santa Anna's opinion, the struggling young country was not ready for democracy: "A hundred years from now my people will not be fit for liberty," he said. "Despotism is the proper government for them." With no legislative branch to regulate him, he exercised the powers of a dictator. When a new Congress reconvened in January 1835, almost all its delegates were military or clerical, ready to do his bidding.

As Santa Anna concentrated authority in Mexico City and abrogated civil and states' rights, a wave of outrage and discontent spread across much of Mexico. Open rebellion occurred in two places: Zacatecas and Texas. Leaving a puppet ad interim president to administrate in his place, His Excellency crushed the uprising in Zacatecas, three hundred miles northwest of Mexico City. Rumors began to spread that his next mission would be to punish the Anglos in Texas. On the last day of August 1835, the government sent a circular to officials throughout the republic.

> The colonists established in Texas have recently given the most unequivocal evidence of the extremity to which perfidy, ingratitude, and the restless spirit that animates them can go, since—forgetting what they owe to the supreme government of the nation which so generously admitted them to its bosom, gave them fertile lands to cultivate, and allowed them all the means to live in comfort and abundance—they have risen against that same government, taking up arms against it under the pretense of sustaining a system which an immense majority of Mexicans have asked to have changed, thus concealing their criminal purpose of dismembering the territory of the Republic.

The statement went on to say that "the most active measures" would be taken to rectify this "crime against the whole nation. The troops destined to sustain the honor of the country and the government will perform their duty and will cover themselves with glory."

His Excellency's dislike of Americans was made even more apparent a few months later. In Mexico City, before an audience of several foreign ambassadors, he talked at length of the United States' involvement in Texas. The shocked U.S. consul, who was also present, wrote to President Andrew Jackson soon after:

> He spoke of our desire to possess that Country, declared his *full knowledge* that we had instigated and were supporting the Revolt, and that he would in due

Season *Chastise us* for it. Yes Sir, he said chastise us:
he continued, I understand that Gen. Jackson sets up a
claim to pass the Sabine, and that in running the
division line, hopes to acquire the Country as far as
the Naches. "Sir," said he, (turning to a Gentleman
present) "I mean to run that line at the Mouth of my
Cannon, and after the line is Established, if the Nation
will only give me the Means, only afford me the
necessary Supply of Money I will march to the
Capital, I will lay Washington City in Ashes, as it
has already been done."

The meaning and intent were clear. Exactly how His Excellency would accomplish his mission—with a depleted army
and an empty treasury—was not.

SANTA ANNA HAD NEVER BEEN a brilliant strategist, but
he led from the front, much like his idol, Napoleon—indeed,
he surrounded himself with books, images, and statues of the
French leader. The confidence and loyalty this inspired in his
men usually overrode his lack of wisdom, for his admiration
of the French military genius did not extend to serious study
of his strategy: he aped the Corsican's style but not his substance. Yet he was also a superb and energetic organizer, and
although he was under no obligation to assume command of
this army, he chose to lead the campaign personally—for his
country, for the glory it entailed, and likely because he did not
trust anyone else to do it right. Santa Anna had never relished
the humdrum duties and routine of the administrative path.
These he left to others, while he sought the spectacular. He
"preferred the hazards of war to the seductive and sought-after
life of the Palace," he would write later. His audacity was the

quality his countrymen found most alluring, and the main reason why he would be reelected several times.

Years of civil war, rebel uprisings, and political turmoil had left the nation almost penniless, and the military had suffered more than most institutions. Legislation during Farías's short-lived federalist regime had downsized the army by demobilizing many veteran units. The standing army was dismayingly small. On paper the military counted 38,715 men, 18,219 of them members of the regular army, but the government would only allow 3,500 of those to be assembled for the Texas campaign — the rest might be needed to quell federalist revolutionary activity in central Mexico. That would not be enough.

After putting down the Zacatecas rebellion in mid-May, Santa Anna had returned to another hero's welcome in Mexico City, then retired to his beloved hacienda in the mountains of Jalapa, ostensibly for health reasons. But when news of the seizure of the Goliad presidio and the confrontation at Gonzales reached the country's interior, he sprang into action. He arrived in the nation's capital by early November to begin assembling the Army of Operations, which would eventually comprise six thousand men and which he planned to deploy against Texas. Financing the expedition was an operation in itself: though Santa Anna had assumed almost absolute authority, there were limits to his power, particularly when it came to the depleted treasury. Later that month, the Mexican Congress authorized the government to furnish him with 500,000 pesos, but the money was never issued. His Excellency took matters into his own hands, negotiating several large loans, and even using his own properties as collateral. One loan of 400,000 pesos with steep interest rates was later rejected by Congress. Somehow, he obtained enough to keep the expedition going, though his exertions to cover payrolls and supplies would involve much juggling and coercion over the next several months—and he would still come up short.

Santa Anna ordered units from around the country to supply conscripts to fill out the skeleton ranks of infantry, cavalry, and artillery forces. The Army of Operations would be almost equally divided between *permanentes,* the regular army forces, and *activos,* the active militia, with some frontier presidial units also present. There was no lack of bodies in the higher ranks: the army was top-heavy with officers, quite a few of them owing their commissions to political connections—one of His Excellency's top aides would later write that there were officers enough for an army of twenty thousand men. Many of these men knew little of their profession.

Most of the higher-ranking officers, however, were veterans who had fought alongside Santa Anna—and sometimes, amid Mexico's near-constant upheavals and ever-shifting allegiances, against him. As his second commander in chief, largely a ceremonial and advisory position, he named Italian-born General Vicente Filisola, a capable administrator but, at forty-six, past his prime as a battle commander. Filisola lacked the respect of his peers, who would never forgive his foreign birth. (Several high-ranking officers were born in Spain or one of its possessions, but they at least shared the same blood and language as their Mexican-born comrades.) General Manuel Fernández Castrillón, the tall, well-educated former royalist who had fought at Santa Anna's side for more than a decade, was appointed aide-de-camp. Born in Cuba, he came to Mexico with the Spanish army, but had changed sides during the revolution. Few men had the courage to stand up to their commander in chief when he turned abusive; Castrillón was one of them.

Serving as chief of staff was Colonel Juan Nepomuceno Almonte, the New Orleans–educated illegitimate son of an early revolutionary hero, José María Morelos. The squat, swarthy Almonte had been sent to Texas in 1834 to infiltrate the province and determine its political attitude. He had seen with his own eyes the colonists' lack of allegiance—and their industriousness in civilizing the province's wilderness. In his report he had presaged the dangers they presented, and recommended that the army be dispatched immediately to control the unruly colonists.

As commanding general of the artillery, His Excellency named the skilled and ruthless Pedro de Ampudia, another Cuban—one of several in positions of high rank. Dozens of other officers rounded out the fifty-man general staff. As the army's commissary general, His Excellency appointed his brother-in-law, Colonel Ricardo Dromundo, who had married his sister Francisca, though Filisola and other officers had reservations about his performance and integrity.

One division of the army was already on the move. Forty-year-old General Joaquín Ramírez y Sesma had commanded the cavalry superbly in the Zacatecas victory in May; he had been rewarded with the governorship of that military department. Despite the fact that he and Santa Anna had opposed each other politically until 1833—he had once issued a manifesto mocking Santa Anna—he enjoyed His Excellency's confidence. He also enjoyed gambling and parties, but he was a brave and determined soldier, though somewhat arrogant. He viewed himself as the Joachim Murat, the dashing French cavalry leader, to Santa Anna's Napoleon, though that opinion was not shared by some of his peers. When news of General Cós's besiegement at Béxar reached the capital, orders were sent to Ramírez y Sesma directing him to march at once to the aid of Cós with three battalions of infantry, one cavalry regiment, and a battery of light artillery. On November 11, he began the long trek from Zacatecas to Laredo, situated on the

Rio Grande, which would serve as the primary base of operations for the march into Texas.

After sorting out the country's political affairs in the capital, Santa Anna rode to the city of San Luis Potosí early in December to begin organizing the army. The troops began assembling there and soon moved to the mile-high mountain city of Saltillo, in Coahuila, about 120 miles farther north, where they would take final shape. Saltillo, a city of almost fifteen thousand, lay in a wide valley flanked by the high peaks of the Eastern Sierra Madres, its old pink marble cathedral and government buildings gleaming in the sun. The area's mild winters reassured Santa Anna of the wisdom of his overland strategy. The line of approach would proceed from Saltillo to Monclova, to Laredo, then to Béxar—some six hundred miles total.

On December 20, when Santa Anna learned of the defeat of General Cós at Béxar, he quickly moved to change his plans. The main portion of the army would now cross the Rio Grande at Guerrero, eighty miles upriver from Laredo—this route, he told his subordinates, would more likely guarantee a surprise attack on Béxar. Just a few days later, Ramírez y Sesma's Vanguard Brigade reached the southern edge of Laredo to find Cós with his bedraggled column entering on the north side. They consolidated, and the Vanguard Brigade shared what they could with Cós's men. Within a week Ramírez y Sesma set out for Guerrero, per His Excellency's orders. Cós and his foot-weary *soldados,* still without their pay, proper food, or sufficient clothing, were ordered to march another two hundred torturous miles to Monclova, there to await the rest of the army.

SOME OF THE UNITS OF THE army moving north boasted experience during the civil wars of the previous half dozen years, but nearly half the soldiers were raw recruits—Indian peasants, vagabonds, prisoners, and the poor of the larger cities and towns—quickly conscripted with no experience and little desire to fight. That trait was shared by numerous veterans, at least in regard to this campaign. The thought of marching almost six hundred miles to Mexico's distant northern frontier to fight *norteamericanos* who posed no direct threat to one's village seemed an abstract cause. Most inhabitants of the sprawling nation still thought of themselves as Oaxacans, or Zacatecans, or Chihuahuans first, rather than Mexicans—the country was still too new, its towns and cities too far from each other, its politics too chaotic. In early December, Santa Anna had directed Ramírez y Sesma to "take advantage of the enthusiasm of the citizenry of the towns along your route by drafting those useful men familiar with firearms into the rank and file as auxiliary volunteers to enlarge the division." The unfortunates thus impressed into service—unwilling conscripts were enlisted for ten years, volunteers for eight—were neither enthusiastic nor volunteers, further eroding the quality and morale of the Army of Operations.

The Mexican soldiers spent most of January 1836 in Saltillo familiarizing themselves with their weapons and learning rudimentary drills—there were, for example, seventy different bugle calls used as field commands. One of them, the *degüello*—"slit throat"—had been inherited from the Spanish, who had borrowed it from the Moors. It signaled "no quarter," and would likely be sounded in earnest before long, since Santa Anna had issued instructions that the foreign rebels be treated as pirates:

The foreigners who wage war against the Mexican
Nation have violated all laws and do not deserve any
consideration, and for that reason, no quarter will be

given them as the troops are to be notified at the proper time. They have audaciously declared a war of extermination to the Mexicans and should be treated in the same manner.

The Anglo colonists, and any other foreigners from the United States or anywhere else who attempted to assist them, would be summarily executed, as befitted such treasonous barbarians.

During their several weeks in Saltillo, the recruits were introduced to the basics of marching and formations, but little more: anything more complicated would normally take a unit months to master. The simple order to load and fire, for instance, required fifteen distinct commands to complete. This series of orders could be reduced to "rapid fire," consisting of a few commands that would result in the soldiers firing at will, but whether their orders were truncated or drawn out, the first time many of these soldiers would ever fire their muskets would be when they confronted the enemy, a prospect that seemed not to bother the commander in chief.

The musket they carried was the India pattern Brown Bess, the standard-issue gun used by British line troops for almost a century—a smoothbore, muzzle-loading, .75-caliber flintlock that was reliable enough but showing its age. Its massive slug could do serious damage, but it generated a powerful kick, and its accuracy range was only seventy yards or so. And because Mexican gunpowder was often inferior—too much sulphur and charcoal—a double load was sometimes used, resulting in a larger powder flash in the pan near the face and eyes, and an even stronger recoil. Because of this, many soldiers fired their muskets from the waist, further reducing any accuracy. Its seventeen-inch bayonet was likely its most effective feature.

The basic army unit was the battalion, and each infantry battalion comprised eight companies of eighty men each, though most averaged half that number. The line units were the six *fusilero* (musketeer), or line, companies—the regular foot soldiers who did most of the fighting. The two other companies were considered the "preferred" units: the best of the line companies were placed in a single company of *granaderos* (grenadiers), veterans usually held in reserve, and the sharpshooters of the *cazador* (hunter) company were the light infantry, or skirmishers. The *cazadores* were better marksmen, and often carried the superior British Baker .61-caliber rifle, accurate up to three hundred yards and easier to load.

Infantrymen wore blue pigeon-tailed jackets with red trim and white crossbelts, and white or blue trousers, though some raw recruits sometimes wore simple white or blue cotton or linen outfits of trousers and a loose shirt. Many of these conscripts wore sandals. All wore a black shako—the stiff, cylindrical, high-crowned hat popular at the time—with a brass plate and small red plume.

The Mexican cavalry was in slightly better shape. Troopers carried short-barreled British Paget carbines and holster pistols, a saber in a waist-belt sling, and a formidable wooden lance—one and a half inches thick and nine feet long, with a red pennant near the end, below the metal point. They wore short red coats and blue cloth trousers, and their black leather crested helmets were decorated with brass plating and a high horsehair comb. Mexican lancers were skillful horsemen and feared opponents.

The artillery corps had suffered the worst during the revolutionary years. A severe shortage of funds and inadequate training for the branch's thin ranks had left it in woeful shape—Santa Anna would head north with only twenty-one pieces of ordnance, the largest being two twelve-pounders, but most of them smaller cannon, scattered among his units.

The officers' uniforms were, in a word, fancier—white or gray trousers; black riding boots; blue pigeon-tailed jackets with scarlet frontpieces, cuffs, and high collars, each embroidered with golden leaves of palm, olive, and laurel; golden epaulets; and a wide blue or green sash around the waist, all quite usual in that era of Napoleonic influence.

There were variations on these uniforms that distinguished the *permanentes* from the *activos,* this state unit from that one, and veterans from recruits, among other distinctions, but the overall effect was colorful and striking, especially against a background of desert tans, oranges, and scrub.

The lack of funds led to serious shortages in every area. The Army of Operations had neither surgeons nor adequate medical supplies. The hospital corps had been abolished in 1833, and interim measures to fix the problem had failed, so medical students and three hundred pesos' worth of drugs obtained at Saltillo—and the occasional village quack impressed into aid—would have to suffice. The quartermaster corps had neither the equipment nor the money to properly equip and supply an army of six thousand. But the army would march north with what could be scrounged together.

Other deficiencies abounded. Because there was a scarcity of mules, hundreds of oxen would be used. They were slow and could only be driven for eight hours a day. The army's train comprised more than two thousand carts. The two months' rations ordered by the commander in chief included flour, corn, beans, rice, and lard, though the largest part of the soldiers' diet would consist of the one hundred thousand pounds of maize hardtack that he had ordered his brother-in-law to have baked. That order would not be completely fulfilled, and eventually the soldiers' daily ration would be cut in half. Officers were expected to provide for themselves out of their regular pay, with no extra campaign allowance, a move that caused much resentment.

Hostile Indians posed an even more significant problem. The army would be moving through territory controlled by the Apaches and Comanches, ferocious tribes that had been active lately. Furthermore, they as well as a handful of other Indian tribes had formed various confederations, an ominous development, since when the Indians were at peace with each other, frontier attacks on colonists increased. Though Santa Anna hoped to persuade them to side with the Mexicans against the *norteamericanos,* and the Texians expected and feared just such an alignment, the Indians refused to aid either side and continued to raid indiscriminately. The Army of Operations would be in great danger of harassment as it moved north.

Several other problems emerged. The road to Béxar manifested a lack of water and adequate pasture for the animals. Through the 150 miles north of the Rio Grande, the route crossed only two rivers dependable year-round for water, and much of the meager winter grass had been burned off by the rebels. Desertions, both by unwilling recruits desperate to leave before entering the emptiness of northern Coahuila and south Texas, and unpaid muleteers, who slipped away with or without their stock, threatened to reduce the effective troop strength by hundreds. The missing mule drivers would force inexperienced and untrained soldiers to take the reins and further slow the columns.

None of this seemed to faze Santa Anna, who showed no alarm and waved off complaints from his aides. There was no time to argue; everything would be taken care of, he maintained, for he personally attended to almost every detail. He issued a steady stream of orders intended to clear up any and all problems, though the specifics of many of these orders remained in question—"Whatever you find available there," read one directive concerning food. Filisola was on the receiving end of many of these commands, but he was unable to comply with some of His Excellency's demands. Many of the necessities — horses, hardtack, uniforms, blankets, and footwear, among them — simply could not be obtained. But orders to alleviate these shortages had been issued, and His Excellency remained confident of their execution.

Before leaving Saltillo, Santa Anna ordered a full-dress parade review of the troops. After witnessing the makeshift army he had attempted to whip into shape — or at least a semblance of such — march through the streets of Saltillo before cheering citizens, he waxed eloquent on its readiness. He reported to Secretary of War José María Tornel that he "had not in years seen in the Republic a more splendid body of troops" — they were well disciplined and equipped, he said, and unanimous in their enthusiasm. Whether he truly believed this, or wrote it to reassure Mexico City of the wisdom of his actions, is unclear, but several of his field officers felt quite differently. Among the various disconcerting issues: the men were owed back pay, were often hungry, and some lacked proper footwear — somewhat necessary for a six-hundred-mile march through desolate terrain.

To bolster enthusiasm for the distant war, Tornel established a Legion of Honor for all soldiers serving in the campaign. It would be Mexico's highest military award, and no doubt the promise of glory and its rewards made up to some extent for the severe shortages and dangerous conditions of the difficult march they were about to undertake. Whether it compensated for the absence of clergy, which for some unexplained reason no one had thought to bring along, was another matter. A dying soldier would not have access to last rites of the Catholic Church, and the solace these rites provided.

A few days after the parade, despite the shortages and looming hardships, the Army of Operations was deemed ready to march north. Several on Santa Anna's staff had advised him to move his men by ship to a Texas port, making troop transportation and resupply much easier, but the commander in chief had overruled them: he wished to make Béxar his base of operations—almost all its inhabitants were Mexican and would, he thought, provide more cooperation and badly needed provisions. Ignoring the importance of having a supply point on the coast flouted every principle of military art, but the fact was that Mexico had no navy to speak of, and certainly no troop ships, not to mention money to charter them.

His Excellency was convinced that the expedition could carry enough provisions for two months and live off the countryside thereafter—after all, it had been done before, when he had accompanied Arredondo's army to Béxar twenty-three years earlier. Several of his commanders advised a southerly route into Texas, nearer the coast, perhaps to the formidable presidio at La Bahía (recently renamed Goliad), which could be used as a base of operations; then adequate supplies could be more easily routed by sea from the states of Tamaulipas and Nuevo León, and even from New Orleans. Santa Anna heard his aides out and continued with his plans: the army would march overland to Béxar.

TWENTY-EIGHT-YEAR-OLD José Enrique de la Peña also disapproved of the decision, though he was not privy to the general staff councils. A former naval lieutenant, he had switched service branches in 1827 and had subsequently received glowing reports from his superiors, including Santa Anna himself, which earned him a brevet promotion to lieutenant colonel. The native-born Mexican had recently been posted overseas as a member of a European diplomatic legation, but on the eve of departure he had changed his mind.

Preparations were under way for an army to march north to chastise the upstart colonists there, to be led by His Excellency, and he wanted to be a part of it. He had admired the flamboyant general since fighting with him at Tampico, where the lieutenant had distinguished himself.

Despite his desire for martial glory, de la Peña was a romantic in every sense of the word. He was keenly aware of the beauty of the natural world: at one point during the march to Texas he would find himself in a field of lilies and poppies whose beauty was so overwhelming that he would ask the soldiers he was with to shoot him—"that I might be buried in this vast garden," he wrote later. He was also madly in love with a young woman named Lucesita, a bewitching beauty who was capricious with her favors. Surely when he returned from this expedition draped with glory, she would yield to his love.

De la Peña had not received his duty assignment yet, but the more he saw of Santa Anna's methods of preparation, the more his admiration for His Excellency waned. The cruel conscriptions, the lack of medical services, the inadequate supplies, the dearth of intelligent planning—these and other aspects of the expedition disgusted the young officer. Like many others, he saw little reason for attacking Béxar, which was of no political or military importance. A strike into the heart of the Anglo colonies would have made more sense. Besides, the young officer was a federalist at heart. As for the comparisons to Napoleon, he thought Santa Anna "as distant from him as our planet is from the sun."

On the last day of January, the main body of the Army of Operations began to leave Saltillo for Monclova, 150 miles to the north, winding its way along El Camino Real, the "Royal Road," between imposing mountain peaks. Three hundred miles beyond that city—about halfway up the portion of El

Camino Real that ran from Mexico City to Nacogdoches in far east Texas—lay Béxar. Santa Anna would lead a five-thousand-man army through the barren semidesert, where there was no forage and little water, in the deepest part of winter, and he would liberate Béxar from the barbarians. He would make an example of them. He knew what had to be done.

If Santa Anna had studied his idol's career more closely, he might have reconsidered his plan. Napoleon had gained his first victories with an experienced army drilled to perfection, whose men had engaged in frequent target and maneuver practice. But his downfall had come after two disastrous invasions. His Iberian peninsular campaign failed because local guerrilla units had harassed the much larger French armies, which had been unable to live off the land in the poor Spanish countryside. And long supply and communication lines, the pitiless Russian winter, and constant guerrilla attacks by the Cossack cavalry had doomed the ill-fated Russian campaign.

An old acquaintance could also have warned him. José Juan Sánchez had returned with Cós's column, and accompanied Cós to Saltillo to meet with Santa Anna. The commander in chief expressed surprise that his old classmate was not wearing a lieutenant colonel's insignia, and granted his request to accompany the campaign. Sánchez would ride with the Second Infantry Brigade, commanded by General Eugenio Tolsa, as General Cós's adjutant. Unimpressed with the army's preparations, he questioned Santa Anna's personal attendance to all matters, no matter how trivial, from grand strategy to quartermaster and commissary duties and muleteer and teamster hirings. Well aware from previous experience of the difficulties of traversing the arid desolation of northern Coahuila and south Texas beyond the Rio Grande, he was especially alarmed. His journey to Béxar with the conscripts had been brutal and

costly. The continual rain and cold, combined with their meager food supplies and inadequate shelter, had almost destroyed
their already low morale—and that had been two months
earlier, in the fall, not the winter. Few of these troops were
from northern Mexico, and these soldiers were unused to
severe cold and uniformed only for mild weather—no heavy
coats or tents were issued. If the weather turned unseasonable,
great suffering and untold deaths could result among the
ranks, to say nothing of the thousands of women and children
following their men.

A potential problem, and another reason for Santa Anna's
haste, was political in nature. If the army did not advance
soon, soldiers might be influenced by some of the revolutionary factions then active. The supporters of federalism were
numerous and active throughout the country, and in the northern departments in particular. It was not unheard-of for an
entire body of troops to desert for political reasons, allying
themselves with another party, especially when they were
unwilling conscripts with little or no reason to maintain allegiance to centralism.

IN LAREDO, SÁNCHEZ HAD SENSED condescension on the
part of the fresh troops for the hungry, near-naked, miserable
soldados from Béxar. News of Cós's surrender there had fostered unofficial accusations of dishonor directed at Cós and
his key subalterns, including Sánchez. It was clear these new
recruits despised Cós's men, and to hear them brag enraged
the captain. General Ramírez y Sesma added further humili-
ation when he expressed serious doubt that the rebels could
stop just a hundred lancers.

Now, the day before the First Infantry Brigade moved out
of Saltillo, Sánchez ran into some old comrades in the street.

They asked him if he was one of the "lost" of Béxar, adding insult to injury. Then General Castrillón inquired about the *norteamericanos*.

"Friend," he said, gesturing toward his troops, "what do you think of these soldiers?"

"That they look good," Sánchez said.

"This will not be anything more than a military parade," explained Castrillón. "Do you know that those wretches ran away without even firing a shot?"

Sánchez protested, but after Castrillón accused him of being frightened in Béxar, the captain returned to his quarters, disgusted. He worried that there were soldiers who thought they could defeat a cunning and stubborn enemy with only bravado.

The next day the troops, like a long line of ants, began moving out through the northern reaches of Mexico toward Monclova. Santa Anna had organized his army into five units. Ramírez y Sesma's Vanguard Brigade of 1,541 men was already at Guerrero on the Rio Grande, having arrived there on January 16. Tolsa's Second Infantry Brigade, consisting of 1,839 men, had left Saltillo a few days earlier, on January 31; the next day, the sixteen-hundred-man First Infantry Brigade, under the command of General Antonio Gaona, departed. Santa Anna, his staff, and his escort of fifty lancers left the same morning. Last was General Juan Andrade's Cavalry Brigade of 437 lancers.

General Cós, accompanied by Sánchez, left Saltillo with a small force on February 6. (General José Urrea's four-hundred-man brigade had set out on January 15 for Matamoros, where 260 Mayan Indian recruits from the warm, humid Yucatán would join him, in response to rumors of a rebel movement toward that city. He would continue up the Atascosito Road, close to the coast, to Goliad and its presidio.) The columns would eventually stretch over hundreds of miles, and face a host of imposing hurdles: inadequate supply lines, desertion, near starvation, extreme weather, dysentery, sickness, savage Indians, plunging morale, and a few corrupt officers who put personal gain above the well-being of their men. Now, as they left the city, they passed a priest, who was blessing them as they filed by.

Fortunately for all concerned, January had been relatively dry, with only the occasional light shower, so the roads between the Rio Grande and Béxar were in good shape—either solid earth, or a mixture of sand and stone that prevented the formation of too much mud when wet. This helped, but if the army was to reach Béxar in decent shape and in decent time, it would largely be due not to the condition of the roads but to the determination and leadership of Antonio López de Santa Anna. Years ago, he had authorized one of his aides to strike him with a pistol if he deviated from his resolve. There would be no need for that now—Santa Anna would surprise the ungrateful Anglo colonists, or many of his men would die trying.

ALMOST FIVE HUNDRED MILES NORTH on El Camino Real lay the objective of Santa Anna's army. Left to defend Béxar was a garrison that by mid-January had dwindled down to eighty men, almost all of them volunteers. Most were dressed in late-summer garb that had worn down to rags after several months of hard fighting and winter weather. The few supplies and clothing sent by the ineffectual government in San Felipe had been rudely appropriated by the Matamoros expedition led by James Grant and Frank Johnson. They had even taken most of the horses, thus preventing effective scouting operations. And though there were plenty of extra muskets appropriated from Cós's forces, good powder was in short supply.

But the Mexican army was not expected until March at the earliest, when the summer grass would begin emerging, and reinforcements and provisions were on the way. The men fortifying the dilapidated mission across the shallow San Antonio River were sure of it.

NINE

The Backwoodsman

Be always sure you're right — then go ahead!

DAVY CROCKETT

If anyone in America could be called an amiable cuss, it was the Honorable David Crockett. On that point virtually everyone, friend and foe alike, agreed. There were only a few for whom the cussedness outweighed the amiability — and one of them was President Andrew Jackson. Once, he had been Crockett's political hero, as well as his commander during the Creek War. But Crockett's allegiance would always be to his poor constituents of west Tennessee, and he had come to realize that Jackson had become an opportunist whose allegiances shifted with the wind, or at least that is what Crockett believed. Over the past five years or so, the congressman from Tennessee's near-constant jabs at Jackson — in the press, in session, in company of every kind — had come to infuriate the president. Jackson's handpicked successor, Vice President Martin Van Buren, was another on Crockett's blacklist. Crockett loathed him, and let everyone know it. For Jackson and Van Buren,

Crockett's defeat in his bid for a fourth congressional term, and the loss of his bully pulpit, was something to be devoutly thankful for.

Jackson's followers had helped bring about that defeat, but it was Crockett himself who would ultimately relieve them of the gadfly who had plagued them for so long. He had told his constituents (or so he claimed later) that if they elected his rival, "You may all go to hell and I will go to Texas." To the surprise of many, he did just that.

EVERY GENERATION HAS ITS LAND OF MILK and honey. In 1835, it was Texas, and had been for more than a decade. And Texas lay to the west. Like his father and grandfather before him, and like their forefathers before them, reaching back many hundreds of years — Celtic warriors and their willful women, who had fought in and conquered the lands from middle Europe westward to the sea, and traveled up the English island to Scotland and over the waters again to Ireland, and then made the great journey across the northern Atlantic to the New World — David Crockett had always been bound westward. It was in his blood, his marrow. Like thousands of others, he was hopeful of finding his fortune by following the sunset. He would encounter something very different.

In common with so many early American frontiersmen, Crockett was of primarily Scots-Irish stock (though he preferred to think the Irish dominated). About 1775, his grandfather David Crockett led his family from the Piedmont region of North Carolina west across the Appalachians into Indian territory. Shortly after settling in what would become eastern Tennessee, the elder Crockett and his wife were massacred by Creek Indians, who were justifiably angry at white encroachment into their land. Some of his children were wounded or captured—one, deaf and mute, resided with the Creeks for eighteen years before his brothers found him and bought him from his captors. But the remaining family refused to leave the area, and on August 17, 1786, a new David Crockett, the fifth of nine children, was born to John Crockett and his wife, the former Rebecca Hawkins, in a log cabin in the hill country, on the Nolichucky River near Rogersville.

John Crockett had fought as a citizen soldier in the Revolution, where he and 1,100 other Tennessee volunteers defeated the British in the bloody battle at Kings Mountain. Later he served as county constable for several terms, and attempted various types of employment—land speculation, working in a gristmill, innkeeping—but he and his family never rose much above poverty, and, if anything, fell deeper in debt. Those financial circumstances would never change, even after he moved farther west in 1796, and on the side of a well-traveled road opened a six-room log tavern that also served as their home. It was a crude existence, the inn catering primarily to a rough trade of drovers and wagoners, and all the children did their share. David would remember later that he and his family made their "acquaintance with hard times, and a plenty of them."

Two years later John Crockett, "being hard run every way," hired out his twelve-year-old son David (a common practice of the time) to a cattle drover named Jacob Siler to help take a herd 225 miles to Rockbridge County, Virginia. Wary of his father's hickory-stick discipline, David went along, even though he would have to make the return trip on his own in winter. Upon arriving at their destination two weeks later, Siler tried to force the boy into indentured servitude. David stayed a month, all the time convincing the man and his family of his cooperation, then snuck out of the house late on a cold Sunday night. After walking seven miles through knee-deep snow, he reached a tavern, where he found a group of travelers who, fortunately and coincidentally, knew his father and arranged his passage south. He arrived home a few weeks later.

David had received no schooling up to that point; there was little opportunity for formal education on the frontier. But the people of the community hired a schoolteacher in the fall of 1799—usually the teacher served in exchange for room and board and a small salary—and the Crockett children dutifully began to attend. Only a few days later a disagreement with his drunken father over his education, and a desire to avoid a severe whipping, led David, now thirteen, to leave once more, again not entirely of his own volition. This time, he hired himself out—to another cattle drover on the way to Virginia.

Over the next two and a half years young David took on odd jobs here and there, learning as he went along how to win friends and attain their approval. When he finally returned home in the spring of 1802 to a touching reunion—even his father was glad to see him—he was sixteen, more man than boy, with a seasoning only the road could supply. He worked off some of his father's debts over the next year, and finally got around to learning his letters by working for a neighboring Quaker in exchange for schooling and board. Six months of four days' lessons a week would be all he would ever know of classwork, but he gained enough knowledge of reading, writing, and arithmetic to stand him in good stead.

The primary aim of his newfound interest in education was to improve his odds among the fairer sex, for he had determined to find himself a wife. At the age of nineteen he became engaged to a young woman and even took out a marriage license. David had begun to spend much of his time hunting, and had become quite good at it. Just a few days before the wedding, after a successful shooting match—he won a whole beef in a competition—he found that his fiancée, perhaps exasperated with having a hunting gun as a rival, had left him for another. His despondency only lasted a short time, and after a quick recovery, he found another young beauty and began courting her. On August 16, 1806, one day before his twentieth birthday, David Crockett married Mary Finley, nicknamed Polly.

They rented a small farm and cabin. In the next few years, two boys, John and William, were born. Crockett soon learned the grimness of his situation:

> We worked for some years [he wrote later], renting ground, and paying high rent, until I found it wasn't the thing it was cracked up to be; and that I couldn't make a fortune of it just at all....I found I was better at increasing my family than my fortune. It was therefore the more necessary that I should hunt some better place to get along; and as I knowed I would have to move at some time, I thought it was better to do it before my family got too large, that I might have less to carry.

So he took his wife and children to the west, following the frontier, in the Crockett way. He left in the fall of 1811, bound for central Tennessee. A year and a half later, he pulled up stakes and moved again, farther west and south to Bean's Creek, almost to the Alabama line, a sparsely settled area where game was still plentiful and a good hunter and marksman like Crockett could supply his family with sufficient meat to get by. Now in his late twenties, he had filled out to about six feet, tall for the time, with lank black hair parted in the middle over an open face of dark blue eyes and light complexion. Despite the time spent outdoors on long hunts and sporadic farming, he would never lose his fair face and rosy cheeks.

Recent clashes between Creeks and whites had led to Indian massacres and retaliatory attacks before Crockett's arrival in the region. The Creek War erupted soon after, when a thousand warriors attacked Fort Mims, in southern Alabama, on August 30, 1813, and killed all but fifty of the 553 men, women, and children gathered there. A few weeks later men began mustering into the militia, and Crockett rode to nearby Winchester to join the Tennessee Volunteer Mounted Riflemen for ninety days. The plan was to march south and meet the Indians before the fight spread north to their homes. The Tennessee men would eventually serve under the command of Major General Andrew Jackson. Crockett participated in some hard fighting, particularly the annihilation of a Creek village full of warriors (including a few women and children), the memory of which would haunt him for a long time. And for a variety of reasons, he also developed a healthy dislike for officers, particularly when one ignored his scouting report until another officer verified it.

He returned home after his hitch was up, but nine months later, in September 1814, he reenlisted as a sergeant to help drive the British and their allies out of Pensacola, in Spanish Florida, on the Gulf Coast. General Jackson took Pensacola on November 7, and proceeded west toward Mobile. Crockett's company arrived on November 8, then was directed to engage in a rear-guard action against the Creeks. They spent the next several months in a fruitless and often aimless Indian chase through the swamps and forests of Florida and Alabama. In January 1815, Jackson decisively defeated the British at New Orleans, but Crockett's unit continued to move north in search of Indians, under the command of a regular army major who kept his troops out even though they were low on rations, suffering from exposure, and exhausted. For weeks they were near starvation; Crockett spent a good amount of the time foraging and hunting, though game was scarce. Sometimes he could only bag squirrels and birds, though his ravenous comrades were happy to get them. Their horses gave out—one day thirteen of them collapsed and were abandoned. By the time Sergeant Crockett returned home—a month early, at the end of February, after hiring a man to serve out the remaining month—he had gained more than enough experience in soldiering.

Polly gave birth to a daughter early that year, and died at the end of the summer of an undiagnosed frontier illness. She left Crockett with three small children, one an infant. Instead of breaking up his family and placing them with friends or relatives, as was the custom, he decided to find another wife. Not far away lived a widow named Elizabeth Patton. Her husband had lost his life in the Creek War, leaving her with two children close to the age of David's boys, the considerable sum of $800 in cash, and a farm worth more than his own (which was failing, to boot). After several months of calculated courtship, he married her in the summer of 1816. Elizabeth—"Bet," as he would sometimes call her—was by all accounts industrious and practical, a capable woman and not a slight one: one frequent visitor to their mill remembered that "Mrs. Crockett was always grinding. She was a woman of great strength and could handle sacks of grain with ease." Though begun as a union of convenience, their marriage would evolve into one of friendship, respect, and love.

A year later Crockett sold the two farms and led his enlarged family eighty miles west, settling on a creek near the small village of Lawrenceburg. His service in the recent war and the fact that his wife came from a well-to-do, prominent family combined to improve his social standing, and despite his distrust of officers he had accepted a lieutenancy in the county militia upon his return. For this and other reasons—his genuine honesty, his forthright manner, and his warm personality, no doubt—his fellow townspeople chose him to be magistrate, an office he accepted in November 1817, a few months after his arrival. The citizens' trust was rewarded when his rulings proved sound and fair: "I gave my decisions on the principles of common justice and honesty between man and man, and relied on natural born sense, and not on law, learning to guide me," he wrote later. The rough backwoodsman was becoming respectable. And though he would never achieve financial independence, always spending more than he made, he would occasionally approach solvency after his second marriage. He would even own a few slaves to help on the farm.

Four months later he was elected lieutenant colonel of his new county's militia regiment, thus acquiring the honorific of Colonel, which would remain with him until the end of his days. Over the next few years, he assumed other town and county administrative positions. In January 1821, encouraged by friends, he resigned his office of town commissioner and announced his candidacy for the state legislature.

Regional campaigning in that time and place consisted of making appearances in local communities, giving speeches, debating, and generally entertaining the crowd. Stump-speaking, as it was called—for the tree stump from which the candidates would address their neighbors—constituted one of the chief forms of social amusement of the day. The political talk usually shared equal time with storytelling, drinking, and tobacco chewing. Crockett by this time had developed a fondness for all three, and he now found he was especially good at the first: his quick wit, flair for repartee, and often self-deprecating humor, all delivered in a backcountry drawl, were qualities to which his listeners responded. He never pretended to be anything more than he was, a simple man like them, and they identified with him. At first he avoided opining on issues of which he knew little, but as he learned more he gained confidence and voiced stronger positions. In August, he won election to the state legislature by a margin of two to one.

Like any poor man—and most of Crockett's life, until he had the good fortune to marry Elizabeth Patton, had been one of crushing poverty—he had desired advancement and respect and a certain degree of affluence. Toward those ends he eagerly climbed each successive rung of the political ladder. Just before his election, he had ambitiously begun construction of a grist-mill, a powder mill, and a distillery on his creekside land—all enterprises typical of a poor man of the time scrambling for a leg up, as they called for the investment of hard work and natural resources more than money. Upon winning his seat he departed for the state capital, Murfreesboro, leaving his wife to handle operations; Elizabeth, a good businesswoman, could do as good a job as he, if not better. But even her skills could not fight nature. No sooner had the mills opened for business than a flash flood washed them away.

That was the end of Crockett's flirtation with entrepreneurship. When he returned after the end of that first legislative session in 1822, he and his family packed up their meager possessions and moved west once more, traveling 150 miles to the westernmost part of Tennessee, where he cleared land and built two connected log cabins on the Rutherford Fork of the Obion River. There were far fewer inhabitants in that region, and game was plentiful. Crockett hunted whenever he got the chance, and every fall after the corn was harvested he retreated to the wilderness for as much as a month or more, killing prodigious numbers of bear, deer, elk, and wolves (the government paid a three-dollar bounty for each wolf pelt). His reputation as a woodsman and hunter spread, abetted no doubt by the tall tales Crockett told of his exploits.

Six years later, after one failed run, he was elected to

Congress. He would be reelected in 1829, lose his seat by fewer than six hundred votes out of the 16,482 cast in 1831, and win it back in another close election (by just 173 votes out of the almost eight thousand cast) in 1833. In Washington he tried mightily to push through passage of a bill that would make land available inexpensively to the poor, particularly those in his western Tennessee constituency who had settled on government land and improved it with their own toil. He believed these "squatters" were the country's true pioneers, risking their lives amid the dangers of the frontier, and should be rewarded for their initiative.

He would not succeed. The relatively guileless Crockett never learned — or never cared to engage in, if it compromised his principles — the art of deal making, the quid pro quo soon to be taken for granted as the price of doing business in Washington. He also refused to sacrifice his principles or the promises he had made to his constituents in the name of party unity. The result was meager support from his fellow Tennessee legislators and other congressmen, since Crockett would not barter votes for bills he did not believe in. The opposition of the Jackson forces also played a part, as Crockett had broken ranks with his old commander as early as 1828, during his first term, after Jackson's election to the presidency. The Jacksonians would gerrymander his west Tennessee congressional district before the 1835 elections, eroding his base further. For these reasons and others, he never garnered the support necessary for his land bill's passage, or for the passage of any other bill he put forward. Unfortunately, he banked his future on getting the bill through to the exclusion of everything else, and that would cost him.

During congressional recesses, Crockett returned home to his family and spent most of his time hunting, farming, and politicking. He enjoyed and excelled at the first; the second was necessary and unenjoyable; the third was necessary to reassure his reelection and enjoyable enough, since it involved socializing, storytelling, and drinking. He spent less and less time at home and saw little of his family—he missed the marriage of his oldest daughter, Margaret, and gave his consent by mail. Fortunately Elizabeth kept the farm going with the help of their children (a total of eight at one point) and a few slaves.

His increasing celebrity pleased Crockett. During his time in Washington his outsize reputation spread from western Tennessee throughout the nation, and he thrived on the larger stage. His colorful oratory, combined with the increasingly mythic tales of his backwoods adventures, made him a popular national figure, particularly in a time when few ordinary folk were involved in government at that level. Jackson's 1828 election had ushered in a new era of the common man in America—he had been the first nonaristocratic elected president, and his populist appeal would never waver—but Crockett even more than the president now personified Jackson's image. In late 1831 a play entitled *The Lion of the West* opened to an enthusiastic reception. The frontiersman protagonist, Colonel Nimrod Wildfire, was clearly modeled on Colonel David Crockett. He dressed in buckskin, wore a wildcat-skin cap, and spoke in a boastful patois sprinkled with colorful phrases. The play both celebrated and ridiculed Crockett with equal fervor.

Crockett's larger-than-life public image was boosted even further with an unauthorized biography released in 1833. The author had talked to friends and acquaintances of the congressman (and even visited Crockett at his home), and combined truth and tall tales into an entertaining and largely flattering picture of his subject as peerless bear hunter, backwoods original, and principled congressman. The book went into several printings.

Crockett was not happy with the book. Not only was it full of semitruths and fantastical fictions; even worse, he earned not a penny from its success. He decided to write his story himself, and enlisted a friend and fellow congressman, Thomas Chilton of Kentucky, to help. *A Narrative of the Life of David Crockett of the State of Tennessee* was released in the spring of 1834 and became an immediate bestseller. Patterned after Benjamin Franklin's autobiography, the book captured Crockett's true voice. Well written (except for the occasional deliberate misspelling and quaint grammar, intended to authenticate his backwoods reputation) and mostly accurate (Crockett changed details about his military service for political reasons), the book was a classic tale of a poor boy from the backwoods who rises to fame through his determination and innate intelligence. Sprinkled through the many stories of bear hunting, Indian fighting, exploring, and other adventures were occasional political jibes and jokes, almost always at the expense of Jackson and Van Buren, for the book was also designed as a campaign tool. And on the title page was the phrase that Crockett had grown most fond of, and adopted as his slogan: "Be always sure you're right—then go ahead!"

By mid-1835, after a whirlwind, two-week book tour of the major cities of the eastern United States—while Congress was in session—Crockett had become one of the most famous individuals in America. But the figure he cut in real life usually fell short of the legend. The half man, half alligator who could whip his weight in wildcats and grin a panther down from a tree was actually a well-dressed, well-mannered gentleman, to the surprise of many, including a woman who saw him in the audience at a ventriloquist's show:

He is wholly different from what I thought him, tall in stature large in frame but quite thin with black hair combed straight over the forehead parted from the middle and his shirt collar turned negligently back over his coat. He has rather an indolent careless appearance and looks not like a "go-ahead man."

That observer was close to the truth. "Go-ahead" though Crockett might be in energy and outlook, he was certainly never going to fit the stereotype of the thrusting, can-do politician— nor did he wish to. Indeed, the more time he spent in Washington, the more disenchanted, impatient, and just plain bored he became with the unpleasant and compromising political process. Crockett was a genuinely honest man, despite the slight autobiographical fiddles he engineered and the occasional harmless trick he played on an opponent to make a point and get a laugh from an audience. Even worse for his political career, he was positively resistant to deal making. "I have always supported measurs [sic] and principles, not men," he wrote, and his political career emphasized the sincerity of that statement.

His disillusionment was all the greater because he had once so admired fellow Tennessean Andrew Jackson. By 1830, during his second term, Crockett was publicly denouncing the president, whom he saw as having been corrupted by Washington and manipulated by the less scrupulous men around him, particularly Vice President Van Buren, a master politician with a reputation as a backroom schemer. That year, Crockett stated, "I am still a Jackson man, but General Jackson is not— he has become a Van Buren man."

In the spring of 1834, Jackson clashed with the Senate over the extent of executive power and control. Some, including Crockett, interpreted these developments as an impending descent into tyranny; many still alive could remember living under the rule of a king, and did not wish for another monarch. They compared Jackson to Julius Caesar and the times to the last days of the Roman Republic. Near the end of the year, in a letter to a friend, Crockett vowed that if Van Buren, Jackson's handpicked successor, was elected, "I will leave the united [sic] States. I will not live under his kingdom."

Nevertheless, Crockett stumped during the late spring and early summer of 1835 with vigor, though he lacked the money for a full-scale campaign. This time his opponents fielded a popular candidate named Adam Huntsman, who gave as good as he got. An attorney with a peg leg, the result of a war injury, he proved adept at savvy disparagement of Crockett, criticizing his lapses in Washington and pointing out his failure to achieve anything of substance during his three terms.

Crockett responded by promising his constituents that he would set out for Texas if he lost the election. But to make matters worse, he had again failed to pass his land bill, despite promising that it would be done, and he had accomplished little else this term save for his tour in support of the book. A mere fifteen months after its publication had established his celebrity, his star was on the decline, and to many, his strident criticism of the president had grown tiresome and his legislation inconsequential. A follow-up narrative of his promotional tour, quickly written (by another ghostwriter, based on Crockett's notes and press clippings) and published to cash in on his fame, resulted in little of the charm and a fraction of the sales of the first. Another book released a few months later, in the summer of 1835, a polemic against Van Buren disguised as a biography of the vice president, turned out even worse. Finally, his vote against Jackson's Indian Removal Act of 1830 had not been popular with his constituents. On the surface it would appear surprising that Crockett, whose grandparents had been massacred by Creeks and who had fought them himself, could summon the compassion to take their side. But Crockett could empathize with the plight of the "civilized" tribes, for they were in the same boat as many of his constituents regarding land. And Indians had saved his life during one of his early hunting trips when a party of them found him in the woods, near death from malaria. Now peaceful and living on ancestral lands, they were protected by treaties that Jackson was choosing to ignore.

Initially, Crockett was confident he would win. As the campaign wore on, however, he suspected he was beaten, though he put on a brave face. On election day he won in eighteen of his nineteen counties. But in the single county Huntsman took, he won handily, and Crockett lost the early August election by 252 votes out of the nine thousand cast. The verdict hit home, and when he walked into his cabin after receiving the news, he told his wife, "Well, Bet, I am beat, and I'm off for Texas." His fourteen-year-old daughter, Matilda, would later recall that he seemed unfazed by his defeat, because "he wanted to go to Texas anyhow." He had given his word, and he would keep it. Another long hunt, another adventure, and a chance to make his fortune in an unsullied land—that was more than enough reason to head west again. Besides, it was surely preferable to the life of a backwoods farmer, which Crockett had never cottoned to and by now was finding intolerable.

At first Crockett suggested that the whole family go together, the sooner the better; but Elizabeth did not like the sound of that idea. "Mother persuaded him to go first and look at the country, and then if he liked it, we would all go," remembered Matilda. "He seemed very confident...that he would soon have us all to join him in Texas." It was settled, then: if the country was as good as the stories he had heard made it out to be, he would stake a claim and come back for his family. On the eve of his departure, he wrote to his brother-in-law George Patton: "We will go through Arkinsaw and I want to explore the Texes well before I return." It would, he hoped, be his last move west.

On an afternoon late in October, a few days before he left, he gave a big barbecue and "bran dance"—that morning they sprinkled the ground liberally with the husks of Indian corn, for a better surface—and invited neighbors and friends from far and near. "They had a glorious time," Matilda remembered. "The young folks danced all day and night and everybody enjoyed themselves finely."

On the morning of November 1, less than three months after his defeat, Crockett said good-bye to his family. Three companions would ride with him: Will Patton, his nephew—"a fine fellow," Crockett thought; Abner Burgin, another brother-in-law; and Lindsey Tinkle, a neighbor and friend. David dressed in his hunting suit and coonskin cap, though he carried finer clothes in his knapsack. The only firearm he carried was his trusted Betsy, the flintlock rifle he had owned for years. He left his nineteen-year-old son, Robert, in charge of the family and farm, said good-bye to Elizabeth, his two teenage daughters, and everyone else, mounted his large bay, and headed southwest to Dyersburg to catch the main road south toward Memphis, about one hundred miles away.

They reached the river town a few days later and soon engaged in a farewell drinking party with some old friends—and some new ones, since Crockett made them as fast as he could meet them, and everyone wanted to meet the famous son of Tennessee. At some point in the evening, he mounted a tavern counter and gave a speech to the crowd who had gathered, concluding with, "Since you have chosen to elect a man with a timber toe to succeed me, you may all go to hell and I will go to Texas. I am on my way now." The next day—their group now doubled in size—they crossed the Mississippi and set out overland for Little Rock, to the west. Overhead, Halley's Comet slowly made its way through the heavens. (Three years earlier, newspapers around the country had carried a story announcing that Crockett had been appointed by the president to "stand on the Allegheny mountains and catch the Comet, on its approach to the earth, and wring off its tail, to keep it from burning up the world!")

If Crockett had not previously given much thought to the political turmoil in Texas, the subject had by now become a rationale for his journey. In Little Rock he gave a speech largely concerned with Texas independence, explaining that he was on his way there "to join the patriots of that country in freeing it from the shackles of the Mexican government," as one local scribe noted. In the weeks previous, the local newspapers had been filled with news from the Mexican province, including a letter from Stephen Austin detailing the October 2 skirmish at Gonzales and a thunderous call to arms from Crockett's acquaintance and fellow Tennessee politician Sam Houston, who had been practicing law in Nacogdoches until the outbreak of hostilities and had recently been elected commander of that town's militia:

> War in defence of our rights, our oaths, and our constitutions is inevitable in Texas!
>
> If *volunteers* from the United States will join their brethren in this section, they will receive liberal bounties of land. We have millions of acres of our best lands unchosen and unappropriated.
>
> Let each man come with a good rifle, and one hundred rounds of ammunition, and come soon.
>
> Our war-cry is "Liberty or death."
>
> Our principles are to support the constitution, and *down with the Usurper*!!!

From Little Rock, Crockett and his Tennesseans proceeded southwest toward Texas and crossed the Red River sometime during the third week in November. He may have been eager to join the Texians in their fight for freedom, but he found time to go on an extended hunt into northeast Texas. Henry Stout, a legend in the area as a hunter and guide, escorted Crockett and company into the Choctaw Bayou area and beyond, into the dense strip of forest known as the Cross Timbers. For two weeks or more they explored a country rich in bison, bear, deer, and other large and small game.

The disappointment of his political defeat was fading: Crockett was in his element, and in fine form and high spirits. The malaria he had contracted twenty years before had troubled him periodically ever since, but now it was only a memory. As he explored Texas south of the Red River, no fever and aches plagued him; he felt in excellent health. And the country was everything he had heard: "I must say as to what I have seen of Texas it is the garden spot of the world the best land and the best prospect for health I ever saw is here and I do believe it is a fortune to any man to come here," he wrote to his oldest daughter, Margaret.

Around the end of December, the party turned south toward Nacogdoches, crossed the Sabine River into Texas, and reached the old Spanish village early in January. At a banquet in his honor given by the ladies of the town, he again told the story that ended with "you may all go to hell and I will go to Texas." (Crockett was never one to waste a good line.) A few days later he rode thirty miles east to the small village of San Augustine, where a cannon's roar announced his arrival, and the requisite welcoming dinner provided another opportunity for a speech.

Already being touted as a local delegate to the constitutional convention scheduled for March 1 in San Felipe—which could not only revive his political career but also help him gain appointment as a land agent for part of the area he had traversed to the north—Crockett decided to make his loyalties official. He could have declined military service due to his age (he would turn fifty in August), or due to his likely election to the convention, but on January 12, Judge John Forbes administered his self-composed oath of allegiance to Crockett, Will Patton, and sixty-six other men. (Friends Lindsey Tinkle and Abner Burgin had decided to return to their wives and children.) They signed up for six months in the Volunteer Auxiliary Corps.

When it came time for Crockett to add his name to the list, he read the oath carefully:

> I do solemnly swear that I will bear true allegiance to the provisional government of Texas, or any future government that may be hereafter declared, and that I will serve her honestly and faithfully against all her enemies and oppressors whatsoever.

Crockett told Forbes that he was only willing to support a "republican government." Forbes inserted "republican" between "future" and "government," and Crockett put his name to the document. With memories of "King Andrew the First" still vivid—and the recollections of life under George III not too far in the past—he had no desire to live under a monarchy, actual or virtual. Now a soldier in the army of Texas, he sent word home. In a letter to Margaret he made clear his enthusiasm for his new cause:

> I am rejoiced at my fate. I would rather be in my present situation than to be elected to a seat in Congress for life. I am in hopes of making a fortune for myself and family bad as has been my prospects... do not be uneasy about me. I am with my friends.

The ex-congressman and his companions soon set out west along the Old San Antonio Road—the Anglo name for El Camino Real—for Washington, 125 miles away on the Brazos River. There they hoped to receive orders from Houston, the recently appointed commander in chief of the Texian army, as to their destination. With Crockett now rode fifteen or sixteen others—"almost all," wrote Judge Forbes of these and other recruits, "gentlemen of the best respectability." Most were educated professionals from Tennessee and Kentucky, several of them lawyers, men who were familiar with Crockett and were honored and delighted to ride with him. They began to call themselves the Tennessee Mounted Volunteers.

Some of these men had come to Texas seeking their fortune. Others came in sympathy with the plight of the people they perceived as their fellow Americans. Daniel Cloud, a young attorney from Kentucky, had journeyed through several states seeking gainful employment; in the Arkansas Territory, he had found what appeared to be a gold mine of opportunity. But upon hearing more about the situation in Texas, he had decided to continue to the Mexican province. "The reason for our pushing still further on," he wrote his brother, "must now be told.... Ever since Texas has unfurled the banner of freedom, and commenced a warfare for liberty or death, our hearts have been enlisted in her behalf." His friend and traveling companion Peter James Bailey, another Kentucky lawyer, shared his sentiments and agreed to join the cause.

For one of their number, the reason lay deeper.

Forty-one-year-old Micajah Autry had lived in a fine white-washed house on the highest hill around Jackson, Tennessee, not far from the home of Andrew Jackson, a neighbor and friend, for whom the town was named. Though frail as a child, Autry had grown to be tall and slender, with dark hair and eyes. As a seventeen-year-old he had served in the army during the War of 1812. He had a loving wife and three children, and a large law practice. But when he gambled a great deal of money speculating in dry goods, the venture failed. He was forced to sell all the property he owned: his house, the land surrounding it, his carriage and horses, and his slaves. Then something far worse happened.

Autry, his wife, Martha, and his family attended a camp meeting a few miles from their house and left their little boy, Edward, in the care of a nurse. They returned home to find the child dead, drowned accidentally after climbing into a bathtub. When a grief-stricken Martha Autry awoke the next day, her glossy hair had turned snowy white. The change in Micajah Autry was no less extreme. "It was on one of his trips north that he became quite enthusiastic over Austin's colony," his daughter, Mary, remembered later, and he made up his mind to "view the prospects himself." He left his wife and children with his stepdaughter — Martha's daughter from her first marriage — and her husband, closed his law practice, and in November 1835 headed for Texas to find a new home for his family.

At Memphis, he boarded a boat and steamed down the Mississippi. Aboard were about twenty other Tennessee men bound for Texas, and Autry fell in with them. The word was that the fighting at Béxar would be over before they got there, but that Santa Anna would invade Texas in the spring. The men had no horses, but they were excited at their prospects. On December 13, they reached Natchitoches, Louisiana, on the Red River. When they found no mounts there, Autry determined to reach Nacogdoches, a hundred miles west, on foot. He followed the Old San Antonio Road to San Augustine, where he joined up with another small company of volunteers, four of whom were lawyers, including Cloud and Bailey, his fellow young Kentuckians. They continued west, slogging their way through torrents

of rain, mud, water, and cold. Autry's new companions alleviated his sorrows somewhat, as did the physical misery—"the
very great fatigue I have suffered has in a degree stifled reflec-
tion and has been an advantage to me," he wrote to his wife
when he reached Nacogdoches:

> I have reached this point after many hardships and
> privations but thank God in most excellent health....I
> go the whole Hog in the cause of Texas. I expect to
> help them gain their independence and also to form
> their civil government, for it is worth risking many
> lives for. From what I have seen and learned from
> others there is not so fair a portion of the earth's
> surface warmed by the sun.

About twenty miles west of Nacogdoches, the piney woods
of east Texas gave way to rolling prairies dotted with clusters
of trees. Along the road, Crockett and his companions found
sustenance and shelter at regularly spaced "stands"—rough
houses that supplied supper, lodging, and breakfast, as well
as corn for the horses, for a dollar apiece. The food was simple
and unvaried: cornbread and meat, never garden vegetables,
and rarely butter or milk. But the stands provided shelter from
the elements and an opportunity to relax after a long day's
ride—and gather around a fire with a cup of coffee or something stronger and listen to Crockett, in that distinctive drawl,
spin more of his yarns.

Near the Trinity River, they left the old road and turned
south toward Washington. There, on a steep slope on the west
bank of the Brazos, the group entered a village of two crude
hotels, a few shops and taverns, and several small residences—
a place so new that there were still stumps standing in the
middle of the only street in town, which was just an opening

cut through the woods up from the ferry landing. Crockett and his men stayed at John Lott's hotel, if it could be called that—"a frame house, covered with clapboards, a wretchedly made establishment, and a blackguard, rowdy set lounging about," according to one visitor. There were not sufficient beds in the large one-room structure, so as many as thirty lodgers shared cots or slept on the floor. The dinner fare consisted of fried pork, coarse cornbread, and bad coffee. Breakfast was the same. The only saving grace was the presence of two large fireplaces, one at each end of the building.

There was another disappointment: Sam Houston was not in town. He had his hands full down near Goliad, trying to stop the Matamoros expedition. In his absence, Lott was the nascent government's local agent, and the man charged with directing recruits to the places where they were needed.

A week or so later, Lott would receive orders from acting governor James Robinson to henceforth direct volunteers to Goliad, or the port of Copano—there were enough troops already at Béxar, or so the advisory committee determined. But now, before the end of January, Béxar was the destination. Word of the Mexican army preparing to march into Texas had recently reached the settlements on the Brazos, and Colonel James Neill was in sore need of men to garrison Béxar. The one thing both deposed governor Henry Smith and his replacement appeared to agree on was the importance of maintaining the post there. As the only town on the main road from Mexico, Béxar served as a picket guard to the Anglo colonies.

That is where Lott sent Crockett and the Tennessee Mounted Volunteers—to Béxar and the old mission turned military post called the Alamo.

TEN

The Road to Béxar

Soldiers! Your comrades have been treacherously sacrificed at Anahuac, Goliad and Bexar; and you are the men chosen to chastise the assassins.

SANTA ANNA TO HIS ARMY, FEBRUARY 17, 1836

From Saltillo, the discrete units of Santa Anna's Army of Operations wound their way toward Monclova, 120 miles north, through the mountain passes on the edge of the Eastern Sierra Madres and to the eastern edge of a huge desert that continued all the way to the Rio Grande. Though most of the region El Camino Real ran through was semiarid and not extreme desert, it was an inhospitable stretch of land. Typical of the region, the weather remained cool at night but warmed once the sun was up. Here, the first cases of large-scale desertions occurred. It was the rare day that did not see missing troops; many mule drivers also disappeared, some taking their animals with them. The problem became so bad that Santa Anna ordered local *presidiales* to patrol the roads and apprehend the deserters. The lack of water and forage could be seen in the condition of the horses and mules, some of which could not continue.

On February 2, a week after leaving Saltillo, Gaona's First Infantry Brigade reached Monclova. Though many citizens of Monclova did not welcome Santa Anna and his *soldados* with open arms—quite a few of them were federalists, and had resisted El Presidente's centralist takeover, though they had stopped short of armed confrontations such as Zacateca's—the authorities had managed to stockpile a considerable amount of basic foodstuffs, most of it seized from the ranches and poverty-stricken villages in the area. (Throughout the campaign, food was hard to find for everyone except those of high enough rank to pay graft, a practice that had reached epidemic proportions.) Along with something to eat, some of the units finally received a portion of their pay. The grateful troops were able to rest a few days before the arduous journey north continued.

Two days later Santa Anna's entourage arrived. For some undisclosed reason, His Excellency was in a foul mood, and officers avoided him whenever possible. Four days later, on the morning of February 8, Gaona's brigade departed Monclova. Santa Anna, in a coach drawn by six fresh mules, his staff, and small escort accompanied the column. The remainder of the expedition was still several days behind. The day before he left, Santa Anna ordered that all troops be placed on half rations of hardtack. His simultaneous assurance to his officers that provisions would be found at the Rio Grande was of little consolation.

General Cós arrived in the city a few days later, accompanied by Captain José Juan Sánchez, his adjutant, and Colonel Nicolás Condelle's weary Morelos Battalion. Cós had lost thirty-two men, women, and children in pressing on through the rough country between Laredo and Monclova to join Santa Anna as ordered, and an irritated Sánchez was puzzled at His Excellency's haste to leave his army behind. Why assemble such a large force if he did not need it? Did he think his name alone was enough to defeat the colonists?

Sánchez would have an opportunity to find out. After eight weeks of near-constant marching through desolate stretches of northern Mexico, Cós and the four hundred men of the Morelos Battalion were officially incorporated into Tolsa's Second Infantry Brigade, and would once more trudge into the wilderness—Sánchez himself on a burro. Their comrades on the long trip from Béxar, most of them cavalry and infantry companies from several different states in northern Mexico, would be posted to other garrisons. Behind them, in a makeshift hospital in Monclova, the army left one hundred sick men, most of them laid low with dysentery and other stomach ailments. Units came together, units came apart, human wreckage was scattered across the desert—such was the dismal pattern.

ON FEBRUARY 8, the same day Santa Anna left Monclova, Ramírez y Sesma received an order from His Excellency directing him to continue to Béxar, making moderate daily marches to conserve his troops. The Vanguard Brigade had reached Guerrero, a small town five miles south of the Rio Grande, in mid-January. They had spent the next few weeks resting and reprovisioning at the presidio there, and gathering intelligence from *soldados* recently arrived from Béxar. The returning soldiers and Santa Anna's spies had told him that there were no provisions there, so Ramírez y Sesma bought what he could and impressed the rest from villages and ranches in the area. Several of the region's presidial companies were gathered at Guerrero, and the general picked up one hundred of the best armed and mounted *presidiales*—they knew the terrain well and were hardy soldiers, long accustomed to fighting Indians.

Santa Anna reached Guerrero on the afternoon of February 12. Ramírez y Sesma had just crossed the Rio Grande five miles away and was on his way to Béxar. Some of the army's mules and horses came down with *telele,* a sickness caused by drinking stagnant water. Others collapsed due to exhaustion and overwork. Almost all suffered badly from lack of forage. An epidemic of dysentery hit the troops after many of them ate the small red berries growing abundantly in the woods along the road. Without even the most basic medical care, several unfortunates died of the ailment.

And while they may have been on Mexican soil, the men were constantly reminded that the region more properly belonged to someone else. One day they marched past a camp of five hundred Lipan Apaches that lay alongside the road. The Lipans were at peace with the Mexicans, but that did not prevent them from stealing mules and horses as the army marched by. Far more dangerous were the Comanches. They could often be seen in the distance, to the rear and on the flanks of the columns, biding their time until they could fall on stragglers and deserters, killing soldiers and *soldaderas* indiscriminately. The Comanches also stole caches of food that had been placed at small ranches along El Camino Real. Improperly packed cases of hardtack soaked by rain went bad and reduced the soldiers' meager rations. Eventually the road north from Monclova was strewn with the detritus of an army in trouble—more like a defeated one in retreat than one advancing.

With the combined effects of malnutrition, disease, Indian attacks, and the elements, the Army of Operations would lose between four hundred and five hundred men on the march to Béxar, and twice as many women and children. Only the weather had so far been largely on their side, delivering cool evenings and pleasant days with only the occasional shower to alleviate the choking dust and ease the noontime heat. That changed on February 13.

The thirteenth dawned cold and wet, and by seven that evening the rain turned to sleet, then thick snow. The Cavalry Brigade promptly got lost in a huge thicket of mesquite. General Andrade ordered a halt in the woods: other units doubled back on the trail. The countermarch quickly degenerated into chaos. Several women and boys attached themselves to one young officer's party, and they all gathered together as he vainly tried to start a fire. Around other flames huddled shivering groups of officers, enlisted men, women, and children, many of them cursing in desperation and anger. Few of the troops were from northern Mexico, and many had never seen snow before. By sunrise, the snow was knee deep and covered everything in sight. Splotches of blood marked where dead horses and mules had expired trying to rip themselves away from their loads. Others had frozen to death or suffocated under the snow.

The snow continued until five o'clock on the fourteenth. Somehow the regiment, and the rest of the Cavalry Brigade, managed to pull itself together and limp on toward the north, but significant damage had been done. Though no snowfall hit Santa Anna's entourage at Guerrero on the Rio Grande, or the Vanguard Brigade, two marches north of the river, Gaona's First Infantry Brigade lost fifty oxen and a large quantity of provisions. Throughout the column, many soldiers, women, and children had died—Santa Anna would later write that four hundred men died in twenty-four hours. Morale plunged with the temperature. Desertions increased, particularly wagon drivers fed up with the grueling conditions and insufficient compensation. Inexperienced soldiers took their places. Their lack of care and a tendency to overwork the slow-moving beasts—the amateur drivers jabbed them from behind with their bayonets and swords in a fruitless attempt to make them go faster—resulted in more problems, further slowing the pace.

Santa Anna remained in Guerrero until the storm was over, firing off what had become a typical barrage of orders and communiqués to his five far-flung brigades. On February 16 he and his staff, and his fifty-man escort of lancers, crossed the Rio Grande and raced after the Vanguard Brigade.

This was, all things considered, a less arduous trek. Though the nights were cold, the simple trail that constituted El Camino Real in south Texas was in good shape; there had been little rain lately, and most of the surface was firm and dry. The towering mountains below the Rio Grande had been left behind, and the road mostly followed a long line of gentle hills. And though much of the range grass had been burned off, and the new shoots had yet to appear, they found enough mesquite grass, a delicacy to mules and horses that matured earlier in the year, for the stock to survive on. But good water was scarce. The wells and pools along the way barely supplied enough for men and livestock, and some were muddy or contaminated by dead animals. So three days later, when the command finally overtook the Vanguard Brigade at the clear Frio River (which, along with the Nueces, was one of only two rivers that ran all year long), there was much rejoicing. They found Ramírez y Sesma's men constructing a new bridge, since the rebels had torn down the old one.

Two days later, just before two o'clock on a cloudy but warm February 21—His Excellency's forty-second birthday—the combined force reached the south side of the Medina River, the official boundary between Texas and Coahuila, a small stream whose banks were lined with pecan trees. Just a few miles away and almost twenty-three years before, a young

Santa Anna had gained the first glory of his storied career as a young officer in Arredondo's army. Twenty-two miles to the east lay Béxar. Though the rest of his force was scattered almost three hundred miles behind him, Santa Anna had somehow managed to cross more than five hundred miles of inhospitable terrain in minimal time and was now poised to surprise an enemy who did not expect him for several more weeks.

While the weary *soldados* pitched camp, nursed their blistered feet, and rested, their commander and his staff deliberated. Santa Anna's spies in Béxar had kept him well posted, and the next day several more sympathetic informers came into camp. One was a priest. Another was Angel Navarro, father of Juana and Gertrudis, who rode out to meet his old friend and apprise him of the situation in town. Santa Anna had become acquainted with the family in 1813 as a young lieutenant with Arredondo's conquering army, and Navarro, unlike his brothers, had remained loyal to Mexico.

The chief reason Santa Anna had chosen Béxar as his base of operations was the loyal citizenry he expected to find. That was not the case, he now discovered. While there were townspeople faithful to the Mexican government, many of Béxar's leading families — the Veramendis, Ruizes, Seguíns, even most of the other Navarros — were aiding the rebels, and a good portion of the populace had followed suit. But Navarro revealed that the Americans would be at a fandango that night, and could be easily taken while they drank and danced.

Santa Anna's instincts warned him better than his spies of the need to hit hard and fast. The Alamo, into which the rebels would doubtless retreat, was no longer a flimsy ruin. Cós had made extensive improvements during his two months in Béxar, and the colonists had spent two more months fortifying it. The old mission was now taking on the look of a credible redoubt.

Here was a golden opportunity. Santa Anna summoned Ramírez y Sesma and ordered him to take 160 lancers of the Dolores Cavalry Regiment and ride into town to surprise the garrison before they could retreat into the Alamo. A singular lack of good pasture had left many of the Dolores cavalry with spent horses, so Santa Anna ordered the infantry officers to give up their fresher mounts. Under a slight drizzle, the cavalry began preparations to march. With any luck, the Mexican tricolor would fly over Béxar the next morning.

ON FEBRUARY 3, William Barret Travis arrived in Béxar to find a bedraggled but determined bunch of volunteers. The decision by Bowie and Colonel Neill to remain, coupled with the recent reports of Mexican troops on the Rio Grande, had infused the undersupplied garrison with a sense of purpose previously lacking. Bowie's letter to beleaguered governor Henry Smith the day before, stating their intention to stay and fight, had motivated the men more than any appeal to patriotism could.

After reporting to Neill, Travis and his twenty-one-year-old slave, Joe, established quarters in town, on Main Plaza. Travis spent several days getting to know the officers, the soldiers, and the situation. A few years previously, he had successfully sued Green Jameson on behalf of a client and won a $50 judgment. Now he found his one-time opponent transformed into a military engineer of near-visionary capability whose ambitious plans to strengthen the mission compound across the river — or Fortress Alamo, as Jameson called it, perhaps in jest — were curbed only by lack of manpower. (Neill needed soldiers for, among other things, scouting the countryside; when Captain John Forsyth and Travis's undermanned legion rode into town two days after Travis did, Neill immediately sent them out.) Even so, Jameson had done his best with what was at hand. Travis would undoubtedly have been impressed.

Jameson's top priority was the battered north wall. During the seven-week siege a few months earlier, Neill's artillery had done significant damage, even though he had not commanded the large cannon necessary for effective siege warfare. When he could muster the men, Jameson kept his crews busy there and elsewhere, fortifying walls, digging outside trenches, and using the dug-up earth to erect banquettes. Some of his other plans—strengthening cannon emplacements, building redoubts, digging deep moats and filling them with water, building sturdy drawbridges over them, and generally expanding on Cós's works—were attended to less assiduously.

The old mission would never become a superior example of a proper fort able to indefinitely withstand a determined and well-equipped army. The compound had not been planned or built with that in mind; it had been built only to protect its inhabitants from Indian attacks, not field artillery. True, the walls connecting the several flat-roofed stone houses erected along the rectangular perimeter were six to nine feet high and almost three feet thick—four feet in the old stone church, the strongest building—but most of the walls were composed of adobe, not stone, and would not withstand heavy bombardment. The north wall had originally been made of limestone, and needed no assistance from artillery to crumble.

The Alamo lacked other features requisite to a proper fortress. There were no parapets atop the walls or banquettes behind them from which defenders could fire their guns without exposure, and there were few defensive positions providing cover for riflemen and artillerists, such as embrasures and portholes. In many sections of the perimeter, defenders attempting to fire on their attackers would be visible targets. There were no outworks, such as moats, mines, and pitfalls, and no protected posts, such as bastions (projections from walls) and bartizans (turrets jutting out from a parapet) — these last two enabling defenders to utilize enfilade, or flanking fire, along the length of an attacking column.

And the space on the north side of the church, behind the two-story barracks, presented special problems of defense. Once used as the monks' cloister, it was now employed as a horse corral; a low wall separated it from a similarly sized cattle pen on its north side that had once been a courtyard. Stone walls surrounded each area, but the cattle pen's was only four and a half feet high and appeared especially vulnerable, though a large field of mud and standing water just to the east might temporarily inhibit an infantry attack.

The previous fall, while besieged by Austin's army, General Cós's men had fortified the compound in certain key places. The main gate was now protected by a strong, well-designed lunette, an outer enclosure surrounded by an outside ditch and a six-foot earthen embankment crowned by a palisade of upright wooden posts. Embrasures had been notched on the east and south sides, through which two smaller cannon could fire. If manned by experienced gun crews, the lunette could be a formidable defensive position. In the church, the stone arches of the unfinished roof had been torn down, and the resulting rubble now constituted a strong base upon which a wooden ramp had been erected, running almost from the front door up to a gun platform above the altar. With great difficulty and without proper tools, Jameson's men had dragged three of the cannon up to the top of the church and positioned them to cover the east and south. The Mexicans had also constructed an elevated wooden tower on the southwest corner of the church, from which a commanding view of all points could be had. And from niches on either side of the doors, the statues of four saints—Francis, Dominic, Ferdinand, and Anthony—gazed down at the activities with apparent indifference.

Along the weakest area of the perimeter—the 115-foot open space between the southwest corner of the church and the two-story building that housed the jail and the kitchen on either side of the porte cochere at the main entrance—Cós's men had constructed a strong palisade of eight-foot-high cedar timbers six feet apart, with an unfinished trench on the outside and a two-foot-high firing step on the inside. About halfway along the palisade was a wooden platform on which Jameson placed a small cannon positioned to fire through an embrasure in the wooden barrier. Just beyond the outer trench, Jameson had fortified the position with an *abatis,* a barrier of felled trees, their heavy branches sharpened and pointed toward the enemy. Such a fortification had proven effective against attacking infantry in several battles of the Revolutionary War and, more recently, during the War of 1812, when a Canadian force in the Battle of Châteauguay had successfully defended its position against an American army almost twice its size.

The entire compound covered almost three acres; a sufficient defensive force would likely number close to a thousand men—or at least five hundred. The rebels were nowhere near that number, nor were they likely to be. The small groups that made their way into Béxar in late January and early February—Philip Dimitt and a few men, William Patton leading eleven more, then Travis with his two dozen—cheered the garrison somewhat but satisfied no one. Near-constant rumors and reports of a large Mexican army on its way into Texas continued to reach Béxar. One of Bowie's Tejano spies had just returned on February 2, fresh from a scout down to the Rio Grande, and brought news of two thousand troops at Guerrero, the presidio across the river, and five thousand more on the march there. One hundred and fifty men, no matter how sure of shot and resolute in conviction, could not hold out long against an army that large and well equipped—especially considering the meager provisions and powder available to them. Yet now they had official orders to do just that. On the recommendation of his advisory committee, acting governor James Robinson wrote Neill on February 2, directing him to remain in Béxar and strengthen the reinforcements.

In the days after his arrival, Travis renewed acquaintances with Bowie, Neill, and others. Bowie he knew well enough— he had handled some minor legal work for him, and had written him to discuss the revolution. But the two were not close friends, due as much to the difference in their interests, ages (Bowie was fourteen years older), temperaments, and overall unfamiliarity with each other as to anything else. Though Travis did not lack for personal bravery, it was of a different sort from Bowie's imposing physicality. While he was far from an uncouth backwoodsman, Bowie owned a reputation as a knife fighter second to none. Travis's nature was more refined, as evidenced in his choice in friends and literature. Both, however, had come to share a single vision of an independent Texas.

FOUR OR FIVE DAYS LATER, another party of volunteers rode into town. It was a small group, but the presence of one of them—a tall fellow in a coonskin cap—was cause for celebration. Jim Bowie might be a living legend along the southwest frontier, but David Crockett's renown was national—indeed, only a handful of Americans were more famous. He arrived with a few of the Tennessee Mounted Volunteers; the rest, led by Captain William Harrison and including Micajah Autry and Daniel Cloud, would join the garrison several days later. Crockett was greeted warmly when he reached Main Plaza. Someone called for a speech, and the crowd took up the cry. Crockett mounted a wooden crate to enthusiastic cheers. He spoke of the new country of Texas, and patriotism, and told several of his tried and tested anecdotes to frequent applause. He alluded to his career as a congressman, and delivered his "go to hell" story, now a staple of all his public utterances. He concluded with words to this effect, wisely chosen for his audience and remembered by John Sutherland:

> And fellow citizens, I am among you. I have come to your country, though not, I hope, through any selfish motive whatever. I have come to aid you all I can in your noble cause. I shall identify myself with your interests, and all the honor that I desire is defending as a high private, in common with my fellow citizens, the liberties of our common country.

"This made many a man who had not known him before Colonel Crockett's friend," remembered Dr. Sutherland.

Crockett lodged at the large stone house of Ramón Músquiz, on Main Plaza, where the doctor and the Dickinsons were staying. His arrival brought some material benefits as well as a boost to morale: Susanna was able to make some money doing the laundry of Crockett and other volunteers.

A few days later, Neill received news by express of an illness in his family at Bastrop. His two boys, Samuel and George, were serving in one of Robert Williamson's ranging companies, but his wife, Harriett, and daughter, Mary, were alone at their homestead. He decided to take a furlough to attend to the problem, promising to be back in twenty days at most. At least one man suspected another motive for Neill's departure: Dr. Sutherland believed he was riding to San Felipe to obtain part of the rumored $5,000 loan to Texas for the Alamo garrison's use. True or not, Neill left knowing the post was in much better shape than when he had inherited it — reinforcements had begun to arrive, Jameson and his crews had made the Alamo more defensible, and strong leaders such as Bowie, Crockett, and Travis were on hand.

Before he left, Neill signed discharges for more than a dozen volunteers who had decided to leave in the next few days — for most of them, their two months was up, and they had received no pay, clothes, or provisions. He also transferred command of the regulars to Travis, the ranking officer at Béxar. Travis also inherited John Baugh as adjutant. The thirty-three-year-old Virginian had been elected lieutenant by his fellow New Orleans Greys, and after the fierce fight for Béxar, Neill had chosen him as his executive officer and promoted him to captain. He was a reliable and loyal man, and not a Bowie acolyte — possibly one of the reasons a problem of command arose.

Most of the men of the garrison, all save Travis's mounted company and a few others, were true volunteers who had remained in Béxar after everyone else had left. They had acknowledged Neill as commander because he had been there from the first, and had proven himself worthy of their respect after four long months of battle and hardship. Bowie, their inspirational leader, also acknowledged his command. They had no such basis of trust with Travis, however. True, he had led a spy company during the siege of Béxar, but he had left after only a month or so. They had not left, and neither had Neill, as their ragged clothing would attest. Besides, Travis was only twenty-six, and not an easy man to warm to. And he was a newly commissioned cavalry officer, with no experience commanding a fort and a formidable array of artillery.

The final sticking point was one the volunteers had been touchy about since the beginning. Travis was a regular army officer, and they had repeatedly made it clear that they would only obey a commander they had elected themselves. As a result, only one of the volunteer companies agreed to serve under him. Some of the men went to Crockett to see if he was interested in taking command. Crockett refused — he was there, he explained, to assist Travis. "Me and my Tennessee boys have come to help Texas as privates," he reiterated.

Travis, appreciative of his "truly awkward and delicate" position, wrote Smith the day after Neill's departure requesting orders. But a reply, if it ever came, would be a week away at best, so on the same day, he issued an order for an election. Only the volunteers voted, naming Bowie as their choice.

Like most men of the time, Jim Bowie imbibed occasionally, but he had never been known as a heavy drinker, as had his friend Sam Houston. Now, though, Bowie responded to his election in an uncharacteristic and spectacularly unfortunate manner. Perhaps the grief in his heart since his wife's death had reached a spillover point as a result of his quartering at the Veramendi house, where they had lived as newlyweds and where the reminders of her presence were constant. The cumulative aches of decades of serious injuries, illness, and wear to his body, or even the pressure of gaining authority, may have led to the snap. In any case, he proceeded to go on a massive drinking bout, accompanied by unseemly behavior.

During his embarrassing two-day rampage, Bowie remained roaring drunk. Out of control, though in command, he told his men to stop the carts of families on their way out of town and prevent them from leaving. He ordered the release from prison of a Mexican convicted of theft by a twelve-man jury — of which he had been a member. He also freed one of Travis's cavalrymen found guilty of mutiny, to loud cheers from the volunteers. For good measure, he set at liberty all prisoners, Tejano or Anglo, who had been placed on work details. When Juan Seguín, acting as the town judge, threw one convict back into jail, a furious Bowie confronted him and demanded the prisoner's release. When Seguín refused, Bowie sent to the Alamo for troops, many of whom were also drunk. The soldiers paraded around Main Plaza under arms—those who had them; some had sold their guns for alcohol—"in a tumultuous and disorderly manner," as Adjutant Baugh put it in a letter to Governor Smith two days later, which expressed his support for Travis. "Things...have become intolerable," he wrote. Travis threatened to move his few loyal troops out of town.

Just when the garrison needed strong leadership—spies rode into town that day with another report of a thousand Mexican soldiers on the Rio Grande poised to invade Texas—a serious schism had erupted. Travis wrote Smith again begging to be relieved of command: "If I did not feel my honor & that of my country compromised I would leave here instantly for some other point with the troops under my command as I am unwilling to be responsible for the drunken irregularities of any man....I do not solicit the command of this Post," he continued. "I will do it if it be your orders for a time until an artillery officer can be sent here." Fannin's commission was in the artillery, and he was only ninety-five miles away, with more than four hundred men. The solution seemed obvious.

Travis went on to request more troops—regulars, to be specific—and he revealed that, despite his disagreements with Bowie, Béxar and its makeshift mission fortress had got into his bones also. "It is more important to occupy this Post than I imagined when I last saw you," he told Smith. "It is the key of Texas from the Interior without a footing here the enemy can do nothing against us in the Colonies."

But before Travis could complete the move of his troops away from town, Bowie sobered up and made amends for his behavior, and the two came to an agreement. The express rider carrying the previous day's letters from Travis and Baugh was detained until he could be given another dispatch, again requesting money and reinforcements, and ending with this pronouncement:

> By an understanding of today, Col. J. Bowie has the command of the volunteers of the Garrison, & Col. W.B. Travis, of the Regulars & Volunteer cavalry.
>
> All general orders, and correspondence, will hence forth be signed by both, until Col. Neill's return —

The letter was in Travis's hand but signed by both men — Travis as commandant of cavalry and Bowie as commandant of volunteers. The crisis was averted, at least for now.

Save for one scrawled signature a week hence, Bowie would not sign any more official correspondence. Some sickness had invaded his body — respiratory, it seems, from the descriptions given later by those who knew him and cared for him — and would soon render him bedridden. Sutherland would later describe the illness as "being of a peculiar nature... not to be cured by an ordinary course of treatment." Other witnesses would describe it as typhoid fever, typhoid pneumonia, or consumption — tuberculosis. Whatever the diagnosis, or lack of one, the final result was an incapacitated Jim Bowie, confined to his bed in the Veramendi house, suffering from an illness that might prove fatal. His sister-in-law Juana Alsbury began to minister to him.

So Travis gradually took over the duties of running the garrison. This time there was little resistance from the volunteers, so vociferous just a few days ago, and there was no election. Bowie, the man they had elected, had agreed to a cocommandancy, and now he was increasingly incapacitated and unable to rise to the demands of the position. Willingly or not, he ceded authority to the young lieutenant colonel.

One of Bowie's last acts as commander involved the near-constant stream of messengers to the east. One morning in mid-February, Crockett and Robert Evans, the tall, black-haired ordnance chief, along with a couple of young volunteers, made their way to the high ground east of town, where many of the horses grazed. They met up with two other soldiers, who asked Crockett if he thought there was any chance of a fight—if not, they were going home. Crockett pointed out that men were leaving as fast as others came in, and remarked that "if he were in command, he would have given them shit long ago," remembered a recent arrival to Béxar named David Harman. They needed someone to "carry orders back to hurry up the drafted men and all soldiers at home," said Crockett. Harman, a stripling of only a hundred pounds, volunteered for the mission. Back in town, Crockett brought him to Bowie, who remarked that Harman looked awfully young to be a soldier. Harman insisted he could handle the job, and Bowie gave him dispatches for the recruiting officers at San Felipe and other towns and sent him on his way.

Under Travis, the work details continued—most important, the shoring up of the adobe walls of the mission, particularly the badly damaged north wall. Jameson had devised a cribbing of log braces along the entire extent, and instructed his men to pack earth between the wall and the wooden supports and bank earth against the exterior. It was nowhere near finished, but a good start had been made on the northeast end. The men dismantled Antonio Saez's blacksmith shop, in La Villita, near the Alamo's south gate, and carried the materials into the compound; old Saez had been repairing their guns since the battle of Béxar, and lately he had been busy preparing *langrage* and canister shot for the artillery. And sixty-five head of cattle were bought from a local rancher at twelve dollars a head. Travis, lacking funds, could only give the man a signed claim for his $780.

Few of the men had any money, but occasionally they scraped together a few coins. Anna Esparza, the wife of Gregorio Esparza, one of Juan Seguín's men, and her oldest son, eleven-year-old Enrique, carried earthen jars full of food over the San Antonio River footbridge to the Alamo. While his mother sold the Americans tamales and beans, they taught the boy a ditty, and laughed and gave him centavos when he sang:

> We are the boys so handy,
> We'll teach Santa Anna to fear
> Our Yankee Doodle Dandy.

Every morning Travis walked from his quarters on Main Plaza to the footbridge across the shallow river and into the Alamo. The last house before the river belonged to Ambrosio Rodríguez, who was friendly to the rebel cause and another of Juan Seguín's horsemen. Travis often stopped to talk to Rodríguez and his wife. Years later the couple's son would recall the tall American. "Colonel Travis was a fine man of more than ordinary height," he remembered. "He was a very popular man and was well liked by everyone." When the elder Rodríguez heard a report that Santa Anna was on the way to Béxar with a well-organized army of seven thousand men, he told Travis and advised him to abandon the town and retreat into the interior of Texas. Travis refused to believe it. Cós had been defeated just two months before. There was no way Santa Anna could have organized such a large force in so short a time.

The scarcity of horses complicated the scouting duties, but

Travis kept as many spies out in the field as he could. Most of them were Juan Seguín's Tejanos, who continued to bring in reports of a large Mexican army on the Rio Grande. Some of Seguín's men requested permission to help move their families out of town, and on February 21 a dozen or so received discharges—a gracious move, but one that further compromised scouting. The reliable Erastus "Deaf" Smith, recently recovered from an injury sustained in the December assault on Béxar, had ranged to a point a few miles from the river, where he spotted Santa Anna's Vanguard Brigade preparing to march north. But Smith rode out of town on February 15 to assist his family, who had departed for the East months earlier, and few non-Tejanos were familiar enough with the area to scout very far from town.

On his way, Deaf Smith agreed to stop in San Felipe first to see Henry Smith and apprise him of the situation in Béxar. But Governor Smith, who had no control over the other two Texian forces—Fannin's at Goliad, and what remained of the Matamoros expedition, commanded by Grant and Johnson— offered no resources, given his almost nonexistent authority. And acting governor Robinson was nearly as hamstrung: the General Council, which had not mustered a quorum since January 18, had substituted an advisory committee of several men that made recommendations to the governor. That board dwindled to two men by mid-February. Some of their suggestions were implemented, some not, but by the end of January, the committee had come to the conclusion that there were enough men at Béxar (likely misunderstanding Neill's request of January 14 that a hundred men be transferred to his command from Goliad or somewhere else), and told Robinson so. The word went out to recruiting agents throughout Texas to stop directing volunteers there.

* * *

AT BÉXAR, small groups of men came and went. Eleven volunteers tired of garrison duty left to scout the area east around Cibolo Creek for their bounty land. A few days later, the garrison's two elected delegates to the convention, Jesse Badgett and Samuel Maverick, prepared to depart for Washington. Badgett left first, but Maverick, who had moved to Béxar a few months before the siege, remained in town to buy another tract of land—his fifth since the rebels had taken command of the city—and did not leave until February 19. John Sutherland continued to assist Dr. Amos Pollard with the two dozen or so sick and wounded men as Pollard moved all of them into the second story of the old *convento* building, where the hospital was located—and found to his surprise that most of the necessary medical instruments were already there.

Among the arrivals were three brothers named Taylor, all in their early twenties, who showed up ready to fight; they had been picking cotton on a farm more than two hundred miles east near the coast when the cry for volunteers reached them. They finished the job, then marched to Béxar. Captain Albert Martin returned from Gonzales, where he operated a store. Martin had been one of the first to join the Army of the People. A native of Providence, Rhode Island, he was a graduate of a respected military academy that emphasized a rigorous physical regimen. He had followed his father and brothers to Texas in early 1835. There Martin lost no time in aligning himself with the independence movement party, and organized a local militia, the Gonzales Ranging Company of Mounted Volunteers. During the siege of Béxar he had somehow cut his foot with an ax and had been forced to return home to heal. Now he was back.

Travis continued to dispatch couriers almost daily with requests for men, ammunition, and provisions. On February 17 he sent James Bonham to Goliad, beseeching James Fannin once more to move all or most of his command to Béxar. Bonham also carried Jameson's latest report on the Alamo's condition, which he would deliver to Governor Smith in San Felipe.

Colonel Fannin, though, would be of no help. Soon after reaching Goliad with his four hundred men on February 12, he began to experience a crisis of confidence. The old Spanish presidio there sat on a rocky hill on the south side of the San Antonio River, overlooking a strategic ford. Its grounds encompassed about three acres, and its ten-foot-high wall was much better fortified than the Alamo; it had been designed as a stronghold from the beginning. But while his men worked to strengthen the old fort, Fannin began to dither. On February 15, he finally received official word from the General Council to abandon the Matamoros plan and "occupy such points as you may in your opinion deem most advantageous," along with a few additional vaguely worded suggestions. "Fortify & defend Goliad and Bexar if any opportunity fairly offers," he was advised. "Now obey any orders you may deem Expedient." Robinson and the council gave him free rein to command—indeed, the acting governor decreed that "all former orders given by my predecessor, Gen. Houston, or myself, are so far countermanded," and even went further: he co-opted Houston's authority by signing the letter "Acting Governor and Commander in Chief of the Army of Texas." Just a few days before, Fannin had been chomping at the bit to assume such power. Now he had second thoughts. He immediately dashed off a reply to Robinson. "I do not desire any command, and particularly that of chief," he wrote.

> I feel, I *know*, if you and the council do not, that I am incompetent. Fortune, and brave soldiers, may favour me and save the State, and establish for me a reputation

far beyond my deserts. I do not covet, and I do earnestly ask of you, and any real friend, to relieve me, and make a selection of one possessing all the requisites of a Commander.... I would feel truly happy to be in the bosom of my family, and rid of the burden imposed on me.

Two days later Fannin requested approval to make his headquarters at Béxar per Travis's suggestion. But Robinson and his two-man advisory board did not approve his plan, and Fannin had no choice but to remain at Goliad and redouble his fortification efforts.

While Fannin's self-confidence—and the confidence of his men in their commander—dwindled, Travis continued to send riders out of Béxar in search of aid. On February 19, he dispatched Captain James L. Vaughan, a veteran of the battle of Béxar, on a risky recruiting trip to the Rio Grande area. Vaughan's mission was to visit several towns south of the river from Guerrero all the way down to Matamoros, which he hoped would be in rebel hands by then. James Grant and others had spread stories of unrest in the region, and Vaughan was directed to sign up as many recruits as possible and send them to Béxar. Travis also sent two Gonzales men, Byrd Lockhart and Andrew Sowell, to their hometown for provisions.

Late in the evening of Saturday, February 20, a young Tejano named Blas Herrera rode into town from the southwest and reported to his cousin, Juan Seguín. Herrera had left the Rio Grande two and a half days before, riding steadily through 145 miles of semidesert. Seguín went straight to Travis when he heard Herrera's report. Assured of the young man's reliability, Travis immediately called a council of war in his room. Before the garrison's officer corps and a few others, Herrera told them what he had seen: a large army, including many mounted men, crossing the Rio Grande. As far as he could tell, the cavalry planned to force-march to Béxar to take the garrison by surprise.

Herrera's report led to much discussion. Some thought it the most authentic intelligence yet received. And it was clear that Seguín believed him. But the opinion of the men was divided. Most labeled this just another wild rumor, like those that reached Béxar almost every day—just one more Tejano false alarm. The meeting broke up before a clear decision could be made. But Travis sent out riders to gather up men on furlough in the area, such as David Cummings, a young surveyor who, with several others, was encamped on Cibolo Creek, staking out a land claim. And though some of the Americans were not convinced by Herrera's story, his relatives were; the Seguín family left town the next morning. Other *bexareños* followed.

The work continued through a wet and overcast Monday, February 22—a day special to the American-born rebels. The date marked the birth of George Washington, the patron saint of the republic to the north, who was just as popular and inspiring to these "sons of '76" in view of their current enterprise. Despite intermittent thunderstorms throughout the day, the men would be attending a fandango in town that evening, and planned to celebrate the occasion properly—and so did the three dozen or so volunteers originally from the British Isles, who had no intention of letting history get in the way of a good time. If the reports of Santa Anna's army were true, it might be the last chance they would have to let loose for a long time.

ELEVEN

Circunvalado

*Béxar was held by the enemy, and it was necessary to open
the door to our future operations by taking it.*

GENERAL SANTA ANNA

The men of the garrison celebrated George Washington's
birthday until very late, eating, drinking, smoking the
locals' cornshuck cigarettes, dancing, and romancing the black-
eyed beauties of Béxar. Most of the artillerymen bunking in the
Alamo eventually made their way down Potrero Street and
across the narrow footbridge and up into the old mission. The
rest of the rebels returned to their quarters in town or found
some shelter to sleep off the effects of tequila, mescal, and corn
liquor. Some of them had barely flopped into their blankets at
dawn on Tuesday when they were awakened by a frenzy of noise
and activity unusual for that early hour. The townspeople were
"in quite an unusual stir," remembered John Sutherland:

> The citizens of every class were hurrying to and fro
> through the streets, with obvious signs of excitement.

Houses were being emptied, and other contents put into carts, and hauled off. Such of the poorer class, who had no better mode of conveyance, were shouldering their effects, and leaving on foot.

When several *bexareños* were detained for questioning, they claimed to be going out to the country to prepare their fields for the summer's crop. Travis issued orders that no further citizens be allowed to leave, hoping to discourage the steady exodus with threats of more drastic measures, to no effect.

At last, near noon, came an explanation for the commotion. A friendly Mexican secretly informed Travis that on the previous night, while the fandango was in full swing, the Mexican cavalry had reached a point just a few hours' ride west of town.

Despite this seeming corroboration of the story told by Blas Herrera just a few days before, Travis was still skeptical. They had been hearing similar stories for weeks. As a precaution he borrowed a mount from Sutherland, who had two with him, and sent a man to drive the main horse herd, grazing a few miles east of town on the Salado River, back to town. He also posted a sentinel in the bell tower of the San Fernando church, the highest spot in town. Travis and Sutherland clambered up there with the soldier, but seeing nothing suspicious, climbed back down. Travis ordered the man to ring the bell at any sign of enemy activity.

Thirty minutes later the church bell rang out, and the lookout shouted, "The enemy is in view!" Sutherland ran across the plaza from his friend Nat Lewis's store to where a crowd was gathering next to the church. Several men scrambled up the scaffold and looked to the west. They saw nothing, and dismissed it as a false alarm. The sentinel insisted he had seen soldiers. "They were hid by the mesquite bushes," he said.

Sutherland proposed to ride west to the Alazán Hills, about

a mile and a half away, if someone who knew the country would accompany him. Garrison storekeeper John W. Smith, "El Colorado," volunteered. He was 6 feet 1 inch and a former county sheriff in Missouri—a good man to have by your side. And he knew the area well, having lived in Béxar for a decade. Sutherland told Travis that if they returned at any gait but a walk, it would be a sure sign that they had seen the enemy.

They splashed across the fifteen-feet-wide San Pedro Creek and trotted past barren cornfields and the Campo Santo burial ground and out of town along muddy Calle Real, the street that became El Camino Real.

BY LATE AFTERNOON of the twenty-second, the weather had again conspired against Santa Anna's Army of Operations. A wave of heavy rain hit the area and transformed the gentle Medina River into a raging torrent. Part of the battalion had already crossed the water, but the ammunition train was left on the opposite bank. At five p.m., despite His Excellency's fury at the decision, Ramírez y Sesma gave the order to stand down. The downpour continued until midnight, when it finally eased up. Ramírez y Sesma led his 160 lancers out of camp soon after.

The rest of the brigade marched out early the next morning, with Santa Anna in the vanguard. They reached a trickle of water called Alazán Creek just after noon. Beyond the stream rose low hills covered with chaparral and mesquite trees. A mile and a half further lay the center of town.

To the surprise of everyone, they found Ramírez y Sesma and his lancers waiting. He had reached the creek at seven a.m., but received conflicting reports from sympathetic *bexareños* and a captured spy. Some gave him directions on where to fall upon the rebels, most of whom had remained in town. But the spy told him the Texians knew of his presence and were planning an attack at that very moment. Ramírez y Sesma, uncharacteristically paralyzed, decided to remain in place until the rest of the brigade arrived.

Santa Anna knew that half the rebels were living in the old mission compound on the east side of town, but that many others were staying in the barracks on Military Plaza and in houses in the area. If he moved fast, there was still a chance he could seize some of them. His Excellency issued orders to march. He dispatched General Ventura Mora to lead his Dolores Cavalry Regiment and some infantrymen and swing down below Béxar to Mission Concepción, the strongest in the chain, to make sure no Texians were there — it was better fortified than the Alamo, and the rebels might have moved down there. To Colonel José Vicente Miñón, he awarded the honor of leading a group of sixty *cazadores* from the Matamoros Battalion into town ahead of the brigade, to take the church. Tall and lean, the Spanish-born Miñón, a twenty-year veteran of the army, was a good choice: as a young second lieutenant during the revolution against Spain, he had led thirty men against four hundred at Querétaro and had taken the town after an all-day battle. His exploits made him a national hero. He had also distinguished himself at Zacatecas the previous May.

While his *soldados* checked their muskets and rifles and prepared for battle, El Presidente donned his finest uniform, belted on his fanciest sword, grasped his gold-plated saddle, and swung onto his horse. It was time to lead his army.

SUTHERLAND AND SMITH GUIDED THEIR horses up the low hill, eventually reaching the crest and peering down on Alazán Creek. Less than 150 yards below them were more than a thousand Mexican soldiers. The sun flashed off the brass buckles of their uniforms and arms. Hundreds of mounted men gripped the long, sturdy lances that were so effective in open-field combat.

The two men wheeled and galloped back down the slope. Rain had fallen the night before, and the horses began to slip on the trail. Sutherland's was smoothly shod, and before they had gone fifty yards tumbled to the ground, throwing its rider ahead and then rolling across his knees. Smith reined in and jumped down. Fortunately Sutherland was not a large man, and Smith managed to pull him out from under his horse. They remounted and loped into town.

Their pace sent the desired message. The church bell was clanging and rebels and townspeople alike were hurrying through the streets when they galloped through Military Plaza and past the church into Main Plaza, where they ran into David Crockett on horseback, heading their way to reconnoiter himself. He told them that Travis was moving his headquarters and the entire garrison to the Alamo. Smith left for his house. Crockett and Sutherland rode over to the mission and made their way to Travis's new quarters in the Trevino family house, along the west wall. As Sutherland dismounted, his right knee gave way and he fell to the ground. His left arm and neck were also injured. Crockett helped him inside, where they found Travis dashing off a brief message to Andrew Ponton, the *alcalde* of Gonzales. He wasted not a word.

COMMANDANCY OF BÉXAR, 3 o'clock P.M. The enemy in large force are in sight. We want men and provisions. Send them to us. We have 150 men and are determined to defend the Alamo to the last. Give us assistance.

P.S. Send an express to San Felipe with news night and day.

Travis needed an express rider, and quick. Sutherland's injuries clearly rendered him unfit for garrison duty. Travis asked him if he was capable of riding to Gonzales with the message and rallying the settlers there to come to his aid. The doctor said he was, and left at once. A few minutes later he ran into Smith, also on his way to Gonzales; his family and pregnant wife were already there, en route to New Orleans. By that time the Mexican cavalry had reached Main Plaza, so the two headed south on the Goliad road until they were out of sight, then struck east for Gonzales.

There was not much time left. Travis dispatched another express rider, cavalryman John B. Johnson, to Goliad with a similar request for aid. He had sent James Bonham there a week earlier, and for the same purpose. Now their plight was much more serious. They would hold out, he wrote Fannin, "until we can get assistance from you, which we expect you to forward immediately. In this extremity, we hope you will send us all the men you can spare promptly. We have one hundred and forty six men, who are determined *never to retreat*." Fannin had previously ignored several requests for aid, so now Travis added a jab to his honor that could not be overlooked: "We deem it unnecessary to repeat to a brave officer, who knows his duty, that we call on him for assistance." There were more than four hundred men at the presidio in Goliad. If Fannin responded quickly and sent even half of them, the Alamo garrison's chances would be improved greatly.

Johnson jumped on a large bay, rode out of the lunette and through the Plaza de Valero, then turned southeast onto the road to Goliad.

Meanwhile Crockett, at Travis's side, was assessing the situation. He was not the official commander of the Tennessee Mounted Volunteers—that honor belonged to Captain William B. Harrison, who had arrived, bringing several more men, a few days after Crockett—but since he had fallen in with them he had occasionally assumed some leadership duties, and this was no time to stand on ceremony. He asked Travis to assign him and his "twelve Tennessee boys" a position to defend. Travis gave the ex-congressman the 115-foot wooden palisade between the church and the low barracks, the most vulnerable part of the perimeter. Crockett's renowned marksmanship could make a difference there.

MIÑÓN LED HIS LINE OF skirmishers over the Alazán Hills, past the Campo Santo cemetery, and into the western edge of Béxar. Crude *jacales* gave way to larger stone and adobe structures as they neared the center of town. The few remaining residents stayed hidden behind closed doors. The *cazadores* waded the shallow San Pedro Creek. The sprawling Plaza de Armas, the Military Plaza, lay less than two hundred feet ahead. They gripped their Baker rifles and Brown Bess muskets tighter.

But no American rebels were in sight, and the only occupants of the barracks were the dozen or so Mexican *soldados*—most of them from the battered Morelos Battalion—too seriously injured in the battle for Béxar in December to leave with General Cós, and the doctor and two interns who had remained behind to tend them in the hospital. The rebel flag had been taken down from the flagpole in the center of the plaza. Miñón ordered his veterans to secure the area and wait for His Excellency to arrive.

AS THE MEXICAN TROOPS ENTERED the west side of town a frenzy of activity engulfed the east. Somehow Bowie found the strength to lead a detachment of his men in breaking into several deserted *jacales* near the Alamo's south gate in a last-minute search for food. They found eighty or ninety bushels of corn, which they carried into the fort. Travis scribbled a receipt for thirty beeves to a local man and ordered them driven into the cattle pen on the eastern side of the compound. The meager horse herd arrived soon after and was guided into the corral adjacent to it.

Half the garrison—artillerymen, primarily—was already quartered in the Alamo. The remainder, most of whom had been bunking in the presidial barracks on Military Plaza, quickly gathered their few possessions and trooped down Potrero Street and across the footbridge on the San Antonio River. As they trudged down the street toward the river they waved to friends among the *bexareños* standing in doorways watching them. "Poor fellows," some of the women cried. "You will all be killed; what shall we do?" At his shop on Main Plaza, bald-headed Nat Lewis, a one-time whaling man from near Nantucket, jammed as many of the most valuable goods he owned into saddlebags and joined the line of people crossing the river.

A few of the rebels were still boys in their teens. Carlos Espalier, the mulatto boy informally adopted by James Bowie and his wife, was now seventeen years old. He had been born out of wedlock to a Louisiana widow and shunted off to live with his aunt in Béxar as a child. Bowie, a friend of the family, and his wife, Ursula, had taken the boy in years ago. At the age of thirteen he accompanied Bowie on the legendary San Saba expedition in 1831, when the Bowie brothers and their comrades held off repeated attacks by more than a hundred Indians. Now he marched into the Alamo to fight alongside the man he called Uncle.

At the Alamo, there was a great deal of activity but little

panic. As the men evacuating Béxar neared the south entrance they could see an artillery captain named William Ward at one of the lunette's cannon. The frequently inebriated Irishman now stood quietly at his post with his battery mates, sober and calm. Inside the compound, everyone was busy. Other gunners were readying the rest of the pieces. A few defenders were storing the bushels of corn in the rooms of the granary, on the north end of the long barracks. Several of the Tejanos were herding the cattle into the pen on the east side. Some of the volunteers who had sold their guns for drinking money — still hungover, no doubt — were scrambling to procure muskets or rifles at the small arms arsenal at the south end of the long barracks, and swearing up a blue streak doing it. Nat Lewis would never forget the vivid profanity he heard that day. He only stayed a short while, but he noticed that not one member of the garrison deserted. He had no horse, so he headed east toward Gonzales on the San Felipe road with his heavy saddlebags over his shoulders.

When the news of the Mexican army's approach reached Captain Almeron Dickinson he galloped up to the Músquiz residence on Main Plaza and yelled for his wife. Susanna appeared with her daughter in her arms. "The Mexicans are upon us," he told her. "Give me the babe, and jump up behind me." She passed Angelina up to him and climbed up behind the saddle, then took her child. Mexican soldiers were across the plaza on Potrero Street, so they made their way to a ford on the south side of town. They splashed across the shallow crossing, then followed the river bend up past the deserted *jacales* of La Villita and into the fort, where Dickinson gave Susanna an embrace and a kiss and left to join his company.

Horace Alsbury had left recently on a journey east to the settlements, to find a wagon to remove his family and their belongings from town. He had not returned, so Juana Alsbury,

Bowie's sister-in-law, also moved into the Alamo, with her eleven-month-old child, Alejo, and her younger sister. Alsbury had placed his new wife under the care of Bowie; now Bowie was under hers.

A dozen or so other Tejano women and children made their way into the Alamo as well, among them Juana Losoya Melton, the new wife of Lieutenant Eliel Melton, a Nacogdoches merchant who served as the garrison's quartermaster. Her mother, Concepción Losoya, was there; so was her brother, defender Toribio Losoya, with his wife and three children. Toribio had been born and raised in one of the Alamo houses, and had still lived in it as a private in the Alamo presidial company; he had left his birthplace only when he had joined the rebels. A few black slaves and servants, two of them Bowie's, entered also. Up on the parapets, men jeered at some of the fleeing merchants as they made their way across the river and out of town, carrying on wagons and their backs as much of their merchandise as they could.

John Smith had left Sutherland in Crockett's care to run by his own place. Then he raced to his friend Gregorio Esparza's house on North Flores Street, north of the plazas, to warn him. Esparza had fought in the battle of Béxar, and Smith was godfather to Esparza's youngest son, Francisco. The family had been preparing to leave for San Felipe after a friend offered the use of his wagon and team. Now it was too late for that.

"Well, I'm going to the fort," Esparza told his wife, Anna.

"Well, if you go, I'm going along, and the whole family," she said. There were four children, including Enrique, the boy who had learned the song from the *norteamericanos*.

The family carried everything they could and made their way down Potrero Street. As they crossed the footbridge they could hear the drums of the Mexican army beating on Military Plaza.

By early evening, when the last courier had been dispatched and all but a few of the rebels were inside the mission, the defenders watched grimly as, five hundred yards across the river, a blood-red banner was hoisted atop the bell tower of the Church of San Fernando. Everyone knew its meaning: *degüello*—no quarter. No mercy would be extended. When the flag was brought to Travis's attention, he ordered a blast from the eighteen-pounder, to the cheers of the gunners at their posts. It was a statement of intent, its meaning as clear as that of the flag: defiance.

The Mexicans quickly unlimbered two howitzers and fired a round from each in response, then another—fused bombs that would explode upon impact, usually to little effect.

Soldados were still pouring into Béxar from the west. From their position on a slight rise across the river, the men on the Alamo walls could see them as they filed into the two plazas flanking the church. There looked to be at least a thousand, including some lancers. A large cloud of dust downriver, somewhere near Mission Concepción, suggested the presence of hundreds more.

Siege etiquette of the time dictated that the attacking army offer the besieged force the opportunity to surrender. A *soldado* displaying a white flag walked down to the footbridge over the river. With him was one of Santa Anna's staff officers.

In the mission, someone told the fatigued Bowie that there had been a Mexican bugle call just before the cannon shot—probably a request for a parley. When he learned of the large numbers of enemy soldiers, it gave him pause. The rebels were seriously outnumbered, perhaps ten to one. It might be worth exploring possible terms—perhaps a parole like the one they had generously extended to Cós in December. After his foraging exertions, Bowie was exhausted and unable to write, but he and Juan Seguín crafted a message to the invaders requesting a parley. When the Tejano captain finished the note he handed it to Bowie, who managed to sign it in a shaky hand, and noticed that Seguín had ended the missive with the traditional "Dios y Federación México." Bowie crossed out the last two words and replaced them with "Texas."

Green Jameson took the letter, mounted a horse, and rode through the front gate and past several *jacales* bordering the west side of Plaza de Valero. He held up his own white cloth as he approached the footbridge, 220 yards from the Alamo. He dismounted and walked over the bridge and handed the communiqué to the officer there, who was none other than Colonel Juan Almonte, well known throughout the colonies after his extensive fact-finding mission in 1834, which had alerted the Mexicans to the colonists' rebellious potential. A decent and cultured man, Almonte had been educated in a Catholic school in New Orleans and spoke English fluently. Squarely built, about 5 feet 6 inches tall, with a round, copper-colored face that betrayed his mestizo blood, he was a good-natured sort. Green could hardly have found more sympathetic hands into which to deliver Bowie's message. Almonte glanced at it, then gave it to the soldier to deliver to Santa Anna.

The letter enraged His Excellency. Perhaps further angered by the insolent claim of "God and Texas," he ordered an aide, Colonel José Batres, to write an uncompromising reply.

At the footbridge, Almonte and Jameson talked while they waited for the response. Jameson revealed to the colonel the bad state of affairs in the fort, and his personal hope that some honorable conditions could be negotiated. When the reply arrived, Jameson carried it back to the mission.

"The Mexican army," read the response, "cannot come to terms with rebellious foreigners to whom there is no other recourse left, if they wish to save their lives, than to place themselves immediately at the disposal of the Supreme Government from whom alone they may expect clemency after some considerations are taken up."

An unconditional surrender at discretion—this meant no guarantees of safety, and possibly mass executions, as had happened twenty-three years ago, when Arredondo had quashed the Republican Army of the North and hanged as many as five hundred rebels and citizens alike. The terms were clearly unacceptable, and Travis, infuriated at Bowie's unilateral decision to request a parley, now sent his own emissary, Albert Martin, down to the bridge. Almonte was still there. This message was oral: if Almonte wished to speak with Travis, he would be received with pleasure. But Almonte could only reiterate His Excellency's terms, and did so.

As his comrades watched from the mission's ramparts, Martin rode back to the fort with the response. When Travis heard the message, he gathered the men together. In a stirring speech, he swore that he would resist to the end. If he had any doubts about the mood of the garrison, they were dispelled now: he received a roar of confirmation in reply.

The formalities having been dispensed with, both sides began settling in for the evening. Santa Anna sent a contingent of *zapadores*—the army's sappers, or engineers, who were also crack troops—upstream to cut off the *acequia* that served as the mission's water supply. Other units moved to designated areas and began to set up camp on the plains around the town. Mora's force, having found no rebels at Mission Concepción, marched upriver to rejoin their comrades.

Inside the fort, the men continued storing supplies and provisions, the newcomers finding a place to sleep in the barracks or elsewhere. In the church, a dozen or so noncombatants were quartered, most of them defenders' families. The women set about making the place as comfortable as they could, arranging hay for bedding and unpacking the food they had brought. Some of the children walked around the mission's large plaza, watching the soldiers at their duties — and a cat that had decided to join the rebels.

Near twilight, the Esparza family approached the Alamo from the south, where they had forded the river out of sight of the Mexican army. They walked up to the main gate to find the semicircular lunette empty and the door and gate closed up tight. Anna Esparza pounded on the door and demanded entry. No one answered.

Someone on the ramparts to the east called to them. Gregorio Esparza shepherded his wife and children past the *abatis* of felled trees and around to the rear of the church. There, on the east wall of the sacristy, a small window seven feet above the ground was opened. One by one, eleven-year-old Enrique and his brothers and sister, then their mother, were passed up to helping hands and pulled into the church. Finally Gregorio scrambled up, after he handed in the few possessions they had brought, and the window was closed tight.

As the sun disappeared below the Alazán Hills west of the city, Mexican soldiers prepared to bivouac at their assigned posts. Some of the men found cots in the presidio on Military Plaza. Officers moved into abandoned houses around the squares, and, in some cases, booted families from their homes. Several of His Excellency's staff decided to make the Church of San Fernando their quarters, and arranged with the custodian's wife for their meals. Colonel Almonte took over the house just west of Main Plaza owned by Major George Anthony Nixon, the commissioner for a land grant company representing several *empresarios*. Nixon had decided he preferred his other residence, in Nacogdoches, for now. For the remainder of the occupation, Almonte would share the house with two other staff officers, Captain Fernando Urriza and the amiable Lieutenant Colonel Marcial Aguirre, a cavalry captain recently given a brevet promotion. With Almonte was Benjamin "Ben" Harris, the Negro freedman cook he had brought back to Mexico from the United States.

The rest of the soldiers drew less luxurious accommodations. The infantry was assigned campsites south of La Villita, along the river. As they and their *soldaderas* set up makeshift shelters and households, the aroma of beef and corn cakes cooking over open fires wafted through the evening, and the sounds of fifteen hundred *soldados* settling in for the night enveloped the Alamo mission. As twilight turned to darkness, the rebels peering over the Alamo walls could see dozens of campfires on almost every side, several hundred yards away. The siege had begun.

TWELVE

"I Am Besieged"

They say they will defend it or die on the ground. Provisions,
ammunition and Men, or suffer your men to be murder in the
fort. If you do not turn out Texas is gone.

LANCELOT SMITHER

Siege warfare had changed little since the introduction of
artillery bombardment centuries before. An attacking
force would begin investment of the defensive position—
surrounding the target and blocking the escape of troops and
the ingress of reinforcements, provisions, and supplies—and
then employ any combination of well-proven methods to
reduce the fortifications and destroy the defenders.

Siege machinery was one option; that meant cannon, primarily, since the invention of gunpowder had allowed artillery
to replace more primitive weapons, such as catapults and tre-
buchets. Mining, or sapping, was another option; this meant
that the attackers would dig tunnels right up to the walls and
place explosive charges under them. The besieging force could

then use the trenches to move men and machines gradually closer to the besieged position. The attackers might also use the technique of deception—seldom quite as simple as the Trojan Horse, but following the same age-old principle: fool the enemy and then infiltrate its defenses. All these devices and more might be put into play, sometimes followed by the slower but no less deadly weapons of starvation, thirst, and disease. (Catapulting corpses of plague victims over the walls, as the Mongols had done, or introducing disease-infected fleas to a fort, thus infesting it with some virulent epidemic, was only for the most impatient; nature could usually do the job unaided.) No single development, however, had changed siege warfare more than the introduction and use during the last half century of large cannon. With heavy siege guns, an army could remain at a safe distance from its target and in a short time batter down almost any fortress wall.

But the weakest branch of the Mexican army was its artillery. Santa Anna had no heavy siege guns. Most of the cannon were leftovers from the royal Spanish army, which during its time in the New World had found few occasions to confront and attack thick-walled fortresses, and thus had little need for very large pieces. The largest tubes carried into Texas were two twelve-pounders, and they were with Gaona's First Infantry Brigade, about a two-week march from Béxar. Those guns were not massive, but they could do some serious damage to the Alamo's walls if positioned near enough. Until they arrived, two howitzers and six smaller cannon—two eight-pounders, two six-pounders, and two four-pounders—were the only ones available, and they would have to be placed extremely close to the Alamo's walls to be effective.

To that end, over the next few days Santa Anna ordered artillery batteries set up west of the Alamo, near the town's

Main Plaza; closer to the river, near Potrero Street, southwest of the fort; and on the Alameda, the road southeast of the fort that led to the old powder house on the hill and then east to Gonzales. The closest emplacement was about four hundred yards away, but the guns were quickly put to work, and on the second day of the siege they succeeded in disabling two pieces, including the big eighteen-pounder, which had been moved to a battery overlooking the southwest corner.

In the meantime, His Excellency would rest his men, reconnoiter, and do what he could to replenish spirits and supplies. In the abandoned mercantile establishment of Nat Lewis and the military storehouse of John W. Smith, his soldiers found a large supply of shoes. Santa Anna looked on as these were distributed to the preferred companies of *cazadores* and *granaderos,* whose footwear had been reduced to shreds after the arduous journey through northern Mexico. He sent patrols out with locals to ranches in the area to procure beeves for his hungry *soldados.*

Most of the occupying army's officers still camped within the town wherever they could find shelter. Many of the houses were abandoned; when they found occupants in others, they booted them out. One family moved into the cellar of a neighboring house, where they would at least be safe from stray gunfire. The great majority of *bexareños* had left town for the safety of the ranches up and down the San Antonio River; others had headed for the Anglo settlements to the east. The few hundred who had elected to stay were told they would be unharmed if they remained indoors. Some of them were conscripted to help care for the injured, cook, and carry equipment around the camps. The rest, especially the women, tried to keep out of sight. The ravenous soldiers commandeered what few supplies still remained in Béxar: beeves, corn, hay, lumber to construct redoubts, and every scrap of anything edible they could find, taking what they wanted without bothering to pay.

The *presidiales* of the Alamo and Béxar companies who had elected to remain in town instead of riding south with Cós in December were now ordered to hold themselves in readiness to join the army for active service. Francisco Esparza—who had stayed at home with his family in his house on North Flores Street—was one of them. Neither he nor his two brothers had joined their sibling Gregorio in the Texian volunteer army, and with the arrival of the Mexican army, Francisco's loyalties might soon be tested: Gregorio and his family were now in the fort with the Americans.

Santa Anna's informants told him the rebels had food for four weeks at most, but His Excellency had no intention of waiting that long. He was conducting this war on a timetable, and it did not allow several weeks for the destruction of one ramshackle fort and fewer than two hundred rebel defenders. Somewhere to the east, he knew from his spies, Sam Houston was gathering a force to march to Béxar. The Alamo and its rebels must be crushed quickly.

DAWN ON THE TWENTY-FOURTH BROUGHT to the Alamo garrison the full realization of their predicament. They were besieged by several Mexican battalions of infantry and cavalry—more than fifteen hundred men, it appeared, with little doubt that several thousand more were on the way. Fortunately, the Alamo was not completely surrounded, and the enemy lines were porous. Messages to and from the town could still get through, with minimal subterfuge required. (In the first few days, Juan Seguín had his meals prepared by a widow named Pacheco, whose young sons delivered them from

Béxar to the fort.) And the pickets toward the east were still few enough that a fast and skillful rider could gallop past them.

But any chance of escape on a large scale was complicated by the presence of two dozen or so wounded and sick and almost as many women and children, whose survival would depend on reinforcements, and soon. Their provisions of cattle and corn, as Santa Anna already knew, could only last a month at most. And while there were plenty of muskets and cartridges on hand, round shot and good powder for the cannon were in short supply.

Still, the defenders believed that, with luck, they would only have to stick it out for a few more days. James Fannin and his four hundred men were just ninety-five miles away—three hard days' march on foot, or maybe four. And somewhere to the east, Sam Houston was surely gathering another army of Texians to come to their aid. Perhaps they were on the move now.

The Mexicans had begun work on another artillery placement on the other side of the river, in the rear of the Veramendi house, less than four hundred yards away. They finished in the afternoon, and started an intermittent but steady bombardment. The Alamo's inhabitants quickly became accustomed to taking cover in the buildings or against the walls at the sound of a cannon or mortar blast. To protect the powder magazines stored in the two small rooms on either side of the church entrance, where the walls were four feet thick, the front windows were covered with masonry. The western walls were in good condition—they had not received the battering that the north wall, still in bad shape, had during the siege the previous fall. Green Jameson, a bit more urgently than before, continued to direct his work crews in its ongoing repairs and fortification.

Travis had spent a good part of the day on the parapets. In the evening, as music from the Mexican battalion bands filled the air, he sat down in his room, dipped his quill in ink, and considered what to write. There was not much news since the day before. Bowie had taken a turn for the worse, and they had moved him away from most of the men lest whatever he had spread to them. He now lay on a cot in a room near the main gate, with Juana Alsbury caring for him. At night she and her sister, Gertrudis, shared a room in a house along the western wall.

Despite the lack of change, the garrison's predicament seemed even more urgent. A message to inspire reinforcements to organize and march in all haste was in order—perhaps publisher Gail Borden might print it in his four-page weekly *Telegraph and Texas Register*. With public consumption in mind, Travis began:

To the People of Texas & all Americans in the world—

Fellow citizens and compatriots—

I am besieged, by a thousand or more of the Mexicans
under Santa Anna—I have sustained a continual
Bombardment & cannonade for 24 hours & have not lost
a man—The enemy has demanded a surrender at
discretion, otherwise, the garrison all will be put to the
sword, if the fort is taken—I have answered the demand
with a cannon shot, & our flag still waves proudly from
the walls—<u>I shall never surrender or retreat. Then,</u> I call
on you in the name of Liberty, of patriotism & everything
dear to the American character, to come to our aid, with
all dispatch—The enemy is receiving reinforcements
daily & will no doubt increase to three or four thousand

in four or five days. If this call is neglected, I am
determined to sustain myself as long as possible & die
like a soldier who never forgets what is due to his own
honor & that of his country — Victory or Death.

William Barret Travis
Lt. Col. Comdt.

P.S. The Lord is on our side — when the enemy appeared
in sight we had not three bushels of corn — we have since
found in deserted houses 80 or 90 bushels & got into the
walls 20 or 30 head of Beeves —

Travis

He underlined "Victory or Death" three times, then signed
the letter. Later that night, Captain Albert Martin burst out
of the main gate and galloped through the Mexican lines
toward his hometown of Gonzales with the missive.

THE EXPRESS RIDER BEARING Travis's first message,
hastily written on the afternoon of the twenty-third, reached
Travis's good friend Robert M. Williamson between Bastrop
and Gonzales. Three-Legged Willie had been placed in charge
of the three ranging companies activated to protect the colonists against Indians while the army was fighting the Mexicans.
Ten days earlier, he had been directed by the General Council
to move his men to the frontier to guard the settlements against
attacks. He was on the upper Colorado River with a company
of rangers when the message from Travis arrived. Williamson
continued on to Gonzales and forwarded expresses to the
Texian government to the east and his ranger forces to the
north, near Bastrop. Indians, especially Comanches, were still

a danger to the frontier communities, but for now the colonists would have to fend for themselves: every man was needed to march to the aid of the Alamo garrison, and Williamson and his ranger company rode to Gonzales.

When the express rider reached San Felipe on the evening of Friday, February 26, the news he brought created a consternation—even more so because five weeks earlier, when Deaf Smith had arrived in town direct from Béxar, he had told Governor Henry Smith that the Mexican army would not arrive in Texas until March, and been so quoted in the February 27 issue of Borden's *Telegraph and Texas Register.* Now the governor quickly directed Borden to print Travis's letter as a handbill, in an edition of two hundred, to be circulated throughout Texas. Residents began preparations to leave town with as many of their possessions as they could carry on carts, livestock, or their shoulders. "The people now begin to think the wolf has actually come at last," wrote an observer in town.

By this time acting governor James Robinson and what remained of the General Council—his advisory committee of two or three citizens—had moved to the rough hamlet of Washington in anticipation of the March 1 convention. Governor Smith, with few resources besides the $5,000 loan delivered to him in January, decided to remain in San Felipe a few more days. The two parties still refused to recognize each other. Delegates from every settlement in Texas were just beginning to arrive in Washington, where they found lodgings hard to come by and comfortable quarters nonexistent; there was only one actual hotel, so many of them boarded at John Lott's one-room house. The two Tejanos representing Béxar, as well as Jesse Badgett, from the Alamo—Samuel Maverick would not arrive until March 3—decided to pay a carpenter to put down wooden planks on the dirt floor of his small workshop, and they rented it from him for a month.

Stephen F. Austin, the first and most successful of the Texas *empresarios*.

Ben Milam, the Kentucky adventurer and failed *empresario* who rallied the Texian rebels at San Antonio de Béxar.

Edward Burleson, Bastrop colonist and seasoned Indian fighter. He was elected commander of the Texian forces surrounding Béxar after Austin's departure.

Erastus "Deaf" Smith, the legendary scout whom William Travis called "the Bravest of the Brave."

Juan Seguín, scion of one of Béxar's most prominent Tejano families. He was a staunch federalist and ally of the Texian rebels.

William Barret Travis, in a sketch by Wylie Martin, a San Felipe friend and neighbor. Though the drawing's attribution is disputed, this is the only known likeness of the Alamo commander.

General Martín Perfecto de Cós, commander of the defeated Mexican army forces at Béxar. He broke his parole and returned to Texas with Santa Anna.

James Bowie, the most dangerous knife fighter in the West: six feet of solid muscle, with eyes that "resembled a tiger's" when he was angered. (Courtesy of Joseph Musso)

The lovely Ursula Bowie, who died of cholera in 1833. (*Courtesy of Joseph Musso*)

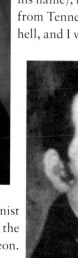

David Crockett (as he always signed his name), three-time congressman from Tennessee: "You may all go to hell, and I will go to Texas."

Dr. Amos Pollard, an abolitionist from Massachusetts, served as the Alamo garrison's surgeon.

Despite his injured leg, Dr. John Sutherland carried the first word of the Mexican army's arrival at Béxar to the east, reaching the town of Gonzales the next day.

There is no known likeness of James Bonham, but the nephew pictured in this photograph, also named James Bonham (shown here at age twenty-eight, the same age as his uncle at the time of the Alamo battle), was said to be "in appearance almost a double of his famous uncle."

Antonio López de Santa Anna: "If I were God, I would wish to be more."

The brave and respected Lieutenant Colonel José Vicente Miñón, hero of the Mexican Revolution. He was often assigned command of the *cazadores*, the army's marksmen.

Colonel Juan Almonte, trusted adviser to Santa Anna. New Orleans–educated and fluent in English, he had gained respect for the colonists during an 1834 fact-finding journey through Texas.

General Vicente Filisola, the Italian-born second commander in chief of Santa Anna's Army of Operations. He was past his prime as a fighting man but more than capable as an administrator, his primary duty.

General Pedro de Ampudia, artillery commander, was Cuban-born and reputed to be skilled and ruthless.

Lieutenant Colonel José Mariano de Salas, commander of the Jimenez Permanente Battalion.

Lieutenant Colonel Rómulo Díaz de la Vega of the Zapadores Battalion.

General José Urrea, commander of the 600-man brigade that swept up the coast, conquering every Texian force it met.

This 1893 German illustration provides a reasonably accurate depiction of Mexican soldiers and officers at the time of the Texas Revolution. *(Courtesy of Joseph Musso)*

David B. Kent, son of Alamo defender Andrew Kent. David had been part of the Alamo garrison but was sent out to gather cattle just before the arrival of the Mexican army. His father insisted he stay in Gonzales to care for their family. *(Courtesy of Chester Wilkes)*

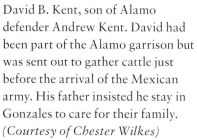

Attorney Robert "Three-Legged Willie" Williamson, good friend of William Travis and commander of an early ranging corps at the time of the Alamo siege.

Colonel James Walker Fannin, well-meaning but dilatory, commanded the men at Goliad.

Sam Houston, the six-foot-two force of nature who was unanimously voted commander in chief of the Texas armed forces.

Susanna Dickinson, wife of artillery captain Almeron Dickinson, survived the battle of the Alamo only to beg Santa Anna to allow her to keep her daughter, Angelina.

The Mexican dictator was charmed by the pretty, blue-eyed child and expressed his desire to adopt her for his own. Angelina was fifteen months old at the time of the Alamo battle.

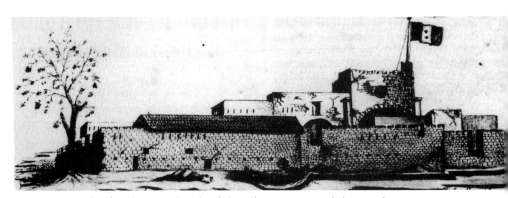

The first known sketch of the Alamo, executed during the 1836 siege by Captain José Juan Sánchez-Navarro. *(Benson Latin American Collection, University of Texas at Austin)*

When the news of the Alamo garrison's besiegement reached Washington a few hours after it arrived in San Felipe, Robinson sent a frantic message to Sam Houston, still parleying with the Cherokees and several associated bands of Indians. "Come quickly and organize our countrymen for battle," the acting governor begged. "Call the militia out en masse.... Say it is done by the order of the Governor & Council & by your own order, and by the unanimous call of Texas." He sent it by express and addressed it "to Gen. Sam Houston Wherever he may be." That rider galloped out of town posthaste, but others directed to bear the news to the north and east did not—the government had no money to pay for them. Only when several citizens pitched in were riders found, paid, and dispatched.

The next morning, Saturday, the citizens of San Felipe met to appoint a committee of twelve to prepare an address and draft resolutions. The meeting adjourned for a while, then reconvened later to adopt the measures. One of the resolutions called for the formation of another committee. Another recommended establishing provision depots on the road to Gonzales. There were eight resolutions in all. None called for an immediate march to Béxar, where 150 men were surrounded by ten times their number, though some of the ladies of the town began to gather clothing just in case.

The fledgling country's severe lack of funds was a chief reason Stephen Austin had been sent, with two other commissioners, to the United States: to drum up support and money. Americans avidly followed the progress of the revolution, and overwhelmingly supported the Texas cause. Most of their information came from newspaper stories, but many learned of the struggle firsthand from Austin and his fellow commissioners, who traveled from New Orleans to Mobile, Nashville, and Louisville on their way to Washington, D.C., speaking of the Texians' grievances to crowds of hundreds or thousands at every stop. They succeeded in acquiring several private loans from individuals and banks, but Austin knew their chances of gaining financial aid and diplomatic recognition from the United States would be slim: the Texians' provisional government had not even issued a declaration of independence, much less established a legitimate, functioning government. Without those essentials, Andrew Jackson and his administration would insist on maintaining neutrality—the last thing they wanted was a war with Mexico. Until then, the unofficial state of Texas would have to go it alone, without official U.S. assistance.

EARLY ON FEBRUARY 25, the morning after Travis wrote his defiant letter, while work was begun on a trench on the east side of the river in the near-empty field east of town known as El Potrero ("the pasture"), Santa Anna ordered the artillery to resume bombarding the Alamo. The rebel cannon returned fire. Overnight, two more Mexican batteries had been erected to the west, and their field of fire controlled the fort's entrance and the road junctions just outside it. His Excellency decided to make use of that advantage—and test the mettle of his troops and of the colonists.

At 9:30 a.m., as the new batteries bombarded the Alamo and Santa Anna watched from nearby, General Castrillón and Colonel Miñón led the Matamoros Battalion and several companies of *cazadores*, the elite light infantry—about three hundred men in total—up through La Villita to within a hundred yards of the rebels. They took possession of several small adobe huts and *jacales* bordering Plaza de Valero and opened a heavy fusillade on the fort's south wall.

A wide ditch almost five feet deep angled out from the main

gate's lunette. A company of rebels in the trench looked over its edge and let loose a hail of well-aimed rifle and musket fire that dropped several attackers. On the walls behind them, more men supplied supporting fire. From the batteries along the south side of the fort and at the lunette, the artillerymen of Captains Almeron Dickinson, Samuel Blair, and William Carey directed a heavy discharge of grapeshot and canister that burst apart and scattered in a wide, deadly arc as they flew from the cannon, much like a massive shotgun. *Soldados* in the open scrambled for cover behind the scattered structures on the south edge of the plaza. The Mexican batteries responded with balls, grapeshot, and canister of their own, and at least one more organized assault was attempted, again repelled by the rebels. The battle raged for two hours until a full retreat was ordered. The attackers fell back out of rifle range, dragging their dead and wounded with them.

Santa Anna's force took the worst of it, with two men killed and six wounded. But he had gained the information he needed. The rebels might be an unruly bunch, but they were good shots, as their reputations suggested; they were well entrenched in a superior position; and they could put up a fight. They clearly would not be overwhelmed by a few weary battalions.

Nine days earlier, while at the Rio Grande, His Excellency had written his secretary of war, José María Tornel, to tell him that Béxar would be taken within fifteen days. The town was in Mexican hands once more—that much was true. But that ownership was in name only as long as the rebels held the Alamo. They constituted not only an impediment but a personal embarrassment. The longer the enemies lived, the more the fame and honor of the Mexican army, and Santa Anna himself, were compromised. And his army's provisions were running out, no new supplies had arrived, and the town had been stripped bare. For more than one reason, he could not afford to remain in Béxar another two weeks.

Santa Anna decided that he could no longer wait for Gaona to arrive with the heavier cannon, which were only twelve-pounders in any case. He dispatched a messenger back down El Camino Real to find the First Infantry Brigade, carrying orders to immediately send Gaona's three best battalions—the Aldama Permanente, the Toluca Activo, and the crack Zapadores—ahead to Béxar under the command of the senior colonel, Francisco Duque. The weaponry would wait.

After this heavy skirmish His Excellency wrote Tornel again: "Up until now they have shown themselves contemptuous, confident of the strong position that they maintain, and basing their hopes upon the great resources of their colonies and of the United States of the North. However, they shall soon be finally disillusioned."

In the meantime, he seized upon an unexpected pleasure. During the morning's fighting, in one of the houses, Castrillón had found the widow of a Mexican soldier and her attractive daughter. The defiant woman told the general that they had no other place to go, and that they were not afraid. Later, when Castrillón told El Presidente of his encounter, Santa Anna expressed a desire to see the girl. Castrillón declined to act as procurer for his commander, but Miñón, untroubled by such scruples, agreed to do it. When he delivered Santa Anna's message, the woman refused to allow Santa Anna any contact with her daughter unless sanctified by marriage. Miñón reported this to his commander in chief, then told him of a man under his command, a well-educated rascal capable of all sorts of tricks—including the impersonation of a priest. Santa Anna gave the order to proceed. The *soldado* borrowed vestments from a priest in town, along with everything else necessary to perform a wedding according to the rites of the Catholic Church. The "nuptials" took place in Santa Anna's quarters on Main Plaza. Afterward, the already married president retired in the company of his young "bride."

A norther blew in about nine p.m. and increased the misery of the troops erecting two more batteries several hundred yards southeast of the Alamo. The Matamoros Battalion set up camp close by, and the Dolores Cavalry Regiment was posted near the hills further east. That night a fresh group of skirmishers was sent against that side of the fort, but grape-shot and small arms fire sent the *soldados* back to their entrenchments. By eleven thirty p.m. most of the Mexican army had retired for the evening.

LATER THAT NIGHT, Travis sat in his quarters along the west wall with pen in hand, the beginnings of a letter to Sam Houston in front of him. Throughout the compound rebels wrapped themselves in blankets and huddled around fires or found a place out of the elements to grab what sleep they could. Even worse off were the sentries on the walls and the pickets outside in the ditches, who had to somehow stay awake and alert. There were now more troops surrounding the Alamo than there were the previous day. Trenches were under construction on the Alameda, to the southeast, and a large force of infantry had moved into them.

Earlier that evening, at a council of war held by the garrison's officers, it was decided that another messenger would be sent to Fannin at Goliad. No one volunteered, so a vote was taken. Juan Seguín was elected to undertake the dangerous mission. Travis objected—no one in the garrison knew the

Spanish language or Mexican customs better, and he might be needed if they were to treat with the Mexican commander again. But his arguments were overruled, and at eight o'clock, after bidding good-bye to his friends and comrades, Seguín sneaked out the main gate and crawled on all fours to the *acequia* east of the fort, then up the waterway and into Béxar. It had been arranged for one of his Tejano horsemen, Antonio Cruz y Arocha, to meet him with a horse. With any luck Seguín would make his way through the Mexican lines and out of town.

The day had been long and exhausting, but Travis's men had acquitted themselves well—"Indeed, the whole of the men who were brought into action conducted themselves with such heroism that it would be injustice to discriminate," he wrote to Houston. But he decided to single out a few, with one receiving the highest praise: "The Hon. David Crockett was seen at all points, animating the men to do their duty." He mentioned several other defenders, including his aide, Charles Despallier, and rifleman Robert Brown: the two had sallied out the main gate and burned the straw-thatched *jacales* and houses around the Plaza de Valero, reducing the cover for any assaults from that direction. Not a single man had been lost; the only injuries were a few scratches from flying pieces of rock. But they were still outnumbered ten to one, if only the able-bodied were counted, and the enemy entrenchments were encroaching. It was bitter cold, and they were running out of firewood. The situation called for another stirring appeal. He ended with this:

I have every reason to apprehend an attack from his whole force very soon; but I shall hold out to the last extremity, hoping to secure reinforcements in a day or two. Do hasten on aid to me as rapidly as possible, as from the superior number of the enemy, it will be impossible for us to keep them out much longer. If they overpower us, we fall a sacrifice at the shrine of our country, and we hope posterity and our country will do our memory justice. Give me help, oh my country!

Once more he ended his letter with: "Victory or Death!" The race for reinforcements was on.

THIRTEEN

"This Time You May See Some Blood"

We have provisions for twenty days for the men we have; our supply of ammunition is limited....If these things are promptly sent and large reinforcements are hastened to this frontier, this neighborhood will be the great and decisive battle ground.

WILLIAM BARRET TRAVIS

Express rider John Johnson arrived in Goliad, ninety-five miles down the San Antonio River, on February 25, two days after leaving Béxar. He exaggerated the size of the enemy force—three thousand or so, he told the men who gathered around him as he entered the presidio—but the news that 156 rebels were holed up in the old Alamo compound stunned the four hundred rebels in the fort. Johnson handed the written plea for help to James Fannin, who was in the middle of penning yet another letter to acting governor James Robinson.

The Goliad commander had received other requests for aid from Béxar, but this one the colonel could not ignore.

Fannin's men had been hard at work fortifying the presidio, and he had been so pleased with the results that two days before, he had conducted a lottery to name the place. "Fort Defiance" won out. When the same day he wrote to Robinson to tell him the news, he again asked to be relieved of his command. "I am a better judge of my military abilities than others," he wrote, "and if I am qualified to command an Army, I have not found it out."

"We deem it unnecessary to repeat to a brave officer, who knows his duty, that we call on him for assistance," read the message from Béxar. Though provisions were scarce, many of his men were dressed in rags, and some were without shoes, Fannin immediately decided that he would respond to the call from the Alamo. One hundred men would stay to garrison the fort; the remainder, about 320 strong, would march north at dawn with four small cannon and several oxcarts of provisions and ammunition. Fannin's decision overjoyed the New Orleans Greys; for at least a month, since the dissolution of the Matamoros expedition, they had wanted to return to their nineteen comrades at Béxar.

The next morning Fannin and his men set out. Two hundred yards from town, three supply wagons broke down. Only by doubling ox teams, and with the greatest difficulty, did they manage to get the artillery across the San Antonio River. By that time it was almost sunset, and a cold wind was blowing in. They returned to the fort to sleep, leaving the supply wagons on the near side of the river and the cannon on the other. During the night some of the oxen strayed off and could not be found the next morning. Without the oxen they would have no provisions, and only the ammunition they could carry.

In the morning Fannin's volunteers requested a council of

war, which convened on the riverbank. Besides half a tierce (about twenty gallons) of rice, they had almost nothing to eat. They were without beef, save for a small portion of jerky, and it would be impossible to obtain any until they had reached the Seguín ranch, Casa Blanca, seventy miles away—and then only if the Mexicans had not already commandeered it. Word had reached them that Santa Anna had dispatched a column down the Goliad road to intercept them. And then there was the condition of the men and their clothing, or lack of it...and the size of the Mexican army they would likely have to fight their way through to reach the Alamo...and the question of what would happen to the Goliad garrison if it fell into the hands of the enemy—the more they discussed it, the more unwise the expedition appeared, until a unanimous decision was reached: they would remain at Fort Defiance. "It was deemed expedient to return to this post and complete the fortifications, etc., etc.," wrote Fannin in a letter to Robinson later that day.

Between San Felipe's resolutions, Fannin's irresoluteness, and the reluctance of Texians to heed the rallying cries of their leaders, it seemed as if there was no one willing to march immediately to the besieged garrison.

But there were a few such men.

ANDREW KENT WAS NOT PARTICULARLY LARGE, nor were his two eldest sons—eighteen-year-old Davy was 5 feet 3 inches, and fifteen-year-old Isaac would be even shorter at full growth—but he was strong, and he knew how to work with wood. Soon after arriving in Green DeWitt's colony in 1830, with the help of his sons, his relatives, his neighbors, and his extensive collection of tools, he began to build a pioneer mansion: a double log cabin with lofts and a dog run and a brick chimney at each end, forty feet apart.

Back in Callaway County, Missouri, Kent had made do with 160 acres. That was enough for a man, but for those who farmed and ranched to feed themselves, it would not be sufficient for his eight children when they became adults and had families of their own. He had heard of the grants in Texas given to men with dependents—4,428 acres, a full league—and had heard the copious praise of the land and its bounties from those who had settled there. After discussing it with a few neighbors, including the Zumwalts—Andrew's wife, Elizabeth, was a member of that extensive clan—they made arrangements for several families to move to DeWitt's colony in Texas. After months of preparations—gathering tools, supplies, and livestock, and building large flatboats—they had made the arduous trip down the Missouri and the Mississippi to New Orleans, and thence by schooner to the mouth of the Lavaca River on the Texas coast. They drove their wagons inland to a choice spot in the bottomlands on the west side of the river, some thirty-five miles southeast of Gonzales. That was in June 1830.

Kent and his sons worked hard on the family homestead, farming cotton, corn, potatoes, yams, and all kinds of vegetables, and raising sheep, hogs, milk cows, and cattle. After a few years he registered his own stock mark and brand. The arrival of two more children meant many mouths to feed, but the land lived up to its legend, and there was enough for everyone, plus extra to barter and sell. Most of their clothes the womenfolk made themselves from cotton and wool spun on their own wheels and woven on their own looms; the family bought little from the stores in Gonzales. It was a hard life but a good one, rewarding honest toil and improving every year.

So upon Santa Anna's rise to power and his severe curtailment of the Texians' rights as guaranteed by the Mexican constitution of 1824, Andrew became increasingly active in politics and supportive of independence—his father, after all, had fought in the American Revolution for similar reasons. He would not accept the possibility of losing everything he had worked so hard for. When a secret meeting was called in July 1835 among the citizens living on the Lavaca and Navidad Rivers, Kent rode thirty-five miles to a neighbor's cotton-gin house to discuss Santa Anna's policies and debate their response. The farmers present put their names to a declaration calling for armed resistance to military occupation. A few months later Andrew and Davy Kent rode with Stephen Austin's Army of the People to Béxar. Father and son participated in the long siege and battle there, but made it home for Christmas, Davy with a slight wound in his shoulder.

About a month later, in late January 1836, eleven men led by Captain William Patton rode up the rough trail from the coast and appeared at the Kent farm. They were on their way to reinforce Colonel James Neill's worn-out garrison at Béxar. The Kents put them up, fed the men and horses, and saw the company on their way the next morning. Patton filled the Kents in on the latest developments and the sorry state of things in Béxar, as reported by Sam Houston. The group's stay was a grim reminder of the increasing hostilities and the mounting threat of all-out war.

Four weeks later, on Sunday, February 21, Andrew Kent rode into Gonzales intending to stay a day or two and return with supplies—his wife needed material to make clothes. After recovering from his wound, Davy, the oldest boy, had followed Patton's company, and was now with the garrison at Béxar, commanded jointly by William Barret Travis and James Bowie. He would turn nineteen in two days. Davy was a good hand with cattle, so he had been sent out to scour the countryside for beeves.

The first thing Andrew heard about that Sunday afternoon

was the attack on a local family east of town earlier in the day. Comanches had ambushed John Hibbens and his family, who were returning home via the Texas coast after a visit to the States. They had killed Hibbens and his brother-in-law and carried off Sarah Hibbens and her two children, a baby and a six-year-old boy. John Hibbens was the second husband Sarah had lost to Indians. Several men had already galloped off in pursuit.

More colonists than usual were present in town that day, there to hear the full report of the ambush and decide what to do. On Monday, Byrd Lockhart secured additional recruits for the Gonzales Ranging Company of Mounted Volunteers, one of three ranger militia groups along the western frontier called for by the provisional government in San Felipe to guard against Indian depredations. Twenty-three men of DeWitt's colony had signed up over the previous two weeks, including Andrew Kent, who now added his son Davy's name and then headed home with several bolts of cloth and news of the Indian attack.

Townspeople were still talking about the Hibbens tragedy two days later, when a pair of exhausted riders from Béxar arrived in town with even more momentous news.

BY THE TIME JOHN SMITH and John Sutherland reached Gonzales, about four p.m. on Wednesday, February 24, the doctor was in bad shape. His leg had begun to stiffen soon after departure, and at the Salado River, five miles east of Béxar, he had almost turned back. Smith had encouraged him to continue, pointing out that the enemy had probably surrounded the Alamo by this time. They had filled their water gourds and continued on until darkness, and the doctor's painful injuries, had persuaded them to stop for the night.

Now, as townspeople gathered around them, the two men

made known their mission, and delivered Travis's message to *alcalde* Andrew Ponton. Within two hours he had dispatched several express riders to the neighboring settlements with news of the Mexican army's arrival and calling for citizens to ride to Gonzales. He also sent messengers to deliver the news throughout DeWitt's colony.

Word spread to the farms in the area, and men began making their way into town. Most of the local mounted volunteers had been notified; though they had been organized with the Indian threat in mind, an invasion by the Mexican army trumped that concern. Among those mustering recruits was George Kimble, recently elected lieutenant. Kimble was a large man, over 6 feet 2 inches and broad-shouldered. He and his partner, Almeron Dickinson, owned the hat shop on Water Street near the Guadalupe River. His pregnant wife, Prudence, was doing the weekly wash in a creek by the house, their two-year-old son, Charles, nearby, when Kimble walked down to tell her what he had to do. He might not get back, he told her, but he owed his life to his country.

More than a dozen other local colonists arrived in town to muster up. Thomas Miller reported for duty. He owned plenty of land in the area, but ever since his much younger wife, Sidney, had divorced him to marry a handsome boy her own age, nineteen-year-old Johnny Kellogg, he had buried himself in business and council work. Miller had just written out his will. Dolphin Floyd, a farmer in town almost four years, rode in with a fine horse and gun. Floyd was a happy-go-lucky fellow who had left his father's Carolina farm a decade before, telling them he intended marrying a rich old widow. When he wrote them years later from Texas, it was with the news that he had married a widow, but she was neither very old nor very rich. Dolphin and Esther had a small daughter and another child on the way.

Late on February 25, a rider made it down to the Kent homestead and others on the Lavaca with the news that the Alamo was under siege, and that the Gonzales rangers had been activated. If Santa Anna was not stopped at Béxar, DeWitt's colony was next, and he would surely come down hard on the town that had started it all.

Kent would have gone anyway, since his boy was working out of Béxar, along with several other DeWitt colonists who were his friends and neighbors. Besides, the men of Gonzales owed a debt they would now repay: many of the Alamo defenders had come to their aid in October, when a hundred *soldados* had arrived on their doorstep and demanded their cannon.

Early the next morning two neighbors, Isaac Millsaps and William Summers, rode up the river and stopped at the Kent place. Summers was a young bachelor, but forty-one-year-old Millsaps, who had fought in the War of 1812 as a teenager, had a blind wife and six children. Andrew Kent said good-bye to Elizabeth and his children and mounted his horse. He turned to the other two men. "This time you may see some blood," he said as they rode away.

They arrived in Gonzales that afternoon to find the streets and stores full, and blacksmith Andrew Sowell busy fixing rifles and pistols. Several members of the Béxar garrison who had been discharged or furloughed in the last week or two were preparing to return — Captain Robert White of the Béxar Guards infantry company had only spent a week at his Gonzales home. Another furloughed volunteer, William Irwin, was doing a brisk business buying up army service chits for ready cash, a rare commodity thereabouts.

Captain Albert Martin had just arrived from Béxar with another express from William Barret Travis. This message gave many more details, and painted a grim picture. Martin told them he had heard a heavy cannonade throughout the day before as he rode to Gonzales—probably an attack on the fort. Despite entreaties from his father, who believed he would be riding to certain death, Martin immediately began preparing to return: he had promised Travis he would bring help. Lancelot Smither had also arrived from Béxar. He took the Travis letter and loped out of town east toward San Felipe, eighty miles away.

Davy Kent was there, too. He had been sent to one of the Tejano farms down the river to drive some cattle into the Alamo, but upon returning to Béxar he found the town teeming with Mexican soldiers. He had hung around in the hills a day or two until he realized he had no choice but to ride to Gonzales.

Andrew Kent was glad to see Davy, but he had sharp words for him when his son said he wanted to ride back to Béxar with the Gonzales ranging company. Between marauding Indians, renegade volunteers, and wandering Mexican soldiers, an isolated farm a day's ride from safety was no place for Elizabeth Kent and her children, especially without a man on the premises. Kent told his son to bring them into Gonzales to stay with Elizabeth's cousin "Red Adam" Zumwalt, who owned a store, a kitchen, and a grog shop in town in addition to a house. After some argument, Davy finally gave in. He would stay. His father would go.

Another volunteer company was being raised, this one solely for the relief of the Alamo. Its elected leader, Irishman Thomas Jackson of Gonzales, was busy mustering in men. His brother-in-law Wash Cottle, the fiddler at the long-ago party at Miller's inn, signed up, along with a few others. Major Robert Williamson had arrived from Bastrop and was busy helping to organize the two companies. Men continued to ride into town from homesteads in the area. Jacob Darst, one of the Old

Eighteen, who had started the revolution by refusing to give up their cannon, signed on. Years before he had fought Indians with the Virginia militia; now he was a freighter whose young son David had recently begun to accompany him on his hauls. He would not allow the fifteen-year-old to ride to Béxar, but a couple of other teenage boys insisted on coming along and had no fathers to prevent them. Sixteen-year-old Galba Fuqua's mother had died when he was eight, and his father two years before. His friend, seventeen-year-old Johnny Gaston, whose mother was a widow, was also determined to go. So was his stepfather, George Washington Davis, and forty-six-year-old John King, the patriarch of the large King family up on the mill road, northwest of town. And Johnny Kellogg had decided to go, despite the fact that his wife, Sidney, was pregnant.

The next day, February 27, as a cold north wind blew through the streets of Gonzales, the men made final preparations. George Kimble bought fifty-two pounds of coffee from Stephen Smith's store—if an army at war needed anything, it was coffee, and the Alamo garrison was low on that staple. Every man carried as many extra supplies as possible. Between them the two companies comprised about twenty-five volunteers, most of them DeWitt colonists.

As the two small companies prepared to leave that afternoon, every man, woman, and child in the town gathered to see the men off. Many of their loved ones, especially the mothers and wives, wept. John W. Smith volunteered to guide them into the Alamo—he knew the area well, and now that he had found his family safe in Gonzales, he felt able to go. They came up with a plan to bypass the regiment of lancers stationed to the east of the compound. To avoid the Mexican mounted patrols, the volunteers would take the mill road, which led up to Joseph Martin's cotton gin and mill and then veered west to Béxar. It was not as well marked or well traveled as Byrd Lockhart's lower road, but it approached Béxar above the town, near the river, which was the least-patrolled area when Albert Martin had left. With any luck, they could sneak down the river to the Alamo.

At two o'clock in the afternoon, they rode out of Gonzales, crossed the San Marcos River, and followed the Guadalupe River west past Green DeWitt's land and the old mill that had been abandoned after Indian trouble a few years back. When they reached the King homestead, a dozen or so miles out of town, sixteen-year-old William King was there to meet them. He persuaded Lieutenant Kimble to let him take his father's place so John King could look after his wife and eight other children, a few of whom were ill. The elder King objected at first, but finally gave in. John and his wife, Parmelia, watched as their son and his comrades disappeared from sight.

ON FEBRUARY 27, as the Gonzales party was making its way to Béxar, Mexican reinforcements were struggling to reach the same destination. Two days after leaving Béxar, His Excellency's courier found General Gaona's First Infantry Brigade 120 miles down El Camino Real, at Peña Creek — "no more than a big puddle of water," remembered one officer. When the courier delivered the orders, and Gaona revealed which units were to force-march to Béxar, "many of the officers in the Aldama, Toluca, and the Zapadores battalions were filled with joy and congratulated each other when they were ordered to hasten their march, for they knew that they were about to engage in combat," wrote de la Peña, attached to the Zapadores. The bulk of the army might have been less than overjoyed at the grueling expedition into Texas, but the elite troops of the Zapadores were eager to fight the ungrateful colonists.

De la Peña's own enthusiasm had been severely tempered by the sorry state of the column. It was in poor shape as a marching unit when he arrived, and over the next few days things got even worse. Almost all the civilian mule drivers had disappeared, their places taken by untrained soldiers. De la Peña was saddened to see how badly they were treating the oxen pulling the carts. The animals received almost no water during the day, and were not pastured properly at night. Like the soldiers in the other brigades, the impatient drivers would stab them with their bayonets or sabers — that is, those oxen that had not drowned crossing the Rio Grande on February 25, and whose carts had to be abandoned. On the twenty-sixth, the powder stores of the Aldama battalion caught fire. The day after that, February 27, they lost more oxen, and the last of the drivers deserted. The brigade looked close to grinding to an ignominious halt. So later that day, when the courier rode into camp with His Excellency's orders, de la Peña and his fellow officers were elated.

Colonel Francisco Duque was put in command of the column, and the selected battalions immediately prepared to march. They would not take supply carts, only pack mules. All told, almost twelve hundred men moved out by two in the afternoon. The three battalions were veteran units commanded by experienced officers: Duque led the Toluca Activo battalion; Lieutenant Colonel Gregorio Uruñuela, a twenty-five-year veteran, helmed the Aldama Permanente battalion; and Colonel Agustín Amat — at fifty-five the oldest battalion commander, with forty years in the army — commanded the Zapadores.

Gaona would continue as best he could with the rest of the brigade. Despite his irritable and haughty character, he had been doing all he could to speed up the slow-moving column, even driving an oxcart. Before the three battalions left, Lieutenant de la Peña suggested bringing the two twelve-pounders along, pulled by good mule teams. Gaona rejected the idea; if Santa Anna had wanted them he would have said so. At San Luis Potosí, Gaona and Santa Anna had engaged in an argument so serious that another general had found it necessary to mediate. Gaona would take no chances this time that he would anger His Excellency further.

When darkness fell on February 27, the men from Gonzales bivouacked for the night a few hours' ride west of town. Early the next morning they continued to follow the crude trail on the north side of the Guadalupe, riding at an easy pace across the gently rolling prairie land and through occasional woods. Early flowers, such as the pink prairie primrose and the yellow huisache daisy, poked out here and there along the path. About forty miles from Gonzales, near the border of DeWitt's colony, the river made a hard turn north. The men crossed and continued westward. By Monday, the twenty-ninth, they had reached the Cibolo, several miles above the place where Byrd Lockhart's well-marked lower road crossed the creek. There they found seven more men who joined the group.

At sunset John Smith led them the last twenty miles to Béxar. By eleven p.m. the moon, almost full, was high above them. An hour after midnight found them in the low hills east of town, where they hid until almost three a.m.

A scout sent ahead came back with good news. The regiment of cavalry that had been bivouacked on the main Gonzales road near the old watchtower was no longer there; Santa Anna had sent it south just a few hours before. But their way was not entirely clear—an infantry battalion was camped to the east of the Alamo, just north of the road. Smith gave the signal and the men mounted their horses and pulled up their collars against the blustery wind. He guided them around the battalion and through the Mexican sentinels over to Powder House Hill. From there they could see the Alamo, and Béxar beyond. They carefully walked their mounts down toward the fort.

Out of the darkness a man on horseback rode up to them and asked in English, "Do you wish to go into the fort, gentlemen?"

"Yes," someone said.

"Then follow me," the rider said, then turned his horse and took the lead of the company.

John Smith sensed something wrong. "Boys, it's time to be after shooting that fellow," he said, but the man put spurs to his mount and galloped into a thicket and out of sight before anyone could train a gun on him. Smith sent a scout ahead, and the band proceeded silently, in single file, toward the old mission.

IN THE THREE DAYS SINCE THURSDAY, February 25, when Travis had dispatched his last two couriers to Gonzales and Goliad, a curious monotony had set in. There were no further attacks on the scale of Thursday's, though at dawn on Friday the Mexicans had made a charge on the east side of the fort, where the corral walls were low; fine sharpshooting and a blast of grapeshot repelled them without further problem. Over the next few days there was only the near-constant, but not particularly destructive, bombardment by the Mexican artillery—complemented by the occasional nocturnal serenade by the battalion bands, no doubt to prevent a good night's sleep for the defenders—or a musket volley accompanied by enough shouting to simulate an attack. Travis ordered his gunners to respond to the enemy's shelling only occasionally, to save ammunition. Every day he sent out parties in search of wood, though without much success—the Mexicans also had sharpshooters, and the parties dared not venture far from the Alamo walls.

The nights were cold, around forty degrees, and the strong wind made it worse. Green Jameson kept his crews working hard day and night on repairs to the walls, particularly the weak area on the north, and on the well in the main courtyard. There were not enough defenders to man the walls in shifts, so most of them slept at their stations, their guns by their sides, though between the Mexican serenading and the intermittent feints against the fort, their slumber was fitful and shallow.

Though the weather, the lack of sleep, the unrelieved diet of beef and cornbread, and the constant exhaustion were taking their toll, the men's spirits were still high. They expected reinforcements any day, from Fannin and his four hundred men in Goliad or the Texian army that was surely gathering in Gonzales. Morale was surprisingly strong, and two natural leaders boosted it even further.

When Bowie had realized the extent of his illness, he insisted that he be moved away from the Alsbury sisters and the rest of the garrison before it spread to them. A couple of his men carried him to a room in the building adjacent to the main gate. As he left, he reassured Juana: "Sister, do not be afraid. I leave you with Colonel Travis, Colonel Crockett, and other friends. They are gentlemen, and will treat you kindly." Anna Esparza and some of the other women staying in the church took over his care. Though Bowie was still in the throes of his sickness, he was occasionally lucid, and during those times he would have some of his men carry him to the long barracks, where he would talk to the people there and remind them that Travis was now their commander.

And Crockett, popular with everyone, encouraged the men constantly. Somewhere he had got hold of a fiddle, and during lulls in the fighting and bombardment he played tunes on it. A Scotsman named John McGregor had brought his bagpipes with him, and occasionally he and Crockett would engage in a musical contest, competing to see who could make the best music, or the most noise. McGregor always won so far as noise was concerned, remembered Captain Almeron Dickinson's wife, Susanna.

On Monday, the weather changed, with a warmer wind blowing in from the west. Except for another Mexican battalion moving their bivouac to the fields east of the Alamo, a quarter mile away, there was little action. Some of the men took potshots at *soldados* in the distance when they approached rifle range, and killed one a couple of hours after sunset.

Around midnight the wind changed direction again, this time from the north. The rebels watched as the cavalry regiment to the east and one of the infantry battalions moved out, marching down the Goliad road—no doubt, those in the Alamo assumed, to intercept Fannin and his men.

A few hours later there was a shot from the walls that roused rebels from their blankets. A sentry had fired at a group of men approaching the fort. Moments later the wooden gate on the western side of the lunette swung open and the big redhead, John Smith, rode in followed by thirty-two men from Gonzales. The sentry's shot had lodged in the foot of one of the riders, but the injury was a slight one. There was much rejoicing as friends and family greeted each other. It was only a reinforcement of thirty-two, but they were good men, many of them veterans of the battle of Béxar, and they told of more on their way, riding to Gonzales from all points. If those reinforcements arrived before the rest of the Mexican army, the rebels might have a fighting chance. Counting effectives and the hospitalized, there were about two hundred men in the garrison—and enough coffee to last them another week or so.

FOURTEEN

"Devlish Dark"

In this war you know that there are no prisoners.

GENERAL SANTA ANNA

For years afterward, *bexareños* would claim that Crockett killed the first *soldado* of the siege, at a range of two hundred yards, and barely missed Santa Anna himself while he was surveying the Alamo in preparation for an attack. The Mexicans learned to keep at a good distance when a tall man in buckskin stepped up on the parapet or lay down on the roof of one of the buildings along the walls.

But the constant confinement, the growing fatigue, the lack of sleep, were taking their toll. There had been no major troop attacks by the Mexicans since the twenty-sixth, though the bombardment continued each day, from early morning until the light dimmed. Although they had not lost a man, the hospital was full—between the casualties from the battle of Béxar and assorted ailments, there were few empty cots, and the overflow had spread down to the first floor of the old *convento*. The thirty-two men from Gonzales had provided a fresh boost in morale. But soon reality set in. Thirty-two more guns were nowhere near the several hundred needed to make an effective defense. Where was Fannin? He and his three hundred should have arrived by now.

Even the perpetually sunny David Crockett was beginning to worry. "I think we had better march out and die in the open air," he said several times during the siege. "I don't like to be hemmed up."

Crockett's statement was rooted in personal experience. During the Creek War, at the Battle of Tallushatchee, he and a group of men had set fire to a house with forty-six Indian warriors trapped inside. The structure, and everyone in it, had burned to the ground. The next day the charred corpses were scattered all across the village, and the hungry soldiers had eaten potatoes—"the oil of the Indians we had burned up on the day before had run down on them," remembered Crockett in his autobiography—from the cellar of a nearby house. The grisly incident had made a lasting impression.

Susanna Dickinson heard Crockett voice his concern more than once. But he was not the only one who felt that way—the little jockey, Henry Warnell, told her something similar, and others surely felt the same. The confinement and the constant reminders of their likely fate were taking their toll on minds as well as bodies.

In the meantime, the overstretched garrison did its best to maintain a routine of sorts. The sentinels had to remain alert, but most of the men still slept at their posts, despite the addition of thirty-two fresh troops. Each evening, a few pickets made their way outside the walls to ditches about seventy yards out, where they shivered in solitude and tried to stay awake so as to alert the fort to any assault under darkness. Green Jameson kept his fatigued crews working through the night in a desperate attempt to bolster the battered north wall with dirt and timbers. And every night the Mexican sappers moved their trenches closer to the Alamo, though they were still several hundred yards away, and the Mexican bands continued to periodically burst into martial music that seemed to announce an attack.

Susanna Dickinson had been overwhelmed upon first entering the compound. Mrs. Esparza had brought her some food that first night. But soon Susanna was helping the other women cook for the men, grinding the corn and cooking it into cakes and tortillas, and roasting the beef. More than two hundred people consumed quite a bit of food each day. In a week or two there would be no more beeves, leaving only corn to eat — or horse meat. Fortunately the well in the courtyard was productive, being so close to the river, so there was plenty of water. Susanna also assisted in the hospital, where Dr. Pollard needed help with his charges, almost three dozen sick and wounded defenders. The good doctor was working tirelessly, but without proper medicines there was little he could do. The Alsbury sisters also attended to the injured. And Angelina, Susanna's fifteen-month-old, charmed everyone, including Colonel Travis, who had a young daughter of his own he had never seen.

Sometimes, between bombardments, Susanna would even make her way up the wooden ramp to the platform atop the church's eastern end to visit her husband. From there she could see the Mexican cavalry to the east. She also met the other artillerymen in her husband's mess, and got to know them. A man from Nacogdoches named Jacob Walker spoke to her of his own four children and his wife, Sara. Another gunner, a tall, dark-haired, eighteen-year-old named William Malone, had not been in Texas long. After a night of wild drinking, and unable to face his stern father, he had run away from his family home in Georgia. The elder Malone followed him to

New Orleans, hoping to persuade him to return to his sorrow-
ful mother; she had recently lost a younger daughter and could
hardly bear losing another child. But William, whether moved
or not by his sister's death, had already taken passage on a
boat bound for Texas, to enlist in the cause. His father returned
home to report his failure. William had managed to write but
one letter to his mother since his arrival in Texas.

At night, when the temperature dropped near freezing, the
women and children in the sacristy burrowed into their blankets and hay and families huddled together for warmth until
the early sun began to melt the night's frost.

The morning of Tuesday, March 1, the cavalry regiment
returned up the Goliad road, seeming none the worse for wear.
Clearly, they had not run into Fannin, which led, again, to the
inevitable question: Where was he?

It was cold all day, but there were clear skies overhead. The
Mexican bombardment continued. To conserve the good powder, Travis directed Captain Dickinson to limit the artillery
response, but sometime during the cannonade, the rebel gunners fired two shots into town, aiming toward the Yturri
house, at the northwest corner of Main Plaza, where a good
deal of activity could be observed. One crashed into the plaza,
the other scored a direct hit.

Wednesday was more of the same—near-constant shelling
by the Mexican batteries but little return fire from the Alamo's
cannon, save the eighteen-pounder's signal rounds, which Travis had told couriers he would set off at morning, noon, and
evening to let others know they still held out. The Mexican
battalion to the east moved their camp to the north side of the
fort, near the tree-covered trail along the *acequia*.

Thursday dawned cold and clear with no wind. About
eleven a.m. a shout came from sentinels on the east walls of
the fort. A lone rider had been spied galloping toward the

Alamo from the hills north of the old powder house on the Gonzales road. As he approached, someone recognized him as James Bonham, and by the time he reined in his horse and turned into the entrance, the gate was open. He entered the compound before a shot could be fired. A crowd gathered round him as he dismounted.

He brought news that cheered the garrison — a message from Robert Williamson, Travis's good friend, who was in Gonzales organizing volunteers. The letter was short, but filled with encouragement. After mentioning sixty men who had set out for Béxar from Gonzales — Albert Martin's thirty or so must have been some of them, and another group of thirty must have tried, without success so far — he had written:

> Colonel Fannin with 300 men and four pieces of artillery has been on the march toward Bexar three days now.... Tonight we await some 300 reinforcements from Washington, Bastrop, Brazoria, and S. Felipe and no time will be lost in providing you assistance.

Williamson had signed his letter "your true friend," and added a PS: "For God's sake hold out until we can assist you."

Travis read the letter carefully. If Fannin had set out on February 27, five days previous, he should have arrived in the vicinity before Bonham. Clearly, something was amiss. But at least reinforcements from Gonzales would soon be on the way — indeed, they might already have left, if the three hundred troops from nearby communities had reached the town as expected.

The news that help was on the way was heartening. It appeared that the garrison might be saved, at least long enough to put up a good fight. In the meantime, they were desperately low on cannon and rifle powder, and ammunition for the rifles and muskets, so their only response to the steady bombardment was a few cannon shots and occasional rifle fire. In the meantime, the Mexicans began work on another battery to the north, less than a hundred yards away.

ON SUNDAY, FEBRUARY 28, the day after leaving Gaona, Duque's column had been joined by General Martín Perfecto de Cós and his small group. Returning with Cós to Béxar was Captain José Juan Sánchez. They marched east with Duque the next morning.

José Enrique de la Peña had been put in charge of the rear guard. A frigid norther enveloped the area that day, followed by a thick snowfall the next day that slowed the column's progress. Just two days before, de la Peña had been glorying in the beauty of Leona Creek: "As one explores it the soul expands and fills with joy...the most delightful feelings follow one another to converge all at once and leave the recipient in a state of sublime ecstasy," he wrote. Now a plethora of problems plagued him, from chasing stray mules and reloading them to the burial of a *soldado* of the Toluca battalion who had succumbed to the frigid weather. But the column trudged on, and at twilight on Wednesday, March 2, they crossed the Medina River and spent the evening there by the water. They were only twenty miles from Béxar—a short day's march. That night a captain of the *granaderos* died of severe gastrointestinal pain: there had been no doctor to attend to him. Duque's column had made good time on their forced march, but a toll had been paid. These deaths and others cast a further pall over troops already cold, weary, and hungry.

A courier rode into camp soon after dark with a message from Santa Anna: Cós was ordered to continue to Béxar that night, so the exhausted general and his aides pushed on. At

Leon Creek, eight miles from town, they could see what resembled a fireworks display—artillery exchange between the Mexican battery near Main Plaza and the rebels in the Alamo, across the river. They reached Béxar at eleven o'clock, after covering fifty miles that day. None of them did much more than find a place to bivouac, wrap themselves in a blanket, and fall asleep.

The next morning was cold, about forty degrees, and blessedly still—the norther they had struggled through only days before was just a memory. After breakfast with General Ramírez y Sesma, Santa Anna expressed a desire to review the camps and batteries. With a small party he crossed the river at ten o'clock, accompanied by Cós and Sánchez, who marveled at how needlessly His Excellency exposed himself to enemy fire. Ramírez y Sesma, Sánchez noticed, took great pains to avoid exposure to the slightest possibility of enemy danger.

The rebels did not show themselves on the walls or parapets. A few hours later, Santa Anna ordered a bombardment that lasted until the news was announced of General Urrea's decimation of a rebel force at San Patricio five days earlier. The San Fernando church bells rang out, and some of the battalion bands began playing. In the middle of all this, the reinforcements under Colonel Duque began entering the west side of town.

The soldiers of Duque's column who had brought dress uniforms had donned them before leaving the Medina River. By five o'clock that afternoon they marched through the streets of Béxar amid the celebration. During the lull, rebels could be seen on the walls of the Alamo, which stood on ground slightly higher than the town.

THE MEN HAD BEEN DISCUSSING Bonham's news when the sounds of bells ringing, men cheering, and band music from town had brought more Texians to the ramparts on the west side to see what was going on. Travis spent some time watching the troops entering Béxar from the west. Then he walked to his quarters and began another letter. The arriving *soldados* strengthened the Mexican army significantly. An all-out assault was clearly brewing, and imminently, especially since the new battery erected just a few hundred yards northeast of the fort—along with the trench by the *acequia,* which was even closer—moved nearer the Alamo each night. Even without heavy siege guns, which could arrive any day, a cannon fired at that distance could inflict severe damage to the weak north wall. Another blood-red banner raised in the Mexican camp above them was a constant reminder of the fate Santa Anna intended for them.

As the sun disappeared in the west, Travis lit a candle and dipped his quill. Addressing the letter to the president of the convention, he summarized the events since his last lengthy report of February 25, and the current situation.

> The spirits of my men are high, although they have had much to depress them. We have continued for ten days against an enemy whose numbers are variously estimated at from fifteen hundred to six thousand.... A reinforcement of about one thousand men is now entering Bejar from the west, and I think it more than probable that Santa Ana is now in town, from the rejoicing we hear. Col. Fannin is said to be on the march to this place with reinforcements; but I fear it is not true, as I have repeatedly sent to him for aid without receiving any....I look to the colonies alone for aid; unless it arrives soon, I shall have to fight the enemy on his own terms....

I hope your honorable body will hasten on reinforcements, ammunition and provisions to our aid, as soon as possible. We have provisions for twenty days for the men we have; our supply of ammunition is limited. At least five hundred pounds of cannon powder, and two hundred rounds of six, nine, twelve, and eighteen pound balls—ten kegs of rifle powder, and a supply of lead should be sent to this place without delay, under a sufficient guard.

If these things are promptly sent and large reinforcements are hastened to this frontier, this neighborhood will be the great and decisive battle ground. The power of Santa Ana is to be met here, or in the colonies; we had better meet them here, than to suffer a war of desolation to rage in our settlements.

He ended this missive, too, with "God and Texas!—Victory or Death!"

On another sheet of paper he wrote to a friend, Jesse Grimes, a convention delegate whose eighteen-year-old son, Albert, was a volunteer in the Alamo: "Let the Convention go on and make a declaration of independence, and we will then understand, and the world will understand, what we are fighting for....If my countrymen do not rally to my relief, I am determined to perish in the defense of this place, and my bones shall reproach my country for her neglect." His grandiose sentiments were purposeful: Travis knew almost every message he sent would be made public and would likely be reprinted and distributed widely.

He drafted two final letters. The first was to his intended, Rebecca Cummings, and for her eyes only. The second, scrawled on a scrap of yellow wrapping paper, was just a short note of two sentences to David Ayres, who was caring for Travis's son, Charles.

> Take care of my little boy. If the country should be saved, I may make for him a splendid fortune; but if the country be lost and I shall perish, he will have nothing but the proud recollection that he is the son of a man who died for his country.

The indefatigable John Smith volunteered to take the missives through the enemy lines to Gonzales. The earlier couriers had carried few letters besides those of Colonel Travis, but now other men, upon hearing that Smith would leave that night, gave the big redhead their own letters to be forwarded to their families. The sight of the Mexican reinforcements, and the attendant signs that a concerted attack was on its way, had induced a sense of impending doom.

Smith knew the area better than anyone in the garrison, but over the last few days the Mexicans had tightened the cordon around the Alamo. He would need help this time, particularly since a full moon would begin rising at seven p.m. Travis ordered a sally on the north side, up toward Zambrano's sugar mill, beyond a loop of the river.

While a squad of rebels jumped the low wall in the cattle pen and moved north, engaging *soldados* and attracting attention with their rifle fire, Smith stole out the main gate and galloped toward Gonzales, disappearing into the night.

THE TWO HUNDRED MEN John Smith left behind him in the fort may not have been well trained or organized, but they were a determined bunch. Beneath the dirt and grime and stubble and rags was a group who had been tested and not found wanting. Many of them had been among the first to answer the call, to join Stephen Austin's Army of the People. These militiamen had hurried to Gonzales at the first request for help and endured much for the cause. They had marched to Béxar and remained there, in cold and rain and wretched conditions, for many weeks. They had stormed the town in the predawn hours of December 5 with Milam and Johnson and Grant, running through the dark cornfields and streets to gain a tenuous foothold on the well-fortified town held by the Mexican army, a much larger, better organized, and better equipped force, battling house by house and room by room for five grueling days.

Some of the colonists had left then, when Cós had surrendered and marched his eleven hundred soldiers out of Texas — gone home to their families and farms. The war was over; they could return to their lives, at least until spring.

Most of the volunteers from the United States, such as the Greys, were young men with no homes to return to. They had left their homes for Texas in response to the call for aid and arrived weeks later to assist their Texian cousins in the ousting of a despot — much as their fathers and grandfathers sixty years before them had rebelled against George III. They saw this cause as similar, the parallels too strong to ignore: a tyrannical dictator running roughshod over the rights of his subjects and violating the covenant accepted by the immigrants and residents alike, whether Anglo or Tejano. Taxation without proper representation, and a complete lack of a representative political system upon the dissolution of the state congresses...the abrogation of the most basic of civil rights, including the absence of trial by jury and the writ of habeas corpus...military occupation that threatened to increase dramatically...the insistence that the colonists deliver up their arms — such burdens these sons of 1776 found intolerable.

So these men had come to Texas to fight for liberty, and also to gain the land that would make them truly free men, earning their living independent of any other and providing a better life for themselves and their families. And they thought these things worth dying for.

The American Revolution had been the first great uprising of modern times, its principles so just and honorable, its conduct so sound and admirable, that a wave of revolution inspired by the American colonists had swept across Europe and the civilized world. It was a movement still finding entire nations of converts in countries such as Greece and Poland.

Americans were beseeched for assistance to these causes, and they had responded. Now their own brothers and sons and cousins and friends and neighbors, their own blood, were fighting for the same cause right next door. And all across the country, from New England to the newest state, Missouri, rallies were held to raise money and soldiers for Texas and its liberty, and thousands of men had answered the call.

Little more than five decades after Americans had secured their freedom, the word "liberty" remained far more than an abstract term, a right taken for granted. Liberty or death, as Patrick Henry put it, represented the American stand on the subject, and in 1836 the cost of freedom paid for with human lives was still vivid in the mind of every citizen and the memory of many. The word represented one of the basic rights every man was entitled to by birth. And the rebels believed passionately, just as Thomas Jefferson had written in the Declaration of Independence, that legitimate political authority rested on the consent of the governed, who retained the right to withdraw their consent and change their government if it threatened those inalienable rights it was formed to protect. As Texians saw it, that was exactly what Santa Anna was in the process of doing.

Linked to this new concept of liberty, this idea of truly free men, and essential to its core, was landownership. Its importance went beyond the desire for riches, or large-scale exploitation of resources in the pursuit of progress. Suffrage, the right to vote and elect representatives, that most essential component of a republic, was even in the United States initially confined to property owners; land meant power. While that requirement had gradually been eliminated in all but a few states, the mindset remained. Too, it was a time, a world, an existence, based on an agrarian way of life—eight of ten men worked the land. To own land in 1836 was viewed by all as an essential condition of liberty. A man without land was nobody.

Eight of the Alamo's defenders were Tejanos who had bravely decided to join the colonists in their rebellion—they, too, were outraged by Santa Anna's actions. But like the great majority of Americans at the time, the rest were of Anglo-Saxon stock. Most of the men in the fort were Scots-Irish whose Scottish ancestors had fought for their freedom from the British at Stirling and Bannockburn, and then fought the Irish at the same time they were marrying and breeding with their women. A dozen or so were Englishmen whose forefathers had defeated the French at Agincourt and Crécy, and beheaded their own king for aspiring to tyranny. And for those who were American-born, 1776 was no such distant memory; there were veterans of that struggle still living. At least fifty of the defenders proudly claimed fathers or grandfathers who had participated in the Revolutionary War. No, whatever else happened, these men would back down from no one.

There were other factors involved. Most of the men, established settlers and fresh volunteers alike, hailed from the contiguous southern states, and many of them considered slavery an accepted part of the order of things. The defense of slavery was at best an underlying cause, not a prime factor, in the Americans' desire to aid their countrymen in gaining their liberty. For that is how they considered their Texian cousins—as Americans, still. But few of the Texian colonists actually owned slaves, and those who did were able to reconcile their adherence to that institution with their belief in the basic rights of man, just as their revolutionary forefathers had. Many colonists considered Mexico's antislavery law hypocritical, given the country's system of peonage, which was used primarily to man the huge haciendas in the south of Mexico. Its victims, who numbered in the tens of thousands, endured many of the same conditions as slaves did: hopeless indebtedness, corporal punishment, and severe penalties for escape; they were even sold as commodities.

Almost all the men from the southern states claimed Scotland and Ireland as their hereditary birthplaces, many of them only one or two generations removed from the old countries. Journeying west—for freedom, for land—was in their blood. And they were fighters. Fighting for these things, and other, sometimes lesser things, too—family, honor, justice, or even sport—was also in their blood. Truth to tell, some of the men had walked or ridden hundreds of miles just for a good fight.

Most of them were not trained soldiers. Save for the New Orleans Greys, they wore no uniforms, and their arms were their own, a mixture of muskets, rifles, shotguns, pistols, tomahawks, and blades. In almost every respect they did not meet the definition of an army. But in a letter to Sam Houston, Green Jameson had summed up their most important quality: "They have all been tried, and have confidence in themselves."

That confidence would soon be tested.

ONE HUNDRED AND EIGHTY MILES to the east, in the town of Washington, other express riders had left with important news of their own.

On the afternoon of March 1, forty-one convention members—enough for a quorum—had met in the unfinished building a quarter mile up from the Brazos River landing. There were no doors, nor was there glass in the windows— only cotton cloth, which did little to keep a below-freezing north wind from entering the unheated hall. "Everybody [was] shivering and exclaiming against the cold," noted an observer. But spirits were high, and compared to the previous Texian political conventions, this one was a model of brisk efficiency. They quickly came to order and elected officers, then began conducting the business at hand. Delegates spoke disapprovingly of the quarrel between the governor on the one hand and the lieutenant governor and the General Council on the other, and refused to hear complaints from either side, calling on each only for their official information.

They wasted little time authorizing a committee of five, headed by George C. Childress, to draw up a declaration of independence. Even the most pacifist among them understood that the time for reconciliation with Mexico was past. The next morning Childress and his committee presented their document, modeled closely on the United States' 1776 declaration. (Childress, an attorney and former newspaper editor, had clearly begun preparing it before he arrived and likely wrote it himself.) The draft was read aloud, and in less than an hour, with no changes made, it was approved.

Only one man rose to speak to the declaration: Sam Houston, representing the citizens of Refugio. His arrival on February 29, fresh from a successfully negotiated treaty with the Cherokees, "created more sensation than that of any other man," wrote an observer; a delegate remembered his appearance as "that of an Indian chief. A piece of red flannel with a hole cut in it for his great head to go through for a shirt with a buckskin over-shirt and buckskin breaches, so eager to fight the massacrerer of the Alamo that he had no time or taste for dress." Houston was waiting for clear authorization from this new legal body before assuming military command; he wanted no repeat of the underhanded shenanigans and schemings of the interim government that had tied his hands so badly. He had learned a hard lesson; this time he would not leave without complete authority over all forces, volunteer or regular. Houston may have been eager to fight Santa Anna, but as yet he had no official title under this new government, and thus no power to command anyone.

That afternoon, Houston's forty-third birthday, enough misspellings were found in the declaration that the signing was delayed until a corrected version was ready. The next day, March 3, every delegate present—including three prominent Tejanos—signed the document, officially declaring independence. Five copies were ordered, to be sent to Brazoria, Béxar, San Felipe, Nacogdoches, and Goliad, and express riders left town for those destinations, announcing the news along the way.

The mood in Washington improved when a courier rode into town with the news that 350 men under James Fannin were on the march to Béxar, and others were on their way. And the latest from Travis—his letter of February 25, which had arrived the previous day, March 2—reported that a Mexican attack had been fought off, and the Alamo garrison was holding its own. The Alamo, it was believed, was safe for the time being. In any case, Houston and many of the other delegates in Washington went on a two-day drinking spree— eggnog fortified with spirits, the libation of the moment—to celebrate the new nation.

WHILE THE TAVERNS OF THE VILLAGE on the Brazos reeled to the merriment of their representatives, the Alamo defenders shivered through another chilly night, another chilling dawn. For them, eggnog was a distant memory, and even coffee now counted as a luxury. But they had cause for celebration, too, though they could not know it. The nature of their struggle had changed. They had been fighting for independence all along. Now, at last, it was official.

FIFTEEN

"His Excellency Expects That Every Man Will Do His Duty"

Our honor, now outraged,
In blood and fire shall be assuaged.

JOSÉ JUAN SÁNCHEZ

Before he left Béxar on February 11, garrison commander James Neill had told his men he would return within twenty days. He would not keep that promise, though for the best of reasons.

After visiting his family in Bastrop and tending to the illness there, Neill had traveled east to San Felipe to see Henry Smith. Though deposed, Smith was still acting as though he were governor, and performing what limited duties he could until he removed to Washington to attend the convention. Neill found him just before he left, and on February 28, Smith gave Neill $600, part of the $5,000 donated to Texas by Harry Hill of Tennessee, for the use of the Alamo garrison. With funds finally in his hands, Neill headed back to Gonzales. A week later Smith would write, "Much confusion prevails among our volunteer troops on the frontier, but, by using much vigilance, I have now got Bexar secure" — sad evidence of his ignorance of the situation 180 miles to the west of him.

Neill arrived in Gonzales a couple of days after the March 1 departure of James Bonham and immediately began purchasing supplies, including much-needed medicines, for his command. Major Robert Williamson had just left to organize his rangers in Bastrop, leaving Neill as the ranking officer in charge. When John Smith made it into town at three p.m. on March 4 with Travis's latest communiqué and reported the size of the Mexican army after the arrival of three more battalions, it was clear that they would need a sizable number of troops to ride to the rescue of the Alamo garrison. Smith, wrote Dr. John Sutherland, "announced that if one hundred men could be raised, that they would be sufficient to sustain the fort, at least until others could reach it, and that he would start with them, as guide, as soon as they could get ready." But one hundred men could not be convinced to ride to Béxar. Fifty would be ready soon, Smith was told, but by the next day the number had dwindled to twenty-five, who would be ready the next day. By Sunday, March 6, they had still not left, though the town was full of men.

Alerted by express riders sent out from Gonzales and San Felipe, companies of colonists within a few days' ride were finally mobilizing and making their way to the small village on the Guadalupe. About two hundred had gathered in Gonzales by the time Neill arrived, but none of them continued on to Béxar. Reports of the size of the Mexican army there went up to six thousand *soldados,* including plenty of the feared lancers. Texians generally derided the bulk of the Mexican army as little more than unwilling, untrained conscripts who marched in chains with whips at their backs, but the cavalry was accorded respect. It would be suicide to attempt to break through the lines with only a couple hundred volunteers.

SOME MEN, however, had left for Béxar since Albert Martin led George Kimble's and Thomas Jackson's companies out of Gonzales on February 27. Not long after Martin's departure, a courier rode into town with a message from James Fannin at Goliad. He had sent an advance party to Seguín's hacienda on the San Antonio River to gather provisions and beef. Fannin and three hundred men would be right behind them, marching to reinforce the Alamo. They would rendezvous with any troops from Gonzales at the Cibolo crossing.

Despite his injuries, Sutherland rode out the next morning, February 28, with Horace Alsbury, who had just returned from the east, and ten other men. They crossed the Guadalupe and waited on Juan Seguín and two dozen of his Tejanos—after his escape from the Alamo on the night of February 25, Seguín had obtained a horse at a nearby ranch and headed south toward Goliad. But he only made it less than halfway there before running into Fannin's foraging company; they had just left Seguín's ranch, where they had collected beeves and corn. Seguín sent an express rider with Travis's oral message to Fannin—beseeching him to march immediately to the Alamo's rescue—and then rode east to Gonzales after gathering some of his men.

They met Sutherland and Alsbury a few days later, and with a force of about sixty men proceeded toward Béxar, to the Cibolo crossing. When Fannin arrived, they would join up with his battalion and ride to the Alamo. Perhaps they could even overtake Captain Martin and the Gonzales men. They reached the Cibolo shortly after dark on Monday, February 29—and just missed Martin's group of thirty-two, who had left a short while ago, at sunset. Sutherland's men bivouacked and waited for Fannin.

But Fannin never came. Sutherland and Seguín waited two days, until the turn of midnight on Wednesday, March 2, then headed back toward Gonzales. They rode into town to find another letter from Fannin, written soon after his previous one, with devastating news. After a council of war, he and his officers had decided to remain in Goliad. There were good reasons for the decision, but it meant almost certain death for the men in the Alamo.

FRIDAY, MARCH 4, dawned windy and cold, in the low forties, in Béxar. The Mexican batteries began their bombardment early. The rebels remained out of sight, not returning fire for several hours, and then delivering only one or two shots. "It is only known that there are men in the Alamo by the cannon and rifle shots that they fire," wrote Captain Sánchez in his diary, "and because no more is heard than the blows of hammers and various obscenities."

In the afternoon, Santa Anna's council of war convened in his quarters at the Yturri house on Main Plaza. Virtually every officer of the rank of lieutenant colonel and above was present: Generals Ramírez y Sesma, Castrillón, and Cós, and Colonels Almonte, Duque, Amat, Uruñuela, José María Romero, Mariano de Salas, and a few others.

As the high command gathered around the detailed map of Béxar and the Alamo prepared by Lieutenant Colonel Ygnacio de Labastida, chief engineer, His Excellency "expounded on the necessity of making the assault," remembered José Enrique de la Peña, who was not present but heard about it later. Everyone agreed on that point—but the question of *how* to make the assault invited more discussion and evolved into one of timing and methods. A few of the officers, including Castrillón, Uruñuela, and Romero, argued for waiting until Gaona and his twelve-pounders arrived—they were expected on Monday, the seventh—and blasting the Alamo walls until a significant breach was made, probably in eight or ten hours. Others agreed with Santa Anna that the assault should be made immediately; after all, the likelihood of rebel reinforcements arriving increased every day.

When someone brought up the subject of prisoners, the discussion became heated. Santa Anna reminded them that there would be no prisoners. Someone cited the example of General Arredondo's conduct in 1813. "He had hanged eight hundred or more colonists after having triumphed," recalled de la Peña, "and this conduct was taken as a model. General Castrillón and Colonel Almonte then voiced principles regarding the rights of men, philosophical and humane principles which did them honor." But their appeals failed to sway Santa Anna. As announced in secretary of war Tornel's December decree, captured rebels were to be considered pirates, and treated as such. They would be executed.

The meeting lasted into the night. When His Excellency finally called it to an end, and his commanders returned to their quarters, no official decision had been made. As was his habit, Santa Anna would make up his own mind, but anyone who had heard him speak knew what that decision would likely be. Earlier that day he had dispatched a courier with a reply to General Urrea concerning the twenty-one prisoners taken at San Patricio. He had reminded the general of Tornel's decree, and added, "An example is necessary, in order that those adventurers may be duly warned, and the nation be delivered from the ills she is daily doomed to suffer." His

Excellency wanted to set his own example by punishing the rebels in Béxar, and he wanted to do it now. One of the maxims of his hero, Napoleon, stated that a general's first duty was to maintain his honor and glory; the safety and preservation of his troops was a secondary consideration. If Mexican soldiers were to die in the taking of the Alamo, so be it.

Outside, once darkness settled on the area, a company of sappers advanced a battery along the *acequia* north of the Alamo. By the next morning, a few of the heavier artillery pieces had been moved there—just two hundred yards from the battered north wall, close enough to inflict serious damage and perhaps effect a breach. The rebels responded with *balas rojas*—hot shot—cannonballs heated to red-hot temperature before firing in order to ignite flammable targets, such as powder magazines. Though no serious damage was sustained, Colonel Ampudia, for one, was outraged: the hot shot, he wrote, was "in violation of the rights of man and of war."

The next day, Saturday, March 5, was warmer, and the skies clear. By midday it had reached sixty-eight degrees. Santa Anna summoned his staff and commanders again and to no one's surprise announced his decision: he would not wait for the siege artillery, but would attack before dawn the next morning. The artillery barrage would stop early in the afternoon, and that night there would be no musical serenades or attacks, feigned or otherwise. With any luck, the exhausted rebel garrison would be caught by surprise and the troops could reach the wall before the formidable cannon of the Alamo responded. His staff proceeded to hash out the details of the assault, and at two p.m. His Excellency's orders, prepared by his secretary, Ramón Caro, and signed by General Juan Valentín Amador, were issued.

Almost every one of Santa Anna's top officers would participate. "The time has come to strike a decisive blow upon the enemy occupying the Fortress of the Alamo," began the orders. "Consequently, His Excellency, the General-in-Chief, has decided that tomorrow, at 4 o'clock a.m., the columns of attack shall be stationed at musket-shot distance from the first entrenchments, ready for the charge, which shall commence at a signal to be given with the bugle from the Northern Battery." The assault would consist of four columns, which would attack from four directions. The greatest force, however, would be concentrated against the further-weakened north wall, which had suffered severe damage that day from the newly advanced battery.

General Cós, with General Amador as his second, would lead the first column, from the northwest, comprising 350 men—all but one company of the Aldama battalion and three line companies of the San Luis Potosí battalion. For Cós, it would be a chance to redeem and repair his badly damaged reputation after his surrender to a smaller rebel force in December.

From the north, Colonel Duque, with General Castrillón his second, would lead the second column: seven companies of the Toluca battalion, and three line companies of the San Luis Potosí battalion, a total of four hundred men. They would compose the critical mass aimed at the ravaged north wall.

The third column, comprising the twelve *fusilero* companies of the Matamoros and Jiménez battalions—about 430 men—would attack from the east, against the formidable battery atop the Alamo church and the vulnerable horse and cattle pens. Colonel Romero would lead them, with Colonel Salas ready to take over if necessary.

The fourth column, from the south, would be the smallest, comprising 125 *cazadores*. Colonel Juan Morales, with Colonel Miñón his second, would lead these elite riflemen against the fort's entrance. "The brave Colonel Morales," as General Urrea described him, was a popular and active commander who had proven himself most recently at Zacatecas. He had specifically requested Miñón, who had also gained glory there.

The four-hundred-man reserve, stationed near the northern battery, would be led by His Excellency himself if called into action, but until then would operate under the direct command of Colonel Amat. These troops would be some of the best—Amat's Zapadores, and the veteran *granadero* companies of the five other battalions.

General Ramírez y Sesma would direct the 375 horsemen of the cavalry regiment, stationed on the east side of the Alamo and charged with preventing the escape of any rebels. If any fled from the fort, his lancers would be ready for them. The cavalry was already commanded by the able General Ventura Mora. His Excellency may have been punishing the general for his tentative actions of February 23—or at least making sure he would not direct any of the assault columns in the same manner.

The only battalion commander not to take part would be Colonel Uruñuela, who was sick. Santa Anna was not happy with Uruñuela's claim of illness, but he would deal with it after the battle. In the meantime, there was much work to be done.

As the orders filtered down through the ranks, the troops readied themselves for battle. Characteristically, His Excellency's directives had covered every detail, down to the proper wearing of chin straps, shoes, and sandals. There were also scaling ladders to be constructed, for the lead units of each column would hurl them up against the fortress walls. Over the following few hours, bayonets were sharpened and straightened, muskets and rifles were readied, cartridges and balls and flints and powder were prepared. While the *soldados* and their line officers busied themselves with these basic practicalities, the principal commanders examined the points of attack.

That afternoon, Francisca, the wife of Ramón Músquiz,

left her house and walked a few doors down to call on Santa
Anna at his quarters on Main Plaza. Her husband, the former
political chief of Béxar, was an avowed centralist, but the
Dickinsons had boarded at her house before the siege, and she
and Susanna had become warm friends. Doña Músquiz knelt
before His Excellency and begged him to spare Mrs. Dickinson and her child, Angelina. After some hesitation, he promised her that no women in the Alamo would be harmed
intentionally.

BY TWILIGHT ON MARCH 5, most of the Mexican preparations had been made, and the troops turned in as ordered.
They would rest until midnight. Some would sleep. Others
would be kept awake by a rumor spreading through camp that
the rebels had mined both the exterior and interior of the fort,
so that attackers and defenders would blow up together. Even
if there was no truth to it, men were bound to die. "Each one
individually confronted and prepared his soul for the terrible
moment, expressed his last wishes, and silently and coolly
took those steps which precede an encounter," remembered de
la Peña. With the other Zapadores, he had originally been
assigned to the reserve column, which might or might not
see action. But over the previous week Colonel Duque had
taken a liking to the young officer and his enthusiasm, and he
had asked Santa Anna personally for de la Peña to be reassigned to his command. The request had been granted. The
excited subaltern would get no sleep that night.

Captain Sánchez would accompany General Cós, who
directed him to march at the head of the column. Sánchez
received the news with mixed feelings—he was not convinced
that the assault was necessary. "Why is it that Señor Santa
Anna always wants his triumphs and defeats to be marked by

blood and tears?" he wrote in his diary that night, and ended with: "God help all of us!"

Accompanied by Colonel Almonte, Santa Anna had spent several late hours overseeing the troop movements and preparations for the assault. It was almost three a.m. when the two returned to His Excellency's quarters. The general was in a foul mood, and threatened to run Almonte's cook, Ben Harris, through with a sword if he did not bring some coffee quickly. Ben was a dapper five-feet-tall gentleman whose services Almonte had taken on in New York two years before. He had been a steward on board several American vessels, and had participated in his share of frontier adventures, but he had never served a president before, and he stepped lively.

AS THE SUN WENT DOWN and the Mexican bombardment ceased, Travis called for his men to assemble in the main courtyard.

During the previous night, the Mexican battery to the northeast had advanced down the *acequia*, to within two hundred yards or so. The artillery at that position, although not consisting of large siege guns, was now close enough to inflict devastating damage to the north wall. Cannonballs consistently crashed through the timber-and-earth-reinforced adobe, and no amount of hasty repairs would have much effect.

In the last few days the situation had become even more critical. Several factors indicated an impending attack. Thursday's reinforcements had almost doubled the Mexican army surrounding them. And the inexorable forward movement of the northern battery, and its relentless pounding, meant a breach could not long be delayed. The men could even make out *soldados* constructing ladders, a sure sign of assault if there ever was one.

Inside the fort, conditions had worsened. The supply of beef was almost gone: feeding two hundred people twice a day required a great deal of meat. That would leave a good supply of corn, but an undernourishing diet. The lack of medical supplies left Dr. Pollard helpless in the face of the various illnesses afflicting the men in the hospital. The poor sanitation—the proximity of the outdoor latrines and the cattle and horse pens, the inadequate facilities for washing and cleaning, and cooking food thoroughly—had no doubt increased the cases of diarrhea, dysentery, and typhoid.

Still, the garrison's spirits were higher than might have been expected—Crockett continued to work hard at keeping them so. Sometimes he would visit the women and children, huddled around their fire, and warm his hands and attempt a few words in Spanish. Bowie, however, was in bad shape, and no longer had himself carried out to visit his men. In one of his better moments he again reminded his men to consider Travis their commander. But most of his hours were spent in delirium, his great chest heaving with the effort to breathe between racking coughs.

The entire garrison was exhausted by the almost constant bombardment during the day and the constant vigilance dictated by the surprise sallies, musket volleys, and music performed by the Mexican battalion bands during the night. Fortunately, the cannon fire had stopped that afternoon. But there was still no sign of help, or word of it. It appeared that the men in the Alamo had been forgotten by the nation they were fighting for.

Travis stood before the men and laid out the situation candidly. He expressed his disappointment that no relief force save the thirty-two men from Gonzales had arrived, though messages received over the past several weeks had promised reinforcements and predicted their timely arrival. He admitted the slim chance that any such forces would reach them before the Mexican attack. He expressed his desire to die for his country rather than surrender—the red flag waving over Béxar made clear the fate of any prisoners—and to sell his life as dearly as possible.

He drew his sword and with its point traced a line in the dirt before him. Then he told them that each could make his own decision, but that he wished every man who would stay and die with him to step across the line. Ben Milam had designated a similar line in rallying the Texian troops before the assault on Béxar.

The first man to do so was one of Captain William Carey's gunners, twenty-five-year-old Tapley Holland, whose father had been one of Stephen Austin's first settlers. Others followed him, even the sick and wounded who had made it down from the hospital. Bowie, on a cot, asked some of the men to carry him across. Four men did so.

Only one remained—Louis Rose, a swarthy old Frenchman from Nacogdoches, where he had lived since 1826, supporting himself through various jobs, such as log cutter and hauler. He had never married, and lived a mostly solitary life, sometimes drinking whiskey to excess, occasionally finding comfort with a woman. When the talk of revolution heated up, he had heeded his old soldier-of-fortune spirit and headed west in October 1835. After the taking of Béxar, he had stayed behind with Neill when Grant and Johnson had led most of the men south toward Matamoros.

Some called the fifty-year-old Rose "Moses," for his age. As a young man, he had fought under his idol, Napoleon, and survived the brutal retreat from Moscow in the icy Russian winter. But he was not ready to die now. He could speak Spanish decently—better than his broken English—and his skin was dark enough to pass for a Mexican. He might be able to escape, with some luck, if he left before the near-full moon rose about nine. He did not cross the line.

Upon full darkness, he scaled the low wall of the cattle pen, carrying only a satchel with his few belongings. He stealthily made his way along the north wall to the *acequia* that ran south near the west wall and followed it to the gently flowing San Antonio River. He waded across the shallow water and walked through the quiet town—to any passing *soldados,* just an old, ragged *bexareño*—and crossed the river again at the ford at the southern side of the loop. He followed the river south out of town for about three miles. Then he struck out east toward the colonies.

That evening, Travis decided on one more desperate attempt to reach Fannin and persuade him to come to their aid. When word spread that he needed another courier, several men volunteered. Travis selected a slight young man with a fleet mare: twenty-one-year-old James Lemuel Allen. He was a graduate of Marion College, near Philadelphia, Missouri, which served as a training school for Presbyterian ministers, the students paying their way by working on the school farm. With a few classmates, Allen had heeded the call for help from the Texian colonies. Upon his arrival in Texas he had volunteered for military service and been sent to Béxar.

There was no need of a written communiqué. The message was simple: Hasten to the aid of your countrymen.

And so, after nightfall, but before moonrise, Allen said good-bye to friends and comrades and mounted his horse bareback, the mare wearing only a bridle—he would need every advantage possible to outrun the Mexican patrols, including the absence of excess weight. After one last look at the Alamo courtyard, he guided his mare through the main gate and out the lunette, leaned down to hug the animal's neck, and at a full gallop man and mount thundered through the Mexican lines and headed southwest, along the San Antonio River, toward Goliad and its four hundred troops.

No one had followed Rose over the walls, but some of the Alamo defenders shared his assessment of their chances. That night, Crockett asked for those of his clothes that the women had recently washed—he expected to be killed the next day, he said, and wished to die in clean clothes in order that he might be given a decent burial. Crockett may have been joking—sometimes it was hard to tell with his dry delivery—but many of the men entrusted their valuables, mostly watches and jewelry, to the women for safekeeping. Juana Alsbury decided to give her share to Bowie's cook, Bettie, in hopes that the *soldados* would be less likely to search her. That night, for the first time, Bettie had been permitted to stay with the other women and children in the sacristy.

While making his rounds, Travis stepped into the sacristy and visited with Susanna Dickinson and her daughter. From his finger he took a gold ring embedded with a black cat's-eye stone, put it on a string, and placed it around the neck of little Angelina. And he directed Robert Evans, the tall, merry, Irish-born master of ordnance, to undertake a desperate task: if and when the fort was overrun, he should light the large store of Mexican powder in the front room of the church. With any luck they would take many more of the enemy with them when they were gone.

Jameson's work crews labored late into the night doing what they could to repair and strengthen the crumbling north wall, which in some places was irreparable. Some of the men took advantage of the lull in bombardment to snatch a much-needed break from their stations. James Bonham shared some tea with Captain Almeron Dickinson, his wife, and the other gunners in Dickinson's mess. Gregorio Esparza turned away from the convivial gathering to seek out his wife—God only knew when he might see her again. That night the couple slept in each other's arms.

Sometime after midnight, most of the exhausted men lay down at their posts and wrapped themselves in their blankets. It was cool but not frigid, and they quickly dropped off to sleep. All but a few fires died out. There was little movement in the fort, and few but the sentinels on the walls and the three pickets in the trenches outside made much of an effort to remain awake.

A few hours before dawn, Captain John Baugh, officer of the day, started on his rounds. The night was quiet — too early in the season for crickets. Along the walls, at each defender's position, lay three or four rifles and Brown Besses primed and ready. The muskets were part of the haul confiscated in December upon Cós's surrender. Some of them came with bayonets, potentially as valuable as their firepower in the fight to come. The moon, almost full, was still high in the sky, but a cloud cover obscured most of its light.

EARLIER THAT NIGHT, Mexican sergeants, with their *bastones* (wooden staffs), had moved among the enlisted men, poking them awake, ordering them to form in ranks. At three a.m. the shivering *soldados* quietly moved through the darkness toward the old mission. They crossed the river and made their way to their designated positions. They were ordered to make no noise, refrain from smoking, and leave their overcoats and blankets in camp lest they impede their own movement. Their chin straps were buckled tight — a properly secured shako could prevent one from getting his head caved in by a blow from a musket or sword. General Cós led his troops to an area about two hundred yards from the Alamo's northwest corner and the battery there. He positioned his eight line companies—since there were only four *fusilero* companies of the San Luis Potosí battalion present, both he and Colonel Duque would each assume command of two, in addition to their full battalions—close to three hundred men, in three parallel lines, each a hundred feet long and two ranks deep. The marksmen of the Aldama *cazador* company would support them as skirmishers. The other columns were deployed in a similar manner to the north, the east, and the south of the fort. The reserves under Colonel Amat waited at the north battery with His Excellency, his staff, and the battalion musicians. General Ramírez y Sesma's cavalrymen and *presidiales,* several hundred yards southeast of the fort, had spread out to encircle it from north to south, outside of rifle distance.

The *soldados* lay with their chests to the ground in the cool morning air, weapons in hand, and waited as silently as possible. Some of those in the front ranks slung their muskets over their shoulders and gripped their ladders—ten ladders in each of the first two columns on the north side. A few in Cós's column also held axes and crowbars, since there were well-fortified doors and gates and blocked-in windows here and there along the walls that might yield to a determined battering. Each man prayed to his Maker, and thought of his loved ones. Men would die in the assault, everyone knew.

At three a.m., near the cottonwood-lined Alameda to the southeast, the cavalry began saddling up. At four a.m., Santa Anna and Almonte quietly made their way across the river and around the fort to the entrenchment a few hundred yards north of the Alamo. The artillery would not be used—the danger of hitting their own infantry was too high—so the cannon there were pulled back from the embrasures to make room for Santa Anna and his staff to observe the attack. The reserves under Colonel Amat and the battalion bands were positioned nearby.

Sometime after five a.m., Mexican skirmishers crept up to

the drowsy rebel pickets stationed in trenches outside the Alamo and dispatched them without alerting the fort's sentinels. A short time later, at 5:30 a.m., Zapadores bugler José María González lifted his horn to his lips.

Two hundred yards north of the Alamo, Lieutenant Colonel de la Peña waited with Duque's column. Like most of the men around him, he could not sleep. Inevitably, his thoughts were somber: that many of those around him who were now breathing would soon be dead, and that others, badly wounded, might wait for hours before aid arrived. And he hoped fervently that the anxiety and uncertainty would end, for the blood of their dead comrades, and Mexican honor, deserved vengeance.

But he was exhausted, and suffering from lack of sleep, and his eyes were just closing when he was jolted wide awake by the bugle sounding the charge, and he and the other men around him jumped to their feet and began to run toward the Alamo.

SIXTEEN

"That Terrible Bugle Call of Death"

A horrible carnage took place.

José Enrique de la Peña

The door to Travis's quarters along the west wall burst open. "Colonel Travis," shouted officer of the day John Baugh as he ran into the room. "The Mexicans are coming!" There had been no warnings from the pickets stationed outside the fort, and the enemy was advancing upon them as he spoke.

Travis threw his blankets aside and leaped to his feet. He grabbed his double-barreled shotgun and sword, yelled at Joe to take his gun and follow him, and ran out into the Alamo courtyard.

It was just after 5:30 a.m. and still dark. To the east, behind the old *convento,* the blackness of the horizon was only barely less intense. Men streamed out of the barracks and granary building to join those who had slept at their posts along the walls. Gunners at the batteries pulled off the leather and lead aprons from their cannon and made preparations to fire canister and *langrage.* Sentinels on the parapets yelled for assistance.

Officers bellowed orders at their men. From outside the walls could be heard the rumble of thousands of pounding feet approaching the fort, and beyond that the ominous strains of the Mexican bands playing the tune they had inherited from the Spaniards, who had borrowed it from their Moorish oppressors: the *degüello*.

Most of the tumult seemed to be coming from the north wall. Travis and Joe ran that way and bounded up the ramp to the battery on the right center of the wall, where three cannon faced the northern approaches. When they reached the parapets and looked out through the darkness and smoke they saw hundreds of *soldados* moving toward them. The moon was low in the western sky and hidden by clouds, but the flashes of massed muskets firing illuminated the scene, aided by rockets shot up into the sky over the town.

Travis took one look and yelled, "Come on, boys, the Mexicans are upon us, and we'll give them hell!"

The gunners barely had time to sight their cannon. Then there was a blast from one of the guns and a load of *langrage* tore into the approaching Mexicans and knocked a score of them to the ground, some screaming, some silent forever. Other guns roared and dozens more fell. But some of the Mexicans had already reached the wall and were under the cannon's reach, since the gunners could not tilt them low enough. Riflemen reached over the edge of the thick wall and fired down into them, but in so doing made themselves silhouetted targets.

Travis stepped past one of the cannon, leaned over the parapet, pointed his shotgun at the men below, and pulled the trigger. At his side, his servant Joe fired his. Before Travis could pull back and reload there was a salvo of musket fire and a slug slammed into his forehead and knocked him back against the gun carriage, lifeless. His shotgun fell into the crowd outside the wall.

Just moments into the battle, the garrison was stripped of its commander. Joe stood transfixed for a moment, then turned and ran down the ramp and across the courtyard to the stone house they had left just minutes ago. Once inside, he locked the door.

THE THREE HUNDRED *SOLDADOS* of the Toluca battalion rushed through the grass and brush toward the north wall. Most of them hurdled the three-foot-wide *acequia,* but in the darkness a few fell into the cold water and then heaved themselves out, staggering to their feet to follow their comrades. Cries of "Viva Santa Anna!" and "Viva la república!" mixed with screams of agony as one of the cannon on the wall roared; meanwhile, jagged pieces of *langrage* ripped into half a company and rifle fire from the rebels on the walls found its mark. At the front of the column, José Enrique de la Peña found himself surprisingly calm, until a hunk of metal slammed into Colonel Duque's left thigh and he tumbled to the grass. Even as some of his men trampled over him in their haste to reach the safety of the wall, Duque yelled at them to keep moving forward. Some of them did, but others stopped when they saw their commander fall. In the semidarkness, *soldados* who had never faced enemy fire panicked; some discharged their muskets from the waist to avoid the gun's nasty kick and sent their shots too high, while others in the rear ranks found targets in their fellow infantrymen charging ahead of them. There was another cannon blast, and Captain José María Herrera, leading the Toluca *cazadores,* fell dead, along with half his sharpshooters. In the field outside the north wall lay scores of men. "Our columns left along their path a wide trail of blood, of wounded, and of dead," recalled de la Peña.

The young officer knelt by Duque's side a moment, then

stood and began making his way through the tangled ranks toward the battery northeast of the fort, where Santa Anna, his staff, and the reserve waited. General Castrillón, Duque's command replacement, must be summoned, thought de la Peña. He fought his way against the tide of men as cannon fire continued to smash into the column, shredding the Mexican lines.

At the sound of the trumpet General Cós, at the head of his first rank, stood and yelled "Arriba!" and the 350 men in his column got to their feet and in tight formation began to follow him toward the northwest corner of the fort and the battery there. Though they were still out of range, some officers ordered their men to begin shooting, so they started firing their weapons while they were still moving. Not many of them had hurdled the *acequia* near the wall before a barrage of cannon and rifle fire ripped into the ranks and swept away most of the men in a single musket company of the Aldama battalion. Another volley of grapeshot took a dozen more. But the three lines remained in good order, and some of the *soldados* reached the wall, stumbling over flattened cannonballs that had crashed into it and fallen to the ground.

The cannoneers and riflemen above them continued to rip into the men in the rear. On Cós's left flank, stray musket fire from Duque's column hit some of the *soldados* there. They were taking too many casualties. Cós ordered an oblique to the right that his men executed smartly, sweeping past the large pecan tree at the corner, and soon they were gathered along the west wall trying to gain entry to the fort. Using picks and axes, they began to bash at the bricks and stones blocking in the windows of the buildings on the west side, and especially at the doors in the rear of the houses. Above them rebels on the roofs leaned over and fired down at them, but in so doing they presented inviting targets, outlined against the cloudy sky, and some muskets—and the more accurate Baker rifles used by some of the *cazadores*—found their marks. A few of the ladder bearers reached the wall, threw the ladders up against the stone and adobe, and held them firm while others began climbing. The walls were lower here, less than ten feet.

On the east side of the Alamo, Colonel Romero's column began advancing against the compound. But the *acequia* there had overflowed into a wide pond, shallow but mucky, and that combined with point-blank blasts from the cannon atop the rear of the church forced them to veer to the right, past the horse and cattle pens. Rifle fire from the roof of the *convento* and the small battery in the cattle yard raked their ranks and pushed them toward the northeast corner, where they slammed into Duque's column and joined the mob of men there. Some *soldados* had begun to climb the crude timber revetments reinforcing the crumbling north wall, since only one ladder was in use—the others had been lost or broken—but so many tried that they knocked others down. The few who reached the top were met with bayonets and pistol fire and fell back into the crowd below. "Disorder had already begun," remembered de la Peña. "Officers of all ranks shouted but were hardly heard" over the "Vivas" and cries of "Muerte a los Tejanos!" and the constant rifle fire from the rebels on the parapets above them. The two columns quickly disintegrated into a disorderly mass. Forward progress halted under the wall.

Meanwhile, to the south, Colonels Morales and Miñón led their 125 men up through the Plaza de Valero toward the Alamo's main gate. But heavy fire from the lunette's cannon and rifle volleys from the palisade forced them to the left, and they ran through the blackened *jacales* ruins toward the shelter of the only structure still standing in the area, a stone house near the fort's southwest corner. Thirty feet away was the large cannon on a platform atop an old building. Morales gathered his skirmishers and prepared to assault the battery. The lunette's cannon faced east and south, so for the moment they were not under artillery fire.

Safer still, in the darkness a few hundred yards away, a quiet force waited: Ramírez y Sesma's cavalrymen. Poised in a long arc east and southeast of the fort, they sat on their horses and watched the infantry's advance, a pageant illuminated by the flash of rifle fire and the flames of the rebel cannon.

CROCKETT AND HIS "TENNESSEE BOYS" — Micajah Autry, Daniel Cloud, and the rest of Captain Harrison's Tennessee Mounted Volunteers — were assigned to defend the wooden palisade running between the church and the gatehouse. But the deadly fire of their long rifles likely helped deflect the *soldados* moving up through the Plaza de Valero, and soon there were no more Mexicans in sight. The bulk of the attack was clearly directed toward the weakened north wall. Following Crockett's lead, most of Harrison's men left the palisade area and hurried in that direction to aid the defenders there. But there was also activity along the west wall, and Crockett turned that way. Some of his companions followed him. He jumped into the battery outerworks on that side and, using Betsy, began shooting at the troops fighting their way in along the length of the wall, firing, reloading, and firing along with his comrades as fast as he could.

Inside the church sacristy, the women and children huddled in the corners, terrified, praying and comforting each other. From time to time the entire room shook, and they looked up at the arched ceiling above them as dust and loose plaster showered down. They could hear the shrieks of the wounded and dying, the uninterrupted roar of rifles and muskets, and the deafening, constant thunder of the Alamo artillery, especially the three cannon almost directly above them.

With the help of Bonham, Walker, Esparza, and his other gunners, Captain Dickinson kept his three pieces atop the church blasting away until the battalions had moved north toward the animal pens and out of his artillery's field of fire. Riflemen near them and on the *convento* roof continued to pour down fire on the *soldados* as they hurried toward the northeast. Now they could only hear the sounds of slaughter at the north wall. Then the question was, should they stay by their guns, or grab rifles and run to the aid of their comrades? Most of the men remained at their posts.

Somewhere out of sight to the north, the Mexican bands stopped playing, and the notes of another charge blared from a single bugle.

FROM THE ENTRENCHMENT NORTHEAST OF the Alamo, Santa Anna observed the progress of the battle, following events by the bright bursts of rebel artillery and the smaller flashes of firearms. "The scene offered by this engagement was extraordinary," he wrote later. The coordinated assault had gone off smoothly, the columns attacking more or less at the same time. But the rebels had responded more quickly than expected and put up a stubborn resistance, and now it appeared that the attack was wavering. It was time to send in his elite troops. He gave the order for the reserves to charge, directing his staff to accompany them. The Zapadores led the way, behind Colonel Amat and General Castrillón, followed by the veterans in the five *granadero* companies.

A blast of shrapnel from a rebel cannon ripped into them,

knocking a dozen Zapadores down along with half their officers. But they forged ahead and reached the wall before another load of grapeshot could find them and pushed as close as they could to the earth-and-wood revetment, where the cannon could not touch them. Somehow de la Peña fought his way through the crowd to find General Castrillón and inform him of Colonel Duque's injury. Meanwhile, some members of Santa Anna's staff pushed through the mass of men at the northeast corner and worked their way down the wall to its weakest area. Setting an example, the staff officers began climbing the ladderlike timber braces reinforcing the wall. One of the first to reach the top of the twelve-foot wall was fifty-five-year-old General Amador. Close behind him were General Ampudia, Lieutenant Colonel Marcial Aguirre, Colonel Esteban Mora, and Lieutenant Colonel Rómulo Díaz de la Vega, de la Peña's good friend. Inspired by the sight of their commanders on the ramparts, the *soldados* rallied and began following them over the wall and overpowering the rebels who remained there.

On the west side, the men of Cós's column spread along the north end of that wall and continued to batter its vulnerable points—the barricaded windows and embrasures. Those who had tools used them; for those who did not, gun butts served as mallets—anything to open up a breach even one or two of them could squirm through. When they finally broke through one of the wooden doors, men began pouring into the Alamo courtyard.

At the southwest corner, Morales and Miñón led a bold assault on the eighteen-pounder there. The fierce battle at the north wall drew some of the rebels away, leaving a thin line to defend the big gun. After picking off the silhouetted riflemen, *cazadores* ran up to the wall, threw their two ladders against it, and stormed the battery. Dozens of men followed them—overpowering the rebels on the platform before they could spike the gun to render it useless—ran down the ramp, and fought their way into the courtyard. Some of them rushed the main entrance, overwhelming any resistance there and opening the main gate and the lunette's timber gate to admit the rest of the column.

Now augmented by the Toluca battalion and the reserves, some of Romero's men followed over the north wall. Others scaled the low walls of the cattle pen and then the horse corral, smashing through a narrow postern at the north end of the granary building to swarm into the fort.

His Excellency continued to observe the progress of the battle. Never lacking in personal courage, he had planned to lead the reserves into action himself, but now he changed his mind, deciding to remain at the northern battery. There was no doubt anymore that the defenders of the Alamo were about to be obliterated.

FROM BEHIND SANDBAGS, defenders on the *convento* roof fired through the thick gray smoke into the Mexican troops on the eastern side even after they climbed into the animal pens. But when *soldados* began streaming into the plaza from every side, those who could left the rooftop to seek shelter below in the second line of defense—the fortified structures along the east side, the granary turned barracks, and the *convento*—slamming and locking the doors behind them. They began firing through the loopholes and windows into the hundreds of Mexicans entering the courtyard.

Not everyone made it even to such temporary safety. A few chose not to try. As the Mexicans overran every position around the perimeter, one knot of rebels remained in place to make a stand in the outerworks along the west wall: David

Crockett and his comrades. And closed doors were no defense for James Bowie. Gasping and too weak to rise from his cot, he had been left alone in his room near the main gate.

A cloud of pungent gray smoke hung over the old mission compound. Rebels and *soldados* howled and swore as they fought now at close quarters with pistols, knives, and swords. With no time to reload, rifles and muskets became clubs and bayonet-tipped muskets deadly lances as the Mexicans took full possession of the courtyard. Many of the remaining defenders made it into the *convento* or the church, but some stood their ground and made isolated stands facing the *soldados* until they were overwhelmed. De la Peña could not help but admire one robust blond *norteamericano* as he fired, ran back a few steps while loading, turned, and fired again, until he finally fell.

The gunners at one battery on the west wall also refused to leave their post. As the Mexicans poured into the fort, these rebels wheeled their cannon around and managed to twice fire down into the enemy before falling to a fusillade of musket fire.

On the platform above the church nave, Almeron Dickinson and his gunners took up their rifles and began firing into the enemy soldiers in the main courtyard. Dickinson ran down the ramp and back through the church into the sacristy, where the terrified women and children cowered in corners. Some of the children hid under the hay they had slept on. Dickinson looked for Susanna and Angelina in the dark and finally found them.

"Great God, Sue, the Mexicans are inside our walls!" he said. "All is lost. If they spare you, save my child." He embraced and kissed both of them, drew his sword, and ran out the door.

Moments later, sixteen-year-old Galba Fuqua from Gonzales burst into the room, pale and haggard. He ran up to Mrs.

Dickinson and tried to tell her something. But his jaw was shattered and blood was flowing from his mouth, and she could not understand him. He held his jaw with his hands and tried again. She still could not make out what he was trying to tell her. He shook his head in frustration, turned, and left.

Outside the church doors, more than sixty defenders had retreated into the fortified area behind the low wall and were taking stock of the situation as they continued to fire into the horde of *soldados* in the courtyard. The fort was clearly lost. A withdrawal into any of the buildings would merely prolong the inevitable. But there were no Mexican troops in sight before the palisade, and the quiet darkness beyond was inviting. Someone opened the two-foot-wide wooden gate at the east end of the palisade, and the men shoved through, forced an opening in the thick branches of the *abatis,* and ran toward the hills to the east. Gonzales and the colonies lay in that direction. Some of them might make it—past the old powder house on the hill, the brush became thick woods, and the Salado River was just a few miles further.

THE HORSEMEN OF THE DOLORES regiment and supporting *presidiales,* almost four hundred strong, had watched and listened to the carnage for half an hour. Now, in the dim morning light, they saw a line of rebels leave the fort through an opening in the *abatis* fronting the palisade, then jump the *acequia* and head for the thicker brush up the hill.

As soon as this was brought to his attention, General Ramírez y Sesma ordered a company of Dolores horsemen after them. Only twelve men in each company carried lances; the remainder brandished sabers. The lancers swooped down on the rebels and "stabbed them to death within moments," wrote the general. Another group burst through the *abatis,* and Ramírez y Sesma waved a second company forward. These *norteamericanos* took refuge in the *acequia* and put up a good fight, but the general ordered thirty-two more men into the fray. Once the rebels fired their rifles, the lancers were upon them before they could reload; their nine-foot spears made short work of them. One was chased down by two riders. He shot and killed the first, but the second speared him while he attempted to reload. Another managed to find a large bush and burrow under it, out of the reach of a lance. He needed to be shot, and that was quickly done. Within minutes, more than sixty rebel corpses lay scattered in the fields east of the Alamo.

ONCE INSIDE THE FORT, General Amador led some men to the battery at the northwest corner. The rebels had evacuated the area so quickly that they had forgotten to spike the cannon. The general ordered the gun there dragged down the ramp and swung around to face the buildings across the plaza. Then he cleared everyone out of the way. His makeshift gun crew loaded the cannon and blasted solid shot into the doors one by one. General Ampudia followed suit with another gun. *Soldados* from the Matamoros and Jiménez battalions, commanded by Colonel Romero, stormed each room, firing through the doorway and then entering bayonet-first, killing every man they came across. Some of the defenders poked their bayonets through a hole or a door with a white cloth to signal surrender—a few even used white socks. When soldiers entered those quarters, other rebels met them with pistol shots and bayonets. Enraged Mexicans killed them all. Amid the chaos, a Tejano named Brigido Guerrero begged for his life, and somehow convinced his captors that he had been held prisoner against his will. He was allowed to live.

Soldados scrambled up the stone stairwell of the *convento* and into the hospital, where they dispatched the bedridden rebels there. In a darkened room below, where fifteen more patients lay, some of the ill or injured fired from their pallets. A group of Mexicans hauled a cannon close to the front door, loaded a double charge of grapeshot and canister, and fired twice. They entered to find all fifteen dead.

On the roof, three Zapadores were killed trying to capture a blue banner waving from a pole atop the *convento* that read FIRST COMPANY OF TEXAN VOLUNTEERS! FROM NEW-ORLEANS. José María Torres, a determined young Zapador sublieutenant, watched them die and decided he would try to reach the foreign flag. He climbed to the rooftop and ran to the flagpole through thick rifle fire. He managed to lower the banner and raise the red, white, and green of his battalion's standard before a rebel round found him. He fell, mortally wounded.

Pandemonium now took over throughout the courtyard as controlled ferocity degenerated into bloodlust. De la Peña was horrified as soldiers "fired their muskets indiscriminately at friend and foe alike," he wrote later. "It seemed as if the furies had descended upon us; different groups of soldiers were firing in all directions on their comrades and on their officers, so that one was as likely to die by a friendly hand as by an enemy." Some of Morales's men jumped into the old, dry *acequia* ditch to avoid being shot by their comrades. The noise was deafening. Officers shouted orders that were either ignored or not understood. De la Peña found General Cós and advised him to order the men to stop firing. Cós grabbed a Zapador bugler named Tamayo and gave the command. No one paid any attention to the call.

The last bastion left was the church. A cannon was wheeled around, and solid shell blasted into the facade. The thick stone walls withstood the large cannonballs, but soon the oaken front doors were obliterated. A horde of attackers rushed through. A moment later, a hail of musket fire hit the rebels below and above on the artillery platform. One Tejano defender made it into a side room off the nave before a bayonet ended his run. Dozens of *soldados* jumped over the sandbags and ran up the long wooden ramp to finish off the rest of the defenders. A tall, black-haired man with a flaming torch in his hand was moving toward the powder magazine at the front, evidently aiming to fire it. He was quickly disposed of. In a matter of minutes every single rebel was shot or stabbed until he was dead, and the floor of the Alamo church was slippery with blood.

IN A HOUSE AGAINST THE northern end of the west wall, the Navarro sisters remained hidden, occasionally peeping out to gauge how things were going, while the sounds of battle roared outside. When the din abated somewhat, and they realized the Texians had been overwhelmed, Gertrudis carefully opened the door. *Soldados* ran up and swore at them, ripping Gertrudis's shawl from her shoulders. Juana stood holding her year-old son tightly to her bosom, fully expecting to be killed any minute. One soldier was demanding her money when a *norteamericano* she knew only by his last name, Mitchell, ran up and tried to protect her. The soldiers bayoneted him until he fell dead at her feet. A young Tejano defender pursued by several Mexicans grabbed her arm and tried to hide behind her. "His grasp was broken," she recalled, "and four or five bayonets plunged into his body, and nearly as many balls went through his lifeless corpse." Then they broke open Mrs. Alsbury's trunk and made off with her money and clothes, and the watches of Travis and other officers.

A Mexican officer walked in, asked some rapid questions,

and told the women to stay there. Another officer came in and told them to leave before a nearby cannon was fired. Finally Gertrudis's brother-in-law Don Manuel Pérez arrived and told one of Jim Bowie's Negro servants, a woman, to take the sisters to their father's house in Béxar.

A few doors down, in Travis's quarters, Joe, too, remained hidden. He had been firing at the *soldados* through a porthole in the door, but had stopped when the battle cooled. Now he heard a Mexican call out in English, "Are there any Negroes here?"

Joe said, "Yes, here's one," and opened the door and stepped out into the courtyard and its chaos. Two soldiers ran toward him. One jabbed him in the side with his bayonet and drew blood. The other fired his musket at him, but only a single buckshot ball pierced Joe's side. Neither wound was serious. The officer who had yelled through the door restrained the soldiers, then escorted Joe to a slender, somewhat tall Mexican in plain black clothes—"like a Methodist preacher," remembered Joe. It was Santa Anna, ready to survey the site of his victory.

The general asked him to point out the bodies of Travis and Crockett. Bowie was well known, and others had already identified the big *norteamericano*. They had found him in the room to the right of the main gate, where he had been killed in his bed. Stories would quickly begin to circulate among the *bexareños* that he had been armed with loaded pistols and managed to kill two *soldados* before he was dispatched. It was the sort of legend Bowie attracted, and one that no other version of his death would ever eclipse.

Joe led the general and some members of his staff between the dead bodies of Mexicans and rebels to where he had left his master on the north wall. Along the way, he noticed a Negro woman lying dead between two cannon—shot accidentally, he guessed, while running across the courtyard. On the north wall platform, Travis lay against one of the cannon there, dead, a hole in his forehead.

The Honorable David Crockett was located with some of the other Tennessee men in the small lunette midway down the west wall, the bodies of several *soldados* scattered around them. Crockett's coat and rough woolen shirt were soaked with blood—either a musket ball or a bayonet had ripped into his chest. He had sold his life dearly, dying in the open air, as he wished—and, as he put it in the final words of his last letter, "among friends."

In the church sacristy, the women and children were waiting, fully expecting to die, when Jacob Walker and three other unarmed gunners burst into the room, chased by several Mexican soldiers. The men were shot and stabbed until thoroughly dead. Then a Mexican officer walked in, asking for Mrs. Dickinson. Susanna, clutching Angelina, identified herself.

In excellent English, the officer said, "If you wish to save your life, follow me."

He led them through the church. Near the door she saw the body of Robert Evans, an extinguished torch in his hand, killed in his attempt to fire the powder magazine. Outside, they walked toward the main gate. Before they reached it, there was the report of a gun and Susanna felt a sharp pain in her right calf. A musket ball had pierced her skin there. She made it outside, where the officer—who introduced himself as Colonel Almonte—helped her into a buggy. She and her daughter were taken to the Músquiz house, on Main Plaza, her home before the siege. As Mrs. Músquiz met her at the door and helped her in, Susanna learned how her friend's visit to Santa Anna had saved her life.

The other women were told to gather their children and belongings and leave the fort. On their way outside, a *soldado* watched as Bettie, Bowie's cook, walked past. All the valuables Juana Alsbury had given her—their jewelry and money, and the watches of their men—she had hidden in her skirt. The *soldado* saw a watch fob hanging down from Bettie's clothes. He ripped it away from her. Other soldiers grabbed the remaining valuables. The rest of the women and children followed Mrs. Dickinson to the Músquiz house, where they were given food and coffee.

More than a thousand Mexicans now crowded the fort. The gunfire finally died down, with only scattered musket shots, as they roamed the courtyard and the buildings, moving among the bodies to gather their wounded and begin reforming in ranks. Those rebels still alive were finished off with a musket shot or a bayonet thrust, and their corpses were stripped of clothing, shoes, and valuables.

Barely an hour had passed since the first bugle call. As the dense smoke began to lift, and the early morning light illuminated a grisly scene strewn with severed limbs, corpses—some naked, others with the burning remnants of clothes still clinging to them—and blood everywhere, a triumphant Santa Anna made his way to the front of his troops.

As His Excellency surveyed the carnage, General Castrillón approached him, followed by five rebel prisoners under guard. Castrillón explained that they had been found hiding. "He was reprimanded severely for not having killed them on the spot," wrote Ramón Caro, Santa Anna's secretary, who stood nearby. Caro watched as Santa Anna barked a command, then "turned his back on Castrillón while the soldiers stepped out of their ranks and set upon the prisoners until they were all killed." Several other officers, de la Peña among them, averted their eyes, disgusted by the barbarity of the act.

"The general then addressed his crippled battalions, lauding their courage and thanking them in the name of their country," remembered de la Peña. The response of the exhausted *soldados*, with almost a hundred of their comrades dead and at least three hundred more wounded, was less than enthusiastic. The expected "Vivas" were offered halfheartedly, and an icy silence followed. A disgusted de la Peña stepped up and called for cheers hailing the republic, then more for the valiant *cazadores* of Aldama, who had paid a heavy toll in the attack on the west wall.

Santa Anna sent for the acting *alcalde* of Béxar, Francisco Antonio Ruíz—who had spent the siege under house arrest, suspected of rebel sentiments—and several other prominent citizens. When they arrived, he directed Ruíz to round up some of the townsmen to bring carts and carry the dead *soldados* to the Campo Santo, the cemetery on the west side of town. Then he told Ruíz to show him the bodies of Travis, Crockett, and Bowie—Joe had identified the first two, but His Excellency desired stronger assurance.

As the corpses were separated and carried outside, another *norteamericano*, a small man named Warnell, was found hiding among the dead bodies and brought before Santa Anna. A Mexican staff officer, Captain Marcos Barragan—who had also found Travis's servant Joe and protected him—interceded. Warnell begged that his life be spared. Santa Anna ordered the American shot, and he was quickly executed.

After the last surviving enemy was dispatched, and all the Mexican dead and wounded had been carried out, Santa Anna ordered wood brought to burn the bodies of the rebels away from the fort. At three p.m. they began laying the wood in two large piles near the Alameda. The Texian corpses were deposited in alternating layers—a layer of wood, topped by a layer of bodies, then another layer of wood, and another of bodies—until the grisly chore was complete.

Before the *bexareños* carted all the dead away, a Béxar

presidial made a special request of General Cós. Francisco Esparza had not participated in the battle, but had remained at his home. Now he and his two brothers asked if they could search for their brother Gregorio and give him a Christian burial. Their request was granted. They found him in a room in the church, a musket ball in his breast and a stab wound in his side, and carried him to the Campo Santo, making him the only rebel to be buried and not burned.

An officer brought a few women he had gathered in town to tend to the dead and dying. They did what they could, bandaging up the wounds of some of the Mexican soldiers and comforting those who had not long to live. The floor of the church "was literally crimson with blood," recalled one *bexareña,* who remembered seeing Crockett "as he lay dead by the side of a dying man, whose bloody and powder-stained face I was washing." Another young Tejana went in and located her dead sweetheart. She wiped the grime from his face, crossed his hands on his chest, and placed a small cross on it. When told to leave, she dipped her handkerchief in his blood, placed it in her bosom, and left.

Santa Anna returned to his quarters in town, summoned Caro to bring pen and paper, and immediately dictated his official battle report. It was addressed to secretary of war José María Tornel. "Victory belongs to the army," he began, "which, at this moment, 8 o'clock A.M., achieved a complete and glorious triumph that will render its memory imperishable." After briefly describing the battle, he summed up the results, albeit with one major embellishment: he tripled the death toll of the enemy to make the victory all the more dramatic, and help to justify his decision to assault the Alamo:

> More than 600 corpses of foreigners were buried in the ditches and entrenchments, and a great many who

had escaped the bayonets of the infantry, fell in the vicinity under the sabres of the cavalry.... We lost about 70 men killed and 300 wounded, among whom are 25 officers. The cause for which they fell renders their loss less painful, as it is the duty of the Mexican soldiers to die for the defense of the rights of the nation....

The bearer takes with him one of the flags of the enemy's battalions, captured today. The inspection of it will show plainly the true intention of the treacherous colonists, and of their abettors, who came from the ports of the United States of the North.

The blue banner of the New Orleans Greys was used to prove that American pirates were aiding the Texians, but the rebels' constitutionalist flag—the Mexican tricolor, with its two stars representing Coahuila and Texas—was destroyed. Such a symbol offered no benefit to Santa Anna, who had dismantled the 1824 constitution and still faced opposition in several Mexican states. He wanted no reminder that the vanquished had considered themselves faithful citizens of their adopted country.

About five p.m. the two funeral pyres, one on each side of the Alameda, were lighted. The bodies, American, Texian, and Tejano, burned for hours, and the large pillars of smoke could be seen for many miles around. Several *bexareños* stood and watched. A few Mexican officers did also, transfixed by the somber scene.

Among them was Captain Sánchez. He, for one, found that pride in this victory was tempered by sadness. The cost had been bitter. He lamented the loss of so many good soldiers— and the gutting of some of the army's best battalions. In the face of a furious and desperate rebel defense, the long-suffering *soldados* of the Army of Operations had fought valiantly. They had paid a stiff price. In addition to the seventy-five killed outright, many of the wounded would soon be dead for lack of proper medical attention. (Only one ineffectual army surgeon — who had remained with the badly wounded from the battle for Béxar in December — was on hand.) As Sánchez and the other staff officers crossed the river to return to town, they passed hundreds of injured men. "Soldiers mutilated and torn stumbled into camp to be bound up," remembered one *béxareño* who was pressed into service. "Dozens and scores were dragged in with gaping wounds through which their life-blood trickled."

Later that night, while His Excellency made plans to move west and strike at the heart of the *norteamericano* colonies, Sánchez ruminated on the day and opened his journal. "With another victory like this one," he wrote, "we may all end up in hell."

SEVENTEEN

The Bleeding Country

Gonzales is reduced to ashes!

SAM HOUSTON

Soon after she was taken to the Músquiz house, Susanna Dickinson asked if she could visit the Alamo. Francisca Músquiz told her it would not be permitted, as the dead bodies—those of her husband, Almeron, and many of their friends—were being burned. As confirmation, she pointed out the column of smoke rising from the Alameda, which occasionally wafted eastward, the stench of charred flesh permeating every part of the city.

On Monday, the day after the battle, Susanna and the other women and children were escorted across Main Plaza to El Presidente's quarters. Francisca Músquiz had provided food for them and some measure of comfort. Now the final disposition of these prisoners would be decided.

Santa Anna interviewed them all, one family at a time. He gave each widow two silver pesos and a blanket after they swore allegiance to him. Eliel Melton's widow, Juana, was terrified that she would be punished for her recent marriage to one of the *norteamericanos,* and begged Anna Esparza not to mention it; Mrs. Esparza promised not to. The only two who escaped the humiliating interview with the general were the two daughters of Santa Anna's old friend Angel Navarro.

Colonel Almonte translated when it was Susanna's turn. Santa Anna seemed taken with the pretty Angelina. He said something in Spanish, and Almonte told Susanna that the general wanted to take her and her child to Mexico with him. Aghast, Susanna protested. Then the general expressed a wish to adopt her little girl—he would see that she was well educated, like his own children. Susanna had no husband, he pointed out, and no money, and would be incapable of caring for her child as Angelina deserved, but as his daughter, "she would have every advantage that money could procure."

Never, said Susanna—she would "rather see the child starve than given into the hands of the author of such horror," she announced, and listened while Almonte pleaded her case. Then she was escorted back to the Músquiz house before a decision was made. She had been numb with shock to this point, but when she realized the grimness of her situation, and possible plight, she broke down. For several days her grief and fear were beyond control.

Almonte finally persuaded Santa Anna to allow her to leave with her child. A few days later, she and Angelina were placed on a pony, given a mule with blankets and food, and started on the road to Gonzales. Almonte's diminutive servant, Benjamin Harris, rode with her, "to assist her safe"—though Ben may have decided to cast his lot, at least for the present, with the Texians rather than risk being run through with a sword, as Santa Anna had threatened the night before the assault; one never knew when His Excellency might change his mind. His extensive experience as steward would guarantee him a job in New Orleans, or elsewhere.

The two rode past the Alamo, passing between the tall cottonwoods lining the Alameda. On each side Susanna could see a large pyre of bones, ashes, charred flesh, and wood—one sixty feet long, the other eighty. Her husband's remains were in one of them.

Just beyond the Salado River, four miles east of town, someone raised his head from the tall grass beside the road and spoke, giving her a fright. It was Travis's slave Joe, also released by the Mexicans.

Joe had been quizzed thoroughly by Santa Anna and Almonte—about Texas, the state of its army, and the number of Americans in it, among other things. Joe told him there were many American volunteers, and that more reinforcements from the United States were expected. The general told Joe that he had enough men to march to Washington if he chose—not the small village on the Brazos but the U.S. capital itself. Joe was made witness to a review of the Mexican troops, and was told there were eight thousand *soldados* on hand. That was about twice as many as there had been when the rest of Santa Anna's army straggled into town in the days following the battle.

Joe and Ben took turns riding as they followed the Gonzales road over the prairies and through woods. Fortunately the cold weather had abated, and though the nights were cool, the days were sunny and warm. At Cibolo Creek, they caught up with a large Mexican force led by General Ramírez y Sesma, which had marched from Béxar that morning. The general gave Ben a proclamation from His Excellency to deliver to the American colonists. It was in English, written by Almonte, and addressed "to the inhabitants of Texas." The missive justified the severe actions of the Mexican army, guaranteed just punishment for the traitorous pirates, and assured citizens that the rights of the innocent would be respected. "The supreme government has taken you under its protection, and will seek for your good," he wrote. "The good have nothing to fear."

The next day, Susanna and her companions pushed on ahead of the column. About midday on March 13, just east of where the road crossed Sandies Creek near the Castleman place, they spied three horsemen in the distance. Joe took to the tall grass and urged Mrs. Dickinson to do the same. He was sure they were Comanches. Susanna refused—she would as soon perish one way as another, she told him.

The three mounted men were not Comanches. They were scouts Deaf Smith, Henry Karnes, and Robert Handy, sent by General Houston to reconnoiter. After hearing her story, Karnes, who was on the fastest horse, galloped back to Gonzales to deliver the news and Santa Anna's proclamation. Smith and Handy escorted the party eastward at a slower pace.

WEARING A RED CHEROKEE BLANKET coat over his buckskins and a feather in his hat, Sam Houston had left Washington on the afternoon of March 6, two days after the convention confirmed him as commander in chief of the army—regulars, volunteers, and militia. That morning, while the delegates were eating their breakfast, an express rider arrived with a letter from Travis dated March 3. While word spread and citizens gathered at the doors to listen, the missive was read before the assembly. When Travis's report of the size of the Mexican force surrounding him and his passionate plea for reinforcements was finished, some of the representatives and citizens doubted the veracity of the dispatch. Only when a delegate familiar with Travis and his handwriting pronounced it genuine did the gathering accept it wholeheartedly.

Someone leaped to his feet and proposed that the entire body adjourn and ride to Béxar. His suggestion was greeted with cheers, and almost every member of the convention announced his intention to immediately depart for the front.

Sam Houston stood and implored them to stay, stressing the importance of finishing the job they had begun. Without a constitution and some sort of government, they would be considered little more than pirates, or an unorganized—even criminal—revolutionary movement. Much-needed American and international support would be minimal. Houston would leave as soon as possible to organize the army and ride to the aid of the Alamo garrison.

The delegates saw the wisdom of his argument and returned to their seats, where they were joined by Samuel Maverick, who had finally arrived in Washington. Houston left that afternoon with a few companions, riding south to San Felipe, then west to Burnham's Crossing on the Colorado. He remained there for two days, much of his time spent dispatching express riders in several directions with orders and requests for reinforcements and supplies. He sent a courier to Fannin with orders to proceed to the west bank of the Cibolo and await the arrival of the forces in Gonzales. At last report, James Neill was there with a small group of men preparing to return to Béxar. But there was no point in rushing to Béxar until a sufficient number of volunteers had mustered.

Two days later, at four in the afternoon of March 11, Houston rode into Gonzales. He found Neill in charge of about three hundred volunteers bivouacked on the southern edge of the town. Most of them had only arrived in the last two or three days. Many were without arms. A few days earlier, on Monday, March 7, John Smith had finally headed west, leading another group of well-armed and well-provisioned volunteers, almost thirty men, with the goal of reinforcing the Alamo.

Houston assembled the men in town. He apprised them of the convention's work and read the declaration of independence, his commission, and his orders. Then, remembered one young colonist, "he delivered a short speech setting forth in stirring words the complications of troubles that threatened our Republic, finally closing with a rousing appeal to every Texan to be loyal and true in that hour of need and peril." They would begin organizing the army the next day.

Around sunset, two Tejanos rode into town from the west. Their names were Anselmo Vergara and Andres Barcena, and the news they brought was dire—"disagreeable intelligence," as the man assigned to record their interview put it. They described the March 6 early-morning assault by Santa Anna's army in sufficient detail, including the most important: "All within the Fort perished."

Despite some contradictions in the men's accounts, Houston suspected the story to be true—Travis had told John Smith that he would fire the eighteen-pounder every morning, noon, and evening as a signal that his garrison still held the Alamo, and no cannon had been heard since early Sunday. To prevent panic, Houston publicly pronounced the two Tejanos spies and ordered them taken into custody. But he could not prevent the spread of the news of the catastrophe to the townspeople of Gonzales. The town had contributed significantly to the Alamo garrison, and if the news was true, a dozen or so women, several of them expecting, were left widowed. "For hours after the receipt of the intelligence," remembered a witness, "not a sound was heard, save the wild shrieks of the women, and the heartrending screams of the fatherless children."

The story was further corroborated later that evening with the return of John Smith and his group of volunteers. On

Tuesday night, they had reached Cibolo Creek, twenty-four miles from Béxar, and bivouacked. A heavy silence raised Smith's suspicions. On Wednesday morning, he sent eight men as scouts toward the town. They had only proceeded six miles when they ran into an advance force of Mexican cavalry, which pursued them. They managed to gallop back to the Cibolo and warn Smith in time for the entire group to escape.

Houston had Captain Juan Seguín send two men to Casa Blanca, Seguín's ranch, to ascertain the truth of the story, though by now he was sure it could not possibly be false. He dispatched another express rider to Goliad with the news of the Alamo's fall and a change of orders: Fannin was to blow up the presidio there—one fort had fallen; they could not afford the fall of another—and immediately go back to Victoria, thirty miles northeast, on the Guadalupe's east bank. "The immediate advance of the enemy may be confidently expected," Houston concluded. "Prompt movements are therefore highly important." Privately, he had no confidence in Fannin, and expected no cooperation from him. He quietly made preparations to retreat with his small army to the Colorado River, which, because it was wide, deep, and swiftly running, would make a more formidable natural defensive line.

The next day was spent organizing the men and electing officers. By Sunday, March 13, Seguín's two Tejanos had not returned. But scouts Deaf Smith, Henry Karnes, and Robert Handy assured Houston that they would get within sight of Béxar, accurately assess the situation, and return within three days. They left that morning.

Sometime between eight and nine o'clock that evening, the redheaded Karnes rode into Gonzales with the news of Susanna Dickinson's approach. Her eyewitness account of the Alamo's fall served as final confirmation. Karnes also delivered more dire intelligence: according to Mrs. Dickinson, as many as two thousand Mexican soldiers were on the march eastward, and had spent the night of March 11 at Cibolo Creek. Santa Anna's army might be just hours away from Gonzales.

Two thousand regulars, including a company of the feared Mexican lancers, against some four hundred untrained and undisciplined volunteers, many of them without arms or ammunition: Houston's decision required little deliberation. "It would have been madness to hazard a contest," he wrote two days later. "By falling back, Texas can rally, and defeat any force that can come against her." Houston gave orders to immediately take up the line of retreat. He also dispatched some two dozen of Seguín's Tejanos to the ranches on the lower San Antonio River to help protect the families there from Indian depredations, and put Seguín in command of the rear guard, with orders not to leave anyone behind. Twenty of Houston's men immediately deserted, either to guard their families or to save their own skins. They would no doubt spread panic among the settlements to the east, which would make recruitment that much more difficult. But there was nothing to be done about that now.

Most of the few wagons Houston had brought with him were given to the families of Gonzales, and it was strongly suggested that they head east also, and as soon as possible. The army moved out around midnight, coming up from their campsite south of town and marching through the streets, most of the houses already empty and dark, others lit as their owners prepared to leave; the army's only remaining cart, pulled by four oxen, carried the force's meager supply of ammunition. With no way to transport their two cannon, the men tossed them into the Guadalupe.

During all this, Deaf Smith and Robert Handy rode in with Mrs. Dickinson, her daughter, Angelina, and their two companions. Wives and mothers surrounded Susanna, screaming and begging for news of their husbands and sons. She could only muster one answer: "All killed, all killed." She was escorted to the house of James Tumlinson, whose wife, Elizabeth, took her in and comforted her. The Tumlinsons' son George was with the Alamo garrison, and on the Sunday previous, they had been awakened by the rumble of distant cannon fire. When it ceased, Tumlinson had said, "Our boy is gone." Mrs. Dickinson told them of the battle, and of the death of every man in the fort. Houston came to the house and listened with tears in his eyes. Then he advised everyone to leave with the rest of the families.

He returned to his men with the proclamation Mrs. Dickinson had carried from Santa Anna, which offered a pardon to all who would lay down their arms and submit, and certain death to anyone who did not. Houston read it to the men, then threw it down and stamped on it, shouting, "Death to Santa Anna, and down with despotism!" The men joined in on the shout. Some of the men were infuriated at the retreat orders. They were convinced they could "whip ten-to-one the carrion-eating convicts under Santa Anna," as one cocky fifteen-year-old, a veteran of the battle of Béxar, would claim years later. A few of them would never forgive Houston, and would continue to criticize his every move over the next several weeks.

Left behind were ten men with orders to burn the town. "Not a roof large enough to shelter a Mexican's head was to be left," recalled one captain. A five-man squad started at each end of the town and with their torches made quick work of it. Kimble and Dickinson's hat factory...the modest hotels of Turner and Smith...the mercantile stores of Miller and Eggleston...Sowell's blacksmith shop...the unfinished log schoolhouse...all these and every residence in sight were set ablaze. Within minutes flames shot up into the sky.

In wagons, on horseback, and on foot, some leading animals

packed with their belongings, the citizens of Gonzales moved eastward, aided by the few able-bodied men left in town. "Red Adam" Zumwalt, assisted by David Kent and a few of the older boys, directed the exodus of his family and the Kents. Byrd Lockhart led his large family and others along the road he had cleared almost a decade ago. Sidney Gaston Miller Kellogg, who had lost a brother and her first and second husbands in the Alamo, carried a baby, John B. Kellogg III, born the night before. Another ten widows walked through the streets of Gonzales with their children, as had the other evacuating families, leaving all they owned except for what they could carry.

Under a moonless sky, they trudged along the San Felipe road for hours, through scattered forests of oak and mesquite and long, open prairies of sandy loam, until they could barely lift their legs. Fortunately, the night was warm. Just before dawn the army halted at Peach Creek, about ten miles from Gonzales. As exhausted soldiers dropped to the ground, and Texian families continued to straggle into camp, a bright orange glow lit up the horizon behind them. When a series of explosions was heard on their backtrail, it touched off a panic. Many feared that the Mexican army and its artillery were close on their heels. Only when someone ventured that the cause of the explosions could have been the powder stores in the shops—someone else said it might have been the whiskey barrels, or barrels of some other liquor—did the bedraggled company settle down to a fitful attempt at rest and sleep.

Ahead of them the deserters and couriers spread the word of the fall of the Alamo and the rapid advance of the Mexican army, and hundreds of families packed up and set out on the roads east, toward the imagined safety of the Sabine River and the United States border. The Runaway Scrape, as the exodus would come to be known, had begun.

*　　*　　*

IN BÉXAR, the disparate elements of Santa Anna's army finally began to arrive in the days after the battle: General Gaona's brigade on March 7, General Filisola on the ninth, Andrade and the cavalry brigade on the tenth, and Tolsa's brigade right behind them on the eleventh. That same day, units began moving out. General Morales left for Goliad to reinforce Urrea's command with two infantry battalions. He was followed by Ramírez y Sesma—with two infantry battalions, fifty cavalrymen, and two cannon—who marched east over Powder House Hill toward Gonzales and the heart of the Anglo colonies: San Felipe. His immediate goal was the destruction of any rebel units, particularly those commanded by Sam Houston. His ultimate destination, if necessary, was Nacogdoches, near the Louisiana border.

Near Santa Anna's quarters on Main Plaza, a tent was set up where various goods and supplies seized from the rebels were sold. They netted only $2,500—the best of the items had already been taken by His Excellency and his favorites.

For the town's residents, life gradually returned to something close to normal. Although the soldiers occasionally took possession of materials and foodstuffs, there was no large-scale sacking, rape, or murder, as had happened in Zacatecas the previous May. So most of the *bexareños* who had fled before Santa Anna's arrival gradually began to return to their homes, finding the town even more battered and shell-scarred than before. Others remained at their houses along the many rivers and creeks in the area—memories of Arredondo's brutal retribution in 1813 were still fresh in their minds, and there were many townspeople who might reveal, to the new centralist authorities, the names of those who had cooperated with the rebels.

For his part, Santa Anna dallied with his young "bride," and planned his strategy. Though some of his officers suggested he lead a fast-moving strike force east to find Houston's army and crush the last of the rebel resistance, he felt no such urgency. The campaign was essentially over, it appeared. The three columns sweeping through Texas—Gaona to the north, up El Camino Real by way of Bastrop; Ramírez y Sesma through the central region, toward San Felipe; and Urrea to the south, along the coast—would quickly mop up the disintegrating colonists and their filibustering friends from the United States.

IN WASHINGTON, the convention had continued to work on hammering out a proper constitution, their work in the unheated hall made more comfortable by the arrival of warmer weather. It had been more than a week since Sam Houston rode out of town on March 6, in response to Travis's stirring plea for reinforcements. Since that day, there had been no further word from the Alamo.

In the afternoon of Tuesday, March 15, a man arrived from Columbia, near the coast, with the news that the Mexican army had attacked the Alamo, but had been repulsed with great loss to the enemy. "The rumor was doubted, on account of the circuitous route by which it came," recorded an observer in his diary. "All hoped it true, but many feared the worst." A half hour later, an express rider rode in from Gonzales with reports from Houston detailing the fall of the Alamo and the death of every man in it save a few Negro servants. A subsequent letter from Juan Seguín to delegates Ruíz and Navarro confirmed the news. "Still some did, or affected to, disbelievement," wrote the diarist.

But most did believe the news, and a panic seized the town. A few members of the convention left to go to their families. A delegate proposed that the proceedings be moved to a safer venue, but it was decided to remain. The arrival of Dr. John Sutherland in town with additional confirmation the next morning put the Alamo's fate beyond any doubt. When more news arrived that the Mexican army was on the march east, the convention made haste to finish its work and at the same time prepared to leave town at a moment's notice.

Late that night, the constitution was finally ready for approval. While rumors spread through town of a large Mexican force fording the Colorado River at Bastrop, some seventy-five miles away, the remaining delegates voted to accept the constitution. One more job remained: to fashion and elect a provisional government. New officers were sworn in at four the next morning, March 17, and the convention soon adjourned. The delegates joined the families and storekeepers of Washington in hastily packing up and fleeing. "The members are now dispersing in all directions with haste and in confusion," wrote an observer:

A general panic seems to have seized them. Their families are exposed and defenseless, and thousands are moving off to the east. A constant stream of women and children, and some men, with wagons, carts and pack mules, are rushing across the Brazos night and day.

The tale of the country is becoming every day more and more gloomy.... An invaded, unarmed, unprovisioned country, without an army to oppose the invaders, and without money to raise one, now presents itself to their hitherto besotted and blinded minds and the awful cry has been heard from the midst of their assembly, "What shall we do to be saved?"

*   *   *

ON MARCH 11, Fannin dispatched a force of some thirty men with wagons to Refugio, thirty miles away, to evacuate Anglo settlers there. It was a foolish endeavor, as recent experience should have made clear to him. A few weeks earlier, James Grant and Frank Johnson had split up their small force at San Patricio, Grant taking twenty-six riders to round up wild mustangs for the Matamoros invasion they still envisioned, Johnson remaining in town to guard the hundred horses they already had. Early in the morning of February 27, in a driving rain, one hundred cavalrymen under the personal direction of General Urrea attacked Johnson and his thirty-four men. By dawn the battle was over. Ten Texians were dead, and eighteen taken prisoner. Only seven men escaped, including Johnson, who reached Goliad two days later. Four days later, on March 2, Urrea and eighty dragoons ambushed Grant and his detachment at Agua Dulce Creek, sixteen miles south of San Patricio, as the Texians herded several hundred horses toward town. The results were equally disastrous: six escapees and only six taken prisoner.

Word of each calamity reached Goliad a few days after its occurrence, as did abundant warning of Urrea's presence in the area as his command swept up the coast from Matamoros. Clearly, small parties of rebels were not safe out in the open. That knowledge had not deterred Fannin.

Led by Captain Amon B. King, a former sheriff from Kentucky, the small company had reached Refugio on March 12. Instead of gathering the families and leaving immediately, King decided to punish loyalist rancheros in the area. When the rebels ran into lead elements of Urrea's cavalry, who pinned them down in a church, King dispatched a courier to Fannin requesting help. William Ward and the Georgia Battalion of eighty men arrived the next day, March 13, and dispersed the

Mexicans. Even then, King refused to return to Goliad, and that night rode out to raid a nearby ranch in search of more spies. The delay enabled Urrea to engage the rebels when they attempted to return to the church the next morning. The Texians established a strong position in a grove of trees along a river. The two forces fought until darkness, with King's long rifles getting the best of it. Both Ward and King were short on powder and ball, and had to make their escape as best they could under cover of a moonless sky. Urrea tracked King's detachment down the next morning and took it without a fight—what little powder they had was wet. By the next day they were back in Refugio, where thirty-three of them were executed. Ward and the bulk of his battalion would manage to evade capture for a week, until they were taken on March 22. They would eventually be returned to Goliad.

Meanwhile, on March 14, Fannin had received Houston's news of the Alamo's fall and his orders to blow up the fort at Goliad and fall back thirty miles east to Victoria, on the Guadalupe. He continued to wait for King and Ward to return, and then postponed a planned departure on the night of March 18, when scouts reported the night too murky. Finally, on March 19, his garrison spiked their heaviest pieces of artillery, loaded their wagons with five hundred extra muskets and as much ammunition as they could carry, put the town of Goliad to the torch, and marched east: about three hundred men, with nine brass cannon, a few howitzers, and several baggage wagons, all drawn by oxen. None of the wagons carried food; in their haste, the soldiers forgot to bring any. The column departed at eight a.m. The twelve-hour delay would prove fatal.

They spent much of the morning crossing the San Antonio River, and entered a large prairie extending twelve miles to

THE BLOOD OF HEROES

heavy timber on Coleto Creek. Some of the unwieldy field-pieces were abandoned along the way, followed by some of the men's personal belongings, and finally a few of the over-stuffed wagons. At noon, just a few miles before they reached the safety of the woods, Fannin called a halt, and the hungry oxen were unyoked and turned out to graze. Some of his officers protested, but Fannin's low opinion of Mexican soldiers had him convinced that they would not dare attack a force of such size. An hour and a half later, when they were about to resume their march, a unit of Mexican cavalry was seen ahead, blocking their way.

Some of his officers advised making for the timber with all speed. But Fannin ordered his men to form a hollow square and prepare for battle. The four remaining cannon were placed at the corners.

The Mexicans, only about 340 of them at first, advanced. Fannin's men held their fire until the horsemen were well within range. The barrage did efficient work on the Mexican ranks. They retreated. Another charge was ordered, then another. The Texian lines held firm, though the Mexican soldiers and cavalrymen fought bravely.

Over the next several hours, until sunset, the battle continued in a desultory fashion. The Mexicans had no cannon, which hindered their attack. But they were soon bolstered by the arrival of reinforcements.

By the time darkness fell, the Texians were low on ammunition and suffering from a severe lack of water — both for their overheated cannon and their wounded, whose cries of agony and discomfort lasted throughout the cold, wet night. The men worked until dawn digging a three-foot trench and erecting fortifications of wagons, dead horses, and even their dead comrades. A council of war was held, and some of the officers argued for a breakout under cover of darkness. But besides ten men killed, there were at least fifty wounded, and with too many of the oxen dead, there was no way to transport them. Fannin, who was injured in the right thigh, refused to consider any plan that would leave the wounded behind. They remained where they were.

Dawn brought the realization of new dangers. Mexican artillery positioned on high ground threatened to do severe damage to the rebels' square. Fannin had hoped that his small force of cavalry, which had escaped, might bring aid from Victoria, about ten miles away, but there was no sign of reinforcements, and now it was clear they were badly outnumbered. After the Mexicans opened up with several barrages of round shot from their brass nine-pounders, a parley was arranged.

With the help of translators, Fannin treated directly with Urrea. Before he limped out to negotiate, he and his men had agreed that they would only surrender under honorable terms—or fight to the death.

Urrea demanded surrender at discretion—unconditional, no guarantees. Fannin insisted his soldiers be treated as prisoners of war. The agreement they signed included both conditions. Urrea, a man of honor, disagreed with his government's policy of execution for the rebels, and promised Fannin he would do what he could to protect them. His own losses included fifty dead and 140 wounded, but he admired the valiant stand put up by Fannin and his men.

Fannin returned to camp and told his soldiers that they were to be treated as prisoners of war and eventually returned to Copano to be shipped to New Orleans under parole, not to fight against Mexican troops. Though some of them—particularly the New Orleans Greys—objected to the surrender, the rebels gave up their arms and were escorted back to Goliad. Ward and his Georgia Battalion were herded into the fort a few days later and joined their comrades confined in the church.

Though the conditions in the church were unpleasant—the men were packed so tightly together that only a few could lie down at one time, and they were only given some meat once a day—hopes were high that they would soon be paroled. Fannin and his adjutant were even escorted to Copano, near the coast, to book passage on a ship to New Orleans. The vessel had sailed, but when they returned to Goliad on Saturday, March 26, "they cheered the men with their good spirits and the kind treatment they had received," remembered one of their doctors. Before retiring, some of the men sang "Home, Sweet Home" in anticipation of their coming freedom.

That evening a member of Santa Anna's staff arrived at the fort with a message from His Excellency. Urrea had left one of his officers, Lieutenant Colonel José Nicolás de la Portilla, in charge and continued his sweep through southern Texas, taking Victoria with no resistance. He had directed de la Portilla to keep the rebels alive, and in a letter to Béxar, he attempted to intercede with Santa Anna for the lives of Fannin and his men. Santa Anna's reply to Urrea was uncompromising: all foreigners captured with arms were to be treated as pirates and executed immediately. His orders to de la Portilla were the same. An hour after Santa Anna's communiqué, a courier rode into Goliad with a message from Urrea: "Treat the prisoners with consideration, and particular their leader, Fanning."

De la Portilla, a twenty-eight-year-old native of Jalapa so darkly complected he was called El Indio, considered himself a soldier, not an executioner. He, too, had been charmed by Fannin—they had recently shared a bottle of wine at dinner, where Fannin had drunk to the health of Urrea. De la Portilla spent a sleepless night agonizing over his choices—the last place he wanted to be was in the middle of a life-or-death argument between two superior officers. In the end, he concluded that he must obey the direct order of his commanding general.

At dawn the next morning, March 27, Palm Sunday, the uninjured Texians—save for a couple dozen spared as physicians, orderlies, or craftsmen—were awakened and divided into four groups. Each was given a different story: they were to march to Copano, or Matamoros, or gather wood, or drive cattle. They were led under heavy guard down three roads in different directions. About a half mile from the fort, each group was halted, then shot at close range. Those not killed on the first volley were shot again, bayoneted, or lanced by Mexican horsemen. Somehow twenty-eight men managed to escape across the San Antonio River.

Back at the fort, some of the fifty wounded, unable to walk, were dragged out and executed against the chapel wall. Others were taken to a spot near the gate, where *soldados* set them on the ground, bandaged their eyes, and shot them two at a time. The rest were slaughtered on their pallets.

Fannin was the last to die. His bravery during the battle had restored much of the confidence the men had lost in him, and indeed his own. Now he asked that his pocket watch be sent to his widow, that the executioners aim at his heart, and that he be given a Christian burial. His watch was kept by the Mexican officer directing the slaughter, and he was seated on a chair and shot in the face. His body was thrown on a pyre and burned with the rest of his soldiers.

When the escapees reached safety and told their tales, and the story of the Goliad massacre spread throughout Texas and beyond, the response in the United States and the rest of the world was outrage. Santa Anna had been considered the ruthless but honorable leader of a young republic fumbling toward the new ideal of liberty and equality. The death of every defender at the Alamo, and the execution of a few prisoners, was defensible; the massacre of almost four hundred unarmed men who had surrendered at discretion but had been led to believe they would be paroled was not. The news of such cruelty and bad faith turned much of the world's opinion against Santa Anna and his troops, and sparked an outpouring of sympathy and a renewed effort throughout the United States to aid the enemies of such a despot. Thousands of volunteers, and hundreds of thousands of dollars, would soon begin making their way into Texas. For now, though, much of the civilian population of the new republic, and its small, irregular army, fled across Texas with Santa Anna's Army of Operations at its heels.

EIGHTEEN

"The Marrow Bone of Texas"

Do everything in your power so that we can push forward on this ragtag rabble, and get it over with, and then we can go home.

GENERAL JOSÉ URREA TO GENERAL JOAQUÍN
RAMÍREZ Y SESMA, APRIL 22, 1836

After forty days spent fleeing before the Mexican army, Sam Houston was ready to fight. Many of his men had been ready long before, and only a few would realize later how close the Texian forces came to mutiny. Their impatience with their commander had been coming to a head since the hurried retreat from Gonzales.

Since leaving that town on the night of March 13, they had retreated steadily through the heart of the Texas colonies, with frightened families all along the roads heading east. On the second night out, while camped on the Navidad River, someone told Houston that another Alamo widow, the blind Mary Millsaps, was missing with her seven children. He dispatched a few men to ride down to her place on the Lavaca River, and the army waited until the Millsaps family had been retrieved before proceeding. Then they continued, Houston riding up and down the slow-moving column, using his penchant for profanity to goad his men into moving faster.

Finally, late on the afternoon of Thursday, March 17, the army reached Burnham's Crossing, on the Colorado River. Houston sent the refugees over first, then crossed his troops on the nineteenth. He ordered the ferry burned behind them. The heavy spring rains of the previous two weeks had left the Colorado near flood level. Houston aimed to consolidate his army on the east side of the swollen river. The Texians were now comfortably closer to the bulk of the Anglo colonies, from which they could draw supplies, provisions, and men.

For volunteers were indeed arriving. At the Colorado, the army numbered six hundred strong. Galvanized by news of the Alamo's fall, and the invasion of their settlements by a large Mexican army, colonists from every municipality were on the march at last. Major Robert Williamson's ranger companies, who had been guarding the Bastrop area against Mexican soldiers and Indian depredations, and helping families evacuate, sunk the ferryboats on the upper Colorado and rode south to join Houston's army. Other companies large and small began arriving in camp. Muddy roads and swollen creeks and rivers slowed every part of the Army of Operations. If the colonists could hold the line at the Colorado, perhaps the Mexican army would be compelled to retreat due to lack of provisions, for their already thin supply lines were stretched to the breaking point.

On March 20, Houston moved his troops down the Colorado thirty miles to Beeson's Ferry, where they would remain for almost a week. There, Houston instituted some much-needed drilling and training. He knew his men would have no chance against an army of regulars unless they had some sense of tactics.

That day, advance units of Ramírez y Sesma's division began to arrive at the west side of the river. They pitched camp just two miles from the Texians, and the two armies spent the next five days facing each other across the wide Colorado. Houston's men, still bitter after retreating from Gonzales amid the wailing of the town's widows, hounded him to fight, but he knew his troops were still not ready, after less than a week of the most basic drills—marching and learning to maneuver company by company. And even if they were to win, there were still thousands more *soldados* on the march. Houston's small army, ill-trained and ill-equipped, could not afford even a victory at this point. It was, in fact, time to fall back even farther.

Houston's decision was made easier by the news, delivered by scouts on March 23, that Fannin's force had been surrounded and attacked a few days earlier by a much larger body of Mexicans. The outcome was not yet known, but Fannin had sustained heavy casualties. Save for a few scattered units here and there, Houston's undisciplined force of volunteers, which had swelled to some fourteen hundred men, was now the only one left to check Santa Anna's advance. But to Houston's mind, they were not ready to fight, particularly without a basic knowledge of the fundamentals of battle formation.

Late in the afternoon of March 26, Houston issued new orders. The army would move out immediately, east toward San Felipe and the Brazos, twenty-five miles away. Before they embarked on their journey, Houston spoke to the assembled men, trying to explain his reasoning:

There are but few of us, and if we are beaten, the fate of Texas is sealed. The salvation of the country depends upon the first battle had with the enemy. For this reason, I intend to retreat, if I am obliged to go even to the banks of the Sabine.

As the grumbling troops packed up and set off, murmurings spread that their commander truly did plan to march to the old Neutral Ground, between the Sabine and the Neches, where U.S. troops on the Louisiana border would cross to attack the Mexican army and deliver Texas to Andrew Jackson.

There was more than a smidgen of fact to the rumor. Houston was in contact with General Edmund P. Gaines, in charge of fourteen U.S. infantry companies moved to the Sabine crossing on El Camino Real, ostensibly to protect settlers in the area from Indian depredations. Gaines was ready and willing to cross over if he found "any disposition on the part of the Mexicans or their red allies to menace our frontier." The approach of Santa Anna's army into the old Neutral Ground, whether in pursuit of Houston's rebel force and fleeing Texian families or not, would surely meet Gaines's criterion.

Rain began to fall. Almost every day near the end of March and the beginning of April would be cold and wet, making the thirty miles to San Felipe particularly grueling for the Texians. The next day they continued to slog over muddy roads until they reached the plantation of Jared Groce, on the west bank of the Brazos River. Houston had traded his Indian blanket for an old black dress coat, and he rode up and down the column, encouraging his men and promising he would not lead them to the Louisiana border.

They made camp in the Brazos bottomlands at Groce's plantation on March 31, just in time to hear the shocking fate of Fannin's men, massacred four days earlier. The news only heightened the panic, and hundreds of Houston's volunteers took furloughs or deserted to assist their families in their flight east. The army shrank to eight hundred stalwarts. Houston spent the next two weeks training his rabble and instilling discipline. While his men talked of mutiny, and of replacing him with someone more aggressive, he spent his nights pondering strategy, usually alone—like Santa Anna, Houston disliked conferring with officers. "I consulted none," he wrote to the interim Texas government, which had recently arrived in Harrisburg, fifty miles to the southeast, near Galveston Bay. "I held no council of war. If I err, the blame is mine."

The heavy spring rains continued, and slowed the progress of the Mexican divisions. Ramírez y Sesma received seven hundred reinforcements, but remained on the west side of the fast-flowing Colorado. Houston continued to drill his men, gradually instilling some understanding of military tactics. And his troops slowly regained their health, recovering from dysentery, measles, colds, influenza, and various other ailments caused by the cold, wet weather, unsanitary conditions, and poor diet. But threats of insubordination and mutiny continued to fester among the more excitable Texians.

Even Houston's superiors made their dissatisfaction known. On April 8, the rebel leader received a letter from the interim president, David G. Burnet: "The enemy are laughing you to scorn. You must fight them. You must retreat no further. The country expects you to fight. The salvation of the country depends on your doing so."

On April 11, Houston broke camp and led the army across the Brazos, then due east. He did not announce a destination. The grumbling in the ranks grew louder, even when the army's first artillery pieces arrived on April 12—two mounted six-pound cannon donated by the citizens of Cincinnati. James Neill was put in charge of the Twin Sisters, as they were dubbed—after the twin daughters of the man who formally presented them to the Texian movement. Houston rode up and down the slow-moving column, his customary profanity betraying his impatience.

Four more days of trudging through mud and rain brought the vanguard of the army to a fateful fork in the road on

April 16. To continue straight would lead them across the San Jacinto River and closer to Nacogdoches and the Sabine—and the United States troops hovering on the border. The road to the right led to Harrisburg, where Houston's scouts had located Santa Anna and 750 of his men racing across Texas to intercept the Texian government and put an end to the revolution. As Houston rode up to the front of the column, the men there turned to the right and marched down the right fork, and shouts of joy spread throughout the ranks. His troops had made his decision for him.

Two days later, on April 18, they reached the small town of Harrisburg, now nothing but charred remains of homes and buildings—a furious Santa Anna had ordered the town burned after just missing the interim government—where fortune smiled on them. That afternoon, scouts Henry Karnes and Deaf Smith captured three Mexican couriers carrying dispatches to Santa Anna. Their contents were invaluable, revealing the strength and plans of the disparate Mexican forces. El Presidente had marched east to the coast, then north through the bayous to Lynch's Ferry, there to rendezvous with General Cós's five-hundred-man division and march on to take Galveston, a rebel stronghold. Santa Anna, it was clear, thought Houston and his army on the way to Nacogdoches. By Houston's own reckoning, he could muster at least twelve hundred men. If he could overtake Santa Anna and capture him...

"We are in preparation to meet Santa Anna," he wrote to a friend the next morning. "It is the only chance of saving Texas.... We go to conquer." To his assembled troops, he gave an impassioned speech, though they hardly needed encouragement at this point. But when Houston concluded by imploring his men, "Remember the Alamo! The Alamo! The Alamo!" they roared back in unison: "Remember the Alamo! Remember Goliad!" The army had found its battle cry.

Everyone was weary of wading through mud and water, but Houston's speech and the promise of revenge after six weeks of a galling retreat was galvanizing. The troops crossed Buffalo Bayou in a leaky ferryboat and continued the march through the night. The exhausted army finally bivouacked in the early morning hours of April 20. Most of the men fell to the wet ground and wrapped themselves in blankets as a late norther blew in.

At daylight, the tap of a drum roused the shivering, hungry Texians. A few hours later they reached Lynch's Ferry. No Mexicans were in sight. Houston "placed his men, gave them his orders, then made them stack their arms in their places and told them to eat their breakfast," remembered a soldier. The rebels had just started their fires when scouts galloped into camp, a tall column of smoke miles behind them evidence of the destruction of New Washington, a village on the coast. The advance guard of the enemy was approaching.

AFTER HIS TRIUMPH AT THE ALAMO, and the capture of the Goliad garrison, Santa Anna had decided to return to Mexico City. His triumphant legions were marching from victory to victory. The American colonists were fleeing the country, and Houston's small, untrained army was doing the same. When they all crossed the Sabine River, Texas would once again be in the hands of Mexican centralists, and Mexican troops posted along the border would keep the Americans out.

Most of his commanders disagreed—few thought it would be that simple—but His Excellency could not be dissuaded. He planned to leave April 1. General Filisola would supervise the final stages of the invasion of Texas.

But when General Ramírez y Sesma reached the west bank of the Colorado on March 21 and sent reports back to Béxar of a strong rebel force across the swollen river—supplying more evidence of his inability to handle problems on his own—Santa Anna changed his plans. His presence and leadership were clearly required to finish the job. Leaving General Juan Andrade in charge of Béxar with more than a thousand men, including most of the cavalry (rendered useless by worn-out, poorly fed mounts), Santa Anna headed east with his staff. After crossing the Colorado, he would personally direct the campaign from San Felipe.

He wasted no time tarrying along the way. His health had been a problem for much of the march north, but now he seemed to be the Santa Anna of old, full of energy and purpose, pushing his men forward by the force of his will. Two days out of Béxar, he ordered his fine carriage returned to San Luis Potosí—with his new "bride" and her mother its passengers. The incessant rains had turned every road into a mud pit and every field into a lake, and anything with wheels was almost immovable. He would proceed on horseback.

But the Texian army was gone by the time he reached the Colorado, so he continued on. When he reached San Felipe and the Brazos River on April 7, he found only ashes—the rebels had put it to the torch to keep it out of Mexican hands. They had also taken every boat with them, and Texian sharpshooters across the Brazos prevented the Mexicans from crossing, even after they had built rafts in an effort to do so. Two days later, with the lower Brazos towns of Columbia and Brazoria his destination, an impatient Santa Anna set out downriver for Fort Bend. The enemy could not man every crossing on the river, and his scouts had discovered the ferry there deserted. Apparently fed up with Ramírez y Sesma's indecisiveness, Santa Anna directed him to remain at San Felipe. From there he would dispatch troops and supplies as needed.

Santa Anna crossed the Brazos at Thompson's Ferry, twenty

miles downriver from San Felipe. He ordered Ramírez y Sesma to join him, and on April 13, he received information from local colonists that would change his plans—and alter the fate of three nations.

The intelligence was tantalizing. Interim Texas president David Burnet and his cabinet had relocated to Harrisburg, near the coast, only thirty miles away. Their capture and execution would likely put an end to the rebellion with a minimum of Mexican lives lost: "A single blow would have been mortal to their cause," Santa Anna wrote later. After dispatching orders to all his commanders to rendezvous at Fort Bend, twelve miles downriver, His Excellency took fifty horsemen and seven hundred *soldados*—most of them preferred companies of *cazadores* and *granaderos* from several battalions—and at three p.m. on April 14 began a hard march over soggy roads to Harrisburg.

When he reached the town the next evening, he found it deserted save for three of Gail Borden's *Telegraph and Texas Register* printers, who had remained there trying to get out one last edition of the paper. They told him the rebel government had left a few hours earlier for New Washington, on the coast less than twenty miles away, there to sail for the safety of Galveston Island. Furious, Santa Anna dispatched Almonte with fifty dragoons after them and ordered Harrisburg burned to the ground. At three p.m., the town in flames behind him, he began marching to the coast. His scouts had told him that Houston, with his puny force, no more than five hundred strong by their count, was on the move, heading once more for the Sabine—and making slow progress due to the families and wagons he was escorting. Houston would no doubt cross the San Jacinto at Lynch's Ferry, at the mouth of the river. The rebel cabinet might still be captured, but if not, here was another chance to end the war in one swift blow: if Santa

Anna could block the ferry and bring Houston's riffraff to battle, he could quit this country by sea—he had already ordered a ship to await him at Copano, down the coast—and return to Mexico City wreathed in glory. He sent a courier to General Cós at Fort Bend with instructions to march with five hundred more *soldados* and join him as quickly as possible.

Santa Anna arrived in New Washington at noon the next day, April 18, to hear disappointing news from Almonte. The colonel had galloped down to the beach to see Burnet and other cabinet members in a skiff about forty yards away, pulling for a steamer out in the bay. They were still within rifle range, and the dragoons took aim, but Almonte pushed one carbine to the side and ordered his men to hold their fire—the gallant colonel had seen a woman aboard. The cabinet, Almonte reported, was likely safe on Galveston Island at that moment.

On the morning of April 20, after looting and burning the town, Santa Anna's division marched up the bayou toward Lynch's Ferry. When advance scouts galloped back to report a large force of rebels up ahead, he was momentarily panicked. But he recovered his composure and continued north toward the ferry. Before noon, they came within sight of the enemy, on the far end of an empty plain almost a mile wide, in front of the road that led to the crossing. Thick woods and marsh surrounded the field of knee-high grass.

Houston had beaten him to Lynch's Ferry, but no matter— Santa Anna was confident that his 750 elite troops, most of them seasoned veterans of the actions at the Alamo, or against Fannin at Coleto Creek, could defeat a rebel army of equal size composed of unruly, untrained farmers and frontiersmen. The imminent arrival of Cós's five hundred *soldados* would guarantee it. Santa Anna posted his troops at the opposite end of the plain from the rebels, on a slight rise at the edge of a small thicket; five hundred yards to their rear lay a boggy marsh and a good-size body of water known as Peggy Lake. He noticed with some satisfaction that Houston was trapped, with his back against Buffalo Bayou—forced either to fight or go into the water behind him on the other side of the road.

Once his men had settled in, Santa Anna ordered a sally against the rebel position—perhaps he could draw the enemy out onto the open prairie between them. His gunners wheeled out their only fieldpiece, a brass nine-pounder that had been hell to drag through the boggy roads from the Brazos, and began blasting away. Two rebel six-pounders in the far-off trees along the road answered in kind. A few men were injured on each side, including Colonel James Neill, who sustained a serious hip wound. He was evacuated to a nearby house and would see no more action on this field of battle.

Near sunset, after a skirmish between Mexican dragoons and Texian cavalrymen that ended with a rebel retreat, both sides retired for the evening. Santa Anna ordered breastworks built, so *soldados* worked into the night erecting a four-foot wall of pack saddles, sacks of flour and corn, supply boxes, and other baggage. He was content with his army's position, but he found it difficult to sleep. He had nothing but contempt for the colonists—minister of war Tornel had described them as "ignorant of the art of war, incapable of discipline, and renowned for insubordination," and Santa Anna agreed with that assessment—but the rebels' restraint during the cannonade, and their daring mounted attack, had surprised him.

GENERAL HOUSTON HAD GIVEN ORDERS to his "ignorant" rabble not to awaken him until eight a.m. It was his first good night's sleep in weeks, and he arose a few minutes before the hour to find the morning clear and the air cool. Reveille for his troops had consisted of a steady tapping on a drum at four a.m., and by the time their commander awoke, they were excited and eager to fight: "Let us attack the enemy and give them hell at once" was frequently heard. Houston was told that five hundred Mexican reinforcements were arriving. He had been expecting them, thanks to the intelligence acquired from the captured courier.

About noon, Houston called six of his senior officers to a council of war to discuss one question: Should they assault the enemy themselves, or await his attack? The subject was put to a vote, which yielded a surprising result, considering the troops' eagerness to fight—all but two were in favor of waiting for the Mexicans to make the first move. One officer was leery of marching across the mile-wide prairie without bayonets; few of the men carried military-issue arms. The other three pointed out the strength of their position and the advantages of defending it.

Houston dismissed his council, then dispatched Deaf Smith with six horsemen to tear down the small bridge over Vince's Bayou. Eight miles southwest down the Harrisburg Road, it constituted the only escape route from the battlefield save for the route to New Washington—and was also the most likely route for any more Mexican reinforcements. He advised Smith to hurry if he wanted to participate in the upcoming battle. The scout rode off with six volunteers and a few axes.

As Smith galloped away, Houston walked among his men, asking if they were ready to fight. The resounding affirmatives were all he needed. "Very well, get your dinners and I will lead you into the fight," he told them. "And if you whip them, every one of you shall be a captain." He conferred with his officers again, who had talked to their men and reported them raring to go. And some Texians who had climbed trees reported no activity in the Mexican camp and no sentries along its perimeter.

At three p.m., Houston ordered his troops paraded for attack in a line a thousand yards long. The men were overjoyed—they were finally going to fight. Houston did not know it, but some of his top officers had made a pledge the night before: they would fight the next day, with or without him. As the men lined up in formation in front of the trees, any thoughts of mutiny disappeared.

Within half an hour they had fanned out into four divisions facing the open prairie, with the Twin Sisters placed in the center. Houston, on a fine-looking light gray stallion named Saracen, rode down the length of the line. As he passed by, one company commander reminded his men that Travis, Bowie, Crockett, and their companions had fought bravely against an enemy force twenty times their number (the number of Mexican troops at the Alamo having been exaggerated in reports). Juan Seguín, who had left those worthies during the siege of the Alamo, stood not far away. He would lead a company of two dozen Tejano infantrymen against their killers.

About an hour later, Houston, in a low but clear voice, gave the order—"Trail arms! Forward!"—and his 930 men began marching quietly through the tall grass with their rifles held low by their sides. The regiment on the left used a line of oaks lining the field to screen their advance. Captains reminded their companies to hold their fire until within fifty yards of the enemy.

Unknown to the Texians, Cós's four hundred *soldados*—he had been forced to leave a hundred men behind to deal with baggage carts bogged down in the mud—had force-marched almost twenty-four hours straight and had not eaten or slept the entire time. They were exhausted and hungry, and, worse, most of them were recent recruits with little experience. Once they had settled in and stacked their arms, Cós asked that his battalion be allowed to eat and rest. Santa Anna was not happy with the quality of the troops, but he granted the request, and as Cós's men and most of the others prepared and ate their midday meals and then relaxed and indulged in their traditional midafternoon siesta, His Excellency followed suit. He lay down to rest in the shade of a tree—he had slept little the night before, and had spent much of the morning on horseback, examining the enemy lines through a spyglass—and was soon asleep. He and his army were stunningly unprepared.

A slight depression running through the field that led up to a low ridge in the middle of the prairie helped shield the Texians from sight as they advanced in two parallel lines under the warm sun. Neill's eighteen-man artillery company used leather straps to pull the two cannon up the slope. Only one company, consisting of Kentucky riflemen, wore anything resembling a proper uniform. The rest of the rebels were dressed in dirty, ragged citizens' clothes, from buckskins to frock coats, mostly dark or gray or brown, more mud-colored than anything else; some in boots, some in shoes, some in moccasins, almost all unshaven, sporting long hair and matted beards, looking more like a band of savages than a proper army. They were two hundred yards from the Mexican lines when the Twin Sisters roared to life and Houston galloped down the line, yelling, "No reinforcements! No reinforcements!"—Deaf Smith had just returned to tell him that the bridge at Vince's Bayou was down. As the men broke into a run, a motley band of four fifers and two drummers began playing a popular and somewhat salacious ballad entitled "Will You Come to the Bower?" and then jumped into "Yankee Doodle," and the attack was on.

Many of the men yelled, "Remember the Alamo!" and "Remember La Bahía!" Others roared, "Remember Fannin!" or "Remember Goliad!" A Mexican bugler finally sounded the alarm, and *soldados* began to jump up and grab their rifles and muskets, but it was too late. The rebels poured over and through the makeshift breastworks and into the Mexican lines. Texian officers ordered their men to "Halt! Fire! And then charge!" but after one shot, few bothered to reload, instead turning their rifles into war clubs and unsheathing Bowie knives. Many of the *soldados* yelled, "Me no Alamo! Me no Goliad!" before they were slaughtered. Some stood and fought, but most turned and ran, panic-stricken. Cós and Almonte, on the right side of the Mexican lines, tried without success to keep their men from breaking—but the Texian assault could not be withstood.

One officer refused to retreat and stood his ground, directing the fire of the Mexican nine-pounder. As rebel fire dropped his gunners and the rest of his men ran for their lives, General Manuel Fernández Castrillón stood on an ammunition box and tried to rally his troops. Moments later he was alone, and he folded his arms and faced forward. A slug ripped into him, then another, then another, and he fell to the ground, lifeless.

The battle itself lasted no more than eighteen minutes, but carnage on a grand scale followed for another hour as the Texians' tenuous discipline gave way to blind bloodlust. Retreating Mexicans reached Peggy Lake and splashed in, attempting to reach the far side, several hundred yards away. Rebels ran up and lined the edges of the water and shot them until the lake ran red; others followed the Mexicans in and took revenge with knives and hatchets. Some two hundred *soldados* died there.

Houston, on his third horse of the day and suffering from a left ankle shattered by a Mexican musket ball, tried to stop the bloodletting, as did other officers. It was no use. All across the field, their men were uncontrollable in their vengefulness. Santa Anna's troops had shown no quarter to the rebels at the Alamo and Goliad. They would receive the same treatment now. "We followed the enemy," remembered one captain, "shooting and killing them, for more than a mile."

By day's end, Texian casualties included seven deaths and more than thirty wounded—four of these so badly that they would die later. At least six hundred Mexicans lay dead on the field, and hundreds had been captured. Only a handful escaped. But the man the rebels wanted most—dead or alive—was nowhere to be found.

WHEN THE SOUND OF GUNFIRE and the roar of cannon awakened Santa Anna from a deep sleep, he leaped to his feet. He made a halfhearted attempt to organize the troops around him, but when a servant offered him a horse, he mounted and fled the battlefield eastward, accompanied by his secretary, Ramón Caro. Sanctuary, and perhaps even victory, was forty-odd miles away, where Filisola and the bulk of his army awaited. Finding the bridge at Vince's Bayou down, and terrified of deep water, His Excellency retreated to a nearby thicket and became separated from Caro. He hid in some brush all night. At daybreak, he exchanged his gaudy clothes for some old slave duds he found in an abandoned shack. Around three p.m., a Texian search party found him hiding in tall grass; ignorant of his identity, they took him to camp. Only when Mexican prisoners began repeating his name as he passed by did his captors realize who he was. They escorted him to Houston, who was lying on a blanket under a tree with his injured leg propped up. Santa Anna grabbed Houston's hand and introduced himself. Then the self-styled Napoleon of the West, the man who bragged that he asked for no quarter and gave none, pleaded that he "be treated as a general should when a prisoner of war."

Hundreds of furious Texians gathered around the two generals, shouting, "Shoot him!" and "Hang him!" But Houston knew what he had: the biggest bargaining chip in Texas, if he could be kept alive. Thousands of Mexican troops were known to be on the Brazos River, or even closer, and an attack in the next few days might be too much even for his ferocious fighters. He ignored his troops' demands for Santa Anna's head, and told him what he needed to do if he wished to live. After two hours of intense negotiation, Houston had Ramón Caro — who had also been found — draft letters from the dictator to General Filisola at Fort Bend, ordering him to withdraw his divisions back to Béxar and Victoria. Three days later, a second message would be sent directing the Army of Operations to continue retreating to the Rio Grande.

When Santa Anna's orders reached Filisola's headquarters, several of Santa Anna's high commanders objected. As a prisoner under duress, he had no authority to issue such orders, they claimed, and Filisola was under no obligation to obey them. Some of them claimed that the war could still be won — they outnumbered Houston's army three or four to one, and in two marches they could reach Lynchburg and bring him to battle. But Filisola was adamant. The army was in no shape to continue a campaign in a hostile country. His men's clothes were reduced to rags, most were barefoot, and their health was poor — many were suffering from dysentery and incapable of battle; provisions, supplies, and ammunition were running out, and their supply lines had dried up; the constant rains had rendered movement in any direction almost impossible. Just as important, all these factors — and the news of His Excellency's defeat and capture — had completely demoralized the troops. Filisola pointed out that the only way to protect their commanding general and the six hundred Mexican prisoners was to withdraw.

So the four-thousand-man Army of Operations began a

slow retreat to Mexico by way of Matamoros, over almost impassable roads and nearly uncrossable rivers and streams. The stoic *soldados* and their loyal *soldaderas* slogged slowly through what Filisola called El Mar de Lodo—the Sea of Mud. One twenty-mile stretch of prairie muck took eleven days to traverse. Over hundreds of miles they abandoned supplies, artillery, wagons, ammunition, supplies, oxen, horses, mules, and booty, and by the time they crossed the Rio Grande and eventually reached their homes in Mexico months later, few of them ever wanted to see Texas again. Indeed, only some of the officers, enraged at the shame brought upon them by the ignominious retreat, wished such a thing.

IN OPELOUSAS, Louisiana, the news of James Bowie's death reached his mother, Elve Bowie, weeks later, when someone knocked on her door and told the seventy-year-old widow the news. A Bowie family historian related that she received the information calmly, only remarking that she would "wager no wounds were found in his back," then stoically returned to her housework. Bowie's brother Rezin—the one to whom he was closest—immediately left for Texas, where he was appointed a colonel in the Texas army.

WHEN WORD OF THE ALAMO'S FALL and the death of David Crockett reached Tennessee around the same time, Crockett's youngest son, Robert, also went to Texas to fight for the country his father had given his life for. He attained the rank of first lieutenant in the cavalry. David's oldest son, John Wesley, took up another of his father's causes. A year later, in 1837, he ran for Congress in his father's old district and was elected when the one-legged Adam Huntsman, who had defeated his father in 1835, decided not to seek reelection. Crockett served two consecutive terms, and in February 1841, he was the driving force behind the passage of his father's land bill, in slightly modified form, which made land cheaply available to the poor in west Tennessee.

José Enrique de la Peña had openly criticized Filisola's decision to return to Mexico, and the endless slog through the Sea of Mud persuaded him to publish an account of his experiences with the Army of Operations to illustrate the "ignorance, stupidity, and cruelty" that led to defeat and disgrace. (The fact that during the retreat he received an emphatic rejection from his beloved but unfaithful Lucesita may have colored his opinions.) He had kept a diary during much of the campaign, and upon his return began work on his book, based largely on his journal but also incorporating newspaper stories as well as reports, accounts, and observations by other officers and even published letters from Travis, Houston, and others, which he translated and included in his book. Early in 1838, while military commander of Mazatlán, he had pronounced his support for his good friend Urrea's armed opposition to the centralist government. Upon the failure of that bloody insurrection in July, he was discharged from the army and spent two years in jail, some of it in ill health. He continued to work on his manuscript while incarcerated, sometimes dictating to another prisoner when he was too weak to hold pen to paper. He became a free man in the spring of 1840 and took an apartment in Mexico City, where he spent the next several months without a job, seeking reinstatement in the army and attempting to recover his back pay.

De la Peña's situation had not improved by October 10. Late in the evening, he became involved in a street altercation, based on a political disagreement, with Lieutenant Colonel José Mariano Cosio, a fellow officer in the Zapadores battalion with whom he had served in Texas—and who had also participated in the attack on the Alamo. In the ensuing struggle, Cosio stabbed de la Peña in the stomach with a sword and killed him. De la Peña was thirty-three years old. His memoir would finally see publication in 1955, more than a century after he wrote it.

Captain José Juan Sánchez would find a brighter future. Despite his objections, and despite a formal request to remain in the Texas campaign, he was sent to Matamoros in April, before the Battle of San Jacinto on the twenty-first, and commissioned to protect the frontier presidios against Indian attacks. He, too, hoped to return to Texas as part of a conquering army set on avenging his nation's honor. Instead, he spent a decade at a job he disliked, though in December 1836 he finally received his long-awaited promotion to lieutenant colonel. In 1844 he was made colonel, and in 1846, he would be chosen by his old officer-school classmate Santa Anna to serve on his staff during the Mexican-American War. He was brevetted a general by war's end, and shortly thereafter was appointed commandant general of the state of Coahuila. He was serving in that capacity when he died on June 2, 1849, at the age of fifty-six.

No SOONER HAD THE Army of Operations returned to Mexico than accusations and recriminations over the decision to retreat began flying hard and fast. Several of Santa Anna's top commanders published books, pamphlets, and articles defending their positions and criticizing their fellow officers. The absent Santa Anna took the worst of it, though public outcry and constant attacks by fellow officers caused Filisola to stand trial for his actions later that year; he was officially exonerated. Though Santa Anna would sign the Treaties of Velasco in May, ending hostilities, Mexico refused to officially recognize Texas independence or accept the loss of her troublesome territory.

Santa Anna would remain in Texas for several months as assurance of the Mexican army's good intentions. In the fall he was transported to Washington, D.C., where he had a conference with President Jackson. After returning to Veracruz in November on a battleship furnished for him, he remained in seclusion, disgraced, at his Manga de Clavo hacienda. That only lasted a year. In November 1837, a desperate Mexican government gave him command of the army, and he led troops against an invading French force at Veracruz. When he lost a leg after being severely wounded by cannon fire, he insisted that it be buried with full military honors. He survived and would serve as president or dictator of Mexico several more times over the next twenty-eight years—in 1853, his final term, he was elected dictator for life, and he demanded that people address him as Most Serene Highness. He was removed from power a year later and spent most of his remaining life in exile. In 1874, he took advantage of a general amnesty and returned to Mexico City. He died there, penniless, in June 1876.

THE TWO YOUNG NATIONS CONTINUED to tussle sporadically until the Mexican-American War ended in 1848, three years after the republic of Texas was admitted as the twenty-eighth member of the United States. For all practical purposes, however, Texas had won its independence on that open field along the San Jacinto River.

But it is doubtful that the Battle of San Jacinto would have happened were it not for the stand made at an old mission compound on the outskirts of San Antonio de Béxar. The siege of the Alamo occupied Santa Anna for two weeks, and for several more days after his March 6 victory. Beyond the battle itself, which killed or injured some of his best troops, the weeks spent in Béxar retarded the Mexican army's progress immeasurably. By the time Ramírez y Sesma's division reached the Colorado River on March 21, heavy spring rains had swelled that river and other waterways to near flood levels and rendered them dangerous and difficult to cross, thus significantly slowing the Mexican advance — which was also checked by Houston's troops stationed at different points on the opposite side of the Colorado. That army of Texians essentially did not exist as an organized military force until a week after the Alamo's fall, and almost certainly would not have been able to stop the Mexican army had it reached a more easily crossed Colorado (and many other more easily crossed rivers and streams) early in March, before the rains began.

Just as important, not until the destruction of the Alamo garrison (and the massacre at Goliad, three weeks later) did most Texian colonists begin to appreciate the seriousness of the situation — that their very lives, and the lives of their loved ones, were at stake — and feel compelled and angry enough to take up arms and join Sam Houston's volunteers to repel an invading army intent on driving them from their homes. (Until then, three-fourths of the Texian forces were recent U.S. volunteers, and only a quarter of them were established settlers; at San Jacinto, those numbers were reversed.) The Alamo and Goliad provided a much-needed rallying cry for the Texian cause. The vengeful fury of San Jacinto would not have existed without them.

Finally, the Alamo garrison bought valuable time for the fledgling Texian government. While the Alamo siege continued, and for ten days afterward, elected delegates at the convention in Washington, representing virtually every municipality in Texas, issued a declaration of independence, crafted and approved a well-constructed constitution, and elected an interim government, measures that significantly legitimized their revolution and greatly assisted them in garnering international political recognition and every kind of assistance and support. Without the stand made by two hundred men at the Alamo, none of that might have happened. More than any other event of the Texas revolution, their sacrifice truly forged a nation that would one day join a country greater than itself.

NINETEEN

Last Rites

They preferred to die a thousand times rather than submit to the tyrant's yoke.

JUAN SEGUÍN, APRIL 25, 1837

On June 4, 1836, Captain Juan Seguín rode down from Powder House Hill at the head of a company of twenty-two Tejano horsemen and approached the outskirts of Béxar. Seven long weeks had passed since their valorous service at San Jacinto, and they were pleased to see the San Antonio River and their town beyond, no matter how battered its structures. All the Alamo's single walls had been torn down and now lay in heaps of rubble. Only the old church, the *convento,* the main gatehouse, and a few of the houses along the perimeter still stood. Seguín halted his men before entering the city and sent one of his troops in with a message ordering any Mexican forces to evacuate.

The Tejanos had spent most of May in the saddle, observing the Mexican army's arduous retreat from Texas. They had been tasked with the unpleasant duty of making sure the *soldados* took no private property with them, including slaves. Worse, they soon found themselves forced to care for the sick and wounded *soldados* and *soldaderas* who could not keep up. Seguín's next orders had been to take possession of Béxar and raise a battalion there to defend the frontier. Comanches were still an ever-present threat, and some believed that the Mexicans would be back.

General Andrade had departed with his thousand men on May 24, headed for Goliad to rendezvous with the remainder of the Army of Operations. Almost a hundred *soldados* stayed in the hospital; the remaining two hundred wounded, some of them on crutches, accompanied him. In the week before leaving, Andrade had overseen the demolition of the Alamo per orders from General Filisola—an especially disheartening task, since his men had spent much of the previous two months improving the fort after the March 6 battle. Behind him he had left a small garrison of eighteen *presidiales* of the Alamo company. Their commanding officer was Lieutenant Francisco de Castañeda, the officer sent to Gonzales to seize the colonists' small cannon the previous September—what seemed a lifetime ago.

Castañeda had lived in Béxar for a dozen years, the last few in his house along the west wall of the Alamo, and he and Seguín had known each other that long. Now Castañeda told him that he could enter the town without opposition. Two days later, the lieutenant and his men left town, bound for Mexico. Several centralist sympathizers and their families departed in the same direction.

The new commandant of Béxar found his family ranch ruined, many of the area fields laid waste, and houses throughout the city little more than rubble—and a citizenry largely unconvinced that the hostilities were at an end. They were thus reluctant to cooperate or assist him in any way, whether it was to join his battalion or just herd cattle to a safer place. A rumor circulated that the Mexican troops had stopped their retreat and were preparing to return. Unable to raise any recruits, Seguín left less than three weeks after his arrival. He returned in November as a lieutenant colonel leading an eighty-man battalion.

Early in January 1837, the Texas high command decided that Béxar would be better off evacuated and destroyed to avoid a second battle of the Alamo if the Mexican army came back. Seguín protested vigorously, and recently elected president Sam Houston reassured his old comrade that the orders would be withdrawn. But difficulties in provisioning, mounting, and paying his men forced Seguín to fall back to Gonzales, whose citizens were only now beginning to return from the east. Before he left, he performed one more important duty.

He ordered a coffin built and covered in black, and placed some of the ashes of the Alamo dead in it; the names of Travis, Bowie, and Crockett were engraved on the inside lid. At four o'clock on the afternoon of February 25, church bells tolled as soldiers carried the coffin to the Church of San Fernando. Accompanied by a procession of other troops, civil authorities, clergy, mourners, relatives, citizens, and a band, they bore it down Potrero Street and across the river. Near the Alameda, at what remained of the largest mound of ashes, three musket volleys were discharged by the entire battalion and the coffin buried with full military honors. In his address, Juan Seguín paid his respects to his fallen comrades. "There are your brothers," he said, "Travis, Bowie, and Crockett, and others whose valor places them in the rank of my heroes."

INSTEAD OF RETURNING TO THE charred ruins of her house in Gonzales, Susanna Dickinson had settled in a new town twelve miles up Buffalo Bayou from San Jacinto, named after the man who had led the Texians to victory—Houston. She was illiterate and destitute, and caring for a small child, so she requested a $500 government donation. After some debate, the measure was voted down. In 1837 she married a man named Williams. He became abusive to her and her young daughter, Angelina, and after five months the union ended unhappily. So did her next marriage, to a man named Frank Herring, who died of drink, and the next, to Peter Bellows, who accused her of abandonment and adultery. Only after she moved to Lockhart in 1857 to set up a boardinghouse there, and met and married one of her boarders—the much younger Joseph Hannig, a gifted cabinetmaker from Germany—did she finally find happiness. They moved to Austin and lived there contentedly in a beautiful home on a bluff overlooking the city.

Susanna did not return to San Antonio de Béxar—which quickly became better known as San Antonio—until almost half a century had passed, and by then the once sleepy little town was a bustling city of twenty thousand. In April 1881, forty-five years after departing on a horse with her daughter clutched to her breast, she returned there and visited the remains of the Alamo with two young nieces, a party of dignitaries, a newspaperman, and the grandniece of Deaf Smith, the man who had found her on the prairie and brought her back to Gonzales. When she walked into the dark room she had occupied during the battle, she cried. The experience released a flood of memories, and she gave the reporter the most detailed account of her ordeal ever made public. She talked of her husband, and the line traced by Travis, and some of the horrors she had witnessed. Then she and her companions retired to the saloon next door, where she soothed her nerves with a glass of wine. After a long illness, she died on October 1, 1883, at the age of sixty-eight.

Angelina Dickinson's life mirrored her mother's in many ways—except for the happy ending. She grew up to be a fun-loving, pretty young woman. After bearing four children by two husbands, she left her children to relatives and took to a life of drifting. The "Babe of the Alamo" turned to prostitution and died of a uterine hemorrhage in Galveston. She was only thirty-four.

AFTER LEAVING GONZALES ON MARCH 13, Susanna's partner in survival, Joe, traveled to the home of plantation owner Jared Groce, on the Brazos River, where a week later he gave a full account of the Alamo battle to an audience that included Texas president David Burnet and his cabinet. Travis's slave was eventually returned to his owner's estate and taken into the possession of John Rice Jones, Travis's executor. On April 21, 1837, exactly one year after the Battle of San Jacinto, Joe and a Mexican working for Jones at his farm near Columbia took two horses and saddles and lit out for another territory—presumably Mexico, which would have meant freedom for both of them. Years later, stories would circulate that Joe had journeyed to the Travis family home in Alabama to relate his master's fate, and in 1875 an Austin newspaper editor would claim to know of his presence near that city. That was the last the public ever heard of Joe.

AFTER LEAVING THE ALAMO ON March 5, Moses Rose traveled only at night, and one evening ran into a thicket of prickly pear cactus that left him with dozens of thorns in his legs. A few weeks and more than two hundred miles later, when he staggered up to the door of a friend's house on Lake Creek, some sixty miles northwest of San Felipe, he could hardly walk. His friend's family took him in and tended to his badly infected wounds, using forceps to extract the thorns from his legs. He stayed there for a couple of weeks, recuperating, then left for his hometown of Nacogdoches. He operated a meat market for a while, and kept to himself. When someone would ask him why he hadn't stayed in the Alamo, his invariable response was, "By God, I wasn't ready to die."

Sometime in the early 1840s, Rose left Nacogdoches and drifted east. Eventually he hired on at the Logansport, Louisiana, plantation of Aaron Ferguson, who allowed him to live in the family home. After a few years, he became bedridden because of his cactus wounds, which had never healed properly. At his request, the Ferguson family moved him from their house to a small wooden shed nearby, where he lived out the last months of his life. They cared for him until he died, and buried him in the family cemetery. More than a century later, an 1813 French coin with an image of Napoleon, the old Frenchman's idol, was found nearby.

ALTHOUGH SUSANNA DICKINSON did not return to Gonzales, most of its surviving residents did, beginning in the spring of 1837. The Runaway Scrape had been especially hard on Gonzaleans. They had no wagons and not enough horses to ride, so most walked and led pack animals. Two of the younger Kent children, seventeen-month-old Phinette and three-year-old Andrew Jackson, died from exposure on the chaotic journey east to Nacogdoches. The oldest three Kent boys, David, Isaac, and thirteen-year-old Bosman, returned before the rest of the family to find their pioneer mansion burned to the ground: only the two large chimneys marked its place. Their stock was dispersed or slaughtered, and all their possessions were taken save for some of their father's tools, a pot, an oven, and a table that had been dragged into the yard. The boys began to plant crops and build another house in preparation for the return of their mother and siblings.

A year later, most of their DeWitt neighbors had made it back to their ruined homesteads—including the widows of Wash Cottle and George Kimble, who had both given birth to twins—and they, too, had begun rebuilding. On the Fourth of July, 1838, the colonists gathered in what was left of their town, now reduced to ashes save for Adam Zumwalt's kitchen, Andrew Ponton's smokehouse, and a few newly erected structures, and observed the holiday with all the festivities they could muster. There was still the threat of another Mexican army returning to claim Texas, and the Comanches continued to be a constant danger. The Texians' lives would be hard for a long time. But they would survive, and, in time, even thrive.

WHEN DAVID CROCKETT HAD LEFT HIS HOME in Tennessee to "explore the Texes," he hoped to return for his wife and family. In 1854, Elizabeth Crockett finally made that journey, with two of her children by David—their son Robert and daughter Rebecca—as well as her son from her previous marriage, George Patton, and his wife. Two years later they settled on a 320-acre tract near Granbury in north Texas, land granted to Elizabeth for her husband's sacrifice. The men built her a home, and Robert farmed the land and cared for his mother, who joined the nearby Methodist Episcopal Church and always appeared in public in her black widow's weeds. She died on January 31, 1860, at the age of seventy-four, after her customary before-breakfast walk, and was buried nearby. Years later a monument was erected at her grave with a statue of her atop it. The pose, her family claimed, was a familiar one on their porch every evening in Tennessee after David left.

Her hand shading her brow, she looks toward the west, watching for his return—the west, where men like David Crockett had always gone in search of those things dear to them, such as liberty, freedom, and fortune. It was inevitable that they would. It was in their blood.

Moses Rose and the Line

Mrs. Dickinson...says that she did not know Rose person-
ally, but recollects that a man escaped at the time mentioned;
that the troops were drawn up in line and addressed by Col.
Travis. Between the time of Rose's escape and the fall of the
Alamo, she heard the men speak of the escape, but none
believed that he would get away alive.

FRANK JOHNSON

Questions abound concerning the siege and battle of the Alamo—the dearth of reliable firsthand accounts guaranteed that. Particularly since every member of the garrison present on the morning of March 6, 1836, died, and since the accounts of survivors Joe, Susanna Dickinson, and others were limited—not only in what they saw (after Travis was killed minutes into the battle, Joe returned to their room and remained there, and the women and children stayed in the church until the battle was over), but in the details they supplied—little is known of what occurred and who actually did it, especially in those last few days after Travis's final message of March 3. No one, it appeared, essayed a proper debriefing of the survivors. (The Mexican after-action reports that have survived—or at least those we know of—are terse and almost completely devoid of the details we crave of who did what, since it was quite dark and none of them knew any of the defenders by sight anyway.) This may seem puzzling to us now, in our media-saturated age—why wasn't every one of the survivors and anyone within a mile of the battle interviewed in depth until every detail had been extracted?—but as historian Walter Lord, author of the best narrative of the battle, wrote in 1968: "The best explanation seems to be the nature of the frontier. People were busy. Research and reporting were civilized luxuries. Who had the time—or even a pencil?"

Without a doubt, the most interesting question—and the one that has been most hotly debated since the nineteenth century—is this one: Did Travis really draw a line a few days previous to the battle and ask those who wished to stay and fight with him to cross it? Since it was first made public in late 1872, reactions to the story, from serious historians as well as the general public, have ranged from enthusiastic acceptance to blind condemnation and every opinion in between. As with much of the Alamo narrative, historians see many limitations, as noted above, to the existing sources of this incident. Still, the image of the line in the dust is extraordinarily vivid and thrilling in what it represents—in this case, life or death, and a willful choice between the two—and thus it has become iconic in popular literature, culture, and phraseology. In the memorable words of historian J. Frank Dobie, "It is a Grand Canyon cut into the bedrock of human emotions and heroical impulses.... Nobody forgets the line. It is drawn too deep and straight."

To answer the question—or attempt to—we must first consider the evidence pertaining to the life of a man named

Louis "Moses" Rose, for his name is inextricably linked with the line.

FROM ITS INCEPTION IN 1857, the annual *Texas Almanac* has included historical and biographical sketches of the Texas Revolution, often written by the participants themselves. In its 1873 edition there appeared an article entitled "An Escape from the Alamo" by a veteran of that conflict named William Physick Zuber. The five-page account related the story of Moses Rose, a Frenchman from Nacogdoches who escaped from the Alamo a few days before the predawn assault on March 6. Zuber claimed that Rose walked to his (Zuber's) parents' house—two hundred miles away, on Lake Creek, some twenty miles northeast of Washington, Texas, on the Brazos River.

Aside from Rose's escape, the most interesting part of the story involves William Barret Travis, the commander of the fort. Two hours before sunset on March 3, he purportedly called his men together and delivered an inspiring speech, imploring them "to remain in this fort, to resist every assault, and to sell our lives as dearly as possible." Then he offered each man the choice of staying or attempting an escape: "Col. Travis then drew his sword, and with its point traced a line upon the ground, extending from the right to the left of the file. Then, resuming his position in front of the centre, he said, 'I now want every man who is determined to stay here and die with me to come across this line. Who will be first? March!'"

Every man who was able to do so crossed, until only a few were left. James Bowie, sick and prostrate on a cot, asked for help across; four men carried him over. The remaining sick were assisted across, leaving only one man—Rose.

When asked why he would not cross, Rose replied that he was not prepared to die. Soon after, he climbed the wall and made his way down the river three miles before heading east. That night he traveled through a thicket of prickly pear cactus, resulting in many thorns in his legs. He continued to head east, avoiding roads for fear of encountering Mexican scouts, and arrived at the home of the Zubers, longtime friends, a few weeks later, lame and in much pain. He rested and recuperated there for a few weeks, the Zubers doing what they could to heal his legs by pulling the thorns out and applying salve to his injuries. During his stay, he retold his story several times until they knew it almost by heart.

William Zuber was fifteen at the time and serving with Sam Houston's army, but when he returned home months later, he heard Rose's account from his parents, Mary Ann and Abraham Zuber—or so he claimed.

Thirty-five years later, in 1871, Zuber set down the story, aided by his aged mother's phenomenal memory. The account appeared in late 1872, upon publication of the 1873 *Texas Almanac*. Zuber's article ended with a signed statement from his mother endorsing it and concluding with the following words: "The part which purports to be Rose's statement of what he saw and heard in the Alamo, of his escape, and of what befell him afterwards is precisely the substance of what Rose stated to my husband and myself."

Reaction to the story was varied then and since. Some believed it, others have not. Three years after its first appearance, Rufus Grimes, brother of Alamo defender Albert Grimes and a neighbor of the Zubers, wrote to Texas governor E. M. Pease to express his support and corroborate the account: "This account is entitled to full credit.... This Wm. P. Zuber is a man of undoubted veracity and when Rose escaped from the Alamo he made his way to the house of Abram Zuber an old friend and acquaintance then living in Roans Prairie in this county (Grimes) where he staid until his feet got well enough to travel again (his feet & legs were full of the cactus thorns), traveling in the night — Zuber tells me of many other interesting statements made by Rose besides what is stated in the sketch." Over the next few decades some Texas historians incorporated parts of Zuber's story into their writings — barely a year after its first publication, James M. Morphis's *History of Texas* (1874) repeated Zuber's account of Travis's speech, the line, and Rose's escape verbatim, though he added: "The writer takes this account of Mr. Rose, *cum grano salis,* though it may be true." Homer S. Thrall, in his *A History of Texas* (1876), also incorporated most of the story into its text as history. And Mrs. Anna Pennybacker included a brief version of Zuber's article in her 1888 publication *A New History of Texas,* which was subsequently adopted for use in Texas classrooms. In her revised edition of 1895, the story was given more space, and Zuber at her request added some details.

Others, however, expressed skepticism. In 1877, the adjutant general of Texas, William Steele, wrote Zuber inquiring about the story's veracity. Zuber replied in a series of letters, often stretching the truth and going to great lengths to defend and explain his clearly embroidered original account. Around the turn of the century, he penned several articles for the *Quarterly of the Texas State Historical Association* in which he continued to defend it. In one, he admitted that his main purpose in writing it was to preserve for posterity Travis's speech, and he had done so by compiling and rewriting his mother's recollections of Rose's "disconnected recitals," as Zuber put it, and combining those with his feel for Travis's style from his dispatches. Zuber also insisted that only one paragraph in the speech was his invention. He never revealed, at least publicly (or privately, in any known correspondence), which paragraph that was—or discussed the line at all. He wrote some good history—his posthumously published auto-biography, *My Eighty Years in Texas,* is well regarded, and his unpublished, 1,500-page collection of Texan profiles is consulted frequently by historians researching the period. But he damaged his reputation by these labored explanations and by two other fanciful accounts of the Alamo that he passed on in published articles. One claimed to be an account of Bowie's death furnished by a young Mexican army fifer, which is absurd on the face of it: when the bedridden Bowie is brought before Santa Anna, he insults the general, who then orders his tongue cut out. The other concerned Crockett's death, and was even wilder and more unbelievable, though Zuber himself explained his contempt for the story, claiming he had only repeated it as an example of the absurd rumors spreading about the Alamo. Nevertheless, since the time of his death in 1913—the last surviving veteran of the Army of San Jacinto—he has been frequently labeled a teller of tall tales, and his story of Rose and the line has been labeled a legend at best.

Without corroborating evidence, historians were increasingly wary even of the existence of Moses Rose. His name was not on either of the two lists of the Alamo garrison—the January 15, 1836, muster roll or the February 1, 1836, election certificate—although other men known to have died in the Alamo were also not listed. (The garrison roster was somewhat fluid in the months between the battle of Béxar and the arrival of the Mexican army on February 23, with volunteers coming and going rather freely.) But the March 24, 1836, *Telegraph and Texas Register* had run a list of the fallen derived from couriers John W. Smith and Gerald Navan that included the entry "Rose, of Nacogdoches." And Susanna Dickinson Hannig had mentioned the line more than once—first, in an interview conducted in September 1877 with someone from the Texas adjutant general's office in which she had related the following:

> On the evening previous to the massacre, Col. Travis asked the command that if any desired to escape, now was the time, to let it be Known, & to step out of the ranks. But one stepped out. His name to the best of my recollection was Ross. The next morning he was missing—During the final engagement one Milton, jumped over the ramparts & was killed—
>
> Col. Almonte (Mexican) told me that the man who had deserted the evening before had also been Killed & that if I wished to satisfy myself of the fact that I could see the body, still lying there, which I declined.

There was no known Ross in the garrison, and it was pointed out that "Ross" could easily have been "Rose" to the illiterate woman, who surely could not have known the name of every man in the Alamo much less recall them after forty-one years. And as Zuber himself later observed, Almonte "would have made the same remark of any other man in the Alamo."

Mrs. Hannig related the story of the line at least two other times. Less than a year after the 1877 interview, a correspondent for the *National Police Gazette* visited her in Austin. His article ran in the May 4, 1878, edition of the paper, and included the following account:

> The chivalrous Travis coolly drew a line, requesting all who would stand by him to step over, a request all but one, without hesitation, complied with. He was permitted to take his departure, but was shot by the enemy in so doing.

She gave only one more newspaper interview. Three years later, in an April 28, 1881, story in the *San Antonio Daily Express*, a newspaperman described his walk through the Alamo with Mrs. Hannig upon her first return to San Antonio since the fall of the garrison there. He related her description of this particular scene:

> But about one hundred and sixty sound persons were in the Alamo, and when the enemy appeared, overwhelmingly, upon the environs of the city to the west, and about where the International depot now stands, the Noble Travis called up his men, drew a line with his sword and said: "My soldiers, I am going to meet the fate that becomes me. Those who will stand by me, let them remain, but those who desire to go, let them go—and who crosses the line that I have drawn, shall go!" The scene is represented by Mrs. Hannig to have been grand—in that its location was above the results and influences of ordinary sentiment and patriotism, and bore the plain tige of that divinity of principle which characterizes the acts of the truly noble and the brave.

True, Mrs. Hannig—or the reporter—got the meaning of the line reversed: in this version, only those men who wished to leave crossed the line. And there is no mention of Rose. But in this account and the previous two, she had remembered that Travis had called the men together, addressed them, and offered each man the choice of staying or going—and included the fact that he drew a line to separate the groups.

Doubters pointed out that she had not mentioned the line, or Rose's escape, before the appearance of the Zuber story in the 1873 *Texas Almanac*. But the fact is that she gave no interviews on the subject before 1873, at least that we know of. Besides a few published lines here and there from people who had talked to her, and a few short depositions concerning land claims for the heirs of three Alamo defenders, there was no extensive interview with or account from her when she died in 1883.

The story of the line, and Susanna's testimony regarding it, was supported by the 1901 publication of *The Life and Writings of Rufus C. Burleson,* a collection of writings by and about an early Texas churchman who arrived in Houston in the late 1840s and later became the second president of Baylor University. In a floridly written (and clearly embellished) sketch of Susanna, he related how he first heard her story in 1849, when she came to hear him preach, and many times after that:

> She has often told me of the solemn hour when the heroic Travis drew a long line with his sword and said, "Now soldiers, every man that is resolved never to surrender, but need be to die fighting, let him cross over this line," and the 182 heroes leaped over the line at once. But the heroic Bowie, lying on his pallet or straw emaciated with consumption, could not stand up, but cried aloud, "Boys, do take me over that line, for I intend to die fighting," and his companions carried him over amid the wildest shouts of applause.

In the first decade of the twentieth century, the story of another Alamo survivor was featured several times in local newspapers. Enrique Esparza was eleven years old (or thereabouts, since reporters claimed a different age in some accounts) when he, his mother, and his siblings endured the siege and battle. In 1907, in his longest interview, a septuagenarian Enrique Esparza told *San Antonio Daily Express* reporter Charles Merritt Barnes his story, including the following:

> Rose left after this armistice had expired and after the others had been sent for succor. Rose went out after Travis drew the line with his sword. He was the only man who did not cross the line. Up to then he had fought as bravely as anyone there. He had stood by the cannon.
>
> Rose went out during the night. They opened a window for him and let him go.

Barnes interviewed several aging San Antonians about their Alamo experiences, and it is clear that he embroidered some of their accounts, adding details, supplying an elegant formality to their phrasing, and maybe prompting these senior citizens to remember events more than six decades removed. But did he insert the story of Rose and the line? Perhaps. Still, Esparza's father, Gregorio, was an artilleryman, so Enrique would likely have been familiar with most of the other gunners, particularly since the families were quartered in the church, almost directly below his father's battery. Esparza also mentioned the line in another account, included in *Rise of the Lone Star* (1936), though it was related to the book's author by her mother, who claimed to have heard it from Esparza:

> When he [Travis] felt that they must fight it out alone, he gave his men a chance to say whether they would stay by him to the end. I saw him draw the line with his sword, and heard him say, "All who are willing to die cross this line." I think all jumped across. Señor Bowie said, "Boys, lift my cot across that line."

The *Daily Express* also ran an article written by another old-timer on June 16, 1912, entitled "Davy Crockett as I Knew Him," by William Alexander Ridgway. In it, the author described his knowledge of the backwoodsman. He also wrote: "In 1880 I travelled in Texas and stopped one day with a man named Smith. He was a very old man.... He also told me of seeing one man many times who, in leaving the fort and making his way through the prickly pear, had suffered terrible torture, all the skin and flesh had come off the forepart of his legs and the bone was naked." Yes, this is secondhand testimony, but if it's authentic, it sounds very much like Rose on his way east.

Ridgway's article was the last known mention of Rose for a while. Zuber's story was edging into mythic territory. In 1908, it was deleted from the Pennybacker history, and when her textbook was replaced by another one in 1913, and that one was supplanted by a newer text in 1932, neither included any reference to Rose or the line. In 1914, there was no mention of it in Frank Johnson's *A History of Texas and Texans* (more about this book later), nor was it mentioned in 1922's *The Republic of Texas* by Clarence Wharton. It appeared that Rose and the line had made the complete transition to myth.

That was how matters stood until the 1930s, when a diligent east Texas researcher and Nacogdoches county clerk named Robert Bruce Blake took it upon himself to transcribe and sometimes translate a massive number of documents from the Nacogdoches and Béxar archives and from various collections—letters, financial records, censuses, muster rolls, family papers, proclamations, and virtually any kind of legal document imaginable. When he finished, the result was ninety-seven large volumes of typewritten transcriptions. He found quite a bit of information on Rose—enough, it appeared, to support the fact of Rose's existence and involvement in some of the events of the Texas Revolution. Intrigued, Blake investigated further, even interviewing older residents of the area whose parents had passed down memories of Rose. Though much of Blake's evidence was secondhand and thirdhand, or circumstantial, it appeared that Louis "Moses" Rose had indeed existed—and had actually escaped from the Alamo before the final assault, if Rose's testimony in a half dozen legal cases involving the lands and heirs of Alamo defenders was any indication:

BLAIR: "Left him in the Alamo 3 March 1836"

CLARKE: "States he saw him a few days before fall of the Alamo—a single Man"

DAY: "Died with Travis in the Alamo"

HASKELL: "Knew him four years, supposes him killed in the Alamo"

SEWELL: "Knew him in the Alamo and left him there 3 days before it fell"

WILSON: "Knew him before the 2nd of May, 1835, was in the Alamo when taken"

It was clear, at least, that the judges in those cases (actually, the three men who sat on the Nacogdoches County Board of Land Commissioners, all distinguished citizens—Adolphus Sterne, later a Texas state congressman and senator; Dr. James Harper Starr, the future Texas state treasurer; and William Hart, the second chief justice of the county) believed Rose's story and testimony to be true: though they rejected dozens of other claims, not one of these claims or the ten others in which Rose was deposed was disapproved. These depositions appear to validate the Zuber account of Rose's escape—perhaps not in every detail but in terms of the larger picture.

Blake found many other documents that testified to Rose's existence and activities in Nacogdoches before October 24, 1835, when he sold some land and his household and personal effects to a neighbor. There is a gap after that until May 10, 1836, when an account in his name appears on the general ledger of a Nacogdoches merchant—silent testimony to (and circumstantial evidence of) his service in Béxar. Soon after his return, Rose opened a butcher shop, and court records and testimony present a picture of a man who kept to himself and maintained a surly temperament that sometimes rubbed people the wrong way—including the Mexican who tried to kill him with a knife and whom Rose then disarmed and injured with the same blade. Another man, a customer, complained about the tough meat Rose sold him: in response, Rose grabbed a Bowie knife and threatened to cut the unhappy customer in two if he ever complained again. When another man made the same complaint, Rose turned around to get a loaded shotgun he kept on a rack. The terrified man ran out the door, jumped a fence, and disappeared.

Rose did not volunteer information about himself, but when acquaintances asked him why he hadn't stayed in the Alamo, his invariable reply was, "By God, I wasn't ready to die."

Blake told of Rose's final years, when he left Nacogdoches in the early 1840s. After a brief stay in Natchitoches, Louisiana, he drifted to Logansport, Louisiana, where he was given a place to stay by Aaron Ferguson, who owned a plantation nearby. He died in 1851 or 1852. Blake wrote that Ferguson's daughter "stated that the old man was a great deal of trouble during the latter years of his life, because of the chronic sores caused by the cactus thorns in his legs, picked up during his flight from the Alamo...that for some time prior to his death, at the age of sixty-odd years, he was bed-ridden by reason of those chronic sores."

Blake wrote a fulsome account of his findings, "Rose and His Escape from the Alamo," though it was never published in his lifetime. (It was not until 2003, in researcher Todd Hansen's monumental and comprehensive compendium of Alamo material, *The Alamo Reader,* that it saw publication.) But a brief overview by Blake (containing little of the background documentation) was included in a 1939 publication of the Texas Folk-Lore Society edited by well-known historian J. Frank Dobie and entitled *In the Shadow of History.* The book also reprinted Zuber's 1873 account and an analysis of the subject by Dobie, an admitted romantic, who believed the story.

Blake's findings were enough to persuade popular historian Walter Lord of the truth of the old Frenchman's story, and he incorporated both Rose and the line into his 1961 book about the Alamo, *A Time to Stand* (although seven years later he professed doubt about Travis's line, or at least about the evidence for it, in an article entitled "Myths and Realities of the Alamo"). But William C. Davis, in his superbly researched book on the Alamo's major personalities, *Three Roads to the Alamo: The Lives and Fortunes of David Crockett, James Bowie, and William Barret Travis,* dismissed the story of Rose and the line. "Nothing in the story stands up to scrutiny," he wrote of the Zuber account in an endnote, and concluded, "So far as this present work is concerned, the event simply did not happen, or if it did, then something much more reliable than an admittedly fictionalized secondhand account written thirty-five years after the fact is necessary to establish it beyond question."

Davis is a rigorous historian, but he wrote that before a few other documents came to light.

AMELIA WILLIAMS, author of the first extensive study of the battle—"A Critical Study of the Siege of the Alamo and the Personnel of Its Defenders," which began life as her doctoral dissertation and from which five chapters were excerpted in modified form over four issues of the *Southwestern Historical Quarterly* in 1933 and 1934 — also dismissed the story of the line, pointing out that she had not found it printed before 1873:

> There is some indication, however, that it was in earlier circulation. Mr. A. D. Griffith...told me in 1929, that he had, in the early sixties, heard the fate of Rose discussed by his uncle, A. J. Griffith, and Captain Frank Dupree. Historians have been divided in their opinion concerning this story, the most careful students having discredited it. At best they consider it a legend, plausible perhaps, but almost certainly the creation of a vivid imagination.

Her statement on historians is accurate. Her private papers and correspondence, however, tell a richer and fuller story. In a 1932 letter, she expanded on what she had heard from Griffith:

> Mr. Griffith [A. D. (Almeron Dickinson) Griffith, grandson of Susanna Dickinson, who was taken by his father after his mother, Angelina, separated from her husband] says that when he was a small boy just after the Civil War, he was wont to sit around and listen to his uncle, H. A. Griffith, and Captain Frank Dupree talk about wars and battles. He says he first heard the Rose story from them. This was down near Matagorda — in the old Caney country. He is quite sure this was before the story was published by Zuber. Mrs. Sterling [Susan Sterling, who lived with her

grandmother Susanna Dickinson as a child] says that she heard her grand mother (Mrs. Dickinson) tell it many times. At first she was positive that she had heard it prior to 1873, but upon several weeks consideration she said she could not be certain whether she heard her grandmother tell the story before 1873 or not.

And in Ms. Williams's handwritten rough notes of an interview with A. D. Griffith (found by Todd Hansen during his research for *The Alamo Reader* but not included there), there is even more:

As young boy sat for hours and listened to his uncle J. D. Griffith and Capt. Frank Dupree talk about early days. Says that some time in 60s heard them talk about Rose.... When he made his appearance at home and told about his escape from the Alamo—told all people he was sure Travis and all his men were dead by that time for there was no chance for them to hold out against St. Ana's force. Said when Travis gave him chance to go he took it.... Capt. Frank Dupree saw Rose—When Rose said when all hope <u>lost</u>—<u>all</u>—Rose—said Rose crawled thru aqueduct after dark—said crawled 4 or 5 hundred yards in thistle—went home. Frank Dupree: You damn dirty coward or you would have stayed; Got chance at life and took it—All against him—worked on him so people talked about mobbing him—Afraid <u>and skipped out.</u> [Griffith] Must have been in 50s for was about 8 or 10 yrs old.

This is a significant document. Captain Frank Dupree (who earned that rank serving with the Texas Cavalry, then part of the army of the Confederate States of America, during the Civil War) told the Griffiths in the 1850s that he talked to Rose, who supplied the details listed above—many years before the Zuber account was published in 1873, and before A. D. Griffith could have heard it from his grandmother, whom he saw very little of as a child. Moreover, some details supplied by Dupree have never been published anywhere before now.

Corroboration of the A. D. Griffith claim appeared the next year from Dobie. In a 1940 *Dallas Morning News* story entitled "The Line That Travis Drew," he wrote: "Charles W. Ramsdell, professor of history in the University of Texas, and one of the pillars in the Texas State Historical Society, married A. D. Griffith's daughter. Ramsdell tells me that he, too, used to hear Griffith relate the story—not however, as coming from Mrs. Dickinson but as coming from his paternal family, who were among the early colonists. When the revolution broke out, they were living in what is now Grimes County. According to tradition in the Griffith family, Rose came to their home on his way east from the Alamo and told of his escape." (More information on the Zuber account—or at least the likelihood that the Rose story could have been accurately passed from Rose to Mrs. Zuber to her son—would be supplied in a July 4, 1967, column by Frank X. Tolbert. He quoted a June 9, 1935, affidavit by a grandson of Mary Ann Zuber, who wrote: "Grandmother had a wonderful memory. She could read any book and recite the gist of it from the beginning to end. I have heard her recite Shakespeare, Byron, or Milton's Paradise Lost line for line. I have heard the Rose story many times and always told as the truth.")

And in another letter, Williams related the opinion of Griffith's sister as to the truth of the line story: "Mrs. Sterling [granddaughter of Susanna Dickinson, and raised by her] avowed that it was."

Hansen found even more corroboration of the Rose story's existence pre-1873 in Williams's papers. She corresponded with a neighbor of the Zubers, W. T. Neblett, who wrote to her in 1935: "Now the Rose story published in 1873 was common Zuber family history and I cannot say definitely when I first heard the story but I feel sure that it was before 1873. I was born in 1857 and between 10 and 16 years old and living within 10 miles which was a neighbor distance in those days; and especially with our families friendly and intimate and my parents educated for those days I feel sure that I heard of it before 1873." And in a subsequent letter, Mr. Neblett relayed a letter received from his sister, Mary Neblett Brown, on the subject:

"Yes, I heard the 'Rose story' from Pa himself. He had gotten it from the Zuber family. I heard Pa speak of it. He believed it. I see no reason to doubt it. Pa died in 1871." [Their father, William H. Neblett, was an attorney who had lived in Texas since 1840 and had practiced law in Grimes County since about 1852.] No doubt I heard this story at the same time that my sister did which must have been 1868 or 69 as I know he had some business with J. R. Edwards, brother-in-law to Zuber, who lived close neighbor to the Zubers.... I know of my own knowledge that the older people of the community and the county talked of the Rose story and regarded it as a fact but I cannot fix on exact date prior to 1873.

Mrs. Brown is most emphatic about whom she heard it from — her father — and remembers quite clearly that "he believed it." Her father died in 1871, before the appearance of the Zuber story in the 1873 *Texas Almanac*.

* * *

As I WAS CONDUCTING THE RESEARCH for the book you hold in your hands, I found a few items that, combined with the previous information, strongly point to the truth of the story of Rose and the line.

Frank Johnson, an early Texas colonist, was one of the firebrands of the Texas Revolution, involved from the outset in the territory's fight for independence. He knew Travis, another member of the war party, well. Johnson moved to Austin in the early 1870s, and began researching and writing a comprehensive history of Texas. Left unfinished at his death in 1884, it would be completed by Eugene C. Barker and Ernest W. Winkler and published in 1914 in five volumes as *A History of Texas and Texans*, a tome well respected for its accuracy, information, and insight.

Johnson's papers, most of them his handwritten notes and transcriptions, fill several boxes in the Dolph Briscoe Center for American History at the University of Texas at Austin. In one file labeled "Historical Notes—Alamo," there is a transcription of Zuber's 1873 Rose story. On the next page, in Johnson's own hand, is written the following:

The foregoing communication was read to Mrs. Dickinson, now Mrs. Hannig, the only living witness of the lamentable and sad catastrophe of the Alamo. Says that she did not know Rose personally, but recollects that a man escaped at the time mentioned; that the troops were drawn up in line and addressed by Col. Travis.

Between the time of Rose's escape and the fall of the Alamo, she heard the men speak of the escape, but none believed that he would get away alive.

We were well acquainted with the elder Zuber, during his lifetime, and knew him as a man of strict veracity. The family is highly respectable, and any statement made by them is entitled to full credit and belief.

Johnson and Susanna Dickinson Hannig both lived in Austin when Zuber's "An Escape from the Alamo" reached the public late in 1872. It seems likely that Johnson—an indefatigable researcher, who died in Mexico while on a research trip—read the Zuber account soon after publication and decided to hear from Mrs. Hannig directly what she thought of the story. Certainly, participants sometimes incorporate the accounts of others into their memories—but Johnson makes clear that this was her first reaction to hearing the Zuber story, not an account rendered months or years later. The extra details she adds ("she heard the men speak of the escape, but none believed that he would get away alive") sound genuine, particularly for a woman who was not known to possess a vivid imagination. (Despite some inconsistencies in interviews, possibly inserted by reporters, there is a conspicuous absence in hers of the absurdities that populate so many other Alamo survivor accounts.)

That Johnson talked directly to Mrs. Hannig, and believed Zuber's story of Rose's escape—at least in its essentials—once he heard her corroborate it, is clear from a December 26, 1875, story in the Galveston *Daily News.* Entitled "Heroes of the Alamo" (and sloppily edited and proofread, with a strikingly large number of misspelled names), it is chiefly concerned with the ongoing attempt by adjutant general William Steele to ascertain a correct roster of Alamo defender names. Steele had enlisted the help of Johnson, and a list is included in the article. On it is "Moses Ross," obviously "Rose" misspelled. And immediately following the list is this: "Col. Johnson says Moses Ross escaped before the assault.... This list Colonel J.

regards as full and complete as any that can be made at this distance of time." The article continues:

The child who survived [Susanna Dickinson], and is now living in Austin, remembers a circumstance which might account for one of the absentees and reduce the number to that extent. The captain of one of the companies, the company being in line, called upon all his men willing to remain and fight to the last to step forward. All responded but one, and he was permitted to go. Whether this was the man sent with dispatches or the one who is reported to have escaped before the assault, or a third person who has never been heard from since, we can not tell. If living even, it is not likely he would at this time step forward to explain.

The reporter obviously talked to or communicated with Johnson, who told him the story of Rose and the line; then he somehow failed to include Travis's name as "the captain of one of the companies" in his retelling. (The possibility exists that the reporter got the line details directly from Mrs. Hannig—"The child who survives, and is now living in Austin, remembers a circumstance"—but this seems unlikely given the context of the article and the lack of any mention of an interview with her.) Johnson, it is apparent, believed the story after talking to Mrs. Hannig.

Finally, there is this. In the September 9, 1901, edition of the *Gonzales Inquirer* there ran a story entitled "The Fall of the Alamo" detailing an interview with David S. H. Darst, a Gonzales resident "who was one of the participants of the struggle for Texas independence. Darst, a former mayor of Gonzales, and one of the founders of the *Inquirer* in 1851, had called at the *Inquirer* office the previous day to deny certain untrue stories and give the true facts." (He was also the son of Jacob Darst, one of the "Gonzales 32," those members of the Gonzales Ranging Company of Mounted Volunteers who had reinforced the Alamo on March 1 and died there five days later. The younger Darst had expressed a desire to go with his father, but had been denied permission.) As related by the reporter:

> Mr. Darst was well-acquainted with Mr. and Mrs. Dickinson before the fall of the Alamo and with Mrs. Dickinson after the fall of the Alamo. He also knew the man referred to as a servant called Rose. Mr. Darst says he saw the man Rose in the year 1840. That he was a Frenchman and was in the Alamo before the fall and the Frenchman gave this version: When the Alamo was besieged by the Mexicans and no help near, Travis drew a line and asked all who would stay with him to come over on his side. All crossed over except himself (Rose) and he decided to try and escape during the night. He made his escape by going down the ditch referred to in the above extract [Zuber's account]. He did not come to Gonzales, the nearest station, but went to east Texas and Mr. Darst did not see him until 1840. This is what Mr. Rose told him.

This article serves as further corroboration of the Rose story by a respected individual, who received it directly from the Frenchman himself.

FINALLY, from a larger perspective, Travis's speech, and the line, make sense. After the arrival of a large Mexican reinforcement on March 3, it must have been increasingly clear that an assault was imminent—and that, despite repeated assurances of Texian reinforcements, none were forthcoming. There are also details that support this knowledge, from Travis giving his ring to Angelina Dickinson and Crockett mentioning his desire to die in his best clothes to the proximity of the Mexican batteries and the knowledge that ladders were being built. And, as Dobie points out, "For Travis to have drawn the line would have been entirely natural.... Travis certainly thought that he was acting a part that the light of centuries to come would illumine." As is abundantly evident from his actions and his dispatches—and his readings, from Porter's *The Scottish Chiefs* to Scott's Waverley novels—he possessed a taste for the romantic and a flair for the eloquently dramatic. The speech and the line would have been entirely in character—and not without precedent in history, from Francisco Pizarro to Ben Milam, who either drew a line in the dirt or asked his men to step across a line or path already there.

As for Moses Rose, he did himself no favors with his story, since he knew others would view his actions as cowardly. It would have made much more sense to either keep his existence in the Alamo quiet or to claim that he had been sent out from the fort as a scout or courier. Instead, he told the truth, and branded himself forever as "the coward of the Alamo"—an unfair legacy for a man who proved his courage many times throughout his life.

THERE ARE HISTORIANS who will complain that much of this evidence is hearsay, or circumstantial, or that post-1873 journalists may have inserted such details into their "interviews," especially with Mrs. Hannig and Enrique Esparza. They will say that there is no direct evidence that Moses Rose escaped from the Alamo, or that he was even there, or that he was even the same individual, if he ever existed, as the Louis/Lewis Rose abundantly documented in the Nacogdoches records—and that there is even less documentation for the story of the line that Travis drew. Those historians would be technically correct.

But much of what we know as accepted history, as perceived truth—particularly involving events before the advent of recording devices in the late nineteenth century—is derived from similar, or even weaker, sources. Whole swaths of history as we know it derive from similarly limited documentation. Historians have often cited hearsay evidence, though of course after applying tests of bias, objectivity, accuracy, and witness proximity.

An important point to bear in mind is this: there is not a single event associated with the siege and fall of the Alamo that has been related in so many independent versions by so many different individuals attesting to its fundamental truth. Furthermore, not a single one of these people had an ulterior motive, e.g., for money or for personal aggrandizement, in supporting Zuber and his 1873 account. There now exists enough reliable evidence to consider the existence of Moses Rose, his escape from the Alamo, and the line drawn by Travis to be acceptable, factual history.

APPENDIX ONE

Mexican Army of Operations
Principal Officers

General Staff, Mexican Army of Operations in Texas
General Antonio López de Santa Anna, commander in chief
General Vicente Filisola, second commander in chief
General Juan Valentín Amador, general staff
General Manuel Fernández Castrillón, aide-de-camp
General Martín Perfecto de Cós, general staff
Colonel Juan Nepomuceno Almonte, general staff
Colonel José Batres, general staff
Colonel Ricardo Dromundo, commissary general
Colonel Esteban Mora, general staff
Lieutenant Colonel Marcial Aguirre, general staff
Lieutenant Colonel Pedro de Ampudia, artillery commander
Lieutenant Colonel José Vicente Miñón, first adjutant, cavalry
Captain Marcos Barragan, cavalry
Ramón Martínez Caro, personal secretary to the commander in chief

Brigade Commanders

General Juan José Andrade, Cavalry Brigade
General Antonio Gaona, First Infantry Brigade
General Joaquín Ramírez y Sesma, Vanguard Brigade
General Eugenio Tolsa, Second Infantry Brigade
General José Urrea (division moving against Goliad)

Battalion/Regiment Commanders

General Ventura Mora, Dolores Cavalry Regiment
Colonel Agustín Amat, Zapadores Permanente
Colonel Nicolás Condelle, Morelos Infantry Permanente
Colonel Francisco Duque, Toluca Infantry Activo
Colonel Juan Morales, San Luis Potosí Infantry Activo
Colonel José María Romero, Matamoros Infantry Permanente
Colonel José Mariano de Salas, Jiménez Infantry Permanente
Lieutenant Colonel José Nicolás de la Portilla, commander, Yucatán Infantry Permanente
Lieutenant Colonel Gregorio Uruñuela, Aldama Infantry Permanente

Others

Colonel Domingo de Ugartechea, military commander, Coahuila y Texas
Lieutenant Colonel José Enrique de la Peña, Zapadores Permanente
Lieutenant Colonel Rómulo Díaz de la Vega, Zapadores Permanente
Captain José Juan Sánchez (Navarro), aide-de-camp to General Cós
Lieutenant Francisco de Castañeda, commander, Alamo presidial company

APPENDIX TWO

Alamo Defenders

Official list compiled by the Daughters of the Texas Revolution (alternate spellings of surnames appear in parentheses)

Abamillo, Juan
Allen, Robert
Andross, Miles DeForrest
Autry, Micajah
Badillo, Juan
Bailey, Peter James III
Baker, Isaac G.
Baker, William Charles M.
Ballantine, Richard W.
Ballentine, John J.
Baugh, John J.
Bayliss, Joseph
Blair, John
Blair, Samuel
Blazeby, William

Bonham, James Butler
Bourne, Daniel
Bowie, James
Bowman, Jesse B.
Brown, George
Brown, James
Brown, Robert
Buchanan, James
Burns, Samuel E.
Butler, George D.
Cain, John
Campbell, Robert
Carey, William R.
Clark, Charles Henry
Clark, M. B.

Cloud, Daniel William
Cochran, Robert E.
Cottle, George Washington
Courtman, Henry
Crawford, Lemuel
Crockett, David
Crossman, Robert
Cummings, David P.
Cunningham, Robert
Darst, Jacob C.
Davis, John
Day, Freeman H. K.
Day, Jerry C.
Daymon, Squire
Dearduff, William
Dennison, Stephen
Despallier, Charles
Dewall, Lewis
Dickinson, Almeron
Dillard, John Henry
Dimpkins, James R.
Duvalt, Andrew
Espalier, Carlos
Esparza, Gregorio
Evans, Robert
Evans, Samuel B.
Ewing, James L.
Fauntleroy, William Keener
Fishbaugh, William
Flanders, John
Floyd, Dolphin Ward
Forsyth, John Hubbard

Fuentes, Antonio
Fuqua, Galba
Garnett, William
Garrand, James W.
Garrett, James Girard
Garvin, John E.
Gaston, John E.
George, James
Goodrich, John C.
Grimes, Albert Calvin
Guerrero, José María
Gwynne, James C.
Hannum, James
Harris, John
Harrison, Andrew Jackson
Harrison, William B.
Hawkins, Joseph M.
Hays, John M.
Heiskell, Charles M.
Herndon, Patrick Henry
Hersee, William Daniel
Holland, Tapley
Holloway, Samuel
Howell, William D.
Jackson, Thomas
Jackson, William Daniel
Jameson, Green B.
Jennings, Gordon C.
Jimenes (Ximenes), Damacio
Johnson, Lewis
Johnson, William
Jones, John

Kellogg, John Benjamin
Kenney, James
Kent, Andrew
Kerr, Joseph
Kimbell (Kimble), George C.
King, William Philip
Lewis, William Irvine
Lightfoot, William J.
Lindley, Jonathan L.
Linn, William
Losoya, Toribio
Main, George Washington
Malone, William T.
Marshall, William
Martin, Albert
McCafferty, Edward
McCoy, Jesse
McDowell, William
McGee, James
McGregor, John
McKinney, Robert
Melton, Eliel
Miller, Thomas R.
Mills, William
Millsaps, Isaac
Mitchell, Edwin T.
Mitchell, Napoleon B.
Mitchusson, Edward F.
Moore, Robert B.
Moore, Willis A.
Musselman, Robert
Nava, Andrés

Neggan, George
Nelson, Andrew M.
Nelson, Edward
Nelson, George
Northcross, James
Nowlan, James
Pagan, George
Parker, Christopher Adam
Parks, William
Perry, Richardson
Pollard, Amos
Reynolds, John Purdy
Roberts, Thomas H.
Robertson, James Waters
Robinson, Isaac
Rose, James M.
Rusk, Jackson J.
Rutherford, Joseph
Ryan, Isaac
Scurlock, Mial
Sewell, Marcus L.
Shied, Manson
Simmons, Cleveland Kinlock
Smith, Andrew H.
Smith, Charles S.
Smith, Joshua G.
Smith, William H.
Starr, Richard
Stewart, James E.
Stockton, Richard L.
Summerlin, A. Spain
Summers, William E.

Sutherland, William DePriest
Taylor, Edward
Taylor, George
Taylor, James
Taylor, William
Thomas, B. Archer M.
Thomas, Henry
Thompson, Jesse G.
Thomson, John W.
Thruston (Thurston), John M.
Trammel, Burke
Travis, William Barret
Tumlinson, George W.
Tylee, James
Walker, Asa
Walker, Jacob

Ward, William B.
Warnell, Henry
Washington, Joseph G.
Waters, Thomas
Wells, William
White, Isaac
White, Robert
Williamson, Hiram James
Wills, William
Wilson, David L.
Wilson, John
Wolf, Anthony
Wright, Claiborne
Zanco (Lanco), Charles
John _____

Additions and Deletions

After two decades of intensive investigation into probate records and archives throughout the United States and Mexico, longtime researcher Lee Spencer White (herself a direct descendant of Alamo defender Gordon C. Jennings and the founder of the Alamo Defenders Descendants Association, as well as the author, with Ron Jackson, of the book *Alamo Survivors*) has determined the following names as those of likely Alamo defenders:

Edwards, Nathaniel
Edwards, Samuel
Gordon, Pelitiah
Kedison, _____
McClelland, Ross

Another Alamo historian, Thomas Ricks Lindley, states in his exhaustively researched book *Alamo Traces,* and in the article "Alamo Sources," that the following men are also worthy of inclusion on the list:

Anderson, A.

Andrews, George

Dickson, James

Edwards, Samuel

Eigenhauer, Conrad

Gordon, Pelitiah

Harrison, I. L. K.

Holloway, James

Hutchinson, Thomas P.

Kedison, _____

McClelland, Ross

Morgan (aka Washington), James

Morman, John

Roth, Jacob

Spratt, John

In addition, Lindley came to the conclusion that the following men on the official Daughters of the Texas Revolution list were probably not at the Alamo at the time of the battle:

Bowman, Jesse B.

Brown, George

Brown, James

Clark, Charles Henry

Day, Jerry C.

Guerrero, José María

Hannum, James

Kellogg, John Benjamin

Robertson, James Waters

Robinson, Isaac

Thompson, Jesse G.

ACKNOWLEDGMENTS

The following individuals and institutions were unfailingly gracious and generous with their time and knowledge: Jim Bradshaw of the Haley Memorial Library and History Center, who directed me to the late historian Marguerite Starr Crain, who told me of the circumstances surrounding the Clarinda Pevehouse Kegans account mentioning Travis and Bonham; Casey Greene, head of special collections at the Rosenberg Library, Galveston and Texas History Center; Pat Mosher at the Gonzales County Archives, who many times went above and beyond the call of duty; Alfred Rodriguez at the Bexar County Archives; Matt De Waelsche, archivist at the San Antonio Public Library; Donald Hoffman of Nixon, Texas, and Pat Meyer of La Vernia, Texas, for their generous assistance regarding the major crossings and *parajes* on the old Bexar–Gonzales road, and for their bonhomie while trudging through brush, grass, forest, and mud in search of historical sites; Steve Davis, Mary E. García, Connie Todd, Katie

Salzmann, and G. G. Mortensen at the Southwestern Writers Collection, Texas State University.

At the Dallas Public Library, the seventh floor's fabulous Texana department, overseen by manager Carol Roark (whose presence, helpfulness, and friendship will be missed) and her excellent staff—Beth Anderson, Brian Collins, Rachel Howell, and Steve Gaither—was very helpful.

I would also like to thank my friend Rick Barrick, for his constant encouragement; my brother, Brian Donovan, and his wife, Bridget, for their forbearance; and my good and longtime friends Pat Ryan and his wife, Julie Lebrun, for the same.

To Jennifer Ohlson and the employees and patrons of the White Rhino coffee house in Cedar Hill, Texas, who provided a suitable level of white noise and plenty of great tea—thank you.

Gratitude is also due to Elisabeth Kimber, who read this book from fore to aft and made it better; to Mike O'Keefe, Melissa Shultz, Rick Barrick, Jim Boylston, Todd Hansen, and Jeff Guinn, who read portions and did the same; to Mark Gardner, for the title; and especially to Tom Kailbourn, whose assistance on many subjects, from the Mexican army to many of the translations from Spanish, was invaluable.

The following people helped in ways too numerous to mention: Roger Borroel, Jim Boylston, Bruce Castleman, Wallace Chariton, Bill Chemerka, Craig Covner, Frank de la Teja, William DePalo, Gregg Dimmick, Bill Groneman, Todd Hansen, Stephen L. Hardin, Alan C. Huffines, Paul Hutton, Jake Ivey, Mike Koury, Mark Lemon, Timothy Matovina, Stephen L. Moore, Joseph Musso, Tim Niesen, Raymond Powell, Richard G. Santos, Skipper Steely, Herb True, Gary Zaboly, and especially Kevin Young, whose steady encouragement and assistance were more valuable than he knows.

My thanks to Catherine Best, Don Carleton, Sarah Cleary,

ACKNOWLEDGMENTS

Matt Darby, Evan Hocker, Kathryn Kenefick, Stephanie Malmros, Linda Peterson, Margaret Schlankey, and John Wheat at the Dolph Briscoe Center for American History, University of Texas at Austin; to Russell Martin and his crew of helpful assistants at SMU's DeGolyer Library; to John Molleston, Kevin Klaus, and Alex Chiba at the Texas General Land Office in Austin; to Jean Carefoot, Sergio Velasco, and particularly Donaly Brice, a fine historian who went out of his way to help a fellow writer, at the Texas State Library and Archives Commission; to Lisa Struthers at the San Jacinto Museum of History's Herzstein Library; to Brenda McClurkin at the special collections section of the University of Texas at Arlington Library; to Michael Toon and John Wilson and their excellent staff, particularly Ellen Kuniyuki Brown, at the Texas Collection at Baylor University; to Christian Kelleher at the Nettie Lee Benson Latin American Collection at the University of Texas at Austin; to Samuel Duncan, library director at the Amon Carter Museum; to Susan Eason, archivist at the Catholic Archives of Texas; to Leslie Stapleton, Stephanie D. Boothby, Caitlin Donnelly, Rusty Gámez, and Martha Utterback at the Daughters of the Republic of Texas Library in San Antonio; and to Doris Wilkes, Elise Kidd, and Mildred Duhon, all Alamo defender descendants, and to Doris's husband, Chester Wilkes, who were all extremely helpful in answering questions and supplying information and materials.

At Little, Brown, thanks are due to my editor, Geoff Shandler — the Sultan of Structure — who helped me make this book better; his assistant, Liese Mayer, a fine editor herself; marketing and publicity wizards Heather Fain, Nicole Dewey, Amanda Tobier, Carolyn O'Keefe, Morgan Moroney, and Amanda Brown, who handle so many of the thankless yet important tasks attendant to publishing a book properly; jacket designer Julianna Lee, for the wonderful jacket; and Michael

ACKNOWLEDGMENTS

Pietsch, the smartest man in publishing, for believing in me. Thanks also to copyeditor Barbara Clark for her great work; Howard David Johnson for the striking cover painting; Jeff Ward for the excellent maps; Marty Brazil for the fine Alamo illustration; Melissa Shultz, for assistance with the photos; my daughter, Rachel, who transcribed some of my handwritten chapters; my wife, Judith Price, for putting up with me; and my literary agent, B. J. Robbins, a whiz of an agent, a good friend and colleague, and a hell of a two-stepper.

Finally, a special thanks to Steve Harrigan, who was supportive of this undertaking from the start, and who spent a great deal of time discussing it, critiquing parts of it, and supplying contacts, ideas, and support: "He could feel his heart beating against the pine-needle floor of the forest...."

To all these people, my sincere gratitude. Thank you.

NOTES

The following abbreviations are used in the notes; these and other sources are listed in the bibliography:

BCAH   Dolph Briscoe Center for American History
TSLA   Texas State Library and Archives Commission
DRT   Daughters of the Republic of Texas Library
GLO   Texas General Land Office
Hansen   Todd Hansen, *The Alamo Reader*
PTR   John H. Jenkins, *Papers of the Texas Revolution* (ten volumes)

PROLOGUE

The account of courier James L. Allen's ride from the Alamo is based on an article by Robert H. Davis entitled "Bob Davis Uncovers an Untold Story About the Alamo," published in the *Fort Worth Star-Telegram* on February 28, 1932, in which he recounts an interview with attorney F. C. Proctor, who as a boy heard the story of Allen's ride from Allen himself. Allen's ride is corroborated by the following sources, whose information was chiefly gleaned from Allen descendants: *Memorial and Genealogical Record of Southwest Texas*, pp. 402–3; Wright, *San Antonio de Béxar*, p. 56; and a letter from Viva Crain Schleicher to Samuel Asbury dated December 16, 1934 (box 2, file 52, Samuel

Erson Asbury Papers, Cushing Library, Texas A&M University), in
which the writer states: "Many years ago I heard an old gentleman,
Mr. Jim Allen, tell how as a boy of seventeen, he carried a message
from Travis in the Alamo to Fannin at Goliad." A May 6, 1938,
affidavit by Thomas M. Stell, one-time treasurer of DeWitt
County, also corroborates Allen's account. In it, Stell writes: "I
first knew Judge Jas. L. Allen in 1868 when I was 12 yrs. old.
Some 2 yrs. later I heard his story from his own lips of his
connection with the Alamo. As I remember it now, his state[ment]
was substantially the same as related by F. C. Proctor [the source
for the Davis story cited above]. He said the reason his name had
never appeared in history was on account of his own negligence in
not taking steps to verify the fact that he delivered Travis' message
to Fannin and remained there one day. When he became convinced
Fannin was not going to Travis' relief he concluded to go to
Gonzales and fall in with Houston's men and he went into the
west side of the Guadalupe River, stopping here and there with the
settlers to acquaint them [with] the desperate situation at San
Antonio.... Judge Allen died in 1901 at the age of 86 yrs., a grave
and dignified gentleman not given to boasting.... Judge Allen
lived and died believing he was Travis' last messenger and I
believe likewise" (affidavit courtesy of Mildred Duhon,
great-granddaughter of James L. Allen; punctuation added).

ONE: THE HOTSPUR
The epigraph is from J. H. Kuykendall's "Sketches of Early
    Texians," p. 6, box 3F82, Jonathan Hampton Kuykendall Papers,
    BCAH.
Sources for this biography of Travis include McDonald, *Travis;*
    Kuykendall, "Sketches of Early Texians"; Mixon, "William
    Barret Travis, His Life and Letters"; Davis, *Three Roads to the
    Alamo;* and Travis's own diary, edited by Robert E. Davis and
    published as *The Diary of William Barret Travis.*
Travis's January 28, 1836, letter is reprinted in Chariton, *100 Days in
    Texas,* p. 176, as is the January 29, 1836, letter, pp. 179–80.
    The quote from his diary can be found in Davis, *The Diary of
    William Barret Travis,* March 9, 1834.
According to Travis's nephew, Mark Travis, almost all the
    Stallworths, who were relations on his mother's side, were
    redheaded (Mark Travis to Samuel Asbury, October 14, 1924,
    box 2J83, William Barret Travis Papers, BCAH). As for his

height, he was slightly above the average height of the period—
most likely approximately 5 feet 10 inches: "tall and manly in
appearance" (Amanda Dorsett Scull, quoted in Sowell, *Early
Settlers,* p. 836) ; "Colonel Travis was a fine-looking young man
of more than ordinary height" (Rodríguez, *Memories of Early
Texas,* p. 7); "In person Col. Travis was rather above the average
height" (Kuykendall, "Sketches of Early Texans," p. 7); "a tall
well-formed handsome man" (Guy M. Bryan to W. W. Fontaine,
June 10, 1890, correspondence 1879–1916, box 2D151, W. W.
Fontaine Papers, BCAH).

The quote from Travis's autobiography, any copy of which no longer
exists, appears in Kuykendall, "Sketches of Early Texians" (he
claimed to have read it). Though Travis would claim later that
there were problems in his marriage, there is little or no evidence
that it was in trouble at the time he left Claiborne: "His
assurances to me, that he would return to his family or send for
them as soon as he could obtain the means to make them
comfortable. He continued to write me affectionately and to
repeat his assurances of unchanging attachment until my brother
Wm [William] took exceptions to his conduct towards me
believing as he did that his intention was to abandon me
altogether and inspire me with the hope that he would return to
us [or] send for me until he could no longer conceal his real
designs of abandoning me altogether" (Rosanna Travis to James
Dellet, September 6, 1834, box 2R207, William Barret Travis
Papers, BCAH). There are many myths and untruths surrounding
Travis's departure for Texas. For an excellently researched,
in-depth discussion of the most prominent of these, see Davis,
Three Roads to the Alamo, p. 635, n. 80.

Bradburn's promised promotion is mentioned in Henson, *Juan Davis
Bradburn,* p. 50. The author's objective (and more sympathetic)
reappraisal of the much-maligned Bradburn brings into question
his long-standing reputation as an arrogant, even brutish tyrant.

The quote about the Texas colonists and their pocket constitutions is
in Jackson, *Texas by Terán,* p. 100. The description of the
Anahuac prisoners threatened with death is from Davis, *Three
Roads to the Alamo,* pp. 38–39; this account of the 1832 Anahuac
disturbance also derives from N. D. Labadie, "Narrative of the
Anahuac, or Opening Campaign of the Texas Revolution," in *The
Texas Almanac* for 1859; F. W. Johnson, "Further Account by
Col. F. W. Johnson of the First Breaking Out of Hostilities," in

The Texas Almanac for 1859; Looscan, "The Old Fort at Anahuac"; and Henson, *Juan Davis Bradburn.*

Details of the steamboat enterprise that Travis was involved in can be found in box 2D157 [papers 1828–29], Benjamin Cromwell Franklin Papers, BCAH.

There is little solid knowledge about Travis's slave Joe. Author Ron Jackson graciously told me that Joe was from Kentucky, a fact he unearthed researching his unpublished biography of Joe. A letter from Travis to David G. Burnet, dated February 6, 1835, is quoted in W. A. Philpott, "Unpriced Inventory of Texana" (1969), where the letter is (in part) summarized as follows: "Travis writes, also, that he recently 'sold My Woman, Matilda' for $700 in Brazoria. He writes 'I hired Joe for a year,' but that he did not know whether or not he 'will sell him'" (box AR507, file 3, Philpott Collection, University of Texas at Arlington Special Collections). The description of Joe is taken from an ad offering a reward for Joe after he ran away in April 1837, which ran in the *Telegraph and Texas Register* from May 26 through August 1837.

William Fairfax Gray's *Diary,* p. 114, notes that Cummings's Mill Creek place was run by "a woman about thirty" and mentions the "warm fire, good supper and comfortable lodging."

The "Victory or Death" countersign is noted in "John W. Moore's The Capture of Anahuac," box 2B120, Eugene Campbell Barker Papers, BCAH.

The August 1835 letter is quoted in Davis, *Three Roads to the Alamo,* p. 458.

Information about Travis's ancestors can be found in *The Alamo Heroes and Their Revolutionary Ancestors,* p. 77.

The "Huzzah for Texas!" quote is in a letter from Travis to J. W. Moore, reprinted in Looscan, "Harris County, 1822–1845," pp. 268–69.

John Forsyth discusses how he has spent all his money on the cavalry company in a letter to the General Council on January 13, 1835, reprinted in PTR 3, p. 504.

TWO: "O! HE HAS GONE TO TEXAS"

The epigraph is from James Hatch's unpublished manuscript "Lest We Forget the Heroes of the Alamo," James Hatch Papers, BCAH.

The May 1820 letter from Jefferson to Monroe is quoted in Walraven, *The Magnificent Barbarians,* p. 25.

NOTES

Washington Davis describes the "fine rich land" of Texas in a March
12, 1831, letter to his wife, Rebecca, in *Southwestern Historical
Quarterly* 44, no. 4 (April 1961), p. 508. The letter discussing
"every poor man" was written on August 14, 1836, and found in
Court of Claims file 1281, GLO. "A vast howling wilderness" is
part of the Hatch quotation that begins this chapter.
The ten thousand Comanche horse soldiers is a median
approximation; estimates vary from six and eight thousand to
twenty thousand. Ruíz, in 1828, wrote that there were "1000 to
1500 families," referring to the Comanches, in Texas at that time
(Ruíz, *Report on the Indian Tribes of Texas in 1828,* p. 8). For a
lengthier discussion of Comanche population in the mid-
nineteenth century, see Noyes, *Los Comanches,* p. 317, n. 12.
Ruíz's book, p. 11, is also the source for the Lobos pledge.
The information on Mexico's peonage system is derived from Knight,
"Mexican Peonage," pp. 44–50.
Santa Anna's statement about the Mexican people being unfit for
democracy is quoted in Brands, *Lone Star Nation,* p. 227.
The account of the battle at Zacatecas chiefly derives from the
excellent material in Roberts and Olson, *A Line in the Sand,*
pp. 15–26; details of the attack on foreigners are from the British
Foreign Office records, 50/95 f148, R. Ogilvie Auld to J.
Backhouse to Foreign Office, Zacatecas, May 20, 1835, courtesy
of Joseph Musso. Santa Anna's quote is from his May 11, 1836,
letter reprinted in the *Mercurio del Puerto de Matamoros,* no. 28
(my translation).
Austin's October 1833 letter to the *ayuntamiento* of Béxar is quoted
in Johnson, *A History of Texas and Texans,* vol. 1, p. 121.
Austin's opinion of Santa Anna's friendship is quoted in Barker,
"Stephen F. Austin and the Independence of Texas," p. 272.
Besides Santa Anna's comparison of himself to Napoleon when
introduced to Sam Houston after the Battle of San Jacinto, another
source for the claim is in Gilliam, *Travels in Mexico,* p. 164, where
the author writes that Santa Anna declared "it was his intention to
march to the city of Washington, and be the Napoleon of America.
A gentleman of Zacatecas informed me that he was present, and
heard the boasted vaunt of the American Napoleon."

THREE: "THE CELEBRATED DESPERADO"
The chapter title phrase can be found in Davis, "A Fortnight with
James Bowie by the Rev. Benjamin Chase," p. 2; after meeting a

helpful stranger, the reverend is told, "That was the celebrated
desperado, James Bowie." The epigraph is from a description of
Bowie reprinted in Speer and Brown, *The Encyclopedia of the
New West*, p. 436.
The account of the Sandbar Fight is based on the following sources:
Batson, *James Bowie and the Sandbar Fight*, which includes most
but not all of the participant accounts of the event that appeared in
the years following; Edmondson, *Mr. Bowie with a Knife*, an
excellent narrative of the fight that draws from the aforementioned
primary sources; Calhoun, "A History of Concordia Parish,
Louisiana"; Caiaphas Ham, "Recollections of Col. James Bowie,
1887," from the John Salmon Ford Papers, BCAH; Thorp, *Bowie
Knife;* a September 20, 1827, letter from Samuel Wells to Josiah
Stoddard Johnston, from the Josiah Stoddard Johnston Papers at
the Historical Society of Pennsylvania; and several primary
accounts from various eyewitnesses that appeared in the Natchez
Ariel on October 19, 1827.
The prediction that Bowie was not expected to recover appeared in
the *Southern Advocate* of October 12, 1826, as quoted in Batson,
p. 4.
Bowie's quote about killing Wright is from Davis, "A Fortnight with
James Bowie by the Rev. Benjamin Chase," p. 4.
The description of James Bowie's upbringing and of his mother, Elve
Bowie, is from two articles written by Bowie's oldest brother,
John: "The Bowie Family," in the Washington, Texas, *Lone Star*
of October 23, 1852, and "Early Life in the Southwest—the
Bowies," in the October 1852 *De Bow's Review*. Bowie's eyes are
described by his close friend Caiaphas Ham in his "Recollections
of Col. James Bowie, 1887," John Salmon Ford Papers, BCAH.
The quote about Bowie's penchant for settling difficulties quickly
is by William H. Sparks, quoted in Ellis, *The Life of Colonel
David Crockett*, p. 214.
Bowie's slave trading and land speculation are best described in Davis,
Three Roads to the Alamo. The information about his informal
adoption of Carlos Espalier derives from Joseph Musso's "James
Bowie's Freed Slaves" and the Carlos Espalier File, Memorials
and Petitions File, TSLA.
Sources consulted for this account of the San Saba fight include
"James Bowie's Indian Fight" by Rezin Bowie, reprinted in
Brown, *Indian Wars and Pioneers of Texas*, pp. 19–23; and
James Bowie's report to the political chief of Béxar, December

10, 1831, Nacogdoches Archives, BCAH, reprinted in Brown, *History of Texas* vol. 1, pp. 170–75.

Though there is no hard evidence for any Bowie progeny, at least two people close to him claimed that his wife, Ursula, bore him two children. One of the people making this claim was Bowie's good friend Caiaphas Ham (Ham, "Recollections of Col. James Bowie, 1887"); the other was his oldest brother, John, who wrote: "Two children sprung from this union died in infancy, followed by the death of their mother in 1833 at Monclova, Mexico" (A. R. Kilpatrick, "Early Life in the Southwest — the Bowies," *De Bow's Southern and Western Review* 1, October 1852). There are no records of baptism for these children, which would be consistent with their dying soon after birth. Bowie's grief concerning his wife is mentioned in the memoirs of José Antonio Menchaca, in the José Antonio Menchaca Reminiscences, 1807–1836, "Memoirs of A. Menchaca," p. 14, A. Menchaca Biographical File, BCAH.

Bowie provides a brief description of his escape from Matamoros in a letter to James B. Miller dated June 22, 1835 (box 2B120 [Transcriptions and Notes, Anahuac, June–August 1835], Eugene Campbell Barker Papers, BCAH).

FOUR: "THE BURLY IS BEGUN"

The chapter title phrase is from a letter by James Fannin, quoted in Young, "James Walker Fannin: The West Point Connection," p. 7. The epigraph is from a letter by Burr Duval to his father, William P. Duval, dated March 9, 1836, and reprinted in PTR 5, p. 35.

The quoted description of the DeWitt colony area is by Elias R. Wightman, Stephen F. Austin's official surveyor, and found in Baumgartner, "History of the Alsey Silvanus Miller Homestead and Surrounding Area, 1700/1992," p. 9.

The only extant mention of Luna is on a map of Gonzales drawn by early resident David Darst that is reprinted in Rather, "De Witt's Colony," and still exists in the Gonzales County Museum. But Adam Zumwalt bought the Luna lot in the town of Gonzales from Benjamin Fuqua in April 1835 (the bill of sale is in the Gonzales County Archives). There was a long tradition of moonshining in the Zumwalt family: another Adam Zumwalt, probably an uncle of Adam Zumwalt of Gonzales, trained as an innkeeper and distiller and set up two still houses in the early 1800s, from which he sold liquor to Black Hawk and other

Indians (Bryan and Rose, *A History of the Pioneer Families of Missouri*, p. 195). According to Gonzales city records, a few years later "John Goss's tavern stand" stood on the same lot (Zumwalt's) as Luna had.

Sources for Gonzales in 1835 include Rather, "De Witt's Colony"; Lukes, *DeWitt Colony of Texas;* and the voluminous vertical files of the Gonzales County Records Center and Archives, primarily the vertical files for Gonzales and the individual files of the many early families of the town. The description of the 1834 ball is from a 1912 manuscript by Walker, "Early Life in Gonzales," pp. 2–3, which derives much of its information from early Gonzales resident David Darst, who also provided the information about Kimble and Dickinson's hats in an interview in the December 8, 1901, edition of the *Houston Daily Post.*

The Gonzales *ayuntamiento*'s resistance to the independence movement is from Barker, "Stephen F. Austin and the Independence of Texas," p. 62. Jesse McCoy's involvement in the Gonzales militia is mentioned in the report of Andrew Ponton to J. B. Miller, chief of the Department of the Brazos, dated July 26, 1835 (Julia Lee Sinks Papers, BCAH). The attack on McCoy is described in an undated letter from Ponton to Ugartechea in the Gonzales *ayuntamiento* minutes (box 3M11, folder 5, Julia Lee Sinks Papers, BCAH).

The actions of the Mexican army at Gonzales are described in an October 1, 1835, report from Ugartechea to Cós, reprinted in PTR 2, p. 12, and in several other Mexican reports included in that volume. Texian eyewitness accounts of the battle of Gonzales include a letter from William DeWees dated December 25, 1835, and reprinted in PTR 3, p. 317, and the report of Andrew Ponton to J. B. Miller (see above). The best recent account is in Hardin, *Texian Iliad*, pp. 7–13, which is based on several earlier Texas histories.

Information about Francisco de Castañeda and his house in the Alamo can be found in the Bexar Archives, BCAH, and Lemon, *The Illustrated Alamo 1836*, p. 46. Castañeda's admission that he, too, was a federalist is in the DeWees letter mentioned above: "The Mexican made answer, that he was himself in favor of the Constitution of 1824."

The number of DeWitt colonists is from Field, *Three Years in Texas*, p. 14.

Sources for the battle of Gonzales include Rather, "De Witt's Colony"; Bennet, "The Battle of Gonzales"; Foote, *Texas and the Texans*, vol. 2; Ornish, *Ehrenberg: Goliad Survivor*; DeShields,

Tall Men with Long Rifles; Johnson, *A History of Texas and Texans*, vol. 1; and the other sources listed above. Turner's hotel as a rallying point is mentioned in the *Gonzales Inquirer* of August 30, 1879, in an article entitled "Thrilling Scenes of Gonzales in Early Days of Texas." Castañeda's report to Ugartechea dated October 3, 1835, in PTR 2, p. 15, mentions the single casualty. The quote concerning the lack of consensus of opinion on Mexico is by Noah Smithwick, from his book *Evolution of a State*, p. 71.

The estimate of the number of Cós's troops is contained in a report from Bowie and Fannin to Austin dated October 22, 1835: "Their whole force does not reach 600, according to the report of a respectable gentleman, who escaped, with his family, from town this morning, and now with us" (PTR 2, p. 191). Another estimate of the number of Cós's troops comes from Samuel Maverick, a resident of Béxar, who counted 647 men on October 18, and seven hundred on October 26 (Green, *Samuel Maverick*, p. 30). The description of Cós is in Robinson, *Mexico and Her Military Chieftains*, p. 46, and also in Kuykendall, "Sketches of Early Texians" (box 3F82, folder 6, Jonathan Hampton Kuykendall Papers, BCAH). In a letter written on September 2, 1835, Béxar resident John W. Smith reported 150 Morelos infantrymen, a third of them officers, and between three hundred and 350 cavalry, "which have come from Monterey and the town on the Riogrande" (box 2B42, Don Carlos Barrett Papers, BCAH).

The Austin broadside is quoted in Barker, "Stephen F. Austin and the Independence of Texas," p. 275. Austin's private letter declaring his feelings about Mexico was written to William Hardin on October 5, 1835 (Hardin Family Collection, BCAH).

The males left in Gonzales after the Army of the People departed for Béxar were described as "12 men, most of them invalids" (in a letter from John Fisher to Stephen Austin dated November 3, 1835, reprinted in Barker, *The Austin Papers*, p. 233). The quotes regarding both the sorry condition of the army's weapons and its appearance can be found in Smithwick, *The Evolution of a State*, p. 75.

FIVE: THE ARMY OF THE PEOPLE

The epigraph is from a letter by William Barret Travis to John Rice Jones dated October 3, 1835, and reprinted in PTR 2, p. 28.

NOTES

The road between Gonzales and Béxar—Lockhart's blazed trail—is
described in Berlandier, *Journey to Mexico,* p. 302.
The lack of tents and shelter is mentioned in Greer, "Journal of
Ammon Underwood," p. 139. Samuel Maverick stated in his
diary on October 18: "The actual number, officers, soldiers,
guards, etc. of Effectives is 647" (Green, *Samuel Maverick,
Texan,* p. 30).
The information regarding Erasmo Seguín's Casa Blanca, and his
treatment by Cós, is from de la Teja, *A Revolution Remembered,*
pp. 5, 88. The fourteen deserters are mentioned in Garcia and
Garcia, *Tejano Participants in the Texas Revolution,* pp. 171–72:
"They were joined by fourteen privates of the old Company of
the Alamo for the most part, sons of San Antonio who deserted
from Mexican forces of General Cos and joined Seguin's
command with arms and baggage." See also "Notes for Manuel-
Antonio-Santiogo Tarin-Leal" in "Descendants of Don Francisco
Joseph de Arocha" at www.somosprimos.com/inclan/arocha.htm,
accessed December 1, 2009.
Charles Ramsdell, in his flavorful *San Antonio: A Historical and
Pictorial Guide,* pp. 4–5, provides an excellent account of the
San Antonio area's early history. Cooley, in "A Retrospect of San
Antonio," p. 55, discusses the width and depth of the San
Antonio River, as does the anonymous author who visited the
town in 1837: "...thirty yards in width and three to four feet in
average depth in the neighborhood of the city" (Muir, *Texas in
1837,* p. 98). The description of the Béxar fortifications is in
Field's *Three Years in Texas,* p. 183.
This account of the Concepción fight derives primarily from James
Bowie's undated report to Austin, in Foote, *Texas and the
Texians,* vol. 2, pp. 121–25; DeShields, *Tall Men with Long Rifles,*
pp. 36–42; Ornish, *Ehrenberg: Goliad Survivor,* pp. 131–33;
Yoakum, *History of Texas,* pp. 373–76; Smithwick, *The
Evolution of a State,* pp. 77–80; "General Austin's Order Book
For the Campaign of 1835"; Austin, "Account of the Campaign
of 1835"; and Hardin, *Texian Iliad,* pp. 77–91. The Bowie quote
is from Smithwick, p. 77.
The tallies of the Mexican dead at Concepción vary, but the estimate
by Alwyn Barr in *Texans in Revolt* seems the most logical and
accurate. Samuel Maverick claimed thirty-eight dead—twenty-
three left dead on the field, and forty-two wounded, of which
fifteen died (Green, *Samuel Maverick, Texan,* p. 33), and both

Bryan (PTR 2, p. 107) and Austin reported sixteen (Gaddy, *Texas in Revolt*, p. 29). Smithwick states: "They left about sixty killed and a number wounded" (Smithwick, *The Evolution of a State*, p. 80); and Taylor writes: "The Mexican loss in this affair is said to have been 60 killed" (DeShields, *Tall Men with Long Rifles*, p. 40). The last two accounts have the ring of rumor and magnification to them, and DeShields may have borrowed the number from Smithwick, since other parts of his book echo Smithwick's. Bowie reported one hundred total casualties and "say 67 killed" (Johnson, *A History of Texas and Texans*, vol. 1, p. 281), likely a gross exaggeration. General Vicente Filisola, who was not there but was diligent in securing accounts from participants, wrote that there were thirteen dead and thirty-five wounded (Filisola, *Memoirs*, vol. 2, p. 68). See Pohl and Hardin, "The Military History of the Texas Revolution: An Overview," for an excellent discussion and analysis of strategy and tactics of this and other battles of the Texas Revolution, and Hardin, *Texian Iliad*, for the best one-volume work on the military side of the revolution.

About Houston's election as general, one council delegate wrote: "Mr. Houston was unanimously elected, there being but one name except his mentioned for the office. That was Robert Potter. Potter was an excellent young man, as loyal and brave as the best" (Dixon, *The Men Who Made Texas Free*, p. 89). Houston's loss of an *empresario* grant is mentioned in Haley, *Passionate Nation*, p. 109, and in McLean, *Papers*, vol. 7, p. 31.

Regarding the number of men in the regular army, Steen writes, in "Analysis of the Work of the General Council," p. 333: "A committee of the Convention reported, March 10, 1836, the number of privates in the regular army as sixty; thirty of whom were stationed at Goliad and thirty at Bexar. The thirty privates stationed at Bexar should not have been counted, for the Alamo had fallen and with it exactly half the enlisted men in the regular army of Texas."

Houston's October 8, 1835, proclamation is reprinted in PTR 2, pp. 68–69.

The Béxar weather is noted in Samuel Maverick's diary, as reprinted in Green, *Samuel Maverick, Texan*, p. 36.

The requisitioned military manuals are noted in Steen, "Analysis of the Work of the General Council," p. 326. The quote about literary tactics is in Smithwick, *The Evolution of a State*, p. 73;

the quote about the obedience of the men is in Joseph Lopez's pension application (reel 226, frames 246–53, ROT [Republic of Texas] Claims, TSLA).

Though the New Orleans Greys were described by more than one eyewitness as wearing a uniform—e.g., "The color of our uniform was a grey jacket and pants with a sealskin cap" (Ebenezer Heath to his mother, March 10, 1836, Harbert Davenport Papers, BCAH) and "Their fine uniform caps and coats attracted the notice of the [Cherokee] chief, Bolles" (Adolphus Sterne, in Morphis, *History of Texas,* p. 121)—it is by no means clear that these were "uniforms" as generally thought of, i.e., manufactured with a military purpose in mind. One surviving Grey, Herman Ehrenberg, said nothing about uniforms when he described their clothing: "All of us had speedily acquired for ourselves clothes suitable for life on the prairie, clothes which we found ready-made in the numerous storehouses. From the grey color of these garments originated the name of our company" (Ornish, *Ehrenberg: Goliad Survivor,* p. 87).

The quote beginning "We then broke into small groups" is from Ornish, p. 133, as is the story of the men blasting cannon shots at the Alamo, p. 135. Another participant described the men chasing down the cannonballs in Crimmins, "The Storming of San Antonio de Bexar," p. 102. The catchphrase "going after that cannon" is found in Smithwick, *The Evolution of a State,* p. 81. The volunteer pay is mentioned in Newell, *History of the Revolution,* p. 67. Austin's request to the General Council to stop sending alcohol is reprinted in PTR 2, p. 322.

The murderer who was convicted and hanged is mentioned in Court of Claims file 2304, GLO. The description of the camp's slaughter area is in Ornish, *Ehrenberg: Goliad Survivor,* pp. 131–33.

Austin's request to be relieved is quoted in Cantrell, *Stephen F. Austin,* p. 326.

The description of Edward Burleson is based on Jenkins and Kesselus, *Edward Burleson: Texas Frontier Leader,* pp. 10–11.

SIX: THE BATTLE OF BÉXAR
The epigraph is in a letter from Edward Burleson to Stephen F. Austin dated December 11, 1835 (but almost surely dated incorrectly; the much likelier date is December 8), PTR 3, p. 155.

This portrait of Ben Milam is based on Garver, "Benjamin Rush Milam." The claim that Milam "would never serve a king" is in the 1857 *Texas Almanac*, p. 137. Smithwick describes Milam as being "near six feet" (*The Evolution of a State*, p. 74). A discussion of the forensic evidence of Milam's arthritis and bad back can be found in Tennis, *Exhumation of a Hero*.

Several witnesses left accounts of Milam rallying the men to attack Béxar. This version, with Milam stepping across a path, was supplied by Creed Taylor on page 20 of John Warren Hunter's "Literary Effort Concerning Activities of Creed Taylor and Others in the Mexican War" (TSLA). Frank Sparks, another Béxar veteran, claimed that Milam drew a line in the dirt—"a mark on the ground"—"and said, 'Who will follow old Ben Milam in to San Antonio? Those who will, cross to my side' " (Sparks, "Recollections of S. F. Sparks"). Milam may have done just that. Writer James DeShields changed Creed Taylor's original account, which described the "line" as a path in front of Burleson's tent, to a description of an actual line in the dirt. It is also possible that Milam was selected by a group of men, probably Greys, and asked to lead them, since that scenario is mentioned in more than one account. See the 1844 letter of Greys leader W. G. Cook in Smither, *The Papers of Mirabeau Buonaparte Lamar*, vol. 4, p. 44, in which he states: "I then marched up and down the lines calling on volunteers to unite with us—We succeeded in raising 300. I then marched to headquarters and halted them, and proposed the name of Benjamin R. Milam as the leader in the attack—He was elected unanimously." Another volunteer, Sherwood Young Reams, claimed that he was the one who hunted up Milam and asked him to lead the men into Béxar (in "Statement of S. Y. Reams," box 2J110, Caryl Clyde Hill Papers, BCAH). Another witness claimed that "a flag was planted and volunteers cald for to attempt to storm the town before day" (letter from Henry C. Dance to an unidentified editor, April 25, 1836, in PTR 6, p. 57). Francis (Frank) Johnson, in his posthumously published *A History of Texas and Texans* (which was completed after his death by Eugene C. Barker and Ernest W. Winkler), vol. 1, p. 352, claims that he himself "suggested to Colonel Milam to call for volunteers." He may have, but he is the only primary source to say so.

Sources employed in the writing of this account of the battle of Béxar include Barr, *Texans in Revolt*; Johnson, *A History of Texas and*

Texans, vol. 1; Yoakum, *History of Texas,* vol. 2, pp. 24–32; DeShields, *Tall Men with Long Rifles;* Ornish, *Ehrenberg: Goliad Survivor;* the reports of Burleson and Johnson as reprinted in Foote, *Texas and the Texans,* vol. 2, pp. 220–28; Garver, "Benjamin Rush Milam"; Smithwick, *The Evolution of a State,* pp. 74–81; Jenkins and Kesselus, *Edward Burleson: Texas Frontier Leader;* Warren, "Col. William G. Cooke"; Crimmins, "The Storming of San Antonio de Bexar in 1835," which includes the account of New Orleans Grey Charles B. Bannister; Henry C. Dance's letter of April 25, 1836, in Smither, *The Papers of Mirabeau Buonaparte Lamar,* vol. 5, pp. 95–99; Joseph Lopez's pension application (reel 226, frames 246–53, ROT [Republic of Texas] Claims, TSLA); and John Warren Hunter's "Literary Effort Concerning Activities of Creed Taylor and Others in the Mexican War" (TSLA).

That some of the men begged Milam's volunteers not to throw away their lives is attested to in a letter from A. H. Jones to William E. Jones dated January 15, 1836, reprinted in PTR 4, p. 31.

Bowie's terse acknowledgment of Austin's orders is found in a letter from Bowie and Fannin to Austin dated October 31, 1835, reprinted in Johnson, *A History of Texas and Texans,* vol. 1, p. 283.

This number of volunteers attacking Béxar is in Steen, "A Letter from San Antonio de Bexar in 1836," p. 514. James Fannin also supports a similar number of attackers—he later wrote, "If 216 could & did take Bejar, how many of Sa. Annas men will be left him, should this force encounter him?" (Fannin to Mexia, March 11, 1836, reprinted in PTR 5, p. 47). Another participant claimed that the volunteers numbered 220, "100 of our men having backed out" (letter from Henry C. Dance to an unidentified editor, April 25, 1836, in PTR 6, p. 57), and another, W. B. Scates, wrote that "216 men, myself among that number, immediately turned out" (1873 *Texas Almanac,* p. 79).

The *bexareño* who invited the Texians to a fandango in the midst of battle is mentioned in Joseph Lopez's pension application, reel 226, frames 246–53, ROT (Republic of Texas) Claims, (TSLA), as is the quote about the house resembling a pigeon nursery. The anecdote about the opponents conducting a discussion while on either side of a wall is in Field, *Three Years in Texas,* p. 21. The actions of William Carey's gun crew are related in a letter from Carey to "Dear Brother and Sister," dated January 12, 1836, as quoted in Chariton, *100 Days in Texas,* pp. 135–36. Although it is not clear on what day these actions of Carey's occurred, this date seems likely.

Evidence that Milam carried a spyglass or some kind of field glasses comes from a letter written by participant Henry Dance: "From his situation with his glasses he was constantly in possession of a full knowledge of our situation" (letter from Henry C. Dance to an unidentified editor, April 25, 1836, in PTR 6, p. 62). Dance, in the same letter, also supplied the quote about Milam's death (p. 59).

The description of Henry Karnes is from a letter written years later by his sister, Mrs. Susan H. Corley: "Fare complexion & blue eyes & very red headed about 6 feet high, wore his hears [hair] verry short divided on each side" (Henry Arthur McArdle, *The Battle of San Jacinto*, McArdle Notebooks, p. 238, TSLA).

The number of wounded is from Warren, "Col. William G. Cooke," p. 214, and Smither, *The Papers of Mirabeau Buonaparte Lamar*, vol. 4, p. 45.

The Mexican reinforcement troops are discussed in a letter from Frank Johnson to Robert Williamson dated November 18, 1835, reprinted in PTR 2, p. 464, and in Filisola, *Memoirs*, vol. 1, p. 91. Sánchez's diary, which also relates the reinforcements' activities, is translated and reprinted in Huneycutt, *At the Alamo*, pp. 3–5. This officer's name is often written today as José Juan Sánchez-Navarro, but he signed his name without "Navarro." Biographical information about him is also derived from his article "A Mexican View of the Texas War," pp. 65–67, and Jackson and Ivey, "Mystery Artist of the Alamo: José Juan Sánchez," pp. 2–3.

The proximity of the attackers' heads to the guns in the windows above them is mentioned in Johnson, *A History of Texas and Texans*, vol. 1, p. 357.

The assault force's lack of ammunition is mentioned in Joseph Lopez's pension application, reel 226, frames 246–53, ROT (Republic of Texas) Claims (TSLA): "We...on the fifth day had not two loads of powder to each man, so short was the Texans of ammunition," and in a letter from a participant that appeared in the *Portsmouth Journal of Literature and Politics* (New Hampshire), February 20, 1836, reprinted in PTR 3, p. 501: "Our little army had but one keg of powder, besides a few rounds in their pouches." The action inside the Priest's House is recounted in Mag Stiff's "Notes on the Storming of San Antonio in

December 1835," PTR 3, pp. 388–92. Sánchez's confrontation with Condelle is recounted in his diary, translated in Huneycutt, *At the Alamo,* pp. 13–18.

That some of the men were unhappy with the agreement is evident in Steen, "A Letter from San Antonio de Bexar," p. 515, quoting a letter from battle participant William R. Carey: "The enemy on the third day of the siege raised a black flag (which says no quarters) and when we had whipped them by washing the flag with the blood of about 300 of them we should have made a Treaty and not a childs bargain...after we took the place and the child's bargain made." However, Sánchez, in his memoirs, wrote: "General Cós approved the provisions with some changes.... Never, never did he promise anything which stained our honor. And he specifically directed that two following ticklish articles be withdrawn concerning our withdrawing with all the honors of war, referring to: 'The señor General, officers, and officials are to bind themselves not to oppose the people if they wish to declare themselves for the Constitution of 1824' " (Huneycutt, *At the Alamo,* p. 30). This indicates that there may have been some misunderstanding as to the exact meaning of this part of the capitulation agreement, perhaps due to faulty translation.

Though several Texian accounts mention figures of one thousand or 1,100 men marching with Cós, the general himself reported that he had 815 men (Cós's report to Santa Anna, December 29, 1836, box 2Q173 [Texas 1835–1836], Archivo General de la Nación México, BCAH). The Mexican casualty figure is taken from Barr, *Texans in Revolt,* p. 69, the best single book on the battle. There is no dispute over the five Texian deaths.

The fact that most of the *presidiales* were unmounted is found in two places: Huneycutt, *At the Alamo,* p. 35, and Cós's report to Santa Anna dated December 29, 1836 (box 2Q173 [Texas 1835–1836], Archivo General de la Nación México, BCAH). The list of captured items can be found in Newell, *History of the Revolution in Texas,* appendix 5.

A list of the supplies sent to Béxar by the provisional government can be found in a letter from army subcontractor Matthew Caldwell to governor Henry Smith dated December 19, 1835 (PTR 3, p. 253).

Details of the New Orleans production of *The Fall of San Antonio* can be found in Huson, *Dr. J. H. Barnard's Journal,* p. 3; PTR 3, p. 382; Helm, *Scraps of Early Texas History,* p. 53; the *New*

York Evening Post, February 1, 1836; Miller, *New Orleans and the Texas Revolution,* p. 141; and the *New Orleans Bee,* January 1, 1836. A listing for the New York production of *The Triumph of Texas* is in Joseph N. Ireland, *Records of the New York Stage, from 1750 to 1860* (New York: T. H. Morrell, 1866), vol. 2, p. 155. The New York newspaper quote is from the *New York Courier and Inquirer* (undated, probably early January 1836), in Gaddy, *Texas in Revolt,* p. 138.

SEVEN: "A MERE CORRAL AND NOTHING MORE"
The chapter title quote is by Ramón Caro, Santa Anna's secretary during the Texas campaign, quoted in Castañeda, *The Mexican Side of the Texan Revolution,* p. 101. The epigraph can be found in a letter from James Neill to Sam Houston dated January 14, 1836, and reprinted in Chariton, *100 Days in Texas,* p. 144.
The quoted description of Neill appears in Stiff, *A New History of Texas,* p. 277. The information regarding William Carey is from a letter from Carey to his brother and sister dated January 12, 1836, and reprinted in PTR 3, pp. 490–95.
Dances and celebrations occurred virtually every night in Béxar. For example: "You will excuse this scrawl as I have danced all night & am indeed exceedingly dull this morning" (Horatio Alsbury to Sam Houston, December 30, 1835, quoted in Chariton, *100 Days in Texas,* p. 78).
Information on Green Jameson's activities as a sales agent is from the Brazoria *Texas Republican,* November 1, 1834, and February 14, 1835. The quote involving his plans is from his plat of the Alamo and accompanying key, reprinted in Hansen, pp. 575–76. Information on the artillery is from Lemon, *The Illustrated Alamo,* pp. 142, 144–45.
Neill's letter to the governor and General Council dated January 6, 1836, is reprinted in Chariton, *100 Days in Texas,* p. 105. His January 8, 1836, letter to the same parties is reprinted on p. 114 of *100 Days in Texas.*
Smith's letter to the General Council is reprinted in PTR 3, pp. 458–60. See also Chariton, *Exploring the Alamo Legends,* pp. 107–15, for a well-reasoned and insightful explanation of this episode.
Proof of Angel Navarro's loyalty to Santa Anna and the centralist cause can be found in a letter from Cós to Navarro dated October 17, 1835, in which Cós acknowledges a patriotic address given by

Navarro to the people of Béxar, reprinted in PTR 2, p. 145, and in a
letter from Navarro to the commandant of Béxar transmitting
evidence in the case of a man leaving Béxar without a passport and
returning with one from the leaders of the revolt; see PTR 2, p. 218.

Details of the vandalism in Gonzales can be found in two letters
written by Lancelot Smither to Stephen Austin on November 4,
1835, reprinted in PTR 2, pp. 318–19. A list of household
possessions Susanna Dickinson left behind in her Gonzales house
can be found in her 1849 petition for relief (folder 7, OS box 8,
Memorials and Petitions File, TSLA).

Neill's January 14, 1836, letter to the governor labeling his men as
"easy prey to the enemy" is reprinted in PTR 4, p. 15. His letter
of the same day to Houston is reprinted in Chariton, *100 Days in
Texas*, pp. 144–45.

The *Telegraph and Texas Register* quote appeared in its issue of
February 27, 1836.

The machinations that resulted in the army having four commanders
are related in Brown, *Life and Times of Henry Smith*, p. 206.
Further evidence that governor Henry Smith did not order the
Alamo to be abandoned, and that Sam Houston knew it, is
Houston's January 30, 1836, letter to Smith, in which he writes:
"Should Bexar remain a military post, Goliad must be
maintained, or the former will be cut off from all supplies
arriving by sea at the port of Copano" (*Life and Times of Henry
Smith*, p. 181). Houston's January 30, 1836, letter to Smith is
reprinted in PTR 4, p. 194.

Johnson's advice to Fannin is contained in a February 9, 1836, letter
from Johnson to Fannin, reprinted in Chariton, *100 Days in
Texas*, pp. 221–22.

Houston's description of his friend Bowie and his orders to him are
from his January 17, 1836, letter to Smith, reprinted in *100 Days
in Texas*, p. 152.

The date of Bowie's arrival at the Alamo has been a matter of minor
dispute. A receipt datelined "January 18, 1836, Bexar," with
Bowie's name on it as "Commandant at the post of Bejar," was
sold at auction and is now in private hands. While it is possible
that Bowie left Goliad sometime on the seventeenth and arrived at
Béxar the next day—riding hard and perhaps changing mounts
somewhere along the way—it seems more likely, at least to me,
that the receipt was either (a) signed by Bowie and predated or (b)
dated in error. The distance from Goliad to Béxar was about

ninety-five miles of rudimentary road, with more than a dozen creeks feeding into the San Antonio River to be crossed—normally two full days of hard riding, and very likely more, if Bowie was traveling with a group of thirty or more men, since a group of horsemen is only as fast as its slowest rider and mount. If Bowie and his men did arrive on January 18, it was at a late hour.

As stated, there is no hard evidence that Bonham (pronounced BEAU-num) and Travis knew each other in Edgefield, South Carolina, though they lived within a few miles of each other until Travis's family left the area when he was nine. But they were acquainted in San Felipe, sometime in December or January, before Travis left for the Alamo in late January, if the memory of one woman, Clarinda Pevehouse Kegans, can be trusted. She was a young girl in 1836, and many years later remembered: "There had been a barbecue at Grandpa's [at San Felipe] the fall before the war began. I remember it so well because it was the best ever held.... Mr. Travis everybody called him Buck except us children and his friend was with him. It was Mr. James Bonham and he was so nice and handsome he caused all the girls to swoon!" ("Memoirs," unpublished manuscript, Haley Memorial Library and History Center, Midland, Texas).

Bonham's letter of December 1, 1835, to Houston is reprinted in Lindley, "James Butler Bonham," p. 3. His announcement of the opening of his law office appeared in the January 2, 1836, *Texas Telegraph and Register*. Evidence that Bonham accompanied Grant to Goliad is in the account of another member of Grant's expedition: "Major Bonham of South Carolina, proceeded with us to Goliad, but returned to the Alamo, as he had received some appointment from Travis" (R. R. Brown, "Expedition under Johnson and Grant," in *Texas Almanac, 1859*, quoted in Mixon, "William Barret Travis," p. 199).

Houston's January 11, 1836, letter to James Robinson commenting on Bonham's influence is reprinted in Chariton, *100 Days in Texas,* p. 126.

On February 2, 1836, Bowie wrote: "Capt Patton with 5 or 6 has come in" (Chariton, *100 Days in Texas,* p. 204), but many years later, sometime after 1860, Sutherland wrote that Patton's company numbered twelve: "I proceeded, in company with Capt. Wm. Patten, and ten others to San Antonio" (Hansen, p. 138), and that number is supported somewhat by Sutherland's audited claim, submitted later in 1836. He also claimed in his account that Patton's company reached Béxar "about the eighteenth of January, 1836" (Hansen, p. 138), but that date is contradicted by his audited claim, in which he states that he was in Gonzales until at least January 27 (Hansen, p. 162), and by the fact that his first entry mentioning Béxar is February 1.

John Sutherland described the garrison's sick and injured in his narrative, written sometime after 1860 and reprinted in Hansen, p. 141. Though Sutherland has been derided as a quack by some historians (most specifically by the late Thomas Ricks Lindley), the fact is that the practice of medicine at the time was primitive, and the Thomsonian system—based on the writings and practice of Samuel Thomson—was quite popular, particularly in the southern and western states. Some of that popularity was due to the fact that the system had achieved a certain degree of success. It was not that far removed from mainstream medicine of the time; there were no internists, and the only surgery was amputation or trephination—cutting a hole in the skull to relieve pressure. The understanding that bacteria and germs were the primary conveyances of disease and illness would not come until some years in the future. Doctors of the time could gain a diploma after two sixteen-week courses that featured no doctoring whatsoever, only solid lecturing and textbook study. Little was known of what caused sickness or health. It was believed (as it had been for centuries) that all disease was caused by an imbalance of the four bodily humors: blood, phlegm, black bile, and yellow bile. Illness was thought to be the result of too much of one of these humors, and recovery depended on righting the imbalance through a variety of practices, such as bleeding, emetics, purging, etc.—a course not too dissimilar from the remedies prescribed by the Thomsonian system, which relied more heavily on the infusion of plant-based medicines. If John Sutherland was a quack, he was no more of one than most other doctors of the day.

The Napoleon statement about artillery is quoted in Stevens, *Artillery Through the Ages,* p. 47.

Neill's estimate that four of five *bexareños* would flock to the Texian banner is contained in his January 28, 1836, letter to the provisional government of Texas, reprinted in Chariton, *100 Days in Texas,* p. 176. Bowie's February 2, 1836, letter to Henry Smith is reprinted in the same volume, p. 204.

John H. Moore's 1835 Indian expedition is discussed in Stephen Moore's superbly researched *Savage Frontier,* pp. 21–29. Further evidence of the ranging service of James Neill's sons can be found in the ROT (Republic of Texas) claims made by Samuel Clinton Neill (reel 77, frame 353) and George Clinton Neill (reel 77, frame 272), TSLA.

Bowie's admiration of the Béxar garrison is from his February 2, 1836, letter to Henry Smith, reprinted in Chariton, *100 Days in Texas*, p. 203. Jameson's similar sentiments are from his January 18, 1836, letter to Houston, in *100 Days in Texas*, p. 155.

The quote beginning "If we succeed, the Country is ours" is by Daniel Cloud, from his December 26, 1835, letter to his brother, I. B. Cloud, reprinted in *100 Days in Texas*, p. 73.

EIGHT: THE NAPOLEON OF THE WEST

The epigraph is quoted in Haley, *Sam Houston*, p. 100.

Several primary sources reported Santa Anna's height at 5 feet 10 inches, including an eyewitness description reprinted in PTR 6, p. 148. Santa Anna's glowing reviews of Texas are quoted in Fowler, *Santa Anna*, pp. 28–29; Fowler's book is also the source of much of this description of the campaign culminating in the Battle of the Medina. The exact size of each of the armies involved, and the casualties incurred, is impossible to verify; I have used the most reasonable numbers, as discussed in Schwarz, *Forgotten Battlefield*, pp. 63–64. See also Hatcher, "Joaquín de Arredondo's Report," pp. 226, 234. The beheadings are mentioned by Navarro in *Defending Mexican Valor*, p. 87, and also in his "Apuntes Históricos Interesantes."

Santa Anna's "end of hatreds" platform is quoted in Hatch, *Encyclopedia of the Alamo*, p. 161. The Texian resolution admiring Santa Anna is quoted in Rives, *The United States and Mexico*, p. 210. Santa Anna's opinion regarding Mexico's readiness for democracy is quoted in Callcott, *Santa Anna*, p. 109, and Wharton, *El Presidente*, p. 64. The government circular discussing the Texian colonists is quoted in Rives, *The United States and Mexico*, pp. 318–19.

The letter from consul Anthony Butler to Andrew Jackson of December 19, 1835, is reprinted in PTR 3, p. 252. Santa Anna's preference for the hazards of war is quoted in Fowler, *Santa Anna*, p. 163. The authorization for the 500,000-peso loan is noted in Filisola, *Memoirs*, vol. 2, p. 126.

This discussion of the 1836 Mexican Army of Operations owes much to the following sources: Hardin, *The Alamo 1836* and *Texian Iliad;*

Santos, *Santa Anna's Campaign;* Castañeda, *The Mexican Side of the Texan Revolution;* Shelby, "Notes"; DePalo, *The Mexican National Army;* Filisola, *Memoirs;* Chartrand, *Santa Anna's Mexican Army;* Young, "Finding a Face"; and Haythornthwaite, *The Alamo and the War of Texas Independence.*

De la Peña, in *With Santa Anna in Texas,* p. 81, notes the shifting allegiances of Santa Anna's top officers: "Nearly all the commanders and officers who were then serving under the orders of our commander had fought against him when they had been in the ranks of the people; hatreds were not completely extinguished, and there were many reasons why they were aroused again." He also notes the fact that Castrillón was one of the few officers who dared to disagree with Santa Anna (*With Santa Anna in Texas,* p. 93).

While English-language narratives (dating back to at least the July 1836 issue of *North American Review,* p. 247) of the battle of the Alamo and the Mexican army's operations in Texas during 1835 and 1836 have often described General Martín Perfecto de Cós as Santa Anna's brother-in-law, no evidence has been found to support that assertion. However, three of Santa Anna's officers on the expedition—all highly familiar with His Excellency—identify Dromundo as his brother-in-law: see the account of Ramón Caro, Santa Anna's secretary, in Castañeda, *The Mexican Side of the Texan Revolution,* p. 100; de la Peña, *With Santa Anna in Texas,* p. 39; and Filisola, *Memoirs,* vol. 2, p. 145. Filisola writes, concerning the stockpiling of supplies for the Army of Operations: "But in the order and manner of handling that [which] was being brought in as well as the manner of receiving it one noted the greatest sluggishness, slowness and lack of organization since the quartermaster named had neither the ability nor the energy necessary for carrying out his duties as he should" (*Memoirs,* p. 139). See also de la Peña, *With Santa Anna in Texas,* p. 59, for that officer's assertion that Santa Anna and Dromundo were plotting to "exploit the sufferings of the soldiers," and Caro in Castañeda, p. 100, for his suspicions of embezzlement by Dromundo.

The biographical information on Ramírez y Sesma is from Valadés, *México, Santa Anna,* p. 160.

Of the conscripts in the Mexican Army of Operations, Santa Anna later wrote: "At least half were raw recruits from San Luis, Querétaro, and other departments, hastily enlisted to fill out the ragged companies" (quoted in Castañeda, *The Mexican Side of the Texan Revolution,* p. 11). See also Filisola, *Memoirs,* vol. 2, pp. 127, 140: "The days that the army spent in Leona Vicario were put to use in the training of the recruits who made up the larger part of the forces"; and Caro in Castañeda, p. 100: "The wretched recruits who in the main were conscripts."

After his capitulation in Béxar and during his march back to Mexico, General Cós described his bedraggled conscript troops as "desnudas, sin instrucción ni amor al Servicio"—naked, without understanding or love for the service (Cós to Santa Anna, December 29, 1835, reprinted in PTR 3, p. 358). Several officers later wrote of the low morale of the troops involved; see, for instance, Castañeda, *The Mexican Side of the Texan Revolution,* p. 100.

Santa Anna's directive to Ramírez y Sesma is quoted in Santos, *Santa Anna's Campaign,* p. 9. His "no quarter" orders are reprinted in the same volume, p. 11. The description of the orders and steps involved in the loading and firing of the Mexican army musket is also in that volume, p. 36.

There were several variations to the basic uniform; see Chartrand, *Santa Anna's Mexican Army,* pp. 28–30, and Kevin Young's excellent "Finding a Face."

The information about the Mexican medical corps, or the lack thereof, is found in Castañeda, *The Mexican Side of the Texan Revolution,* pp. 100–101, as is the information concerning the rations.

The Indian confederations and their impact on their raiding is noted in Shelby, "Notes," p. 13.

Santa Anna's orders about "whatever you find available there" is reprinted in Filizola, "Correspondence of Santa Anna," p. 21. His letter to Tornel commenting on the splendid appearance of the army is quoted in Shelby, "Notes," p. 52. The lack of proper footwear is noted in Castañeda, *The Mexican Side of the Texan Revolution,* p. 100. The discussions about the proper route to Texas are from Filisola, *Memoirs,* vol. 2, p. 119.

José Enrique de la Peña's *With Santa Anna in Texas* is a well-written, sharply observed memoir of the author's participation in the Texas campaign. His notion to ask his soldiers to shoot him so that he "might be buried in this vast garden," p. 102, is typical of his romantic inclinations. For other rapturous descriptions of nature, see pp. 34–35 and 112–13.

Besides de la Peña's reconstructed memoir, I have relied on the diligent research into de la Peña's life and writings conducted by

Roger Borroel, who has published his findings in several volumes, chief among them *The J. Sánchez Garza Introduction to the Rebellion of Texas: The Diary of Lt. Col. José Enrique de la Peña.*

De la Peña's opinion of the Santa Anna–Napoleon comparison is in *With Santa Anna in Texas,* p. 12. For a good discussion and analysis of Napoleon's strategy, tactics, and overall career, see Ross, *From Flintlock to Rifle,* chapter 3, "Napoleonic Warfare."

Filisola discusses the ill effects of the conscripts' journey to Béxar in his *Memoirs,* vol. 2, p. 73.

The possibilities of a civil war within Mexico are noted in Shelby, "Notes," p. 48, and Castañeda, *The Mexican Side of the Texan Revolution,* p. 8. The accusations of dishonor regarding Cós and his officers are mentioned in Filisola, *Memoirs,* vol. 2, p. 120.

Ramírez y Sesma's humiliating comment, and the discussion between Sánchez and Castrillón, are related in Sánchez-Navarro, *La Guerra de Tejas,* pp. 68, 77 (my translation).

Santa Anna's order to his aide to strike him with a pistol is mentioned in de la Peña, *With Santa Anna in Texas,* p. 83.

NINE: THE BACKWOODSMAN
This sketch of Crockett is based on the following sources: Crockett's *A Narrative of the Life of David Crockett;* James Shackford's *David Crockett;* Joseph Arpad's dissertation "David Crockett"; Mark Derr's *The Frontiersman;* James R. Boylston and Allen J. Wiener's *David Crockett in Congress;* Manley F. Cobia's *Journey into the Land of Trials;* and William C. Davis's *Three Roads to the Alamo.*

The epigraph, Crockett's famous line about Texas, can be found in Shackford, p. 212.

Crockett in his autobiography claimed that his father was of Irish descent (Crockett, p. 14). His quotes regarding his acquaintance with hard times, and his father being "hard run," are also from his book (p. 22), as is his quote about family and fortune (p. 68). Recent scholarship points to some French ancestry also.

The description of Elizabeth Crockett is found in Ellis, *The Life of Colonel David Crockett,* p. 58.

Crockett's quote concerning his method of justice is from his autobiography, p. 135.

The description of Crockett at the ventriloquist's show is in a letter from Helen Chapman to Emily Blair dated May 1, 1834 (box

2C433, William W. Chapman Papers, BCAH). She also mentions his "drawling accent."

Crockett's quote about supporting measures and principles rather than men is in Boylston and Wiener, *David Crockett in Congress*, p. 217, as is his quote about leaving the United States (p. 319), and his still being a Jackson man (p. 112).

Cobia, in *Journey into the Land of Trials*, p. 15, makes a convincing case that Crockett most likely made a public pronouncement in which he said his opponent could go to hell and he would go to Texas—or something similar to it.

The details of the scene of Crockett coming home after receiving the election results is from an 1882 newspaper interview with his daughter Mrs. Matilda Fields in the David Crockett file, DRT, as are the details of his barbecue and bran dance. "Bran dance" has usually been regarded by twentieth- and twenty-first-century historians as a misspelling of "barn dance," and corrected accordingly—and almost surely in error. A bran dance was a frequent occurrence on the southern frontier, where the absence of a proper building or plank floors obliged dancing to be performed outdoors. Here is one definition: "A plat of land was cleared off and leveled down hard and smooth, after which a layer of one or two inches of wheat bran was scattered over the surface, and the 'ballroom' was declared completed, and ready for the dancers" (*History of Newton, Lawrence, Barry and McDonald Counties, Missouri*, p. 124). An account and description of a bran dance is rendered in the anonymously written 1833 biography of Crockett, *Sketches and Eccentricities of Col. David Crockett, of West Tennessee* (London: O. Rich, 1834), p. 148, and there is an illustration of a bran dance on p. 157 of Sherwood Bonner's *Dialect Tales* (New York: Harper and Brothers, 1883).

The quote from the letter Crockett wrote on the eve of his departure is in Shackford, *David Crockett*, p. 210. Crockett's description of William Patton is quoted in Boylston and Wiener, *David Crockett in Congress*, p. 285.

Crockett's daughter Matilda remembered, many years later, that he wore his coonskin cap, and she did not talk of it as if it were something new (1882 newspaper interview with Mrs. Matilda Fields in David Crockett file, DRT). A young man who saw Crockett in Memphis a few days later confirmed this costume, writing: "He wore that same veritable coon-skin cap and hunting shirt" (as quoted in Cobia, *Journey into the Land of Trials*,

p. 36). A woman who saw him a few weeks after that in Texas wrote, years later: "Crockett was dressed like a gentleman, and not as a backwoodsman. He did wear a coonskin cap" (*Dallas Morning News*, January 6, 1894). Several other descriptions of Crockett later in his journey also mention his coonskin cap. That Crockett took his trusted Betsy with him is confirmed by an account written by John Swisher, a young man living in Texas at the time, who spent a few days in Crockett's company. Years later, Swisher wrote: "His rifle I well remember. It was ornamented with a single silver plate, let into the stock, upon which was engraved 'David Crockett'; and he called it 'Bessie' "—clearly meaning "Betsy" (Colonel John M. Swisher, *The Swisher Memoirs* [San Antonio, TX: The Sigmund Press, 1932], p. 19).
Matilda Crockett Fields's account refutes the claim, frequently accepted as fact, that Crockett was estranged from his wife and family and lived elsewhere, a claim that was first mentioned, at least to my knowledge, in Shackford, *David Crockett*, p. 149, where the author based his assumption on the fact that no known letters from Crockett to his second wife, Elizabeth, survive (though she was almost surely illiterate). Shackford further states that "when [Crockett] was at home his letters were generally written from Weakley County, though his wife and children were living in Gibson County.... [This] is evidence that he maintained a dual residence and suggests unamicable relations between Crockett and his wife and a consequent dwelling under separate roofs. However, there is no positive evidence for this conclusion." This despite a footnote in Shackford's book referring to the 1831 sale of Crockett's land in Weakley County: "The land deed was certified for registration in both Weakley and Gibson Counties, and we have another indication that David was living in two counties or that the land sold lay first in the one and then in the other" (p. 306, n. 32). Further evidence of this confusion is supplied by Mark Derr in his Crockett biography, *The Frontiersman*, pp.108–09: "As the population grew, the legislature created Gibson and Weakley counties, whose boundary with Carroll [county] cut through the Patton-Crockett farms. David and Elizabeth also purchased additional land and built new homes in each of the jurisdictions, leaving census takers, local officials, and the Crocketts themselves confused over which county was theirs, a circumstance that over the years has led some scholars to conclude erroneously that they maintained

separate residences." Another possible source of confusion, based on the various Weakley/Gibson County addresses on Crockett's correspondence, is that Crockett lived in one county and used a post office in the other. In short, there is no reliable evidence at all that there was an estrangement, and Mrs. Fields's account makes clear the fact that the family, including Davy, was living together when he left for Texas. (Thanks to Crockett expert Jim Boylston for his information and opinions regarding this subject.)

Robert P. Crockett discusses his father's departure in a letter to Smith Rudd dated December 30, 1879 (Rudd Manuscripts, Lilly Library, Indiana University). There is no hard evidence that they rode to Dyersburg first, but there are several good-size rivers and creeks south of Rutherford, and no roads through the area at the time; since they were planning on exploring Texas, and not southwest Tennessee, I believe the Dyersburg route is much more likely. See also Zaboly, "Crockett Goes to Texas."

Crockett's Memphis speech containing his reference to "a man with a timber toe" is quoted in Shackford, *David Crockett*, p. 212. The newspaper quote concerning Halley's Comet is in Cobia, *Journey into the Land of Trials*, p. 26, as is the quote from Crockett's Little Rock speech in which he discussed Texas independence (pp. 44–46).

The Houston call to arms is reprinted in PTR 2, p. 47.

Crockett's final letter home, dated January 9, 1836, is reprinted in McLean, *Papers*, vol. 12, p. 618 (punctuation added).

Crockett may have signed the oath of allegiance a few days earlier than the date given here, which is the accepted one; contemporary and reminiscent accounts disagree as to the exact date. See Cobia, *Journey into the Land of Trials*, pp. 106–10, for a cogent summary of potential explanations. The oath was reprinted in *Niles' Register* on June 23, 1838.

Crockett's letter to his daughter Margaret is the same January 9, 1836, letter referenced above.

Judge Forbes's description of Crockett's comrades is quoted in Cobia, p. 128.

Crockett's exact route from Nacogdoches to Béxar, and the identity of whom he traveled with and when, is not clear, but the best evidence indicates that Crockett traveled from Washington to Bastrop and thence to Béxar—the route of El Camino Real, though he may have made a detour or two along the way. Noah Smithwick, in *Evolution of a State*, p. 81, writes: "I was taken down with fever while in Bastrop, but was convalescent when Crockett came on, and wanted to return with him to San Antonio, but seeing I was not in condition to do so, he persuaded me to wait for another party to arrive a few days later"; further evidence is found in Leonie Rummel Weyand and Houston Wade, *An Early History of Fayette County* (La Grange, TX: La Grange *Journal*, 1936), p. 283 (see note concerning John Lott and the advisory committee below). See also Cobia, *Journey into the Land of Trials,* pp. 121–64.

Daniel Cloud's December 26, 1835, letter to his brother is reprinted in Groneman, *Alamo Defenders,* p. 132. Information on Autry is drawn from Looscan, "Micajah Autry"; "Sketch of My Life" by Mary Autry Greer, Autry's daughter (box 32, James L. Autry Papers, Fondren Library, Rice University); and the letters he wrote home, reprinted in many books and articles. Autry's January 13, 1836, letter to his wife is quoted in Looscan, pp. 319–20.

The information about the stands along El Camino Real is taken from Jenkins, *The General's Tight Pants.*

The description of Washington, the town on the Brazos River, is in Gray, *Diary of Colonel W. F. Gray,* pp. 107–8. It was not referred to as Washington-on-the-Brazos at this time.

That John Lott was the provisional government's local agent in Washington is evidenced from reports reprinted in PTR 3, p. 181, and PTR 9, p. 153. The advisory committee's report concerning their determination that Béxar had enough troops is quoted in Binkley, *Official Correspondence,* p. 372, in a letter from the advisory committee to J. W. Robinson dated January 31, 1836: "The advisory Committee are of opinion that no further necessity exists of increasing the number of troops now at Bejar, beyond those that are already there, or on their way to that place,—and therefore advise that an express be sent immediately to the Town of Washington, requiring John Lott the Government [agent] at that place, to direct all volunteers from the United States or elsewhere, passing through that place, to proceed direct to Goliad or Copano, where the Government supplies are generally stored and where they will receive orders for their future movements." Along the left-hand margin next to this recommendation is written "Order issued No. 15." Another indication that the provisional government's recruiting agents were sending men to Béxar, at least in January and early

February, is this quote from Weyand and Wade, *An Early History of Fayette County,* p. 283, in a profile of area resident James Seaton Lester: "In January and February 1836, our hero was stationed at Bastrop where he was acting as a kind of recruiting agent for the garrison at Bexar, the object of which was to strengthen that outpost as much as possible. While acting in this capacity he met David Crockett and his men in the upper edge of Hill's Prairie and sent them on to reinforce Travis and help defend the Alamo." Lester's ROT (Republic of Texas) pension claims, which can be found online at the Texas Library and Archives Commission website, support the fact that he was assigned by Sam Houston to duty in the recruiting service.

TEN: THE ROAD TO BÉXAR

The epigraph, from Santa Anna's address to his army, is reprinted in PTR 4, pp. 373–74.

In Juan Almonte's journal entry for February 22, 1836 (Asbury, "The Private Journal," p. 16), he writes: "The troops cleared their arms and dryed their clothes; no desertions whatever or sickness." This is the only entry during the army's march north in which the lack of deserters is mentioned. Many of the details noted in this account of the march derive from Almonte's journal; Sánchez's journal; Filisola's *Memoirs,* vol. 2; Santos, *Santa Anna's Campaign;* de la Peña, *With Santa Anna in Texas;* Filizola, "Correspondence of Santa Anna"; and Castañeda, *The Mexican Side of the Texan Revolution,* which includes the memoirs of Santa Anna and his secretary, Ramón Caro.

Sánchez's puzzlement over Santa Anna's haste to leave his army behind is mentioned in his journal, translated in Huneycutt, *At the Alamo,* pp. 54–55.

The date of February 8 for the arrival of Santa Anna's orders to Ramírez y Sesma is an estimate; the order was issued from Monclova, 120 miles away, on February 5. The details of *telele* and dysentery are found in Filisola, *Memoirs,* vol. 2, pp. 143, 160. The loss of more than a thousand women and children (1,300, actually) is mentioned in Salas, *Soldaderas,* p. 29.

De la Peña recorded vivid details of the February 13 snowstorm. That the other units of the Army of Operations did not experience snow, or the same extremes of cold weather, is noted in several sources. De la Peña wrote: "This unexpected storm did not cause the other brigades the damage that it caused the cavalry" (*With*

Santa Anna in Texas, p. 28); Juan Almonte, traveling with Santa Anna, noted in his diary on February 13: "weather stormy; thermometer 51°" (Asbury, "The Private Journal," p. 14); and the February 13 entry in the logbook of the San Luis Potosí battalion, which was part of the Vanguard Brigade, states: "North with rain. Extreme cold" (Borroel, *The Itineraries of the Zapadores,* p. 17).

The deaths of four hundred men in a span of twenty-four hours is mentioned in a letter that Santa Anna wrote in 1852 (Valadés, *México, Santa Anna,* p. 166).

The mesquite grass that enabled the stock to survive is noted in Chariton, *Exploring the Alamo Legends,* p. 159.

Santa Anna's friendship with the Navarro family is related in Lozano, *Viva Tejas,* p. 30.

Regarding Santa Anna's plan to surprise the rebels early on the morning of February 23, it must be pointed out here that one or two of the sources for this plan state that the fandango occurred on the night of Sunday, February 21, and that Santa Anna ordered Ramírez y Sesma to advance with the cavalry that night. Santa Anna himself wrote, in a report dated February 27, 1836: "My objective had been to surprise them early in the morning of the day before, but a heavy rain prevented it" (quoted in Hansen, p. 332). But the bulk of sources mention the night of February 22—including Santa Anna himself, who wrote in his "Manifesto," a defense of his handling of the Texas campaign published in 1837: "I entrusted, therefore, the operation to one of our generals, who with a detachment of cavalry, part of the dragoons mounted on infantry officers' horses, should have fallen on Béxar in the early morning of February 23, 1836" (translated in Castañeda, *The Mexican Side of the Texan Revolution 1836,* p. 13). The Mexican secretary of war, José María Tornel, wrote an account of the campaign in 1837 in which he stated: "A division of the army was to surprise Béxar early the morning of the 23rd of February, 1836, but for some reason yet unknown the orders of the General were not carried out" (quoted in Castañeda, p. 351). Francisco Becerra, an infantry sergeant with the Vanguard Brigade of Ramírez y Sesma, wrote or dictated an account in which he said: "On reaching Medina river Santa Anna halted one day to reunite and rest his army. Señor Navarro and a priest met him there. He received them well. The priest told the President there were two hundred and fifty Americans in the

Alamo; that they were at a fandango that night, and could be easily surprised. Santa Anna intended to make a forced march for that purpose. A wet norther had been blowing during the day, the Medina river had risen suddenly, the ammunition train had been left on the opposite bank, and could not be crossed. His Excellency was very mad, but there was no remedy, and he had to abandon the enterprise. The Medina had fallen the next evening, and every thing was passed over safely. The march was resumed the next day" (quoted in Hansen, p. 455). Clearly, since they marched from the Medina into Béxar on February 23 ("the next day"), the fandango was being held on the previous day, February 22—the actual birthday of George Washington and the day that Americans celebrated the occasion.

The fragile condition of the Alamo's north wall is discussed in Ivey, *Mission to Fortress,* chapter 7, p. 26.

The four saints in the niches on either side of the Alamo's main entrance are listed in Ivey, "The Search for the Saints."

The two rows of timber stakes are mentioned in Jack Eaton's 1980 excavation research report, quoted in Hansen, p. 737. John Sutherland also described the palisade as having two rows (Hansen, p. 175). However, two leading Alamo researchers, James Ivey and Mark Lemon, have concluded that there was only one row of stakes.

The information supplied by the Tejano scout was forwarded by Bowie in his February 2, 1836, letter to Henry Smith, reprinted in Chariton, *100 Days in Texas,* p. 204.

Robinson's February 2, 1836, letter to Neill is quoted in Binkley, *Official Correspondence,* vol. 1, p. 372. Though the physical letter has disappeared, the council's recommendation to Robinson is still extant, and has a note on it stating: "Col. Neill written to Feb 2d 1836."

Crockett's arrival and this portion of his speech are related in Sutherland, *The Fall of the Alamo,* pp. 11–12.

Evidence of the service of the Neill sons is at TSLA (ROT audited claim 558, reel 77, frame 353), and it states that Samuel Clinton Neill served as a private in the mounted rifle corps under Colonel John Moore and Williamson, and that George Jefferson Neill "served 14 days in Williamson's corps" plus "two months in Hunt's company" (frame 272). The exact dates of service are unavailable, but it is clear that the two were actively engaged in defending the frontier area around Bastrop in the early part of

1836. The rumor that Neill had also left to procure money for the garrison is noted in Sutherland, *The Fall of the Alamo,* p. 8. See Hardin, "J. C. Neill," for an excellent and judicious appraisal of Neill that refutes Walter Lord's description of Neill in *A Time to Stand* as a "good second-rater" who was "gently nudged aside" by Travis, Bowie, and Crockett.

There are records for at least fifteen discharges at this time. See TSLA records for John T. Ballard, M. B. Atkinson, David Davis, Jabez Fitch, Chester Gorbit, T. Harris, Thomas Hendrick, Jonathan Hobbs, William Irwin, David Murphree, Preston Pevyhouse, John Pevyhouse, Felix Taylor, and Robert White (plus Neill's February 14, 1836, discharge for Marcus Sewell). All these men were on the muster roll of Alamo defenders taken by Neill in mid- to late January (John T. Ballard likely was "J. Bartlett" on the list, especially since he is on the February 1 Alamo election return and "Bartlett" is not). See Chariton, *100 Days in Texas,* pp. 148–49, for the mid-January list, and n. 81 on p. 191 of that work for further explanation. Additionally, several men on the muster roll are known to have left the Alamo (TSLA records of them exist), though their discharges could not be found, including F. W. Jackson, Peter Conrad, John Johnston, Gerald Navan, William Bell, Thomas Ryan, and John Pickering. Based on the dates of most of these discharges—February 14—researcher nonpareil Thomas Ricks Lindley concluded in his book *Alamo Traces* that Neill left on the eleventh, made it to Gonzales, but was persuaded by a rider from Béxar to return and sort out the command problem. This may have happened, but due to the complete lack of corroborating evidence in the record—no account, letter, or report mentions anything of the sort—I find it unlikely.

Crockett's statement affirming his rank of private is quoted in Sutherland's early draft account, reprinted in Hansen, p. 178.

Travis's February 13, 1836, letter to Henry Smith regarding his awkward position is reprinted in Mixon, "William Barret Travis," p. 227, as is Baugh's letter of the same date to Smith (p. 229). The February 14, 1836, letter from Travis and Bowie to Smith that relates their agreement is reprinted in Hansen, pp. 24–25.

Sutherland's tantalizingly brief and enigmatic description of Bowie's illness is in *The Fall of the Alamo,* p. 13. See Reid, "What Ails You," for a succinct account of the various diagnoses of Bowie's condition, and the author's conclusion that it was probably typhoid pneumonia, from which sufferers often recovered after an acute period lasting a few weeks. Supporting this diagnosis somewhat is what Susanna Dickinson supposedly told her grandchildren—that at "lucid moments when the fever was somewhat abated, his soldiers would bring his cot to the main building" (Hansen, p. 57), since delirium, according to Reid, invariably accompanied the sickness. Two medical authorities also weighed in with a diagnosis of pneumonia: Dr. Joseph Field mentions "pneumonia typhoides, or bastard pleurisy" as a common Texas affliction of the time in his book *Three Years in Texas,* p. 37, and the author of *The Medical Story of Early Texas,* Patrick Ireland Nixon, concludes: "It is likely that Bowie contracted pneumonia ten days before his death" (p. 182). But historian John S. Ford, who interviewed Juana Alsbury, who may or may not have been familiar with the diagnosis, quoted her as saying that "Col. Bowie was very sick with typhoid fever" (Hansen, p. 87).

Most writers on the subject claim that Bowie did not become bedridden until the second day of the siege, February 24, citing Reuben Potter's "The Fall of the Alamo" as their source. But circumstantial and oral evidence strongly points to an earlier date, as much as a week previous, or to a day or two after the cosigned dispatch of February 14. Virtually all accounts by participants mention Travis as being in command at the time of the retreat into the Alamo, and sometimes before. John Sutherland, who was there until the siege began, wrote (in what is likely his earliest account, sometime soon after 1860): "Col. James C Nail [Neill] was the Commander, by leave of absence, Col. Jas. Bowie, was entitled to the command; but owing to sickness previous to the commencement of the siege, he requested in presence of the writer of this, Col Travis (who had but recently arrived at San Antonio) to take the command, which he did" (Hansen, p. 167). In another section of the same account, he writes: "All in the Alamo at the fall One hundred & eighty seven men; forty of which when the writer left were on the sick list. (Col Bowie with the sick)" (Hansen, p. 179). In his more polished account, published by his daughter in 1936, he writes: "By Colonel Neill's absence, Colonel James Bowie was left in command but he was shortly afterwards taken sick and confined to his bed" (Sutherland, *The Fall of the Alamo,* p. 8), which certainly sounds as though Bowie was bedridden soon after Neill's departure on February 11 and several days before the arrival of the Mexican army on February 23. (And since Sutherland left the Alamo on the afternoon of February 23, the simple fact that he discussed and attempted to diagnose Bowie's illness indicates that Bowie was seriously ill before that date.) Another witness was Juana Alsbury, who in the fall of 1838 visited the Alamo with Béxar resident and historian Mary Maverick, wife of Samuel, and described Bowie's death to her. Mrs. Maverick wrote: "Mrs. Allsbury went into the Fort with Bowie to care for his comfort, he being in feeble health, & having had to resign command to Col. Travis" (Green, *Samuel Maverick*, pp. 55–56). And affidavits from Juan Seguín, on behalf of some of his Tejano horsemen seeking pensions years later, mention Travis and not Bowie in connection with the men receiving furloughs at the time: "After the capitulation of Gen'l. Cos he [Jesus Hernandez] continued in the same volunteer service till the beginning of February at which time B. Travis who was in superior command gave leave of absence sine die, to a large portion of volunteers whose services were no longer needed" (affidavit of Juan Seguín, Jesus Hernandez pension claim, reel 220, frame 270, ROT [Republic of Texas] Claims, TSLA), and: "After the capitulation, he [Macedonia Arocha] continued in the military service, until the middle of the month of February 1836 at which time he received from Col. Travis leave to retire" (affidavit of Juan Seguín, Macedonia Arocha pension claim, reel 201, frame 372, ROT [Republic of Texas] Claims, TSLA). A Tejano in Seguín's company testified that "the commanding officer B. Travis dismissed indefinitely good many volunteers" (affidavit of Clemente Bustillo, Jesus Hernandez pension claim, reel 220, frame 269, ROT [Republic of Texas] Claims, TSLA), and on February 22, Travis signed a receipt for forty *fanegas* of corn appropriated from Antonio Cruz (Antonio Cruz pension claim 4469, reel 23, frame 13, ROT [Republic of Texas] Claims, TSLA). In November 1837, Captain William H. Patton signed a receipt stating: "This will certify that I was present when Capt. Francis Desauque loaned Col. Travis at Bexar two hundred dollars on act. Of the Texian Gov't." (Desauque audited claim, reel 25, frame 531, ROT [Republic of Texas] Claims, TSLA). There are no doubt other examples as well. There are at least three pension claim affidavits from men of Seguín's command who, many decades later, testified that they were dismissed or received permission to leave the Alamo garrison from both Bowie and Travis (José Alameda, Agustin Bernal, Matias Carillo); only one claimed he was dismissed by Bowie and not Travis (Manuel Cerbera). The point is that there is virtually no evidence that Bowie exercised command, or shared it with Travis, after the February 14 cosigned letter.

After that letter, Travis wrote and/or signed every letter, order, or receipt through February 24 (a total of at least eleven extant, including two receipts recently made public in the November 9, 2011, auction conducted by RR Auction of Amherst, New Hampshire—both with the header "Commandancy of Bexar"), plus a few others known to have been written to James Fannin at Goliad but not extant. Bowie's shaky signature at the bottom of the February 23 letter to Santa Anna—actually penned by Juan Seguín—evidences the only known letter he had anything to do with, though he may have cosigned, with Travis, a letter to Fannin on the same day. There are three pieces of evidence for that letter. One is in Foote, *Texas and the Texans*, vol. 2, p. 224: "The Commandant at Fort Defiance had received the express of Travis and Bowie requesting his aid, on the 25th of February," which is followed by the text of said letter. The second is the fact that Fannin, in a letter to Robinson on February 25, 1836, wrote: "The appeal of cols Travis & Bowie cannot however pass unnoticed..." (Chariton, *100 Days in Texas*, p. 272). The third is Travis's statement in his March 3, 1836, letter: "On the arrival of the enemy in Bejar ten days ago, I sent an express to Col. F., which arrived at Goliad on the next day, urging him to send us reinforcements— none have yet arrived" (quoted in Hansen, p. 36). (Note that Travis did not write "Col. Bowie and I sent an express," which may or may not be construed as support for this argument, but is certainly no support for Bowie having written it; another possibility is that Bowie merely signed the letter, as he did on February 23.) Additionally, in every account by a credible eyewitness (Dickinson, Dimitt, Esparza, Highsmith, Seguín, Sutherland, etc.), Bowie is rarely if ever mentioned in connection with any command activities in the week preceding Santa Anna's arrival on February 23—or mentioned at all. In a February 28, 1836, letter to James Kerr, Dimitt wrote: "On the 23rd, I was requested by Colonel Travis to take Lieutenant Nobles and reconnoitre [sic] the enemy" (Huson, *Captain Philip Dimitt's Commandancy*, p. 236). Susanna Dickinson is quoted in 1874 as saying: "On February 23rd, 1836, Santa Anna, having captured the pickets sent out by Col. Travis to guard the post from surprise..." (Hansen, p. 45). And Juan Seguín, in a June 7, 1890, letter, wrote: "Col. Travis had no idea that Santa ana [sic] with his army, would venture to approach the city of Bexar, (now San Antonio) and for this reason, only a watch was kept up on the church tower.... In the act of the moment, Col. Travis resolved to concentrate all his forces within the Alamo, which was immediately done" (Hansen, p. 197).

Crockett's earthy opinion concerning the men leaving the garrison appears in an affidavit of David Harman (David Harman Donation Voucher File, GLO). I have corrected the spelling of "shit," which in the written affidavit was euphemized as "sheet."

Details of Antonio Saez's blacksmith shop are from the Antonio Saez File, TSLA. The claim for the sixty-five head of cattle is in the February 19, 1835, pension claim by Felipe Xaimes (audited claim 813, reel 130, frame 606, ROT [Republic of Texas] Claims, TSLA).

The ditty taught to young Enrique Esparza was related by Esparza in an interview reprinted in Hansen, pp. 113–14.

The footbridge across the San Antonio River has often been described and portrayed as a sturdy bridge wide enough for a cart to cross, but John Sutherland specifically wrote of "the footbridge from the city leading to the Alamo (there was no wagon bridge then)" (Hansen, p. 179). J. M. Rodriguez, who was a child at the time and lived close to the bridge, described it as "the footlog across the river" (*San Antonio Daily Express*, May 28, 1905). Additionally, Captain José Juan Sánchez's map/illustration of the area clearly shows a small plank bridge, and his description reads: "Board bridge to facilitate the passage of the people from Béxar to the Alamo." The next entry in his descriptive list concerns the ford lower on the river, which he describes as a "ford for vehicles and horses going toward La Villita," indicating that he would probably have used similar language for the Potrero Street bridge if it deserved such a designation (Hansen, p. 409). And de la Peña writes of the morning of the attack: "The columns were set in motion, and at three they silently advanced toward the river, which they crossed marching two abreast over some narrow wooden bridges" (de la Peña, *With Santa Anna in Texas*, p. 46).

The description of Travis is from J. M. Rodriguez's memoir, reprinted in Hansen, p. 507.

Deaf Smith's objective of seeing Henry Smith is noted by James Neill in his January 14, 1836, letter to Houston, reprinted in Chariton, *100 Days in Texas*, p. 145.

The advisory committee's mistaken impression that there were enough men in Béxar likely stems from Neill's letter, in which he wrote: "I hope you will send me one Hundred men from Goliad, unless they have been already sent from some other quarter, as it is absolutely necessary for the support of this place" (Neill to Sam Houston, January 14, 1836, in Chariton, *100 Days in Texas*, p. 145). To the best of my knowledge, Manley Cobia, author of *Journey into the Land of Trials*, was the first historian to notice this (p. 152).

The source for the eleven defenders who left to scout for their bounty lands is a February 14, 1836, letter from David Cummings to his father, reprinted in Chariton, *100 Days in Texas*, p. 234.

There is some disagreement about the date of Samuel Maverick's departure; see Marks, *Turn Your Eyes Toward Texas*, p. 52, and Agatha Maverick Welsh's letter to Charles W. Ramsdell, November 7 (?), 1931 (box 3L74, BCAH). In *Samuel Maverick, Texan*, author Rena Maverick Green makes the case that Maverick remained in the Alamo until several days into the siege; this assumption is apparently based on his late arrival, on March 6, to the convention. But in a letter to a friend in 1847, Maverick wrote: "I was almost a solitary escape from the Alamo massacre having been sent by those unfortunate men only four days before the Mexican advance appeared, as their representative in the convention which declared Independence" (Green, *Memoirs of Mary A. Maverick*, p. 134). And Mrs. Welsh, Maverick's granddaughter, discussed the subject with Maverick's eldest son, her uncle, who told her: "He [Maverick] had said that he had had a long talk with Travis just before he had left the Alamo, that he was sitting sideways on his horse with one leg caught around the pommel of his saddle, Travis leaning with his arm on the horse's neck..." This sounds much more like a man leisurely preparing to leave an uninvested Alamo rather than a man about to gallop through an enemy cordon.

Amos Pollard mentions having plenty of instruments but little medicine in his February 13, 1836, letter to Henry Smith, reprinted in Chariton, *100 Days in Texas*, p. 145.

The story of the three Taylor brothers is in Sowell, *Early Settlers and Indian Fighters*, p. 838.

While there are no extant records offering solid proof that Albert Martin attended or graduated from Partridge's school, revolutionary firebrand (and later historian) Frank Johnson, who doubtless knew Martin, wrote that Martin was a "graduate of Capt. Partridge's Military school in Connecticut" (Johnson, *A History of Texas and Texans*, vol. 1, p. 269).

James Robinson's February 13, 1836, letter to Fannin is reprinted in Chariton, *100 Days in Texas*, p. 230. Fannin's letter to Robinson of the next day, February 14, 1836, is reprinted in the same volume, p. 232.

Details of Travis's instructions to Vaughan are in his February 19, 1836, letter to Vaughan, reprinted in Chariton, *100 Days in Texas*, p. 246. Travis sending out Sowell and Lockhart for provisions is noted in Sowell, *Rangers and Pioneers*, p. 136. Details of Blas Herrera's scouting trip and the February 20 council of war are related in Sutherland's unpublished narrative reprinted in Hansen, pp. 142–43.

Though some histories of the Alamo claim that the fandango attended by the defenders occurred on the evening of Sunday, February 21, there are several contemporary accounts that strongly indicate that it occurred on Monday, February 22. De la Peña writes: "When General Ramírez y Sesma sighted the town, the enemy was still engaged in the pleasures of a dance given the night before" (*With Santa Anna in Texas*, p. 57); though de la Peña was not with Santa Anna and Ramírez y Sesma's Vanguard Brigade at that time, he would surely have heard details of its arrival in Béxar. (See also note on p. 416.)

ELEVEN: *Circunvalado*

Circunvalado is Spanish for "surrounded"; it is used in Ramírez y Sesma's March 11, 1836, report (Archivo General de Mexico, Secretaria de Guerra y Marina, Book 335, pp. 166–68, BCAH). The epigraph is from Santa Anna's "Manifesto," published in 1837 and translated in Castañeda's *Mexican Side of the Texan Revolution*, pp. 12–13.

The scene of Béxar on the morning of February 23, 1836, and most of the details of the Texians' move into the Alamo are related in Sutherland's unpublished narrative, reprinted in Hansen, p. 142.

The description of John W. Smith is taken from "Incidents in the Life of John W. Smith" (Frank M. Gillespie Papers, BCAH).

The decision of Ramírez y Sesma to refrain from attacking on the morning of February 23 is discussed in de la Peña, *With Santa Anna in Texas*, pp. 56–57.

The information on Miñón derives primarily from his self-penned service record in Borroel, *Field Reports of the Mexican Army,* vol. 6, pp. 25, 27, 35.

A conversation with Elise P. Kidd, great-granddaughter of John Sutherland, revealed that one of her grandparents told her that Dr. Sutherland was "short to medium in height."

Travis's February 23, 1836, letter to Andrew Ponton is reprinted in Hansen, p. 28.

John Sutherland detailed his injuries in an 1854 petition for bounty land reprinted in Hansen, p. 164, and in an undated draft of his story (Hansen, p. 171).

John Sutherland insisted that a man named Johnson was the first express rider to Goliad, though he could not remember his first name (see Sutherland's unpublished narrative, reprinted in Hansen, p. 146). Lindley's well-reasoned conclusion in *Alamo Traces* (pp. 89 and 109, n. 20) that this express rider was most likely John Johnson, a member of the garrison as listed on the February 1, 1836, Alamo election return, seems reasonable. The Mistress Kenner pension claim in the TSLA files (audited claim 100, reel 56, frame 324) shows that John B. Johnson was a member of Travis's cavalry, pressing a horse belonging to Mistress Kenner for $30.

The February 23, 1836, letter from Bowie and Travis to Fannin is quoted in Foote, *Texas and the Texans,* vol. 2, p. 224. The original of this message is not extant; Foote's use of it in his 1840 history is its earliest known publication, and the only source for it.

Though Crockett was not the official commander of the self-styled Tennessee Mounted Volunteers, he clearly assumed some leadership duties of the group, or a portion of them, and was considered its leader by the members. Confirmation of this fact includes the following: (1) a volunteer named Charles Lewis Brown stated in an affidavit years later that he "served under Colonel David Crockett" (Brown pension claim, reel 205, frame 59, ROT [Republic of Texas] Claims, TSLA); (2) in a letter to the editor of the *Austin City Gazette* signed by a "Volunteer of 1836," published in the April 14, 1836, issue of that newspaper, the anonymous author claimed he had left Nacogdoches in February 1836 with a company of "about sixteen men under the command of Col. Crockett"; (3) in an audited claim signed by Sam Houston, a volunteer named Peter Harper wrote that on

January 8 he "commenced at Nacogdoches under Col. Crocket" (reel 41, frame 350, ROT [Republic of Texas] Claims, TSLA); and (4) one volunteer who rode with Crockett and died in the Alamo, B. Archer M. Thomas, signed a receipt in Washington as "one of D Crocketts Com[mand]" (Chariton, 100 Days in Texas, p. 171).

Sutherland's unpublished narrative is the only source for Crockett's assigned position in the Alamo (reprinted in Hansen, p. 176).

Thomas Ricks Lindley discusses the Mexican wounded left behind in his well-researched three-part article "Mexican Casualties at Bexar."

In a series of handwritten revisions and additions made to the original text of his 1860 pamphlet "The Fall of the Alamo," Reuben Potter made the sources for his version of some of the events clearer: "When Mr. [Nat] Lewis visited the Alamo, the town was in possession of the enemy, the confusion which prevailed there beggared description. Bowie with a detachment was engaged in breaking open deserted houses in the neighborhood and gathering corn. Another squad was driving some cattle into the inclosure...East of the Long Barrack."

Juan Seguín's June 7, 1890, letter, in which he describes the women lining the streets as the men left Béxar for the Alamo, is reprinted in Matovina, The Alamo Remembered, p. 91.

Nat Lewis's background as a whaling man from near Nantucket is noted in his obituary in the San Antonio Daily Express of October 23, 1872.

The source for the information on Carlos Espalier is Musso, "Col. Bowie's Freed Slaves," and the Antonio Menchaca affidavit, Carlos Espalier File, Memorials and Petitions File, TSLA.

Nat Lewis's memories of the morning—including recollections about William Ward, and the profanity—are in Potter, "The Fall of the Alamo," p. 7, and Potter's notes to it, cited above.

Some later accounts claim that Alsbury was in Béxar on February 23, went into the Alamo with his wife, and rode out later as a courier. But Mrs. Alsbury told a later interviewer: "When the news of Santa Anna's approach, at the head of a considerable force, was verified in San Antonio, Dr. Alsbury proceeded to the Brazos river to procure means to remove his family, expecting to return before Santa Anna could reach the city. He failed to do so; and his wife went into the Alamo where her protector was, when the Mexican troops were near by" (Hansen, p. 87). And an

August 1, 1888, *Dallas Morning News* story about Mrs. Alsbury published soon after she died quotes from a story published in the *Hempstead Advance-Guard,* "edited by a nephew of Horace A. Alsbury": "When she was within the walls of the Alamo, she was Mrs. Alsbury, wife of Dr. Horace A. Alsbury, who had placed her under the protection of Col. James Bowie when San Antonio was expecting the invasion of Santa Anna." Additionally, there is this comment written by Dr. Joseph Barnard in his journal (Barnard was saved by a Mexican officer from the Goliad massacre and then moved to Béxar to assist with the wounded there): "Tuesday, [April] 17th, —Dr. Alsbury came into town to-day from General Filisola, now commander in chief, with a pass. He (Dr. Alsbury) is son-in-law to Angelo Navarro, with whom I live. His wife and sister, together with a Negro of Bowie's, were in the Alamo when it was stormed. He has come in order to look after his family and take them off" (quoted in Hansen, p. 612). Finally, John Sutherland writes in an early draft of his account written soon after 1860: "On Sunday morning [February 28, 1836] the writer in Company of Dr Alsbury & ten other Americans crossed the Guardaloup River at Gonazales & fell in with and waited on Capt John N Seguin" (Hansen, p. 179). It is clear from these accounts that Alsbury was not in the Alamo or Béxar on February 23.

That there were several black servants inside the Alamo, enslaved or otherwise, seems fairly certain. Joe, in his first account to the convention on March 20, 1836, was quoted by a reliable witness as relating that "the negroes, for there were several negroes and women in the fort, were spared. Only one woman was killed, and Joe supposes she was shot accidentally, while attempting to cross the Alamo. She was found lying between two guns" (Hansen, p. 78). Mary Maverick, the wife of Samuel Maverick and a resident of San Antonio soon after the battle, wrote: "The survivors were...2 negro servants of Bowie," and then identified her source: "This present writer visited the site [of pyres] with Dr. and Mrs. Allsbury in Fall of 1838" ("Fall of the Alamo," an account by Mary A. Maverick "compiled from H. Yoakum and Oral Testimony," in Green, *Samuel Maverick, Texan,* p. 55). A doctor stationed in Goliad and sent to Béxar after Fannin's surrender wrote: "Tuesday, [May] 17th—Dr. Alsberry came in to town to-day....His wife and sister, together with a Negro, [of] Bowie's, were in the Alamo when it was stormed" (Joseph H.

Barnard, in Huson, *Dr. J. H. Barnard's Journal,* p. 42). And according to Juana Alsbury, after the battle, "Don Manuel placed them in charge of a colored woman belong to Col. Bowie, and the party reached the house of Don Angel Navarro in safety" (Hansen, p. 88). Finally, Sam Houston, in a letter from Gonzales penned soon after information was received of the Alamo's fall, wrote: "Three negroes and Mrs. Dickinson were all in the fort, who [es]caped Massacre as reported!" (Houston to Raguet, March 13, 1836, reprinted in Hansen, p. 518).

The scene of the Alamo defenders jeering at the fleeing merchants is related in a July 29, 1876, letter from Reuben Potter to William Steele (AGO Attorney General Office File, TSLA).

The details of the Esparza family's movements are from a 1902 interview of Enrique Esparza, reprinted in Hansen, p. 97.

The brief negotiations between the Texians and Santa Anna are described in Santa Anna's February 27, 1836, report, reprinted in Hansen, pp. 332–33, and Reuben Potter's 1878 article, "The Fall of the Alamo," reprinted in part in Hansen, p. 697.

Juan Díaz, whose father was the church custodian, remembered his mother preparing meals for the Mexican officers; his interview is reprinted in Matovina, *The Alamo Remembered,* p. 94. Details of the Mexican officers' boarding arrangements are in Asbury, "The Private Journal of Juan Nepomuceno Almonte," p. 17.

TWELVE: "I AM BESIEGED"

The chapter title is a phrase in W. B. Travis's public pronouncement of February 24, 1836, reprinted in Hansen, p. 32. The Smither quote is from a note he appended to the letter, reprinted in Chariton, *100 Days in Texas,* p. 269.

The artillery emplacement locations are derived from Asbury, "The Private Journal of Juan Nepomuceno Almonte," pp. 17–18, and Labadie, *La Villita Earthworks.*

The various hardships suffered by *bexareños* are described in various San Antonio newspaper articles reprinted in Matovina, *The Alamo Remembered,* pp. 91, 54, 100, 34.

Travis's February 24, 1836, public pronouncement "to the people of Texas and all Americans in the world" has been reprinted countless times. The copy in my collection was supplied courtesy of the TSLA.

Williamson's activities during the early days of the siege are related in Robinson, *Judge Robert McAlpin Williamson,* p. 129.

The quote regarding the panic in San Felipe is from William Fairfax
  Gray's diary, reprinted in Chariton, *100 Days in Texas,*
  p. 277. Robinson's February 26, 1836, letter to Houston is
  reprinted in the same volume, p. 278. The San Felipe citizens
  committee report is also reprinted in that volume, pp. 281–82. The
  March 5, 1836, *Telegraph and Texas Register* reported: "Many
  other ladies are doing every thing in their power in providing
  clothing, and articles of equipment for those going to the field."
The various sources for the February 25 skirmish are summarized in
  Huffines, *Blood of Noble Men,* pp. 50–54, and also in an
  extensive illustration caption by Gary Zaboly in the same
  volume, p. 53. The ditches are mentioned by Santa Anna's
  secretary, Ramón Caro, in his account of the Texas campaign
  published in 1837: "Around the fortress there were ditches which
  were used by the enemy to fire upon our troops, while our
  soldiers, in order to carry out their orders to fire, were obliged to
  abandon the protection that the walls afforded them, and
  suffered the loss of one or two men, either killed or at least
  wounded, in each attempt to advance" (quoted in Castañeda, *The
  Mexican Side of the Texan Revolution,* pp. 101–2). Another
  source is General Ampudia's report of May 6, 1836 (Secretaria de
  la Defensa Nacional, Archivo Historico Militar Mexicano,
  Expediente 1655, pp. 58–61, translated by Tom Kailbourn).
Santa Anna's report to Tornel is reprinted in Filisola, *Memorias,* vol.
  2, p. 168.
Sources testifying to Santa Anna's "marriage" include Francisco
  Becerra (reprinted in Hansen, pp. 459–60), Maria de Jesus
  Buquor (*San Antonio Daily Express,* July 19, 1907), and Juana
  Alsbury (reprinted in Hansen, p. 88). Caro also refers to it —
  somewhat obliquely, in a reference to someone departing for
  Mexico in Santa Anna's carriage, with this titillating footnote:
  "Decency and respect for public morals do not permit further
  details to be given" — in his account of the campaign; see
  Castañeda, *The Mexican Side of the Texan Revolution,* p. 108.
There are many versions of the manner in which Seguín left the
  Alamo and escaped from Béxar. His own account, translated and
  included in de la Teja, *A Revolution Remembered,* is one of the
  least reliable. See also Huffines, *Blood of Noble Men,* pp. 60–61;
  and Hansen, pp. 192–200, 699–700.
Travis's letter to Houston of February 25, 1836, is reprinted in
  Chariton, *100 Days in Texas,* p. 271.

THIRTEEN: "THIS TIME YOU MAY SEE SOME BLOOD"

The chapter title phrase was uttered by Andrew Kent just before
riding off to the Alamo with the Gonzales Ranging Company of
Mounted Volunteers, as remembered by his eight-year-old
daughter, Mary Ann, who passed her reminiscences down to her
descendants. See the Kent Family Biographical Files, Gonzales
County Archives; also see "Remembers Bloody Days of Texas
Republic," *San Antonio Light,* August 13, 1911. The epigraph,
from Travis's letter to the president of the convention dated
March 3, 1836, is reprinted in Hansen, p. 36.

Fannin's February 22, 1836, letter to Robinson is quoted in Hansen,
p. 251.

The message from Béxar was the letter to Fannin from Travis and
Bowie, reprinted in Foote, *Texas and the Texans,* vol. 2, p. 224.

The Greys' desire to reunite with their comrades at Béxar is
mentioned by New Orleans Grey Herman Ehrenberg in Ornish,
Ehrenberg: Goliad Survivor, pp. 195, 205–6.

Fannin's February 26, 1836, letter to Robinson is reprinted in PTR 4,
pp. 443–44.

Details of Andrew Kent's story were obtained from Kent Family
Biographical Files, Gonzales County Archives, and the dedicated
research of Chester Wilkes, husband of Doris Wilkes, Andrew
Kent's great-great-granddaughter, particularly his article "Mary
Ann Kent Byas Chambers Morriss," revised in July of 1994, a
copy of which is in my collection. Wilkes based details of the
Andrew and David Kent story on an interview he conducted in
the early 1960s with Oliver Byas, who related the story as told by
his grandmother Mary Ann Kent Byas, who was Andrew Kent's
daughter.

The Patton company's stay at the Kent homestead is testified to in
John Sutherland's audited claim of 1836 (reel 102, frames 300–
311, ROT [Republic of Texas] Claims, TSLA). For the date of
January 25, there is the following entry: "for cash paid at Kents
for the use of Troop to reinforce Col. Neil at the Alamo—P
[paid] 13.50." The going rate at that time and place for room,
board, and corn for one man's horse was a dollar, so this
payment jibes with Sutherland's statement that Patton led him
and ten other men to the Alamo. The next two entries are also
for similar services in the Gonzales area—one at John McCoy's
on January 25, and the next for "Gonzales—corn & Bord at
Hensleys—P 16.25."

In mid-February, thirteen Comanches killed John Hibbens and his
brother-in-law George Creath, and took Sarah (Creath) Hibbens
and her two children (one a baby and one six years old, the latter
from her previous husband, who was also killed by Indians) to
the Comanche encampment six miles above the village of Sweet
Home—which was within fifteen miles of the Hibbens home, on
the east side of the Guadalupe River near the present town of
Concrete. The attack occurred near Rocky Creek, and the
Comanches moved northwest. On the second day in camp, the
Comanches brained the infant on a tree when it would not stop
crying. A few weeks later, Mrs. Hibbens escaped near the future
site of Austin, leaving her six-year-old son, John McSherry, with
the Indians. He was later rescued. (See Brown, *Indian Wars and
Pioneers*, p. 89; *Telegraph and Texas Register*, February 27,
1836.)

Details about George Kimble and his statement to his wife are related
in the *Seguin Enterprise* of October 15, 1937. Thomas Miller's
will is mentioned in Baumgartner, "History of the Alsey Silvanus
Miller Homestead," p. 21.

The audited claim for Lewis Boatwright (audited claim 2163, reel 138,
frame 156, ROT [Republic of Texas] Claims, TSLA) places
White in Gonzales from February 18 through February 24,
solidifying the probability that he left for the Alamo with the
Gonzales relief force a few days later.

Several Republic of Texas claims attest to William Irwin's purchasing
the chits of other soldiers, among them Lewis Boatwright
(audited claim 2163, reel 138, frame 156, ROT Claims, TSLA),
Jabez Fitch (reel 153, frame 062, ROT Claims, TSLA), and John
Harris (reel 159, frame 495, ROT Claims, TSLA).

Recently, some researchers (chief among them the late Thomas Ricks
Lindley) have suggested that about sixty men left Gonzales on
February 27 in this group, which comprised two separate
companies, and that only half of them made it into the Alamo.
Offered as evidence are two documents. The first is Robert
Williamson's March 1 letter to Travis (translated from the
Spanish-language version in a Mexican newspaper, though the
original has not been found), in which he states that "sixty men
have set out from this municipality and in all human probability
they are with you at this date" (reprinted in Hansen, p. 601). But
Williamson did not specify that the sixty men set out together, a
point that will pertain later in this endnote. The other source is a

July 1836 obituary for Albert Martin printed in the
Manufacturers and Farmers Journal and the New Orleans *True
American,* which states of Martin: "He had left the fortress and
returned to his residence, where he was apprized of the perilous
situation in which his late comrades were placed. His
determination was instantly taken. In reply to the passionate
entreaties of his father, who besought him not to rush into
certain destruction, he said, 'This is no time for considerations. I
have passed my word to Colonel Trav[is] that I would return, nor
can I forfeit a pledge thus given.' In pursuance of this high
resolve he raised a company of sixty-two men and started on his
way back. During the route, the company, apprized of the
desperate situation of affairs, became diminished, by desertions,
to thirty-two. With this gallant band, he gained the fort and the
reinforcement, small as it was, revived the drooping spirits of the
garrison" (as quoted in Moore, "Texas Rangers at the Battle of
the Alamo," p. 16, although no source for these statements is
given). The evidence for two separate companies, detailed in
Moore's excellently researched article, is convincing and I accept
that conclusion. But save for the two questionable documents just
mentioned, there is no evidence or indication that sixty men, and
not about half that number, around thirty—as mentioned twice
by Travis in letters written on March 3—left the town of
Gonzales on February 27 in response to Travis's request for help.
(Enrique de la Peña wrote that "about sixty men did enter one
night" [de la Peña, *With Santa Anna in Texas,* p. 41], but since
he was not present in Béxar at the time, and does not specify the
date of the reinforcement, he was almost surely repeating, much
later, the information from Williamson's letter, which was printed
in a Mexican newspaper; de la Peña collected many other
Mexican newspaper stories about the Texas campaign and likely
was aware of this one.) The supporting evidence for the number
of men being twenty-five to thirty-two, on the other hand, is
convincing. In the earliest extant draft of his account, John
Sutherland (who was in Gonzales at the time) writes in two
places of twenty-five men leaving: "John W Smith left Gonzales
on Saturday, with the 25 men before named" (Hansen, p. 179),
and then relates: "On Sunday morning the writer in Company of
Dr Alsbury & ten other Americans crossed the Guardaloup River
at Gonzales & fell in with and waited on Capt John Seguin, who
with twenty-four of his men were getting ready to go on to meet

Col Fannins division, but Capt Seguins men detained so long in getting ready that we failed overtaking Smith with the 25 men alluded to before at the Cibolo crossing" (Hansen, pp. 179–80); he repeats this information, with the same numbers, in slightly different language, a few paragraphs later (Hansen, pp. 180–81). The total here is sixty-three, very close to Williamson's sixty, and exactly the total in Martin's obituary. Appearing to support Sutherland's account is the fact that Juan Seguín claimed, in one dictated account: "I arrived safely in the town of Gonzalez, and obtained at [once] a reinforcement of thirty men, who were sent to the Alamo, and I proceeded to meet Sam Houston" (Hansen, p. 198). However, the phrasing of the next sentence in Seguín's letter appears to indicate that he may have been referring to the men led into the Alamo by John Smith, which is highly unlikely, if not impossible, and unsupported by any other account: "When the notice of the arrival of the thirty men was given to Santana, it is said, he gave orders, to allow them entrance stating that he would only have that many more to kill." Since the letter was written on June 7, 1890, fifty-four years after the fact, it is more likely that the eighty-three-year-old Seguín's memory was faulty. Also, other accounts by men in Gonzales or the vicinity around the same time are unanimous in mentioning a similar number of men — about thirty — leaving Gonzales with Smith. John Jenkins, for instance, who arrived in Gonzales on March 3 or 4, about a week after the force had departed town, writes: "While at Gonzales awaiting recruits, tidings came to us of the fall of The Alamo on the 6th of March, and of the terrible loss of 180 men, besides the band of 27 Texans, who during the siege made their way into the Fort and were all slain" ("Personal Reminiscences," box 2R65, John Carmichael Jenkins Family Papers, BCAH). Colonist John Swisher related: "We arrived at Gonzales on the fifth of March and found about two hundred volunteers from the Colorado and the more contiguous points already there.... Only a few days previous thirty-two men, residents of that place, in fact the very flower of its male citizens, had gone to the relief of the besieged fort at San Antonio" (Swisher, *The Swisher Memoirs,* pp. 29–30). Another colonist, Robert Hancock Hunter, wrote a narrative in about 1860 based on a diary he kept. In late February or early March he joined Captain Bird's company at San Felipe and rode west. He related: "There was a company of 32 men made up from Gonzales. The first of March they got in the Alamo, threw the enemy safe to Travis" (Hunter, *Narrative of Robert Hancock Hunter,* p. 14). In a March 6, 1836, letter to James Fannin, acting governor James Robinson wrote: "This moment information has been given that about 30 men has thrown themselves into Bears for its relief from Gonzales," almost surely referring to the group Smith guided into the Alamo; this is information possibly gleaned from Smith himself after his return to Gonzales on March 4 (the letter appears in PTR 5, pp. 5, 10). More corroboration is found in a June 9, 1836, letter written by Dr. John H. Barnard, who was with Fannin in Goliad but was spared due to his medical training and later sent to Béxar to help treat the Mexican wounded in the Alamo battle. Barnard remained in Béxar for five weeks, and as historian Kevin Young points out, "stayed in the home of Angelo Navarro and interacted frequently with the Navarro family and that of Dr. Horace Alsbury"—which included Alsbury's wife, Juana Navarro Alsbury, who was not only Navarro's daughter but also in the Alamo during the siege and would have known of the Gonzales reinforcement. In the letter, Barnard writes: "The Texian force here was 120 men—30 more fought their way in, after a few days; making 150 in all" (Young, "Joseph Henry Barnard Letter"). In the August 18, 1912, *San Antonio Light,* in a story entitled "Frontier Days of Texas," Andrew J. Sowell wrote of Travis's first written request for aid: "A gallant response met the appeal, and soon thirty-two men and boys of DeWitt's colony were ready to start....David Darst, one of the Colonists, told the writer that he was a boy at the time, saw them start, and that they were under the command of Capt. George C. Kimble. All of the men, women and children in the town were present, bidding farewell to loved ones." Darst's father, Jacob Darst, was among the group; David, who was fifteen at the time, would surely have known if anywhere near sixty men left Gonzales. Further, in the March 12, 1836, issue of the *Telegraph and Texas Register,* published in San Felipe, this information was published: "We also learn, by letter, that John W. Smith, who previously conducted 30 men into the Alamo, would be entreated with the hazardous enterprise of conducting 50 more"—the "30 men" clearly referring to the group Smith led out of Gonzales on Saturday, February 27. At least one man, John T. Ballard, claimed later that he had been a member of Thomas Jackson's company, but had been run off by Mexican cavalry near the

Alamo, and a few others may have had the same thing happen.
But Sutherland received his information about the entrance of the
"Gonzales Thirty-Two" into the Alamo from John W. Smith, and
it seems reasonable to believe that Smith would have told
Sutherland if anything like sixty men had approached the Alamo
but only half had made it in. Finally, in the Texas Collection at
Baylor University, there is a March 8, 1907, clipping from a
newspaper (possibly published in Houston) containing a story
under the headline "The Real Alamo," which consists primarily
of a letter from A. C. Gray, a one-time resident of San Antonio.
He writes: "On March 3, after the investment of the Alamo by
Santa Anna, Travis sent out his famous last appeal for relief, and
because of his success in bringing in a party of thirty-two men
on the 1st, Travis selected Captain John W. Smith to take this
last appeal and letters to Washington on the Brazos, where the
convention was in session. Smith did so unwillingly, and having
performed his mission hurried back with additional men; but the
assault took place sooner than was expected, and his aid came
too late. I got this information from Captain Smith himself, who
was a very quiet, unpretentious gentleman, loath to talk for
publication, but always willing to entertain his friends with
reminiscences. If he were alive now and knew I was quoting him,
he would not thank me.... Captain Smith had been a resident of
San Antonio since before the Texas revolution, and had married
a Mexican lady. They had a son and daughter, with whom I
became acquainted and through them with their father." Thus
the overwhelming evidence available supports a group of between
twenty-five and thirty men leaving Gonzales on February 27, in
two companies headed by George Kimble and Thomas Jackson.
The scene of the Gonzales townspeople seeing off the relief force is
briefly described by eyewitness David Darst (son of Alamo defender
Jacob Darst) in the *San Antonio Light* of August 18, 1912.
There is little reliable information on the route and makeup of the
Gonzales relief force. The route to San Antonio here posited—
the mill road rather than the better-marked and more heavily
traveled road cleared and marked by Byrd Lockhart—is based on
the fact that the King residence was on this route. As it was most
likely a rougher road (probably a trail hard to follow at some
points, and even more so at night), it probably took the force
longer to make the trip, thus explaining their arrival at the
Alamo at three a.m. on March 1. Evidence of the road's existence

can be found on several maps of the period, in Byrd Lockhart's "Notes Related to Land Distribution," dated November 1831 (file SC 000119:2, GLO), and on a map in Hunt and Randel, *A New Guide to Texas.*

The King family story is related in an undated transcript of a newspaper story entitled "Wm. P. King, Youngest Martyr To Die In Alamo," in which a story supplied by Captain William L. Foster, who married King's sister, Eliza Ann, is related (TSLA; also in file 5, box 1039, Lindley Papers, Southwestern Writers Collection, Texas State University). It is also corroborated in a speech given by Captain H. E. McCullough on July 22, 1857, and reported in the Seguin *Mercury* on April 7, 1858 (reprinted in Sowell, *Rangers and Pioneers of Texas,* p. 145).

The description of Peña Creek is in de la Peña, *With Santa Anna in Texas,* p. 33; he also noted the eagerness of the soldiers (pp. 20 and 40) and the reluctance of Gaona to incur Santa Anna's displeasure (p. 33). Santa Anna did reprimand Gaona for his column's slow pace when he reached Béxar.

As noted above, several period maps illustrate the upper road, or the mill road, from Gonzales along the Guadalupe to Béxar, showing where it crosses the Cibolo a few miles north of the spot where the lower road fords the creek and also showing where it intersects the lower road a few miles west of the Cibolo. For one example see the map of Texas in Hunt, *A New Guide to Texas.*

The arrival of the Gonzales relief force at the Alamo is described by John Sutherland, who doubtless received his information from his friend John W. Smith, the group's guide. See Sutherland, *The Fall of the Alamo,* pp. 25–26, and Sutherland's unpublished narrative, reprinted in Hansen, p. 147.

Bowie's reassurance to Juana Alsbury was described in her account of events, reprinted in Hansen, p. 87. His appearances while sick are related by Susanna Dickinson in a remembrance to her grandchildren, reprinted in Hansen, pp. 57 and 58. She also told them many times of the fiddle playing of Crockett and the bagpipe playing of McGregor (see Hansen, pp. 58 and 60), and she also related it in an interview with James Morphis, who published it in his 1874 *History of Texas;* her account therein is reprinted in Hansen, p. 75.

Almonte, in his journal, notes that Ramírez y Sesma left on February 29 and returned early the next morning (reprinted in Hansen, p. 364).

At the beginning of the siege Travis reported, in an express to Fannin at Goliad, 156 "effective men" (John Sowers Brooks to his father, February 25, 1836, reprinted in Chariton, *100 Days in Texas,* p. 274). Both John Sutherland and Susanna Dickinson reported between two and three dozen ill or injured men, as did Green Jameson, who on January 18 counted "114 men counting officers, the sick and wounded which leaves us about 80 efficient men" (Hansen, p. 571), though it is not clear if he was including Seguín's Tejanos. Most of the Tejanos left the Alamo before the battle, and at least fifteen defenders left the garrison about February 14; for these reasons and others, it is impossible to come up with an accurate count of the garrison at the time of the battle. But several letters written from Goliad after the arrival of courier James L. Allen on March 8 mention the Alamo garrison as consisting of about two hundred men, information clearly derived from Allen, who left the Alamo on the evening of March 5 (see Chariton, *100 Days in Texas,* pp. 349–57). Thus, with the arrival of the "Gonzales Thirty-Two" early in the morning of March 1, the Alamo defenders, not counting women and children, likely comprised about two hundred volunteers, give or take a courier or two. For two good discussions of the subject, see "The Alamo Numbers Game" chapter in Chariton, *Exploring the Alamo Legends,* and the essay "Numbers of Combatants" in Hansen, pp. 758–62.

Regarding the supply of coffee, the existence of a promissory note signed by Travis on February 20, 1836, to a local merchant for 640 pounds of coffee, 370 pounds of tobacco, three large bars of lead, and twenty-five pounds of powder was recently made public (in the November 9, 2011, auction conducted by RR Auction of Amherst, New Hampshire). If legitimate, it would indicate that the garrison had a supply sufficient for quite a while. But it appears doubtful that Kimble would go to the trouble of buying and carrying fifty-two pounds of coffee unless one of the couriers—John Sutherland, John W. Smith, or the more recently arrived Albert Martin—made it clear that the coffee supply was low. If the 640 pounds were indeed delivered to the garrison, part or all of it may have been left in Béxar in the haste to move into the Alamo upon the arrival of the Mexican army.

FOURTEEN: "DEVLISH DARK"

The chapter title phrase is from the *Arkansas Gazette* of April 19, 1836: "To use the language of one of our correspondents, the

atmosphere of Texas is becoming 'devlish dark.'" The epigraph is
from Santa Anna's February 29, 1836, orders to Ramírez y
Sesma, reprinted in Hansen, p. 335.

These stories of Crockett's expertise are in Field, *Three Years in
Texas,* p. 17; Muir, *Texas in 1837,* p. 113; and Captain Rafael
Soldana's account of the Alamo siege and battle in DeShields's
Tall Men with Long Rifles, reprinted in Hansen, p. 470.
Crockett's statement about being hemmed up was remembered by
Susanna Dickinson in an interview granted to historian James
Morphis and published in his 1874 *History of Texas* (reprinted
in Hansen, p. 46). Her recollection of Henry Warnell's similar
statement first appeared in an 1860 deposition, reprinted in
Hansen, p. 45. Details of Crockett's War of 1812 experiences can
be found in his *Narrative,* p. 90.

The information on William Malone is found in G. A. McCall,
"William T. Malone," *Quarterly of the Texas State Historical
Association* 14 (April 1911), and in the deposition of Mary
Malone in the case of *Malone et al. v. Moran et al.,* case number
3644, on file in the district court of Parker County, Texas.

The move of the Mexican battalion is noted in Almonte's diary,
reprinted in Hansen, p. 365: "The President discovered, in the
afternoon, a covered road within pistol shot of the Alamo, and
posted the battalion of Jimenes there."

Williamson's March 1, 1836, letter to Travis is reprinted in Hansen,
p. 601.

De la Peña's quote, and the details of the Duque-led battalion's force-
march to Béxar, are found in his *With Santa Anna in Texas,* pp.
35 and 36.

Travis's March 3, 1836, letter to the president of the convention is
reprinted in Hansen, pp. 35–36. His letter of the same date to
Jesse Grimes is reprinted in Hansen, p. 37. His letter to David
Ayres of the same date is reprinted in Hansen, p. 38.

This reconstruction of the events of March 3 is based on the known
circumstances and events of that evening. Almonte wrote in his
journal, "The enemy attempted a sally in the night at the Sugar
Mill, but were repulsed by our advance" (Hansen, p. 365). The
possibility of this action being used as a diversionary tactic is
first mentioned in Santos, *Santa Anna's Campaign,* p. 72.

The cold weather in Washington, Texas, is noted in William Fairfax
Gray's diary, which is quoted in Chariton, *100 Days in Texas,*

p. 293; his description of Houston's arrival there is also noted in his diary, *Diary of Colonel W. F. Gray,* p. 122.

For convincing circumstantial evidence that George Childress was likely the sole author of the declaration, see Greer, "The Committee," pp. 244–45. His dress is described in a January 24, 1888, letter from William C. Crawford to Henry McArdle, in Account Papers, Undated, W. W. Fontaine Papers, BCAH.

The two-day eggnog-drinking spree in Washington was revealed in Mary Austin Holly's interview with Sam Houston, conducted on April 7, 1844, and reprinted in Hansen, p. 621.

FIFTEEN: "HIS EXCELLENCY EXPECTS THAT EVERY MAN WILL DO HIS DUTY"

The chapter title phrase is from Santa Anna's general orders for the attack on the Alamo, as reprinted in Hansen, p. 338. The epigraph, Sánchez's quote, is reprinted in Chariton, *100 Days in Texas,* p. 320.

Henry Smith's February 25, 1836, letter to Bryan is quoted in Lindley, *Alamo Traces,* pp. 121–22.

The John Sutherland quote about John W. Smith's attempt to round up one hundred men, and the details of that attempt, are found in his unpublished narrative, reprinted in Hansen, p. 152. The number of men in Gonzales at the time Neill returned is from Colonel John M. Swisher, *The Swisher Memoirs* (San Antonio, TX: The Sigmund Press, 1932), p. 29.

Details of Sutherland and Alsbury's failed relief force are found in Sutherland's draft account, reprinted in Hansen, pp. 179–81.

The March 4 quote by Sánchez is from Huneycutt, *At the Alamo,* p. 64. The de la Peña quotes regarding the council of war are in *With Santa Anna in Texas,* pp. 43 and 44.

The Santa Anna quote is from his March 3, 1836, letter to Urrea, as reprinted in Chariton, *100 Days in Texas,* p. 309.

The hot shot is mentioned in Kailbourn, "Lt. Col. Pedro Ampudia's After-action Report." As the author points out, despite Ampudia's outrage, "apparently there was no international ban on the use of that type of ammunition during this era.... The customs of war condemned the use of such projectiles as chain shot, bar shot, bits of scrap metal fired en masse, and jagged shot, but not specifically hot shot. However, during some conflicts the use of hot shot had been prohibited by treaties or military arrangements."

Santa Anna's general orders for the attack on the Alamo are in
Filisola, *Memorias,* pp. 7–9, translated and reprinted in Hansen,
pp. 337–38.

Urrea's description of Morales can be found in his own diary of the
Texas campaign, reprinted in Castañeda, *The Mexican Side of
the Texan Revolution,* p. 223.

Santa Anna was skeptical of Uruñuela's illness and initiated an official
investigation after the battle; the result was Uruñuela's
banishment to the frontier village of Guerrero, near the Rio
Grande and adjacent to the Presidio de San Juan Bautista del Rio
Grande (Gregorio Uruñuela, compiled personnel file, entries of
May 3, 1837; August 21, 1837; and December 20, 1837; Archivo
de Cancelados, Secretaría de la Defensa Nacional—thanks to
Tom Kailbourn for assistance in translating).

Details of Francisca Músquiz's plea to Santa Anna to spare Susanna
Dickinson and her daughter are in Hansen, p. 59, and in a letter
from Amelia Williams to Samuel Asbury dated May 3, 1832
(Amelia Williams Papers, BCAH).

The rumor that the Alamo was mined is related by Sánchez, in
Sánchez-Navarro, *La Guerra de Tejas,* p. 83.

De la Peña's quote regarding the Mexican soldiers and their thoughts
on death is in de la Peña, *With Santa Anna in Texas,*
p. 45. Duque's request for de la Peña is related by Duque in Borroel,
*The Papers of Lieutenant Colonel José Enrique de la Peña,
Selected Appendixes from His Diary,* p. 19, and in *With Santa
Anna in Texas,* p. 47.

Sánchez's puzzlement over Santa Anna's penchant for blood and tears
is from his journal, in Sánchez-Navarro, *La Guerra de Tejas,* p.
84 (my translation).

Biographical details about Benjamin Harris are from "Documents of
the Texian Revolution," *Alamo Journal* 142 (September 2006),
and Newell, *History of the Revolution in Texas,* p. 88.

The weak condition of the north wall is noted in two letters written by
a man named John Sowers Brooks, who was stationed at Goliad.
The first is to James Hagarty, written on March 9, 1836: "He
[Santa Anna] has erected a battery within 400 yards of the
Alamo, and every shot goes through it" (reprinted in Hansen, pp.
605–6), and the second is to A. H. Brooks, written on March 10,
1836: "Every shot goes through the walls" (reprinted in Hansen,
pp. 606–7). Brooks was repeating information heard from a
courier from the Alamo—likely James L. Allen.

That the Alamo defenders could see ladders being constructed is
noted in John Sutherland's draft account, reprinted in Hansen,
p. 179.

For a discussion of Ben Milam's line in the dirt, see notes for chapter
6, above.

Biographical details regarding Louis "Moses" Rose can be found in
Blake, "Rose and His Escape from the Alamo," part of which is
reprinted in Hansen, pp. 274–82, and Zuber, "The Escape of
Rose from the Alamo," reprinted in Hansen, pp. 245–50. See also
the Afterword for a discussion and analysis of the evidence for
the line. In an interview conducted in September 1877, Susanna
Dickinson said: "Col. Almonte (Mexican) told me that the man
who had deserted the evening before [March 5, the night before
the attack] had also been Killed & that if I wished to satisfy
myself of the fact that I could see the body, still lying there,
which I declined" (reprinted in Hansen, p. 48).

Crockett's request for a clean change of clothes is related in Dr. J. H.
Barnard's June 9, 1836, letter from Velasco, published in the
August 26, 1836, *Missouri Argus,* in which he states of the
Alamo battle: "The Americans fought to the last, and were killed
to a man. There were several friends who were saved, and who
informed me that the men, with the full prospect of death before
them, were always lively and cheerful, particularly Crockett, who
kept up their spirits by his wit and humor. The night before the
storming, he called for his clothes that had been washed, stating
that he expected to be killed the next day, and wished to die in
clean clothes, that they might give him a decent burial." (Thanks
to Kevin Young for generously providing a copy of this item.)

Details of the men entrusting their valuables to the women, and Bettie
being allowed to stay with the women, are in file 3 (Notes,
Handwritten, Interview with Enrique Esparza), box 2M129
(Descendants of Gregorio Esparza), Adina de Zavala Papers,
BCAH.

For a discussion of the ring that Travis gave to Angelina, see Hansen,
p. 62.

Susanna Dickinson related that Robert Evans was given orders to set
fire to the gunpowder; her accounts are reprinted in Hansen, pp.
55 and 59. She is also the source for the story of Bonham sharing
some tea with Almeron Dickinson's mess, in an account she gave
to Bonham's younger brother, Milledge Luke Bonham, reprinted
in Hansen, p. 706.

The final column assignments and deployments are discussed in Tom
Kailbourn's unpublished "Concordance Comparing Troop
Assignments per Column in Alamo Assault," as well as in several
other sources. José Juan Sánchez's two map indexes (1836–39
and 1840)—as translated in Ivey, "¡Viva la Patria es nuestro el
Alamo!"—describe slightly different final column assignments,
but the San Luis Potosí battalion daybook (original translation by
Gregg Dimmick, revisions by Tom Kailbourn) lists the
assignments I have used here. The fact that only four line
companies of the San Luis Potosí battalion were present in
Béxar was ascertained by Kailbourn from a report on officers
who passed in review in Béxar in March 1836, found in
Expediente 1713, SEDENA files, beginning on p. 528, online at
www.archivohistorico2010.sedena.gob.mx/busqueda/busqueda
.php (accessed December 13, 2011).
De la Peña's final thoughts on the battle can be found in *With Santa
Anna in Texas,* pp. 46–47.

SIXTEEN: "THAT TERRIBLE BUGLE CALL OF DEATH"
The title phrase is from de la Peña, *With Santa Anna in Texas,*
p. 47, as is the de la Peña epigraph, p. 51.
There is no primary source to definitively support the playing of the
degüello save for one account by a certain Madame Candelaria
(Hansen, p. 303), and it is highly unlikely that she was in the
Alamo during the battle. But she could certainly have heard it
from Béxar. Additionally, Reuben Potter, the first serious student
of the battle, claimed that the air was played, and he talked to
Juan Seguín (and several others who may have heard of its
playing from residents of the city) as well as officers and enlisted
men of the Mexican army who were present at the battle
(Hansen, p. 701). It is clear that the Mexican regimental bands
played martial music throughout the siege and during the March
6 assault, and researcher Kevin Young wrote that "Mexican
cavalry manuals of the 1840s carried the bugle call, El Deguello,
which was to be blown at the climax of a cavalry charge to
signify no quarter to the enemy" (Young, "Finding a Face").
Young has also pointed out to me that the *degüello* is mentioned
in an 1824 cavalry manual, *Reglamento para el ejercicio y
maniobras de la caballeria* (Mexico: Martin Rivera, 1824).
The presence of rockets was noted by several observers, including Ben
(both in Newell, *History of the Revolution in Texas,* p. 88, and

Colonel Edward Stiff, *The Texan Emigrant* [Cincinnati, OH: George Conclin, 1840], p. 314) and Susanna Dickinson (Hansen, p. 47). That the Mexican army possessed signal rockets and used them is evidenced by a quote in Samuel Maverick's diary entry for November 8, 1835, during the siege of Béxar, in which he notes the Mexican army firing them off (Green, *Samuel Maverick, Texan,* p. 37).

Travis's actions during the battle, and his rallying cry as he stood upon the north wall, was remembered by Joe in his account, reprinted in Hansen, p. 74. The location of Travis's body was described by Francisco Ruíz in his "Fall of the Alamo," originally appearing in the 1860 *Texas Almanac* and reprinted in Hansen, pp. 500-501. This placement of Travis's body, and thus the site of his death, is reinforced by Reuben Potter's "Attack and Defence of the Alamo" in the *San Luis Advocate* of November 18, 1840, the existence of which has been overlooked by modern scholars, though the eminent Texas historian Eugene Barker wrote a summary of it that is among his papers (Alamo File, box 2B120, Eugene Campbell Barker Papers, BCAH). An incomplete copy of the article is part of the holdings of the BCAH, though the issue is not included on the microfilm copy of the newspaper's files. Unfortunately, the actual text of the pertinent part of the article is missing due to a large tear, but this is Barker's summary: "Heard different stories as to where Travis fell, the most [illegible] says that he was found dead at breach of a gun near where right column entered." Earlier in the article, Potter's description of the attack makes fairly clear that what he designates as the right column was the column led by Colonel Duque toward the northeast part of the north wall. Potter in the story claimed to have talked to several members of the Mexican army present during the attack, and it is doubtful that he had visited Béxar at this point, making it unlikely that his source was Ruíz, whose account confirming Travis's position would not appear until twenty years later.

De la Peña's quote regarding the trail of wounded and dead left by the columns is in *With Santa Anna in Texas,* p. 47. The anonymous author of the newsletter account of the battle published in *El Mosquito Mexicano* on April 5, 1836, remembered Cós shouting "Arriba!" De la Peña's quote about the disorder in the Mexican ranks is in *With Santa Anna in Texas,* p. 48. "Muerte a los Tejanos!" was heard by *bexareño* Juan Vargas and related in a 1910 interview reprinted in Hansen, p. 538.

Ruíz, in "Fall of the Alamo," reprinted in Hansen, p. 500–501, locates
Crockett's body "toward the west, and in the small fort opposite
the city." Early Alamo researcher Reuben Potter, who claimed to
have talked to several members of the Mexican army (including
some officers) who participated in the attack, also located
Crockett in the area: "Crockett's body was found, not in an angle
of the fort, but in a one-gun battery which overtopped the center
of the west wall, where his remains were identified by Mr. Ruiz, a
citizen of San Antonio, whom Santa Anna, immediately after the
action, sent for and ordered to point out the slain leaders of the
garrison" (*Magazine of American History*, February 1884, p.
177). Two and a half years later, Potter wrote a letter to the
editors of another magazine, *The Century*, to correct some facts
about Crockett that had previously appeared in that magazine.
Wrote the editors: "Captain Reuben M. Potter, U.S.A., writing to
correct some statements in an account of the fall of the Alamo
that appeared in an article on General Sam Houston, in *The
Century* for August, 1884, states that Crockett was killed by a
bullet shot while at his post on the outworks of the fort, and was
one of the first to fall" (*The Century*, October 1886).
Santa Anna's quote describing the "extraordinary" scene is from his
March 6, 1836, letter to Tornel reporting the taking of the
Alamo, reprinted in Hansen, p. 341.
De la Peña mistakenly claimed a blond defender in the courtyard was
Travis in *With Santa Anna in Texas*, p. 50. Potter, in his 1878
account, recounted the Texians on the west wall who turned
their cannon around to fire upon the Mexicans in the courtyard
(reprinted in Hansen, p. 702).
Almeron Dickinson's last words to his wife were remembered by her
in an interview conducted before 1874 and published in Morphis,
History of Texas, pp. 174–77. Her description of Galba Fuqua
and his broken jaw appears in Sowell, *Rangers and Pioneers*, pp.
138–39.
In his 1840 article "Attack and Defence of the Alamo," Reuben Potter
provides some details of the battle that were not included in his
later accounts, including that of the Texian chased down by two
lancers and killed.
Several Mexican sources support this late breakout. In Ramírez y
Sesma's March 11 report to Santa Anna, reprinted in Hansen,
pp. 369–70, he describes three separate breakouts, though the
number of escapees is provided for only one group ("about

fifty"). Manuel Loranca, a sergeant in Ramírez y Sesma's Vanguard Brigade, says in an 1878 newspaper article that "sixty-two Texans who sallied from the east side of the fort, were received by the Lancers and all killed.... These were all killed by the lance, except one, who ensconced himself under a brush and it was necessary to shoot him" (June 23 or 28, 1878, *San Antonio Daily Express*, reprinted in Hansen, p. 475). These retreating defenders are also mentioned in the San Luis Potosí daybook: "Regiment of Dolores. *Presidiales* and pickets of the regiments of Tampico and Veracruz under the command of General Ramírez, who spread out during the campaign in order to pursue the dispersed [Texians], of whom they killed 68" (de la Peña Papers, BCAH, translated by Gregg Dimmick and Tom Kailbourn). Additional references without specific numbers are in Almonte's diary: "At half past 5 the attack or assault was made, and continued until 6 A.M. when the enemy attempted in vain to fly, but they were overtaken and *put to the sword*" (Asbury, "The Private Journal," p. 23); de la Peña, *With Santa Anna in Texas*: "Those of the enemy who tried to escape fell victims to the sabers of the cavalry, which had been drawn up for this purpose, but even as they fled they defended themselves" (p. 52); Sánchez, who in an anonymously written letter refers to "the ones who sought safety in flight" (published in the April 5, 1836, *El Mosquito Mexicano* and reprinted in Hansen, pp. 486–87), and who, in the legend for his 1840 map of the battle, writes of the palisade: "At this point, some colonists attempted to escape" (reprinted in Nelson, *The Alamo*, p. 59); and, finally, Santa Anna himself, in his March 6, 1836, battle report: "a great many who had escaped the bayonets of the infantry, fell in the vicinity under the sabres of the cavalry" (reprinted in Hansen, p. 341).

Sánchez's 1836 map of the Alamo and its legend, in which he writes, "Barracks for the troops. Col. José María Romero with the Battalions 'Jimenez' y 'Matamoros' assaulted and entered," is reprinted in Nelson, *The Alamo*, p. 58.

The scene of the cannon firing into the hospital is from an interview with Mexican soldier Francisco Becerra, reprinted in Hansen, p. 457.

The taking of the Alamo flag is related in Lamego, *The Siege and Taking of the Alamo*, p. 38, and by de la Peña in Borroel, *The J. Sanchez Garza Introduction*, p. 24. See also Groneman, "The Taking of the Alamo Flag."

De la Peña's quote regarding the chaos in the courtyard in the last
    minutes of the battle is in *With Santa Anna in Texas*, p. 51.

The story of the Navarro sisters is drawn from Juana Alsbury's
    account, reprinted in Hansen, pp. 87–88. Joe's story derives from
    his account, reprinted in Hansen, pp. 74–76.

The description of Crockett's injuries is related by Eulalia Yorba in
    her account published in the *San Antonio Daily Express* of April
    12, 1896.

The earliest mention of Robert Evans and his attempt to fire the
    powder magazine is in the March 24, 1836, *Telegraph and Texas
    Register* article on the battle, details of which were supplied by
    John W. Smith and Gerald Navan after talking to Susanna
    Dickinson: "Major Evans, master of ordnance, was killed in the
    act of setting fire to the powder magazine, agreeably to the
    previous orders from Travis." Mrs. Dickinson also told her
    grandchildren about Evans and his mission (Hansen, p. 59).

The scene of the Mexican soldiers grabbing the valuables from Bettie
    is related in file 3 (Notes, Handwritten, Interview with Enrique
    Esparza), box 2M129 (Descendants of Gregorio Esparza), Adina
    de Zavala Papers, BCAH.

The description of the fort after the battle, and the soldiers stripping
    the corpses, is related by de la Peña in *With Santa Anna in Texas*,
    p. 52 ("Quite soon some of the bodies were left naked by fire,
    others by disgraceful rapacity, especially among our men"), and
    Ivey, "¡Viva la Patria es nuestro el Alamo!" p. 13, in which he
    translates Sánchez's journal: "the troop was allowed plunder."

An hour as the total time elapsed since the beginning of the attack
    until the battle's end is from Almonte's journal, quoted in
    Lamego, *The Siege and Taking of the Alamo*, p. 37: "By six-
    thirty in the morning not a single enemy existed."

The scene of the execution of the captured Texians is in Caro's
    account, translated and quoted in Castañeda, *The Mexican Side of
    the Texan Revolution*, p. 106. See also the anonymous Mexican
    account quoted in Huffines, *Blood of Noble Men*, p. 182.

David Crockett is frequently cited as being one of the prisoners
    brought before Santa Anna and executed. Since the publication of
    With Santa Anna in Texas, the English translation of José
    Enrique de la Peña's reconstructed memoir of the 1835–36 Texas
    campaign, several historians have used that account and a half
    dozen other second- and thirdhand accounts to write, as history,
    that David Crockett did not perish in the Alamo battle but was

executed afterward with a few other defenders. But if these accounts are examined critically, there is little evidence to support such a scenario—certainly not enough to write it as history. Each of the accounts has serious credibility problems.

Though unsubstantiated rumors placing Crockett among the executed began to circulate just weeks after the battle, the claim took root in the public mind soon after the appearance of the 1975 English translation of *With Santa Anna in Texas,* first published in Spanish in Mexico City in 1955. De la Peña was an officer in Santa Anna's Army of Operations who took part in the assault on the Alamo—and who was also an observant, eloquent, and passionate writer. In one passage, he claimed to have witnessed the execution of "some seven men" who "had survived the general carnage" and had been brought before Santa Anna. One is described at great length and identified as "the naturalist David Crockett, well known in North America for his unusual adventures, who had undertaken to explore the country and who, finding himself in Bejar at the very moment of surprise, had taken refuge in the Alamo, fearing that his status as a foreigner might not be respected." Santa Anna orders the troops closest to him to execute Crockett (and presumably the other men); neither these men nor their officers support the order, but several nearby officers draw their swords and fall upon the defenseless men, hacking them to death.

If Crockett really was one of the executed prisoners, for some reason it was not mentioned in the accounts and reports of several members of the Mexican army present, including Colonel Almonte, Santa Anna himself, and his secretary, Ramón Caro, all of whom wrote accounts of the campaign and the Alamo battle shortly after their return to Mexico. Neither did José Juan Sánchez, who kept a journal of his experiences, mention it, though his reference to "the death of an old man named Cocran" has been used as evidence of a Crockett execution and indeed is one of the Mexican accounts often cited by the Crockett execution theorists. A Crockett execution is not mentioned in an account by Sergeant Manuel Loranca, who does relate the finding in the *convento* of "all refugees which were left," and says that Santa Anna "immediately ordered that they should be shot, which was accordingly done." It's also not mentioned by General Vicente Filisola, Santa Anna's second in command, who wrote a detailed account of the campaign and the Alamo battle gleaned from participants' oral and written accounts. In short, several high-ranking witnesses who would have been aware of such an event never mentioned Crockett as being one of the executed, even though most or all of them would have had good reason to. And neither in his March 6 report, written just an hour or two after the battle, nor in his lengthier 1837 account did Santa Anna ever mention Crockett's execution—though in his March 6 report, he listed Crockett as "among the corpses" and in his memoirs, written much later in life, he wrote of the rebels, "Not one soldier showed signs of desiring to surrender." Santa Anna would have been eager to brag about killing such a prominent U.S. citizen, particularly since it would have been further evidence of a claim he was constantly making—that many of the rebels were American citizens. And the others were all highly critical of Santa Anna in the years after the campaign, and would have gladly seized on such a cold-blooded act to make him look worse in the eyes of the world. But none of them mentioned Crockett as one of the executed. Also worth considering is the fact that in the extensive (more than two-hour) interrogation of Santa Anna immediately after he was captured, and during the seven months in which he was a captive in Texas and the U.S., there was no mention, or at least none was recorded, of Crockett being one of the men executed after the battle—by him or his interviewers.

The heavy reliance of Crockett execution theorists on the de la Peña memoir is weakened by several facts. We must keep in mind that, although popularly referred to as a "diary," the manuscript is clearly a reconstructed memoir, written in the years after the battle and based on a reworked diary that de la Peña only began months after the battle. Following common practice at the time, de la Peña incorporated (a) various Mexican accounts he gathered from disparate sources, such as other army officers and newspaper accounts, and (b) letters and reports written by Texians such as Travis and Houston. (De la Peña's original holograph diary is not known to exist.) As William C. Davis, author of *Three Roads to the Alamo*, points out in his article "How Davy Probably *Didn't* Die": "De la Peña openly admitted that he did not see all that he recounted and that he had adopted the recollections of others. The highly derivative and contradictory nature of his Crockett account suggests powerfully that it is one of those episodes 'to which I have not witnessed.'"

NOTES

Though I am convinced of the authenticity of the de la Peña materials—yes, they were written (or dictated; there are at least three or four different hands) in the de la Peña manuscript written in the years after the campaign and before his death in 1840—their accuracy in several places is highly questionable, and sometimes demonstrably wrong. For instance, de la Peña claimed to have seen Travis, "a handsome blond," shot in the Alamo courtyard, though no historian argues against the traditional location of his death as testified to by Joe, Travis's slave, and acting *alcalde* of Béxar, Francisco Antonio Ruíz: on the north wall. He also wrote that "all of the enemy perished, there remaining alive only an elderly lady and a Negro slave," though it is generally accepted that there were as many as twenty survivors. Counting against the veracity of de la Peña's Crockett execution scene are these points: first, the brief account of Crockett's execution is contained on a single slip of paper—the verso of folio 35—and was not only written on a different kind of paper from the rest of the manuscript (consisting of 105 folded "quartos" of four pages each) but was also written in a different hand. Folio 35 was tucked into the manuscript just as several other slips of paper were—suggesting that it was one of many accounts, rumors, and stories obtained from other sources and inserted where it belonged chronologically, rather than with accounts of episodes witnessed by de la Peña himself. In addition, de la Peña did not mention Crockett's execution in a pamphlet he published in 1839, *Una Víctima del Despotismo* (A Victim of Despotism), which discusses the execution of "a few unfortunates" but does not name David Crockett as one of them, though he describes "a man who pertained to the natural sciences"—a brief description of an unnamed defender who somehow became Crockett in de la Peña's note tucked into his manuscript. And, just as telling, he does not claim to have witnessed the executions himself in *Una Víctima del Despotismo*. Furthermore, neither Crockett's name nor the executions are mentioned in de la Peña's rewritten diary, supposedly the source of his main narrative—that manuscript doesn't even contain entries for the dates from March 3 through March 7. Moreover, on that slip of paper (folio 35), de la Peña (or someone) claims to have witnessed the execution, and in the same sentence disingenuously suggests that General Ramírez y Sesma—an

449

officer de la Peña despised, as he makes abundantly clear in his narrative—was one of the attacking officers, though de la Peña says he "will not bear witness to this, for though present, I turned away horrified in order not to witness such a barbarous scene." That de la Peña the eyewitness would not have known if this was true is hard to believe on the face of it, but it's highly unlikely that Ramírez y Sesma was there, since he was in command of the Mexican cavalry outside the fort and was quite busy overseeing the corralling and killing of some sixty Texian defenders there.

The other Mexican accounts cited by Crockett execution theorists are even weaker—all hearsay, second- and thirdhand accounts purportedly derived from Mexican soldiers (supposedly six officers and one sergeant), most of them so shaky as to emphasize the fact that few of those who cite them have examined them closely and critically. On the surface, as researcher Bill Groneman has pointed out in *Death of a Legend,* the most thorough examination of the accounts, "Six officers and a sergeant are a pretty impressive array of witnesses when taken at face value. However, when you scratch the surfaces of these accounts they reveal themselves to be other than pristine firsthand accounts." The Dolson account, supposedly given to a Texan army sergeant, George M. Dolson, by an anonymous officer of Santa Anna's, contains only a few historical inaccuracies (Crockett and five others are found in "the back room of the Alamo"; "Santa Anna's interpreter knew Crockett," a highly unlikely situation; and the captives are "marched to the tent [or possibly the flag, depending on the translation] of Santa Anna")—but its author's anonymity makes it highly suspect as a reliable source. The Colonel Urriza account—reported from memory twenty-three years after the battle by a man who claimed to have heard it from Urriza in 1836—tells of Castrillón leading "a venerable-looking old man by the hand" to Santa Anna, who orders his soldiers to shoot the prisoner, of whom the narrator says, "I believe...they called him Coket." This vaguely worded identification ("I believe"? Who are "they," and why were they qualified to identify him as "Coket," and why would this mean "Crockett" and not "Cochran" or anyone else?) is little support for Crockett execution theorists. Even the staunchest of them, Dan Kilgore, author of *How Did Davy Die?,* labeled the Urriza account as "a controversial remembrance perhaps erroneously perceived and personally biased"—though he proceeded to cite it as one of the accounts supporting Crockett's execution. Speaking of "Cochran," another account offered as evidence—that of José Juan Sánchez—states: "Some cruelties horrified me, among them the death of an old man they called 'Cochran' and of a boy approximately fourteen years." No executions are described, and of course "Cochran" is assumed to be Crockett.

Another account, this one attributed to General Cós, is just as unlikely, with Cós "searching the barracks" when he comes across "alive and unhurt, a fine-looking and well dressed man, locked up, alone, in one of the rooms." When Cós asks him who he is, the defender in a lengthy answer reveals that he is Crockett, a noncombatant, who has been prevented from leaving the fort. When he is brought before Santa Anna, he draws a knife and leaps at Santa Anna, but is himself bayoneted. The historian who related the story, William P. Zuber (he of Moses Rose fame), denounced it as a gross falsehood, yet Kilgore presented it as supporting evidence for David Crockett's execution. And the Sergeant Becerra account offers more absurdities: Becerra kills Bowie, then discovers Travis and a sleeping Crockett in another room, where Travis pulls out a large roll of money that he hands to Becerra in an attempt to buy his freedom. Then three Mexican generals and a colonel enter the room, and that's when it really gets outrageous. That these last two accounts are cited as evidence of Crockett's execution is especially shameful—and shameless. Todd Hansen, the highly respected author of *The Alamo Reader* and an impressively impartial analyst, rates the reliability of these accounts as either "rejected," "poor," or "marginal," with only the Sánchez account receiving a "good" rating. (And to my knowledge, no one save Bill Groneman has pointed out that Crockett execution theorists conveniently ignore the fact that several other Mexican accounts testify to Crockett dying in combat—Madame Candelaria [Andrea Castañón Villanueva], Sergeant Felix Nuñez, Captain Rafael Soldana, and an unidentified Mexican army captain—accounts that suffer from some of the same reliability problems as those listed above.)

What seems never to have occurred to Kilgore, who claimed that these clearly faulty accounts were "mutually corroborative," is that several of them derive from one rumor or fabricated story—a story either (a) based on erroneous or conflated information or (b) deliberately fabricated by a captive for his own purposes—to damage someone, most likely Santa Anna himself, or simply to curry favor with his captors. (William C. Davis, in "How Davy Probably *Didn't* Die," explains how and why some of these scenarios likely occurred, and how such a story could easily have spread.) As several historians have pointed out, from Walter Lord to Davis and Wallace Chariton, several of these Mexican accounts were rendered soon after San Jacinto, when imprisoned Mexican soldiers would say anything to their captors that might please them. (Another question never answered or even brought up by most Crockett execution theorists is how the Mexicans knew who Crockett was or what he looked like, though convoluted explanations of Almonte's knowledge of him, sometimes involving paintings of Crockett that Almonte may have seen on a visit to the United States, have been made.)

The final argument against the Crockett execution theory is the fact that two men—Joe, Travis's slave, and Béxar's acting *alcalde,* Francisco Antonio Ruíz—were asked to identify Crockett's body after the battle and did so, and they described their identification and the location in a manner that makes it extremely difficult to accept his death as being the result of a post-battle execution. Clearly, Santa Anna would not need Crockett's body identified if he had just witnessed his execution. And Susanna Dickinson, in her earliest accounts of the battle, claimed that "he [Crockett] and his companions were found surrounded by piles of assailants." Joe also described Crockett's body as being found with the bodies of a few of his friends, with twenty-four dead Mexican soldiers around them, and Enrique Esparza (albeit in an account rated "marginal" by Hansen) also placed Crockett in front of the church's large double doors, surrounded by a heap of slain attackers. Ben, Almonte's servant, was also said to have pointed out the body of Crockett, whom he knew by sight, and to have found "no less than 16 dead Mexicans around the corpse of Colonel Crockett and one across it with the huge knife of Davy buried in the Mexican's bosom to the hilt"—hardly the scene of an execution. Finally, Joe is quoted in Niles, *A History of South America and Mexico,* p. 327, as giving this information: "One man alone was found alive when the Mexicans had gained full possession of the fort; he was immediately shot by order of the Mexican chief"—no mention of Crockett being executed.

As Michael Lind points out in his article "The Death of David Crockett," to believe the Crockett execution theory, "one must believe that Santa Anna executed the famous David Crockett, but neglected to mention the fact in his after-action report an hour or so later; that his personal secretary, describing and denouncing the execution of Texian prisoners in 1837, also failed to mention this fact; and that Enrique de la Peña himself neglected to mention it, in his account of the executions written in 1839."

Clearly, the documentation presented thus far by the Crockett execution theorists falls far short of the level necessary for it to be considered fact. David Crockett may have been executed after the battle, but until stronger evidence is presented, let history show that he died fighting with his comrades.

For further information on the subject, see Chariton, *Exploring the Alamo Legends* ("Crockett vs. Kilgore, Santos, et al.: Davy's Last Fight," pp. 37–63); Chemerka, "The Death of Davy Crockett at the Alamo"; Connelly, "Did David Crockett Surrender at the Alamo?"; Crisp, "Davy in Freeze-Frame," "Documenting Davy's Death," "An Incident at San Antonio," and *Sleuthing the Alamo;* Davidson, "A Forensic Look at Crockett's Death," "How Did Davy Really Die?" and "When Propaganda Becomes History"; Davis, "How Davy Probably *Didn't* Die"; Dettman, "Davy's Death"; Durham, "*Where* Did Davy Die?"; Groneman, *Death of a Legend,* "A Witness to the Executions?" and "Some Problems with the 'Urriza' Account"; Hansen, *The Alamo Reader,* chapter 5 ("Special Commentary: Deaths of Travis, Bowie, and Crockett," pp. 783–798); Harburn, "The Crockett Death Controversy"; Hawkins, "How Did Davy Die?"; Kilgore, *How Did Davy Die?;* Lind, "The Death of David Crockett"; and Lindley, "Killing Crockett," parts 1–3.

De la Peña's description of Santa Anna addressing his men is from *With Santa Anna in Texas,* pp. 52–53.

Joe (as heard by two independent witnesses who set down what they heard) described the single survivor who was executed as "a little man named Warner" and "a little weakly body, named Warner" (Hansen, pp. 75, 70) — an accurate description of Henry Warnell, the small former jockey. The execution of "Warner" was also mentioned in one of the earliest newspaper stories about the battle, which appeared in the March 24, 1836, *Telegraph and Texas Register,* details of which were provided by John W. Smith after talking to Susanna Dickinson. As far as is known, no one named Warner died at the Alamo.

Francisco Esparza's request for his brother's body is given in his 1859 deposition, reprinted in Matovina, *The Alamo Remembered,* p. 34.

Crockett's dead body is described by Eulalia Yorba in her 1896 account, reprinted in Hansen, p. 527. Though Susanna Dickinson in one interview located Crockett's body as "lying dead and mutilated between the church and the two story barrack building and [I] even remember seeing his peculiar cap lying by his side" (reprinted in Hansen, p. 46), in another interview she said of Crockett, as related by the interviewer, "He was killed, [I] believe" Hansen, p. 48), which sounds as though she didn't know where Crockett's body was. But the account of acting *alcalde* Francisco Antonio Ruíz, in which he says that he was asked by Santa Anna to identify the bodies of Travis, Bowie, and Crockett—"On the north battery of the fortress lay the lifeless body of Col. Travis on the gun-carriage, shot only in the forehead. Toward the west, and in the small fort opposite the city, we found the body of Col. Crockett" (reprinted in Hansen, p. 501)—is to me highly credible. Ruíz was most likely referring to one of the batteries or entrenchments along the west wall of the fort. His location is corroborated by the first serious historian of the battle, Reuben Potter, who talked to several Mexican soldiers, including some officers, during the research for his three extensive accounts, written in 1840, 1860, and 1878. In his final account, he wrote that "the body of Crockett was found in the west battery just referred to," that being "the twelve-pound carronade which fired over the centre of the west wall from a high commanding position" (reprinted in Hansen, p. 702). However, in two subsequent commentaries, Potter refined the location. In the January 1884 *Magazine of American History,* he wrote a letter to the editor (in response to an article about Crockett) in which he said, "Crockett's body was found, not in an angle of the fort, but in a one-gun battery which overtopped the center of the west wall, where his remains were identified by Mr. Ruiz." Finally, in his last known comment on the subject, he wrote another letter to the editor, this one in response to an article on Sam Houston. The letter was published in the October 1886 issue of *The Century,* where the editors related: "Captain Reuben M. Potter...states that Crockett was killed by a bullet shot while at his post on the outworks of the fort, and was one of the first to fall"—a location that appears to match Ruíz's "small fort opposite the city," most likely the outer half-circle entrenchment delineated on the map and view of the Alamo drawn by José Juan Sánchez (see Nelson, *The Alamo,* pp. 58–59), though the artillery battery atop the center of the west wall is also a possibility.

The account of the young woman dipping her handkerchief in her
  sweetheart's blood is reprinted in Hansen, p. 469.
Santa Anna's March 6, 1836, report to Tornel is reprinted in Hansen,
  pp. 340–41.
The number of the Mexican dead and wounded has been a point of
  mild controversy since the battle. The first reports making their
  way east to the colonies grossly exaggerated the casualties, which
  were often reported to be in the thousands—in one of the first
  newspaper stories about the battle, in the March 24, 1836,
  Telegraph and Texas Register, "about 1500 killed and wounded"
  Mexicans were reported. The most reliable Mexican accounts tally
  between sixty dead and 251 wounded (Andrade report, Hansen,
  p. 393) and about seventy dead and three hundred wounded (Santa
  Anna to Tornel, March 6, 1836, reprinted in Hansen, pp. 340–41);
  Almonte tallied sixty-five dead and 223 wounded (Hansen, p. 367).
  But Joseph Field, a physician captured at Goliad and sent to Béxar
  to minister to the many Mexican soldiers wounded in the Alamo
  battle, wrote on April 21: "There are now about one hundred here
  of the wounded. The surgeon tells us that there were five hundred
  brought into the hospital the morning they stormed the Alamo, but
  I should think from appearances there must have been more. I see
  many around the town who are crippled,—apparently two or
  three hundred,—and the citizens tell me that three or four
  hundred have died from their wounds" (Hansen, p. 612). Those
  figures are supported by a Mexican casualty report noted in Davis,
  Three Roads to the Alamo, p. 739, n. 22 (Mariano Arroyo report
  from the military hospital at Béxar, August 1, 1836, Expediente
  XI/481.3/1151, Secretaría de la Defensa Nacional, Archivo
  Historico Militar Mexicano; also in Hansen, p. 378), which
  documents a total of 456 men treated from March 6 to August 1 in
  the Mexican hospital at Béxar (though that number includes the
  wounded men of Cós's command from the Battle of Béxar in
  December—probably approximately sixty), seventy-five of whom
  died from their wounds. But as Todd Hansen points out in his
  thorough analysis of the subject (Hansen, pp. 778–783),
  "Undoubtedly many other sick were treated during the period
  covered"; he suggests that those additional men might be half the
  total number listed as treated. I suggest, for no concrete reason
  save that Hansen's number of additional sick men seems somewhat
  high, that a figure closer to one hundred might be more accurate.
  Thus, total casualties likely comprised about seventy-five killed

during the battle and approximately three hundred wounded, some seventy-five of whom died later of their wounds—figures in line with accounts by Santa Anna, Andrade, de la Peña, and Filisola. See also Thomas Ricks Lindley's three-part article "Mexican Casualties at Bexar."

The quote describing the Mexican army returning to Béxar after the battle is from Juan Vargas's account, reprinted in Matovina, *The Alamo Remembered*, p. 101.

Sánchez's journal diary decrying the empty victory is in Sánchez-Navarro, *La Guerra de Tejas*, p. 85 (my translation).

SEVENTEEN: THE BLEEDING COUNTRY
The chapter title phrase is from Sam Houston, who referred to Texas as such in his March 2, 1836, proclamation: "The patriots of Texas are appealed to in behalf of their bleeding country" (reprinted in Houston, *Texas Independence*, p. 151). The epigraph is from Houston's March 15, 1836, letter to James Collinsworth, reprinted in Chariton, *100 Days in Texas*, p. 370.

Susanna Dickinson's post-battle ordeals were described to her grandchildren, whose memories, recorded years later, are reprinted in Hansen, p. 59, and in Williams to Asbury, January 31, 1934 (box 2, file 52, Samuel Erson Asbury Papers, BCAH), and in several of her interviews, primarily the one conducted on March 14, 1878, and reprinted in Hansen, p. 50. "Assist her safe" are the words of historian Edward Stiff, who also interviews her in *A New History of Texas*, p. 312.

Santa Anna's missive, which begins "The General-in-Chief of the Army of Operations of the Mexican Republic to the Inhabitants of Texas," dated March 7, 1836, is reprinted in Chariton, *100 Days in Texas*, pp. 345–46. That Ben was given this message and delivered it to Houston is corroborated in two places. Houston, in his March 15, 1836, letter to James Collinsworth, wrote: "Enclosed you will receive the address of General Santa Anna sent by a negro to the citizens. It is in Almonte's handwriting" (reprinted in *100 Days in Texas*, p. 370), and a letter written by Joaquín Ramírez y Sesma to Santa Anna on March 15, 1836, says: "I ordered at once the proclamation to them in English that Your Excellency has served to direct to the people of Texas" (reprinted in Borroel, *Field Reports of the Mexican Army*, vol. 1, p. 19). Finally, Yoakum, in *History of Texas*, vol. 2, p. 106, writes: "Mrs. Dickinson brought with her a boasting proclamation of Santa Anna, which she had received from the hands of General Sesma, then at the Cibola, on his route, with the advance of the enemy, to Gonzales." Yoakum was Houston's friend and law partner at the time of writing, and had excellent access to the general, as is evident from the wealth of reports, orders, and memoranda included in the book's appendixes.

That the veracity of Travis's March 3, 1836, letter was questioned is noted in Lancelot Abbotts's letter to General Steele of January 26, 1876 (box 1037, file 19, Lindley Papers, Southwestern Writers Collection, Texas State University).

John W. Smith's March 7 departure with a group of twenty-five to fifty men is mentioned in several sources, the earliest being Smith's letter of March 7, 1836, to the president of the convention, which is cited in Yoakum, *History of Texas,* vol. 2, p. 104, though the original copy of this letter is not known to exist, and Yoakum only summarizes its contents in a footnote ("It is proper to state that Captain John W. Smith, after conducting the thirty-two Texans from Gonzales to the Alamo, returned on the 4th of March and started again on the 7th with fifty more from the same point; but it was too late.—Smith to the President of the Convention, March 7, 1836"). This letter of Smith's was the likely origin of a brief note in the March 12, 1836, *Telegraph and Texas Register*: "We also learn by letter, that John W. Smith, who had previously conducted 30 men into the Alamo, would be entrusted with the hazardous enterprise of conducting 50 more." Further, a letter from Captain Moseley Baker to Jones, Gray, and Pettus, dated March 8, 1836, corroborates the claim that Smith left Gonzales on March 7 with fifty men: "On day before yesterday I arrived here....I found about one hundred sixty men here, which, with our force, made about two hundred and seventy, fifty of which started on yesterday for the Alamo" (reprinted in Chariton, *100 Days in Texas,* p. 346). However, some twenty-four years after the battle, John Sutherland wrote that Smith left on Sunday, March 6, with twenty-five men as well as Captains Desauque and Chenoweth (Hansen, pp. 157, 180), and Houston, in a letter to James Collinsworth written on March 13, 1836, mentioned "the repulse of a party of twenty-eight men, the other day, within eighteen miles of Bexar" (Hansen, p. 516)—almost certainly a misdated reference to Smith's reinforcement that left Gonzales on Monday, March 7, 1836. Finally, in a letter published in the 1872 edition of the *Texas Almanac,* in an article entitled "Survivors of

the Texas Revolution," a volunteer named Connell O'Donnell
Kelly claimed that he "went to Gonzales, where volunteers were
called for to go to the assistance of Travis, and volunteered as one
to go; went to Leon, where we saw about one thousand Mexican
camp fires; when they, the Mexicans, opened fire on us, and our
party being too small, retreated to the Cibolo, under Capt. W.
Smith, where we remained but a short time, and returned to
Gonzales, where Gen. Sam Houston had just arrived from
Washington, Texas, when our captain informed him that the
Alamo had fallen." In another letter written by Kelly, published in
the *San Francisco Examiner* (the clipping is undated, but the
letter must have been written sometime in the late nineteenth
century), he stated: "I first joined the 'Mobile Greys,' under the
command of Captain Burke and two other Companies
commanded by Captain Moseley Baker and John W. Smith, and
upon the call for volunteers at Gonzales to go to the assistance of
Travis, Bowie and Crockett, I was one of the twenty-five who
responded." And in a letter written on December 28, 1883, to
Texas governor Ireland, he wrote: "We started for Gonzales and
arrived there at the time that Captain W. Smith was calling for
Volunteers to go that evening to the assistance of General Travers
[Travis] Boya [Bowie] and Crockett. And I was the only man out
of Capt Mosley Bakers Company along with 25 others who
volunteered to go we went as far as the Saylow [Salado]. There the
Mexican troops saluted us with grape and canister and run us to
the Sea willow [Cibolo]. We remained there a few minutes to hear
our cannon but no response came then we retreated to Gonzalas.
General Sam Houston just arrived from Washington Texas to
Gonzalas and took command of the few little companies and
ordered a retreat to Judge McClure ranch on Peach Creek" (Louis
Wiltz Kemp Papers, BCAH). Thus I have opted to go with the
lower number of twenty-eight, though the possibility exists that as
many as fifty men left with Smith on March 7.
Houston's address to the men in Gonzales is related in Jenkins,
    Recollections of Early Texas, p. 37, and in Houston, *Texas
    Independence,* p. 153.
The March 11, 1836, letter relating the news from Vergara and
    Barcena is reprinted in Hansen, pp. 509–10. Both of these men's
    names were misspelled by Anglos unfamiliar with Spanish spelling
    when their accounts were written down upon their arrival in
    Gonzales. Anselmo Vergara's name was initially recorded as

"Ansolma Bergara," and later writers such as John Linn and Reuben Potter, who also talked to him, recorded it as Anselmo Borgara. In his memoirs, published in 1858, Juan Seguín used the correct spelling. Andres Barcena's name was originally spelled as "Andrew Barsena," and is likewise spelled correctly by Seguín.

The description of the grieving widows and children is from John Sharpe's account, reprinted in Foote, *Texas and the Texans,* vol. 2, p. 268.

The results of John W. Smith's March 7, 1836, reinforcement attempt is related in John Sutherland's unpublished narrative (Hansen, p. 157); John Sutherland's draft account (Hansen, pp. 180–81); and a letter from Sam Houston to James Collinsworth dated March 13, 1836 (Hansen, p. 516). Sutherland wrote that Smith was on the Cibolo, twenty-four miles from Béxar, and sent an eight-man scouting party toward town. "They had only gone about six miles, when they met the advance of the enemy" — putting them eighteen miles from Béxar, matching Houston's report of "the repulse of a party of twenty-eight men, the other day, within eighteen miles of Béxar."

Francis Desauque's identity as the bearer of Houston's letter to Fannin is mentioned in Niles, *History of South America and Mexico,* p. 332, and also in Johnson, *A History of Texas and Texans,* vol. 1, p. 428. Desauque was executed at Goliad.

Houston's March 11, 1836, letter to James Fannin is reprinted in Hansen, p. 513; his lack of confidence in Fannin is noted in his March 13, 1836, letter to James Collinsworth, reprinted in Hansen, p. 515. He wrote of his decision to fall back from Gonzales in his March 15, 1836, letter to James Collinsworth, reprinted in Chariton, *100 Days in Texas,* pp. 369–70.

The scene of Susanna Dickinson at Stephen "James" Tumlinson's house is related by Mrs. Annie E. Cardwell, a stepdaughter of Tumlinson, in a story in the Gonzales *Daily Inquirer* of June 7, 1911, and in a story in the *San Antonio Light* of August 18, 1912. Mrs. Cardwell was eleven at the time.

The scene of Houston reading Santa Anna's letter is found in Alexander Horton's memoir of October 18, 1891, reprinted in the section entitled "Short Memoirs and Sketches from Old Texians," located on the "Sons of DeWitt Colony Texas" website, http://www.tamu.edu/faculty/ccbn/dewitt/dewitt.htm (accessed July 15, 2010). Creed Taylor, the cocky fifteen-year-old, is quoted in Haley, *Sam Houston,* p. 125.

The quoted description of the burning of Gonzales is from John
  Sharpe's account, reprinted in Foote, *Texas and the Texans,*
  vol. 2, p. 268.
The sale of the Texians' supplies and goods is mentioned by Ramón
  Caro in his account, reprinted in Castañeda, *The Mexican Side
  of the Texan Revolution,* p. 107, and by de la Peña in *With Santa
  Anna in Texas,* p. 62.
The diary quotes describing the reaction to the early news of the
  Alamo's fall, and the panic that seized the residents of
  Washington, are from William Fairfax Gray's diary, quoted in
  Chariton, *100 Days in Texas,* pp. 368, 374–75.
The doctor's quote regarding the cheered men at Goliad is in Joseph
  Barnard's account, "Fannin at Goliad," in Wooten,
  Comprehensive History of Texas , vol. 1, p. 626.
The message from Urrea to de la Portilla, and de la Portilla's
  admission that he, too, was charmed by Fannin, is related in
  "Extract from the Diary of Lieutenant Colonel Portilla," *The
  United States Magazine and Democratic Review* 3, no. 10
  (October 1838), p. 144.

EIGHTEEN: "THE MARROW BONE OF TEXAS"
The chapter title phrase is in a May 17, 1836, letter from soldier
  Moses Lapham to Amos Lapham: "Our number was somewhere
  about 700....It consisted in part of the marrow bone of Texas"
  (Louis Wiltz Kemp Papers, BCAH). The epigraph is from Urrea's
  April 22, 1836, letter to Ramírez y Sesma, reprinted in PTR 6,
  p. 21.
This summary of Houston's march across Texas and the San Jacinto
  campaign derives chiefly from Stephen L. Moore's superbly
  researched *Eighteen Minutes.*
Houston's address to his men on March 26, 1836, is quoted in Haley,
  Sam Houston, p. 131.
Gaines's statement to U.S. secretary of war Lewis Cass of his intent to
  move into Texas if provoked is quoted in Haley, *Passionate
  Nation,* p. 178.
Houston's March 29, 1836, letter to Thomas Rusk, noting his
  reluctance to seek the counsel of others, is reprinted in PTR 5,
  pp. 234–35. David Burnet's April 7, 1836, letter to Houston
  insisting that he fight is quoted in Hardin, *Texian Iliad,* p. 189.
The incident of the army's turn toward Harrisburg is detailed in
  Moore, *Eighteen Minutes,* pp. 222–27, and in Haley, *Sam*

Houston, pp. 139–42. Houston's April 19, 1836, letter to Henry Raguet, in which he notes the army's readiness to fight Santa Anna, is reprinted in PTR 5, p. 504.

The scene of the Texian army roaring its battle cry is quoted in Hardin, *Texian Iliad,* p. 200. The soldier's remembrance of reaching the San Jacinto bivouac is quoted in Moore, *Eighteen Minutes,* p. 255.

The departure of Santa Anna's carriage, carrying its scandalous passengers—undoubtedly the young "bride" of His Excellency, and probably her mother—is noted by Ramón Caro in his account, reprinted in Castañeda, *The Mexican Side of the Texan Revolution,* p. 108. He wrote: "The general-in-chief and his staff left on the 31st, and I accompanied the second in command in his carriage. On the second day's journey, His Excellency ordered his carriage to return to Béxar from where it was to proceed to San Luis. It was to be used by some travelers to whom 2,000 pesos had been given by His Excellency, who in turn had received this sum from Colonel Ricardo Dromundo. From what funds this money was taken, I do not know." In a footnote, Caro added: "Decency and respect for public morals do not permit further details to be given."

Santa Anna's April 8, 1836, letter to Filisola noting his orders to Ramírez y Sesma is quoted in Santos, *Santa Anna's Campaign Against Texas,* p. 94. His understanding of the importance of capturing and executing David Burnet and his cabinet, written a year later, is in Castañeda, *The Mexican Side of the Texan Revolution,* p. 22.

Santa Anna's procurement of a ship to await him at Copano is noted by Caro in his account, reprinted in Castañeda, *The Mexican Side of the Texan Revolution,* p. 111. His Excellency's surprise at the restraint shown by the colonists during the April 20 cannonade is noted in his account in the same volume, p. 113. Tornel's contempt for the Texian colonists is quoted in Hardin, *Texian Iliad,* p. 98.

The quote concerning the army's eagerness to attack is in Nicholas Labadie's "San Jacinto Campaign," originally published in the 1859 *Texas Almanac* and quoted in Moore, *Eighteen Minutes,* p. 286. Labadie is also the source for Houston's orders to his men to eat first before fighting (see Moore, *Eighteen Minutes,* p. 309).

Several accounts make note of Mexican soldiers crying out "Me no Alamo!" I have found at least half a dozen, and there may be more: (1) "As we rushed over, they fell on their knees, and with uplifted hands, cried out: 'Me no Alamo! Me no Alamo!'" (Mrs. Fannie A. D. Darden, "Extracts from the Manuscript of Moseley Baker," in Stewart, *Gems from a Texas Quarry*, p. 287); (2) "The Mexicans would fall down on their knees, & say me no Alamo me no Laberde" (Hunter, *The Narrative of Robert Hancock Hunter*, p. 24 [Hunter was not at the battle, but arrived at the battlefield later that night]); (3) "The Mexicans cried for quarter, but it was long before they received any; the cry of the Texian was 'Alamo', 'remember the Alamo', and the Mexican soldier would cry 'me no Alamo' (Abram Marshall to Ann Marshall, May 15, 1836, box 1027, Lindley Papers, Southwestern Writers Collection, Texas State University); (4) "When the charge was sounded we rushed upon them; the cry of 'The Alamo and La Bahía' sounded throughout the lines.... The poor devils of Mexicans would hold up their hands, cross themselves and sing out: 'Me no Alamo,' but nothing could save them..." (*The Albion*, June 11, 1836, reprinting a letter from an unknown correspondent on Galveston Island, May 6, 1836, which was in turn reprinted in the *U.S. Telegraph* [based in Washington, D.C.] on June 14, 1836, under the heading "From the *New York Courier*" [folder 5, box 15, Nell Goodrich DeGolyer Papers, DeGolyer Library, Southern Methodist University]); (5) "Me no Alamo! Me no Goliad!" (Mary J. Briscoe, detailing the account of her husband, Andrew, regarding San Jacinto, is in the Louis Wiltz Kemp Papers, BCAH); (6) "As we overtook them, we felt compelled to kill them, and did so, on their knees crying for quarter, and saying, 'Me no Alamo—me no Bahia'" ("Pursuit of Santa Anna and His Cavalry," published in the 1868 *Texas Almanac*, p. 43); (7) "They would dismount get on their knees begging for their lives denying at the same time that they were not connected with the two massacres Alamo or Goliad. They would exclaim in broken inglish me no Alamo me no labida" ("William S. Taylor's Report or Account of the Battle," in Henry Arthur McArdle, *The Battle of San Jacinto*, McArdle Notebooks, p. 238, TSLA); and (8) "In answer to our yell, 'Remember the Alamo!' 'Remember Labadie' the Mexicans would say, 'Me no Alamo' 'Me no Labadie' but the memory of those recent butcheries were too fresh in our minds and the excitement of the occasion was not such as to arouse our sympathy" (James Monroe Hill, published in an Austin, Texas, newspaper on June 22, 1894).

NaNNOTES

Captain William Heard remembered chasing down the Mexican soldiers for more than a mile, and is quoted in Moore, *Eighteen Minutes*, p. 346.

Santa Anna's request to be treated as a general is quoted in *Eighteen Minutes*, p. 382.

The Elve Bowie quote regarding her son upon hearing of his death is in Bowie, *The Bowies and Their Kindred*, p. 262.

Rezin Bowie's service in the Texas army is mentioned in PTR 5, p. 402; PTR 6, p. 126; and Yoakum, *History of Texas*, vol. 2, p. 152. His commission as a colonel appears to have been used chiefly for publicity purposes in connection with enlistment.

De la Peña's opinion of the reasons for the campaign's failure are in *With Santa Anna in Texas*, p. xxvii. Much of de la Peña's post-campaign activity, and the details of his eventual fate, was unearthed by historian Roger Borroel, whose research efforts concerning the Mexican army have added much valuable information; see Borroel, *Field Reports of the Mexican Army*, vol. 6, pp. 1–20.

Sánchez's later years are discussed in Sánchez-Navarro, "A Mexican View of the Texas War," pp. 64–68.

The proportions of established Texian colonists to newcomers in the Texian army before San Jacinto and at that battle are from Lack, *The Texas Revolutionary Experience*, pp. 123 and 127.

NINETEEN: LAST RITES

The epigraph and the other Juan Seguín quotes are from his speech given upon burying the remains of the Alamo defenders; it is reprinted in the *Telegraph and Texas Register* of April 4, 1837.

Susanna Dickinson's 1881 return to the Alamo was chronicled in the April 28, 1881, *San Antonio Daily Express*. Details of her daughter's tragic life are in the *Austin American-Statesman* of October 14, 2000.

Details of Joe's escape are given in the ad taken out by Travis's executor, John Rice Jones, which ran in the *Telegraph and Texas Register* from May 26, 1836, through the month of August, 1836; Joe's alleged sighting in the Austin area is noted in Pittman, "One Did Survive!"

The details of Louis "Moses" Rose's ordeals, and his later life, are in "Documents from Nacogdoches County Records Relating to Moses (Louis) Rose," Robert Bruce Blake Collection, BCAH, reprinted in Hansen, pp. 274–82; in Jelinek, *Survivor of the Alamo,* pp. 201–5; and in phone conversations during September 2011 with historian Raymond Powell of Mansfield, Louisiana, who generously supplied his notes on the subject. Although Jelinek adds some fictional touches to Rose's story, the basic elements are rooted in fact, as he interviewed descendants of the Ferguson family. See also the Afterword.

The information regarding Gonzales after the Texas Revolution, and the activities of the Kent family, are from Wilkes, "The Andrew Kent Home," and Bennet, "The Battle of Gonzales."

The Crocketts' move to Texas, and details of Elizabeth Crockett's life and death there, are from Lake, "David Crockett's Widow."

AFTERWORD: MOSES ROSE AND THE LINE

The epigraph is from a Frank Johnson note in "Historical Notes— Alamo," p. 773 (box 2D187, Francis White Johnson Papers, BCAH).

The Walter Lord quote explaining the paucity of primary accounts of the Alamo is in Lord, "Myths and Realities of the Alamo," p. 18.

The J. Frank Dobie quote about the line is reprinted in Hansen, pp. 286–87.

The William P. Zuber article "An Escape From the Alamo" was first printed in the 1873 *Texas Almanac,* which is available at the Portal to Texas History website, http://texashistory.unt.edu/.

The July 20, 1876, letter from Rufus Grimes to E. M. Pease is in the AGO File, TSLA.

The *cum grano salis* comment is in Morphis, *History of Texas,* p. 187.

The September 1877 Susanna Dickinson Hannig interview with the Texas adjutant general's office is reprinted in Hansen, p. 48. The September 14, 1877, letter of William P. Zuber to General William Steele commenting on the interview and Almonte's quote in it is in the AGO File, TSLA.

The interview in the *National Police Gazette* has not been reprinted since its May 4, 1878, appearance; thanks to Joseph Musso, who supplied it. The May 19, 1881, interview in the *San Antonio Daily Express* was Mrs. Hannig's last and most extensive.

As an old man, Enrique Esparza was interviewed several times. The May 19, 1907, *San Antonio Daily Express* interview by Charles Merritt Barnes was his last and longest; it is reprinted in Matovina, *The Alamo Remembered,* p. 82.

The account by Esparza in Driggs, *Rise of the Lone Star,* is reprinted in Hansen, p. 117.

The Robert Bruce Blake information about Rose can be found in the Proceedings of the Board of Land Commissioners, Nacogdoches County Clerk's Office, which can be found in Blake's "Documents from Nacogdoches County Records Relating to Moses (Louis) Rose," Robert Bruce Blake Collection, vol. LXI: pp. 126–40, BCAH, and are also reprinted in Hansen, pp. 273–74, 278.

In his book *Alamo Traces,* Thomas Ricks Lindley argues that Blake misrepresented his original sources. But the crucial documents cited by Blake that Lindley claims do not exist — specifically, the Proceedings of the Board of Land Commissioners — were found by Todd Hansen in the office of the county clerk in Nacogdoches County. Hansen was allowed to photocopy excerpts from the original proceedings; he subsequently transmitted a copy to the Daughters of the Republic of Texas Library at the Alamo on June 11, 2005, for their vertical file on Moses Rose, and verified that Blake's transcript accurately reflects his cited source.

Blake's "Rose and His Escape from the Alamo" is reprinted in Hansen, pp. 274–82.

More evidence of Rose's nature is evident in a document I recently found, dated October 31, 1834. It is a petition signed by fifty-two of the town's citizens, addressed to the Department of Nacogdoches political chief, Henry Rueg, requesting permission for Louis Rose to be allowed to make a living by supplying the town with fresh beef (another citizen had managed to obtain an exclusive license to do the job). The signatories state their wish to see "Louis Rose occupied as usual instead of stalking unemployed about the streets and stores" (Nacogdoches Archives, pp. 244–248, BCAH).

The Davis quote concerning his disbelief in the line is in *Three Roads to the Alamo,* pp. 731–32.

The first Amelia Williams quote about A. D. Griffith and the line is from her groundbreaking "A Critical Study of the Siege of the Alamo," p. 31. The second Williams quote about Griffith (and his sister, Mrs. Susan Sterling) is found in a letter from Williams to Samuel Asbury, dated February 1, 1932 (box 2A138, Samuel Erson Asbury Papers, BCAH). The Williams notes from her interview with Griffith are in folder 6 (Dickinson), box 2N492, Amelia Worthington Williams Papers, BCAH.

The Dobie column about Charles Ramsdell appeared in the *Dallas Morning News* of March 31, 1940.

The Amelia Williams quote stating that Mrs. Sterling "avowed that it was" when asked about the truth of the line story is in a letter from Williams to Samuel Asbury, dated November 7, 1933 (box 2A138 [the Alamo File], Samuel Erson Asbury Papers, BCAH).

The two letters from W. T. Neblett to Amelia Williams are dated April 4, 1935, and April 26, 1935, and are in the General Correspondence folder for 1935 (box 2N490, Amelia Worthington Williams Papers, BCAH).

The Frank Johnson quote is found in the file entitled "Historical Notes—Alamo," p. 773 (box 2D187, Francis White Johnson Papers, BCAH).

See chapter 15 endnotes for details and citations regarding the last night in the Alamo.

Dobie's discussion of the line is reprinted in Hansen, p. 286.

For more on Rose and his foolhardiness in claiming to be a deserter rather than an Alamo scout, see Lon Tinkle's entertaining but fanciful *13 Days to Glory,* pp. 184–85, where he makes this point in a discussion of the Zuber account. A final tantalizing tidbit can be found in the BCAH files, in the Samuel Erson Asbury Papers. Asbury, a leading historian of the Texian revolution, corresponded with many other historians, including Roy F. Hall, author of *Collin County: Pioneering in North Texas* (Westminster, MD: Heritage Books, 1975), who lived in McKinney, Texas. At one point, Hall was heavily into research for a book on the battles of Texas, and in a letter to Asbury dated August 26, 1933, he wrote: "By the way, I recently unearthed something which hints that one man from the Alamo made his way through the lines on the 3rd of March, and this was written [in] 1848!" (this letter is in box 2A141, Samuel Erson Asbury Papers, BCAH). When Hall's manuscript was finished, he sent it to his publisher, who lost it. Apparently it was the only copy. Hall's papers were burned in a fire in his widow's house in 2002.

BIBLIOGRAPHY

BOOKS

Baker, DeWitt Clinton. *A Texas Scrap-Book*. New York: A. S. Barnes, 1875.

Bancroft, Hubert Howe. *History of the North Mexican States and Texas*. 2 vols. San Francisco: A. L. Bancroft, 1884.

Barker, Eugene C., ed. *The Austin Papers*. 3 vols. Austin: University of Texas Press, 1927.

Barr, Alwyn. *Texans in Revolt: The Battle for San Antonio, 1835*. Austin: University of Texas Press, 1990.

Batson, James L. *James Bowie and the Sandbar Fight*. Madison, AL: Batson Engineering and Metalworks, 1992.

Baylor, George Wythe. *John Robert Baylor: Confederate Governor of Arizona*. Tucson: Arizona Pioneers' Historical Society, 1966.

Berlandier, Jean Louis. *Journey to Mexico During the Years 1826 to 1834*. Austin: Texas State Historical Association, 1980.

Binkley, William C. *Official Correspondence of the Texan Revolution 1835–1836*. 2 vols. New York: Appleton-Century, 1936.

Blair, E. L. *Early History of Grimes County*. Austin, TX: privately printed, 1930.

Borroel, Roger, ed. *Field Reports of the Mexican Army During the Texan War of 1836*. 9 vols. East Chicago, IN: La Villita Publications, 2001–2008.

————, ed. *The Itineraries of the Zapadores and San Luis Battalions During the Texas War of 1836*. Vol. 1 of *Mexican Battalion Series at the Alamo*. East Chicago, IN: La Villita Publications, 1999.

————, ed. *The J. Sanchez Garza Introduction to the Rebellion of Texas: The Diary of Lt. Col. José Enrique de la Peña*. East Chicago, IN: La Villita Publications, 1998.

————. *Mexican Accounts of the Battle of the Alamo: A Collection and Critical Analysis*. East Chicago, IN: La Villita Publications, 1998.

————, ed. *The Papers of Lieutenant Colonel José Enrique de la Peña: The Last of His Appendixes*. East Chicago, IN: La Villita Publications, 2001.

————, ed. *The Papers of Lieutenant Colonel José Enrique de la Peña: Selected Appendixes from His Diary, 1836–1839*. East Chicago, IN: La Villita Publications, 1997.

————. *The Texan Revolution of 1836: A Concise Historical Perspective Based on Original Sources*. East Chicago, IN: La Villita Publications, 1989.

Bowie, Walter Worthington. *The Bowies and Their Kindred: A Genealogical and Biographical History*. Washington, D.C.: Cromwell Brothers, 1899.

Boylston, James R., and Allen J. Wiener. *David Crockett in Congress: The Rise and Fall of the Poor Man's Friend*. Houston: Bright Sky Press, 2009.

Brands, H. W. *Lone Star Nation: How a Ragged Army of Volunteers Won the Battle for Texas Independence—and Changed America*. New York: Doubleday, 2004.

Brister, Louis E., ed. *In Mexican Prisons: The Journal of Eduard Harkort, 1832–1834*. College Station, TX: Texas A&M University Press, 1986.

Brown, Gary. *The New Orleans Greys*. Plano, TX: Republic of Texas Press, 1999.

Brown, John Henry. *History of Texas, from 1685 to 1892*. 2 vols. St. Louis, MO: L. E. Daniell, 1893.

————. *The Indian Wars and Pioneers of Texas*. Austin, TX: L. E. Daniell, 1896.

————. *Life and Times of Henry Smith, the First American Governor of Texas*. Dallas: A. D. Aldridge and Company, 1887.

Bryan, William S., and Robert Rose. *A History of the Pioneer Families of Missouri*. St. Louis, MO: Bryan, Brand and Company, 1876.

Callcott, Wilfrid Hardy. *Santa Anna: The Story of an Enigma Who Once Was Mexico*. Norman: University of Oklahoma Press, 1936.

BIBLIOGRAPHY

Campbell, Randolph B. *An Empire for Slavery: The Peculiar Institution in Texas, 1821–1865*. Baton Rouge: Louisiana State University Press, 1989.

Cantrell, Gregg. *Stephen F. Austin: Empresario of Texas*. New Haven, CT: Yale University Press, 1999.

Carreno, Alberto M. *Jefes del ejercito Mexicano en 1847*. Mexico City: Imprenta y Fototipia de la Secretaría de Fomento, 1914.

Castañeda, Carlos, trans. *The Mexican Side of the Texan Revolution 1836*. 1936. Reprint, Washington, D.C.: Documentary Publications, 1971.

Chabot, Frederick. *With the Makers of San Antonio*. San Antonio, TX: privately printed, 1937.

Chariton, Wallace O. *Exploring the Alamo Legends*. Plano: Wordware/Republic of Texas Press, 1992.

———. *100 Days in Texas: The Alamo Letters*. Waco: Texian Press, 1968. Reprint, Plano: Wordware/Republic of Texas Press, 1990.

Chartrand, René. *Santa Anna's Mexican Army 1821–48*. Oxford, UK: Osprey Publishing, 2004.

Chemerka, William R. *Alamo Almanac & Book of Lists*. Austin, TX: Eakin Press, 1997.

Chipman, Donald E., and Harriet Denise Joseph. *Notable Men and Women of Spanish Texas*. Austin: University of Texas Press, 1999.

Cobia, Manley F., Jr. *Journey into the Land of Trials: The Story of Davy Crockett's Expedition to the Alamo*. Franklin, TN: Hillsboro Press, 2003.

Crisp, James E. *Sleuthing the Alamo: Davy Crockett's Last Stand and Other Mysteries of the Texas Revolution*. New York: Oxford University Press, 2005.

Crockett, David. *A Narrative of the Life of David Crockett, of the State of Tennessee*. 1834. Reprint, Lincoln: University of Nebraska Press, 1987.

Daughters of the American Revolution. *The Alamo Heroes and Their Revolutionary Ancestors*. San Antonio, TX: privately printed, 1976.

Davis, Robert E., ed. *The Diary of William Barret Travis, August 30, 1933–June 26, 1834*. Waco: Texian Press, 1966.

Davis, William C. *Three Roads to the Alamo: The Lives and Fortunes of David Crockett, James Bowie, and William Barret Travis*. New York: HarperCollins, 1998.

De Bruhl, Marshall. *Sword of San Jacinto: A Life of Sam Houston*. New York: Random House, 1993.

de la Peña, José Enrique. *With Santa Anna in Texas: A Personal Narrative of the Revolution.* Expanded edition. College Station: Texas A&M University Press, 1997.

de la Teja, Jesús F., ed. *A Revolution Remembered: The Memoirs and Selected Correspondence of Juan N. Seguín.* Austin, TX: State House Press, 1991.

———. *San Antonio de Béxar: A Community on New Spain's Northern Frontier.* Albuquerque: University of New Mexico Press, 1995.

DePalo, William A., Jr. *The Mexican National Army, 1822–1852.* College Station: Texas A&M University Press, 1997.

Derr, Mark. *The Frontiersman: The Real Life and the Many Legends of Davy Crockett.* New York: William Morrow, 1993.

DeShields, James T. *Tall Men with Long Rifles: The Glamorous Story of the Texas Revolution, as Told by Captain Creed Taylor, Who Fought in That Heroic Struggle from Gonzales to San Jacinto.* San Antonio: Naylor Company, 1935.

Dimmick, Gregg J. *Sea of Mud: The Retreat of the Mexican Army after San Jacinto, an Archeological Investigation.* Austin: Texas State Historical Association, 2004.

Dixon, Sam Houston. *The Men Who Made Texas Free.* Houston: Texas Historical Publishing Company, 1924.

Driggs, Howard R. *Rise of the Lone Star: A Story of Texas Told by Its Pioneers.* New York: Frederick A. Stokes, 1936.

Duval, John C. *Early Times in Texas, or the Adventures of Jack Dobell.* 1892. Reprint, Lincoln: University of Nebraska Press, 1986.

Edmondson, J. R. *The Alamo Story.* Plano: Republic of Texas Press, 2000.

———. *Mr. Bowie with a Knife: A History of the Sandbar Fight.* Haltom City, TX: Watkins Printing Services, 1998.

Ellis, Edward S. *The Life of Colonel David Crockett.* Philadelphia: Porter and Coates, 1884.

Field, Dr. Joseph E. *Three Years in Texas.* Greenfield, MA: Justin Jones, 1836.

Filisola, Don Vicente. *Memoirs for the History of the War in Texas.* Translated by Wallace Woolsey. 2 vols. Austin, TX: Eakin Press, 1985.

———. *Memorias para la historia de la guerra de Tejas.* Mexico: Imprenta de Ignacio Cumplido, 1849.

Fish, Carl Russell. *The Rise of the Common Man, 1830–1850.* Vol. 6 of *A History of American Life.* New York: Macmillan, 1927.

Foote, Allan D. *The Defiant Dozen: New Yorkers at the Alamo.* Whitesboro, NY: Mohawk Valley History Project, 2005.

Foote, Henry Stuart. *Texas and the Texans*. 2 vols. Philadelphia: Thomas, Cowperthwaite and Company, 1841.

Fowler, Will. *Santa Anna of Mexico*. Lincoln: University of Nebraska Press, 2007.

Fox, Anne A. *Archaeological Investigations in Alamo Plaza, San Antonio, Bexar County, Texas, 1988 and 1989*. Archaeological Survey Report no. 205. Center for Archaeological Research, University of Texas at San Antonio, 1992.

French, Janie Preston Collup, and Zella Armstrong. *The Crockett Family and Connecting Lines*. Vol. 5 of *Notable Southern Families*. Bristol, TN: King Printing, 1928.

Frenzel, Victoria Eberle. *Gonzales: Hope Heartbreak Heroes*. Gonzales, TX: privately printed, 2008.

Fulton, Maurice Garland, ed. *Excursions in Mexico and California*. Vol. 2 of *Diary and Letters of Josiah Gregg*. Norman: University of Oklahoma Press, 1941.

Gaddy, Jerry J. *Texas in Revolt: Contemporary Newspaper Accounts of the Texas Revolution*. Fort Collins, CO: Old Army Press, 1973.

Garcia, Robert, and Sylvia Jean de Jesus Garcia. *Tejano Participants in the Texas Revolution of 1835–1837*. San Antonio, TX: Los Bexarenos Genealogical Society, 2004.

Gilliam, Albert M. *Travels over the Table Lands and Cordilleras of Mexico, During the Years 1843 and 44*...Aberdeen, Scotland: G. Clark and Son, 1847.

Gladden, Sanford Charles. *Durst and Darst Families of America*. Boulder, CO: privately printed, 1969.

Goodspeed Publishing Co. *History of Newton, Lawrence, Barry, and McDonald Counties, Missouri*. Chicago: Goodspeed Publishing, 1888.

———. *Memorial and Genealogical Record of Southwest Texas*. Chicago: Goodspeed Publishing, 1894.

Gray, William F. *Diary of Colonel W. F. Gray: From Virginia to Texas, 1835–'37*. Houston: Fletcher Young Publishing, 1965.

Green, Rena Maverick, ed. *Memoirs of Mary A. Maverick*. Lincoln: University of Nebraska Press, 1989.

———. *Samuel Maverick, Texan: 1803–1870*. San Antonio: privately printed, 1952.

Groneman, Bill. *Alamo Defenders: A Genealogy*. Austin, TX: Eakin Press, 1990.

———. *Death of a Legend: The Myth and Mystery Surrounding the Death of Davy Crockett*. Plano: Republic of Texas Press, 1999.

———. *Eyewitness to the Alamo*. Revised edition. Plano: Republic of Texas Press, 2001.

Haley, James L. *Passionate Nation: The Epic History of Texas*. New York: Free Press, 2006.

———. *Sam Houston*. Norman: University of Oklahoma Press, 2002.

Hansen, Todd. *The Alamo Reader: A Study in History*. Mechanicsburg, PA: Stackpole Books, 2003.

Hardin, Stephen L. *The Alamo 1836: Santa Anna's Texas Campaign*. Oxford, UK: Osprey Publishing, 2001.

———. *Texian Iliad: A Military History of the Texas Revolution*. Austin: University of Texas Press, 1994.

Harris, Charles H., III. *A Mexican Family Empire: The Latifundio of the Sánchez Navarro Family, 1765–1867*. Austin: University of Texas Press, 1975.

Hatch, Thom. *Encyclopedia of the Alamo and the Texas Revolution*. Jefferson, NC: McFarland and Company, 1999.

Haythornthwaite, Philip. *The Alamo and the War of Texan Independence 1835–36*. London, UK: Osprey Publishing, 1996.

Helm, Mrs. Mary S. *Scraps of Early Texas History*. Austin, TX: Privately printed, 1884.

Henderson, Timothy J. *A Glorious Defeat: Mexico and Its War with the United States*. New York: Hill and Wang, 2007.

Henson, Margaret Swett. *Juan Davis Bradburn: A Reappraisal of the Mexican Commander of Anahuac*. College Station: Texas A&M University Press, 1982.

Hobsbawm, Eric. *The Age of Revolution, 1789–1848*. Reprint, New York: Vintage, 1996.

Houston, Andrew Jackson. *Texas Independence*. Houston: Anson Jones Press, 1938.

Huffines, Alan C. *Blood of Noble Men: The Alamo Siege and Battle*. Austin: Eakin Press, 1999.

———. *The Texas War of Independence 1835–1836: From Outbreak to the Alamo to San Jacinto*. Oxford, UK: Osprey Publishing, 2005.

Huneycutt, C. D., ed. and trans. *At the Alamo: The Memoirs of Capt. Navarro* (New London, CT: Gold Star Press, 1988).

Hunt, Richard S., and Jesse F. Randel. *A New Guide to Texas*. New York: Sherman and Smith, 1845.

Hunter, Robert Hancock. *Narrative of Robert Hancock Hunter 1813–1902*. Mesquite, TX: Ide House, 1982.

Huson, Hobart. *Captain Philip Dimitt's Commandancy of Goliad*. Austin: Von Boeckmann-Jones, 1974.

———, ed. *Dr. J. H. Barnard's Journal*. Refugio, TX: privately printed, 1949.

Jackson, Jack, ed. *Texas by Terán: The Diary Kept by General Manuel de Mier y Terán on His 1828 Inspection of Texas*. Austin: University of Texas Press, 2000.

Jackson, Ron. *Alamo Legacy: Alamo Descendants Remember the Alamo*. Austin, TX: Eakin Press, 1997.

Jelinek, Donald A. *Survivor of the Alamo*. Berkeley, CA: Beard Books, 1999.

Jenkins, John H., and Kenneth Kesselus. *Edward Burleson: Texas Frontier Leader*. Austin, TX: Jenkins Publishing Company, 1990.

Jenkins, John H., ed. *The General's Tight Pants: Edward Warren's Texas Tour of 1836*. Austin, TX: Pemberton Press, 1976.

———. *The Papers of the Texas Revolution*. 10 vols. Austin, TX: Presidial Press, 1973.

———. *Recollections of Early Texas: Memoirs of John Holland Jenkins*. Austin: University of Texas Press, 1958.

———. *The Texas Revolution and Republic*. Austin, TX: Jenkins Company, 1986.

Johnson, Frank. *A History of Texas and Texans*. Edited and updated by Eugene C. Barker. 5 vols. Chicago: American Historical Society, 1916.

Kavanagh, Thomas W. *The Comanches: A History 1706–1875*. Lincoln: University of Nebraska Press, 1996.

Kilgore, Dan. *How Did Davy Die?* College Station: Texas A&M University Press, 1978.

King, C. Richard. *James Clinton Neill: The Shadow Commander of the Alamo*. Austin, TX: Eakin Press, 2002.

———. *Susanna Dickinson: Messenger of the Alamo*. Austin, TX: Shoal Creek, 1976.

Labadie, Joseph H. *La Villita Earthworks, San Antonio, Texas: A Preliminary Report of Investigations of Mexican Siege Works at the Battle of the Alamo*. San Antonio: Center for Archaeological Research, University of Texas at San Antonio, 1986.

Lack, Paul D. *The Texas Revolutionary Experience: A Political and Social History 1835–1836*. College Station: Texas A&M University Press, 1992.

Lemon, Mark. *The Illustrated Alamo 1836: A Photographic Journey*. Abilene, TX: State House Press, 2008.

Levy, Buddy. *American Legend: The Real-Life Adventures of David Crockett*. New York: Putnam, 2005.

Lindley, Thomas Ricks. *Alamo Traces: New Evidence and New Conclusions*. Plano: Republic of Texas Press, 2003.

Lockhart, Dr. John Washington. *Sixty Years on the Brazos: The Life and Letters of Dr. John Washington Lockhart*. Los Angeles: privately printed, 1930.

Lord, Walter. *A Time to Stand: The Epic of the Alamo*. New York: Harper and Row, 1961.

Lozano, Ruben Rendon. *Viva Tejas: The Story of the Tejanos, the Mexican-Born Patriots of the Texas Revolution*. San Antonio, TX: Southern Literary Institute, 1936.

Lukes, Edward A. *De Witt Colony of Texas*. Austin, TX: Pemberton Press, 1976.

Lundy, Benjamin. *The War in Texas*. 1836. Reprint, Upper Saddle River, NJ: Gregg Press, 1970.

Marks, Paula Mitchell. *Turn Your Eyes Toward Texas: Pioneers Sam and Mary Maverick*. College Station: Texas A&M University Press, 1989.

Marshall, Bruce. *Uniforms of the Alamo Defenders and the Texas Revolution and the Men Who Wore Them 1835–1836*. Atglen, PA: Schiffer Publishing, 2003.

Matovina, Timothy M. *The Alamo Remembered: Tejano Accounts and Perspectives*. Austin: University of Texas Press, 1995.

McDonald, Archie P. *Travis*. Austin, TX: Pemberton Press, 1976.

McGraw, A. Joachim, John W. Clark Jr., and Elizabeth A. Robbins, eds. *A Texas Legacy: The Old San Antonio Road and the Camino Reales*. Austin, TX: State Department of Highways and Public Transportation, 1991.

McLean, Malcolm D., ed. *Papers Concerning Robertson's Colony in Texas*. 19 vols. Arlington: University of Texas at Arlington Press, 1987.

Miller, Edward L. *New Orleans and the Texas Revolution*. College Station: Texas A&M University Press, 2004.

Montaigne, Sanford H. *Blood Over Texas: The Truth About Mexico's War with the United States*. New Rochelle, NY: Arlington House, 1976.

Moore, Stephen L. *Eighteen Minutes: The Battle of San Jacinto and the Texas Independence Campaign*. Plano: Republic of Texas Press, 2004.

———. *Savage Frontier: Rangers, Riflemen, and Indian Wars in Texas*. Vol. 1, 1835–1837. Plano: Republic of Texas Press, 2002.

Morphis, J. M. *History of Texas from Its Discovery and Settlement*. New York: United States Publishing Co., 1874.

Muir, Andrew Forest, ed. *Texas in 1837*. Austin: University of Texas Press, 1958.

Navarro, José Antonio. *Defending Mexican Valor in Texas: José Antonio Navarro's Historical Writings 1853–1857.* Austin, TX: State House Press, 1995.

Nelson, George. *The Alamo: An Illustrated History.* 2nd ed. Dry Frio Canyon, TX: Aldine Press, 1998.

Nevin, David. *The Texans.* New York: Time-Life Books, 1975.

Newell, Rev. Chester. *History of the Revolution in Texas.* New York: Wiley and Putnam, 1838.

Nichols, James Wilson. *Now You Hear My Horn: The Journal of James Wilson Nichols, 1820–1887.* Austin: University of Texas Press, 1967.

Niles, John M. *A History of South America and Mexico.* Hartford, CT: H. Huntington Jr., 1838.

Nixon, Patrick Ireland. *The Medical Story of Early Texas, 1528–1853.* Lancaster, PA: Mollie Bennett Lupe Memorial Fund, 1946.

Nofi, Albert A. *The Alamo and the Texas War for Independence.* Conshohocken, PA: Combined Books, 1992.

Noyes, Stanley. *Los Comanches: The Horse People, 1751–1845.* Albuquerque: University of New Mexico Press, 1993.

Ornish, Natalie. *Ehrenberg: Goliad Survivor—Old West Explorer.* Dallas: Texas Heritage Press, 1997.

Peterson, Harold L. *Round Shot and Rammers: An Introduction to Muzzle-Loading Land Artillery in the United States.* Harrisburg, PA: Stackpole Books, 1969.

Poyo, Gerald E. *Tejano Journey, 1770–1850.* Austin: University of Texas Press, 1996.

Procter, Ben. *The Battle of the Alamo.* Austin: Texas State Historical Association, 1986.

Ragsdale, Crystal Sasse. *Women and Children of the Alamo.* Austin, TX: State House Press, 1994.

Reid, Stuart. *The Secret War for Texas.* College Station: Texas A&M University Press, 2007.

———. *The Texan Army 1835–46.* Oxford, UK: Osprey Publishing, 2003.

Reséndez, Andrés. *Changing National Identities at the Frontier: Texas and New Mexico, 1800–1850.* New York: Cambridge University Press, 2005.

Rios, John F., ed. *Readings on the Alamo.* New York: Vantage Press, 1987.

Rives, G. L. *The United States and Mexico, 1821–1848.* 2 vols. New York: Charles Scribner's Sons, 1913.

Roberts, Randy, and James S. Olson. *A Line in the Sand: The Alamo in Blood and Memory.* New York: Free Press, 2001.

Robinson, Duncan. *Judge Robert McAlpin Williamson: Texas' Three-Legged Willie*. Austin: Texas State Historical Association, 1948.

Robinson, Fayette. *Mexico and Her Military Chieftains, from the Revolution of Hidalgo to the Present Time*. Philadelphia: E. H. Butler, 1847.

Rodríguez, J. M. *Memoirs of Early Texas*. San Antonio: Passing Show Printing Co., 1913.

Ross, Steven T. *From Flintlock to Rifle: Infantry Tactics, 1740–1866*. 1979. Reprint, London: Frank Cass, 1996.

Ruíz, José Francisco. *Report on the Indian Tribes of Texas in 1828*. New Haven, CT: Yale University Library, 1972.

Salas, Elizabeth. *Soldaderas in the Mexican Military*. Austin: University of Texas Press, 1990.

Sánchez-Navarro, Carlos. *La Guerra de Tejas: Memorias de un soldado*. 2nd ed. Mexico City: Editorial Jus, 1960.

Santos, Richard G. *Santa Anna's Campaign Against Texas 1835–1836*. 2nd ed. Waco: Texian Press, 1968.

Schoelwer, Susan Prendergast. *Alamo Images: Changing Perspectives of a Texas Experience*. Vol. 3 of the DeGolyer Library Publications Series. Dallas: Southern Methodist University Press, 1985.

Schwarz, Ted. *Forgotten Battlefield of the First Texas Revolution: The Battle of Medina, August 18, 1813*. Austin, TX: Eakin Press, 1985.

Shackford, James Atkins. *David Crockett: The Man and the Legend*. 1956. Reprint, Chapel Hill, NC: University of North Carolina Press, 1986.

Shiffrin, Gale Hamilton. *Echoes from Women of the Alamo*. San Antonio: AW Press, 1999.

Smith, Justin Harvey. *The War with Mexico*. 2 vols. New York: Macmillan, 1919.

Smith, Richard Penn, ed. *On to the Alamo: Colonel Crockett's Exploits and Adventures in Texas*. 1838. Reprint, New York: Penguin Books, 2003.

Smither, Harriet, Charles Adams Gulick, Katherine Elliott, and Winnie Adams, eds. *The Papers of Mirabeau Buonaparte Lamar*. 6 vols. Austin: Texas Library and Historical Commission State Library, 1921–27.

Smithwick, Noah. *The Evolution of a State, or Recollections of Old Texas Days*. 1900. Reprint, Austin: University of Texas Press, 1983.

Sowell, A. J. *Early Settlers and Indian Fighters of Southwest Texas*. 1900. Reprint, New York: Argosy-Antiquarian, 1964.

————. *Rangers and Pioneers of Texas*. San Antonio: Shepard Bros., 1884.

Speer, William S., and John Henry Brown. *The Encyclopedia of the New West*. Marshall, TX: U.S. Biographical Publishing Co., 1881.

Steuart, Ella Hutchins. *Gems from a Texas Quarry*. New Orleans: J. S. Rivers, 1885.

Stevens, Phillip H. *Artillery Through the Ages*. New York: Franklin Watts, 1965.

[Stiff, Edward]. *A New History of Texas*. Cincinnati: George Conclin, 1847.

Sutherland, Dr. John. *The Fall of the Alamo*. San Antonio: Naylor Publishing, 1936.

Swisher, Mrs. Bella French, ed. *The American Sketch Book*, vol. 6. Austin, TX: Sketch Book Publishing House, 1881.

Swisher, Col. John M. *The Swisher Memoirs*. San Antonio: The Sigmund Press, 1932.

Tennis, Cynthia L. *Exhumation of a Hero, Colonel Ben Milam*. Archaeological Survey Report no. 223. Center for Archaeological Research, University of Texas at San Antonio, 1995.

Thorp, Raymond W. *Bowie Knife*. Albuquerque: University of New Mexico Press, 1948.

Tijerina, Andrés. *Tejanos and Texas Under the Mexican Flag 1821–1836*. College Station: Texas A&M University Press, 1994.

Tinkle, Lon. *13 Days to Glory: The Siege of the Alamo*. New York: McGraw-Hill, 1958.

Todish, Tim J. and Terry S. *Alamo Sourcebook 1836: A Comprehensive Guide to the Alamo and the Texas Revolution*. Austin, TX: Eakin Press, 1998.

Trammell, Camilla Davis. *Seven Pines: Its Occupants and Their Letters, 1825–1872*. Dallas: Southern Methodist University Press, 1986.

Uecker, Herbert G. *The Archaeology of the Alamo: A Self-Guided Walking Tour and Personal Account*. Bulverde, TX: Monte Comal Publications, 2001.

Valadés, José C. *México, Santa Anna y la guerra de Téxas*. 3rd ed. Mexico City: Editores Mexicanos Unidos, 1965.

Walraven, Bill and Marjorie K. *The Magnificent Barbarians: Little-Told Tales of the Texas Revolution*. Austin, TX: Eakin Press, 1993.

Weber, David J. *The Mexican Frontier 1821–1846: The American Southwest Under Mexico*. Albuquerque: University of New Mexico Press, 1982.

Weddle, Robert S. *San Juan Bautista: Gateway to Spanish Texas.* Austin: University of Texas Press, 1968.

Weyand, Leonie Rummell, and Houston Wade. *An Early History of Fayette County.* LaGrange, TX: LaGrange Journal, 1936.

Wharton, Clarence. *El Presidente: A Sketch of the Life of General Santa Anna.* Austin, TX: Gammel's Bookstore, 1926.

Wooten, Dudley G. *Comprehensive History of Texas 1685 to 1897.* 2 vols. Dallas: William G. Scarff, 1898.

Wright, Mrs. S. J. *San Antonio de Béxar.* Austin, TX: Morgan Printing, 1916.

Yoakum, Henderson. *History of Texas from Its First Settlement in 1685 to Its Annexation to the United States in 1846.* 2 vols. 1855. Reprint, Austin, TX: Steck Company, 1937.

Young, Kevin R. "Finding a Face: *El Soldado Mexicano 1835–1848.*" Appendix C in *A Thunder of Cannon: Archeology of the Mexican-American War Battlefield of Palo Alto* by Charles M. Haecker (Santa Fe, NM: National Park Service Divisions of Anthropology and History, 1994). http://www.nps.gov/history/history/online_books/paal/thunder-cannon/appc.htm.

ARTICLES

Anonymous. "The Release of Stephen F. Austin from Prison." *Texas Historical Association Quarterly* 14, no. 2 (October 1910).

Asbury, Samuel E. "The Private Journal of Juan Nepomuceno Almonte." *Southwestern Historical Quarterly* 48, no. 1 (July 1944).

Austin, William T. "Account of the Campaign of 1835." *Texana* 4 (Winter 1966).

Barker, Eugene C. "General Austin's Order Book for the Campaign of 1835." *Quarterly of the Texas State Historical Association* 11, no. 1 (July 1907).

———. "Stephen F. Austin and the Independence of Texas." *Texas Historical Association Quarterly* 13, no. 4 (April 1910).

Bennet, Miles S. "The Battle of Gonzales, the 'Lexington' of the Texas Revolution." *Texas Historical Association Quarterly* 2, no. 4 (April 1999).

Bishop, Curtis. "King of the Wild Frontier." *True West* 2, no. 6 (July–August 1955).

Bonham, Milledge L., Jr. "James Butler Bonham: A Consistent Rebel." *Southwestern Historical Quarterly* 35, no. 2 (October 1931).

Bostick, Sion R. "Reminiscences of Sion R. Bostick." *Texas Historical Association Quarterly* 5, no. 2 (October 1901).

Boyle, Andrew A. "Reminiscences of the Texas Revolution." *Texas Historical Association Quarterly* 4, no. 4 (April 1910).

Boylston, Jim. "Another Look at the Perry Account." *The Alamo Journal* 139 (December 2005).

Bugbee, Lester G. "Slavery in Early Texas." *Political Science Quarterly* 13, no. 3.

Caine, Jerry. "Alamo Flags." *The Alamo Journal* 131 (December 2003).

Calhoun, Robert D. "A History of Concordia Parish, Louisiana." *Louisiana Historical Quarterly* 15 (January 1932).

Casso, Raul, IV. "Damacio Jimenez: The Lost and Found Alamo Defender." *Southwestern Historical Quarterly* 96, no. 1 (July 1992).

Chemerka, William R. "The Brown Bess Musket of Santa Anna's Army." *Alamo News* 44 (April 1985).

———. "The Death of Davy Crockett at the Alamo." *The Alamo Journal* 136 (March 2005).

———. "More Alamo Defenders." *The Alamo Journal* 127 (December 2003).

Clopper, J. C. "J. C. Clopper's Journal and Book of Memoranda for 1828." *Texas Historical Association Quarterly* 13 (July 1909–April 1910)

Cohen, Hennig, ed. "Seven Patriotic Poems from New Orleans Newspapers on the War for Texas Independence." *Southwestern Historical Quarterly* 54, no. 3 (January 1951).

Connelly, Thomas Lawrence. "Did David Crockett Surrender at the Alamo? A Contemporary Letter." *Journal of Southern History* 26, no. 3 (August 1960).

Cooley, Mrs. Emily B. "A Retrospect of San Antonio." *Texas Historical Association Quarterly* 4, no. 1 (July 1900).

Corner, William. "John Crittenden Duval: The Last Survivor of the Goliad Massacre." *Texas Historical Association Quarterly* 1, no. 1 (July 1897).

Costeloe, Michael P. "The Mexican Press of 1836 and the Battle of the Alamo." *Southwestern Historical Quarterly* 91, no. 4 (April 1988).

Crimmins, M. L., ed. "John W. Smith, the Last Messenger from the Alamo and the First Mayor of San Antonio." *Southwestern Historical Quarterly* 54, no. 3 (January 1951).

———. "The Storming of San Antonio de Bexar in 1835." *West Texas Historical Association Year Book* 22 (October 1946).

Crisp, James E. "Davy in Freeze-Frame: Methodology or Madness." *The Alamo Journal* 98 (October 1995).

———. "Documenting Davy's Death: The Problematic 'Dolson Letter' from Texas, 1836." *Journal of the West* 46, no. 2 (Spring 2007).

———. "An Incident in San Antonio: The Contested Iconology of Davy Crockett's Death at the Alamo." *Journal of the West* 40, no. 2 (Spring 2001).

———. "Trashing Dolson: The Perils of Tendentious Interpretation." *The Alamo Journal* 99 (December 1995).

Davenport, Harbert. "The Men of Goliad." *Southwestern Historical Quarterly* 48, no. 1 (July 1939).

Davidson, Richard. "A Forensic Look at Crockett's Death." *The Alamo Journal* 128 (March 2003).

———. "How Did Davy Really Die?" *The Alamo Journal* 78 (October 1991).

———. "When Propaganda Becomes History." *The Alamo Journal* 127 (December 2003).

Davis, William C., ed. "A Fortnight with James Bowie by the Rev. Benjamin Chase." *The Alamo Journal* 126 (September 2002).

———. "How Davy Probably *Didn't* Die." *Journal of the Alamo Battlefield Association* 2, no. 1 (Fall 1997).

de la Teja, Jesús F., and John Wheat. "Bexar: Profile of a Tejano Community, 1820–1832." *Southwestern Historical Quarterly* 89, no. 1 (July 1985).

Dettman, Bruce. "Davy's Death: A Common Sense Approach." *The Alamo Journal* 91 (April 1994).

Dobie, J. Frank. "Jim Bowie—Big Dealer." *Southwestern Historical Quarterly* 60, no. 3 (January 1957).

———. "No Help for the Alamo." *True West* 6, no. 5 (May–June 1959).

Drake, David. "'Joe' Alamo Hero." *Negro History Bulletin* 44, no. 2 (April–June 1981).

Durham, Robert L. "Once More Against the North Wall." *Journal of the Alamo Battlefield Association* 3, no. 1 (Fall 1998).

———. "*Where* Did Davy Die?" *The Alamo Journal* 104 (March 1997).

Gaddy, Jerry J. "The Alamo—Another View." *By Valor and Arms* 1, no. 2 (January 1975).

Garver, Lois. "Benjamin Rush Milam." *Southwestern Historical Quarterly* 38, no. 2 (October 1934).

Gates, Paul Wallace. "Private Land Claims." *The Journal of Southern History* 22, no. 1 (February 1956).

Gracy, David B., II. "Just as I Have Written It: A Study of the Authenticity of the Manuscript of Jose Enrique de la Peña's

Account of the Texas Campaign." *Southwestern Historical Quarterly* 105, no. 2 (October 2001).

Green, Michael Robert. "El Soldado Mexicano 1835–1836." *Military History of Texas and the Southwest* 13, no. 1 (1995).

———. "Two Contemporary Views of Texas Revolutionaries." *Military History of Texas and the Southwest* 14, no. 4 (1978).

Greene, Col. A. A., trans. and ed. "The Battle of Zacatecas." *Texana* 7, no. 3 (1969).

Greer, James K. "The Committee on the Texas Declaration of Independence." Pt. 1. *Southwestern Historical Quarterly* 30, no. 4 (April 1927).

———. "Journal of Ammon Underwood, 1834–1835." *Southwestern Historical Quarterly* 32, no. 2 (October 1928).

Groneman, Bill. "Jim Bowie—A Popular Leader?" *Alamo News* 34 (December 1984).

———. "Some Problems with the 'Urriza' Account." *The Alamo Journal* 87 (July 1993).

———. "The Taking of the Alamo Flag." *The Alamo Journal* 154 (September 2005).

———. "A Witness to the Executions?" *The Alamo Journal* 88 (October 1993).

Guarnieri, Phil. "Some Thoughts on the 'Second Reinforcement Theory.'" *The Alamo Journal* 138 (September 2005).

Hansen, Todd. "A Summary Critique of Thomas Ricks Lindley's Second Reinforcement Theory." *The Alamo Journal* 157 (June 2010).

Harburn, Todd E. "The Crockett Death Controversy." *The Alamo Journal* 76 (April 1991).

Hardin, Stephen L. "The Félix Nuñez Account and the Siege of the Alamo: A Critical Appraisal." *Southwestern Historical Quarterly* 94, no. 1 (July 1990).

———. "J. C. Neill: The Forgotten Alamo Commander." *The Alamo Journal* 109 (May 1989).

———. "A Volley from the Darkness: Sources Regarding the Death of William Barret Travis." *The Alamo Journal* 59 (December 1987).

Hatcher, Mattie Austin, trans. "Joaquin de Arredondo's Report of the Battle of the Medina, August 18, 1813." *Texas Historical Association Quarterly* 11, No. 3 (January 1908).

Hawkins, Nigel. "How Did Davy Die? He Died Fighting!" *The Alamo Journal* 69 (December 1989).

Heiser, Lisa, and William Bor. "Military Health Care During the Texas Revolution." *The Alamo Journal* 148 (March 2008).

Huffines, Alan C. "Mexican Cavalry at the Alamo." *Journal of the Alamo Battlefield Association* 2, no. 1 (Fall 1997).

Ivey, James E. "Archaeological Evidence for the Defenses of the Alamo." *The Alamo Journal* 117 (June 2000).

———. "The Search for the Saints." Alamo de Parras website (2000).

———. "South Gate and Its Defenses." *Alamo Lore and Myth Organization* 3, no. 4 (December 1981).

———. "Southwest & Northwest Wall Gun Emplacements." *Alamo Lore and Myth Organization* 3, no. 3 (September 1981).

———. "¡Viva la Patria es nuestro el Alamo!" *The Alamo Journal* 123 (December 2001).

———. "West Wall's Brief History." *Alamo Lore and Myth Organization* 1, no. 4 (December 1979).

Jackson, Jack, and James E. Ivey. "Mystery Artist of the Alamo: José Juan Sánchez." *Southwestern Historical Quarterly* 105, no. 2 (October 2001).

Kailbourn, Tom. "Lt. Col. Pedro Ampudia's After-Action Report of the Siege and Capture of the Alamo." *The Alamo Journal* 159 (December 2010).

Knight, Alan. "Mexican Peonage." *Journal of Latin American Studies* 18, no. 1 (May 1986).

Lack, Paul D. "Slavery and the Texas Revolution." *Southwestern Historical Quarterly* 89, no. 2 (October 1985).

Lake, Mary Daggett. "David Crockett's Widow." *The Texas Monthly* 2, no. 5 (December 1928).

Lee, A. J. "Some Recollections of Two Texas Pioneer Women." *Texas Methodist Historical Quarterly* 1, no. 3 (January 1910).

Lemon, Mark. "The Artillery of the Alamo and Its Placement." *The Alamo Journal* 146 (September 2007).

———. "An Unexpected Find." Pts. 1–3. *The Alamo Journal* 153–155 (July 2009–December 2009).

———. "Where's Juana? A Case for Locating Juana Alsbury in the Final Assault." *The Alamo Journal* 145 (June 2007).

Lind, Michael. "The Death of David Crockett." *Wilson Quarterly,* Winter 1998.

Lindley, Thomas Ricks. "Alamo Sources." *The Alamo Journal* 74 (December 1998).

———. "Analysis of the 'Lancer' Account of David Crockett's Death." *The Alamo Journal* 138 (September 2005).

———. "Davy Crockett: The Alamo's High Private." *The Alamo Journal* 64 (December 1988).

———. "Documents of the New Orleans Greys." *The Alamo Journal* 140 (March 2006).

———. "Drawing Truthful Deductions." *Journal of the Alamo Battlefield Association* 1, no. 1 (Summer 1995).

———. "James Butler Bonham, October 17, 1835–March 6, 1836." *The Alamo Journal* 62 (August 1988).

———. "Killing Crockett." Pts. 1–3. *The Alamo Journal* 96–98 (May 1995–October 1995).

———. "Making It Right." *The Alamo Journal* 130 (September 2003).

———. "Mexican Casualties at Bexar 1835–1836." Pts. 1–3. *The Alamo Journal* 121–123 (June 2001–December 2001).

———. "William B. Travis: Father of the Texas Revolution." *The Alamo Journal* 132 (March 2004).

Looscan, Adele B. "Harris County, 1822–1845." Pt. 1. *Southwestern Historical Quarterly* 18, no. 3 (January 1915).

———. "Micajah Autry, a Soldier of the Alamo." *Texas Historical Association Quarterly* 14, no. 4 (April 1911).

———. "The Old Fort at Anahuac." *Texas Historical Association Quarterly* 2, no. 1 (July 1898).

Lord, Walter. "Myths and Realities of the Alamo." *The American West* 5, no. 3 (May 1968).

Lundstrom, John B. "Assault at Dawn: The Mexican Army at the Alamo." *Campaign: The Magazine of Military History,* no. 1 (Summer 1973).

Miller, Thomas Lloyd. "Mexican-Texans at the Alamo." *The Journal of Mexican American History* 2, no. 1 (Fall 1971).

———. "The Roll of the Alamo." *Texana* 2, no. 1 (Spring 1964).

Moore, Stephen. "Texas Rangers at the Battle of the Alamo." *The Texas Ranger Dispatch* (Spring 2004).

Musso, Joseph. "Col. James Bowie's Freed Slaves." *The Alamo Journal* 142 (September 2006).

Navarro, José Antonio. "Apuntes Históricos Interesantes de San Antonio de Béxar." *San Antonio Ledger,* December 12, 1857.

Pittman, Ruth. "One Did Survive!" *Elks Magazine* (May 1982).

Pohl, James W., and Stephen L. Hardin. "The Military History of the Texas Revolution: An Overview." *Southwestern Historical Quarterly* 89, no. 3 (January 1986).

Potter, R. M. "The Fall of the Alamo." *Magazine of American History* 2, no. 1 (January 1878).

Powell, Raymond. "The Traitor of the Alamo." *North Louisiana Historical Journal* 4, no. 4 (Summer 1973).

Presley, James. "Santa Anna in Texas: A Mexican Viewpoint." *Southwestern Historical Quarterly* 62, no. 4 (April 1959).

Raines, C. W. "Life of Antonio Lopez de Santa Anna." *The Texas Magazine* 1, no. 1 (May 1896).

Ramsdell, Charles. "The Storming of the Alamo." *American Heritage,* February 1961.

Rather, Ethel Zivley. "De Witt's Colony." *Texas State Historical Association Quarterly* 7, no. 2 (October 1904).

Reid, Stuart. "The Second Reinforcement: A Re-Appraisal of the Evidence." *The Alamo Journal* 137 (June 2005).

———. "What Ails You Jim, Exactly?" *The Alamo Journal* 143 (December 2006).

Rowe, Edna. "The Disturbances at Anahuac in 1832." *Quarterly of the Texas State Historical Association* 6, no. 4 (April 1903).

Sánchez Lamego, Miguel A. *Apuntes para la historia del arma de ingenieros en México: Historia del Batallón de Zapadores.* Mexico City: Secretaría de la Defensa Nacional, 1943.

———. *The Siege and Taking of the Alamo.* Santa Fe, NM: Press of the Territorian, 1968.

Sánchez-Navarro, José Juan. "A Mexican View of the Texas War: Memoirs of a Veteran of the Two Battles of the Alamo." Trans. by Helen Hunnicutt. *The Library Chronicle of the University of Texas* 4, no. 2 (Summer 1951).

Scruggs, Thomas E. "Davy Crockett and the Thieves of Jericho." *Journal of the Early Republic* 19, no. 3 (Fall 1999).

Sears, Edward S. "The Low Down on Jim Bowie." *Texas Folklore Society Publications* no. 19 (1944).

Sparks, S. F. "Recollections of S. F. Sparks." *Texas Historical Association Quarterly* 12, no. 1 (July 1908).

Steen, Ralph W. "Analysis of the Work of the General Council, Provisional Government of Texas, 1835–1836." *Southwestern Historical Quarterly* 41, no. 4 (April 1938).

———. "Notes and Documents: A Letter from San Antonio de Bexar in 1836." *Southwestern Historical Quarterly* 62, no. 4 (April 1959).

Stout, S. H. "David Crockett." *The American Historical Magazine* 7, no. 1 (January 1901).

Stulting, Tommie. "A Pioneer Woman and Her Family." *Plum Creek Almanac* 8, no. 1.

True, Herbert E. "The Early Siege of the Alamo: Feb. 23–March 6, 1836." *The Alamo Journal* 156 (March 2010).

Warren, Harry. "Col. William G. Cooke." *Texas Historical Association Quarterly* 9, no. 3 (January 1906).

Williams, Amelia. "A Critical Study of the Siege of the Alamo and of the Personnel of Its Defenders." Pts. 1–5. *Southwestern Historical Quarterly* 36, no. 4–37, no. 4 (April 1933–April 1934).

Williams, Robert H., Jr. "Travis—a Potential Sam Houston." *Southwestern Historical Quarterly* 40, no. 2 (October 1936).

Wilson, Francis W., MD. "Medical Service in the Texas Revolution." *Plum Creek Almanac* 4, no. 2 (Fall 1986).

Young, Kevin R. "James Walker Fannin: The West Point Connection." *The Alamo Journal* 33 (July 1983).

———, ed. "Joseph Henry Barnard Letter." *The Alamo Journal* 159 (December 2010).

———ed., and David McDonald, trans. "The Siege of the Alamo: A Mexican Army Journal." *Journal of the Alamo Battlefield Association* 3, no. 1 (Fall 1998).

Zaboly, Gary S. "The Abatis." *The Alamo Journal* 139 (December 2005).

———. "Crockett Goes to Texas: A Newspaper Chronology." *Journal of the Alamo Battlefield Association* 1, no. 1 (Summer 1995).

Zuber, W. P. "The Escape of Rose from the Alamo." *Texas Historical Association Quarterly* 5, no. 1 (July 1901).

———. "Notes and Fragments." Pts. 1–3. *Texas State Historical Association Quarterly* 5, no. 2–6, no. 1 (October 1901–July 1902).

THESES AND DISSERTATIONS

Adams, Allen. "The Leader of the Volunteer Grays: The Life of William G. Cooke, 1808–1847." Master's thesis, Southwest Texas State Teacher's College, 1939.

Alexander, Gladys. "Social Life in Texas, 1821–1836." Master's thesis, East Texas State Teacher's College, 1942.

Arpad, Joseph John. "David Crockett: An Original Legendary Eccentricity and Early American Character." PhD Diss., Duke University, 1968.

Filizola, Umberto Daniel. "Correspondence of Santa Anna During the Texas Campaign, 1835–1836." Master's thesis, University of Texas, 1939.

Garver, Lois Antoinette. "The Life of Benjamin Rush Milam." Master's thesis, University of Texas, 1931.

Mixon, Ruby. "William Barret Travis: His Life and Letters." Master's thesis, University of Texas, 1930.

Tolson, Marjorie Cain. "Gonzales, Birthplace of Texas Independence, 1825–1865." Master's thesis, University of Texas, 1966.

Turkovic, Robert J. "The Antecedents and Evolution of Santa Anna's Ill-Fated Texas Campaign, 1835–1836." Master's thesis, Florida Atlantic University, 1973.

Williams, Amelia. "The Siege and Fall of the Alamo." Master's thesis, University of Texas, 1926.

UNPUBLISHED MANUSCRIPTS

Andrassy, Richard, and Clyde Hagood Jr., MD. "Amos Pollard: Chief Surgeon of the Alamo." Pollard Vertical File, Daughters of the Republic of Texas Library, San Antonio, TX.

Baumgartner, Dorcas Huff. "History of the Alsey Silvanus Miller Homestead and Surrounding Area, 1700/1992." Gonzales County Records Center and Archives, Gonzales, TX.

Blake, R. B. "Rose and His Escape from the Alamo." Samuel Erson Asbury Papers, Cushing Memorial Library, Texas A&M University, College Station, TX.

Brierley, Ned F. "The Journal of Sergeant Santiago Rabia." Santiago Rabia Papers, Daughters of the Republic of Texas Library, San Antonio, TX.

Choquette, Clifford J. and Marcelle R. "Ashburnham to Alamo: Amos Pollard, M.D." Clifford J. Choquette Research Papers, Daughters of the Republic of Texas Library, San Antonio, TX.

Harrigan, Stephen. "The Last Days of David Crockett." Unpublished manuscript.

Hatch, James. "Lest We Forget the Heroes of the Alamo." James Hatch Papers, Dolph Briscoe Center for American History, University of Texas at Austin.

Henson, Margaret Swett. "List of Mexican Officers Killed or Captured at the Battle of San Jacinto, Plus Biographical Notes." Unpublished manuscript.

Ivey, James E. "Mission to Fortress: An Architectural History of the Alamo." Unpublished manuscript.

Jackson, Jack. "Week of Work at Archivo Historico of Secretaria de la Defensa Nacional, July 2000." Lindley Papers, Southwestern Writers Collection, Texas State University, San Marcos, TX.

Kailbourn, Tom. "Concordance Comparing Troop Assignments per Column in Alamo Assault." Unpublished manuscript.

Kuykendall, Jonathan Hampton. "Sketches of Early Texans." Kuykendall Papers, Dolph Briscoe Center for American History, University of Texas at Austin.

Lindley, Thomas Ricks. "True as Steel: Character and Destiny in the Texas Revolution." Lindley Papers, Southwestern Writers Collection, Texas State University, San Marcos, TX.

Shelby, Charmion. "Notes on the Mexican Army of Operations in Texas, 1835–1836." Charmion Shelby Papers, Dolph Briscoe Center for American History, University of Texas at Austin.

Walker, R. H., Jr. "Early Life in Gonzales." Vertical Files, Gonzales County Records Center and Archives, Gonzales, TX.
Wilkes, Chester. "The Andrew Kent Home." Unpublished manuscript.
———. "Mary Ann Kent Byas Chambers Morris." Unpublished manuscript.
Young, Kevin R. "Understanding the Mexican Army." Unpublished manuscript.

NEWSPAPERS
Dallas Morning News
Gonzales Inquirer
Houston Daily Post
The Lone Star (Washington on the Brazos)
El Mosquito Mexicano
New Orleans Bee
Niles' Register; The Weekly Register; Niles' National Register; Niles' Weekly Register
San Antonio Daily Express
San Antonio Light
Telegraph and Texas Register
Western Texian (San Antonio)

PERIODICALS
The Alamo Journal
Alamo Lore and Myth Organization
Journal of the Alamo Battlefield Association
The Texas Almanac

COLLECTIONS AND ARCHIVES
At the Nettie Lee Benson Latin American Collection, University of Texas at Austin
Antonio López de Santa Anna Papers, Genero García Collection
At the Dolph Briscoe Center for American History, University of Texas at Austin
Samuel Erson Asbury Papers
Eugene Campbell Barker Papers
Don Carlos Barrett Papers
Bexar Archives
Robert Bruce Blake Papers
John Henry Brown Papers
Adina Amelia de Zavala Papers
Burr H. Duval Papers
W. W. Fontaine Papers

John Salmon Ford Papers
Benjamin Cromwell Franklin Papers
George Pierce Garrison Papers
Hassell Family Papers
James Hatch Papers
Mary Austin Holley Papers
James Jackson Family Papers
John H. Jenkins Reminiscences
Francis White Johnson Papers
Louis Wiltz Kemp Papers
Jonathan Hampton Kuykendall Papers
Ira Randolph Lewis Papers
Walter Lord Archive
Ruby Mixon Papers
Ben Caldwell Prather Papers
Charmion Clair Shelby Papers
Julia Lee Sinks Papers
William Barret Travis Papers
Amelia Worthington Williams Papers
William Physick Zuber Papers

At the Cushing Memorial Library, Texas A&M University, College Station, TX
Samuel Erson Asbury Papers

At the DeGolyer Library, Southern Methodist University, Dallas
James DeShields Papers

At the Albert and Ethel Herzstein Library, San Jacinto Museum of History, La Porte, TX
Louis Wiltz Kemp Papers

At the Southwestern Writers Collection, Texas State University, San Marcos, TX
Thomas Ricks Lindley Papers

At the Texas State Library and Archives Commission, Austin
Harbert Davenport Collection

INDEX

INDEX

INDEX

Nacogdoches *(cont.)*
and El Camino Real, 33, 138;
establishment of, 26; and Houston,
70, 159, 324; and Nixon, 204; and
Ramírez y Sesma, 309; and Rose,
270, 348, 353, 356, 363, 374; and
Texas declaration of independence,
256
Napoleon I (emperor of the French):
and artillery strategy, 113–14; and
Louisiana, 27; as Santa Anna's
model, 40, 94, 125, 128, 133, 137,
138, 264, 334, 391n
Navarro, Angel, 102, 173, 403–04n
Navarro, Gertrudis, 102, 103, 212,
290–91
Navarro, José, 102
Neblett, William H., 368
Neblett, W. T., 368
Neill, George, 115, 179, 417–18n
Neill, Harriett, 115, 179
Neill, James C.: and Alamo garrison,
96, 97, 98–101, 102, 103–04, 108,
111, 113–14, 115, 165, 174–75, 178,
186, 227, 418n, 423n; and battle
of Béxar, 80, 88, 95; family
background of, 95–96; furlough to
Bastrop, 179–80, 259, 419n; and
Gonzales hostilities, 60; injuries
of, 329; and Twin Sisters, 323; and
volunteers for Alamo, 303
Neill, Mary, 179
Neill, Samuel, 115, 179, 417–18n
Neutral Ground, 27, 322
New Orleans Greys: and battle of
Béxar, 79, 88–89, 92, 97, 180, 251,
399n; clothing of, 72, 398n; and
defense of Alamo, 224, 296, 430n;
and Fannin, 315; and Texian
army, 72, 75
New Spain, 25–29
Nixon, George Anthony, 204

Old Three Hundred, 31, 103

Paine, Thomas, 22
Panic of 1819, 28–29
Patton, George, 157, 349
Patton, William, 108, 109, 111, 112,
115, 177, 227, 405–06n
Peace Party, 20
Pease, E. M., 354

Pedraza, Manuel Gómez, 122
Pennybacker, Anna, 355, 361
Pérez, Don Manuel, 291
Pizarro, Francisco, 25, 373
Pollard, Amos, 83, 111–12, 187, 243,
269, 423n
Ponton, Andrew, 195–96, 229, 349
Porter, Jane, 10, 373
Potter, Reuben, 419n, 426n, 442n,
443n, 444n, 454n
Potter, Robert, 397n
Presidio La Bahía, 64

*Quarterly of the Texas State Historical
Association,* 355

Ramírez y Sesma, Joaquín: and Alamo
siege, 3, 247, 262; and attack on
Alamo, 174, 266, 274, 282,
287–88, 416–17n, 424n, 444–45n,
449–50n; camp on Colorado
River, 321, 323, 325–26, 340; and
Cós, 128–29, 139; and drafting
recruits, 130; and march to
Béxar, 169, 170, 172, 193–94;
march to San Felipe, 309, 310,
326; and Santa Anna's
proclamation to Anglo colonists,
301–02, 456n; and Texas
campaign, 111, 140
Ramsdell, Charles W., 367
Reams, Sherwood Young, 399n
Republican Army of the North,
120–21, 203
Ridgway, William Alexander, 361
Robinson, James: and convention in
Washington, 214; and Fannin, 188,
223, 224, 225, 434n; and Houston,
111, 215; and Lott, 165, 414n; and
James Neill, 165, 178, 186
Rodríguez, Ambrosio, 185
Romero, José María, 262, 263, 265,
281, 288
Rose, Louis "Moses," 270–72, 347–48,
353–56, 358, 360, 361–74, 441n,
463–64n, 465n
Ruíz, Francisco Antonio, 294, 449n,
452n, 454n
Runaway Scrape, 307–08, 348

Saez, Antonio, 184–85, 422n
Salas, Mariano de, 262, 265

496

ABOUT THE AUTHOR

As a literary agent over the past nineteen years, James Donovan has sold several bestselling nonfiction titles; previous to that he was a buyer for a chain of bookstores and a trade book editor. He lives in Dallas with his wife, Judith, and his daughter, Rachel.

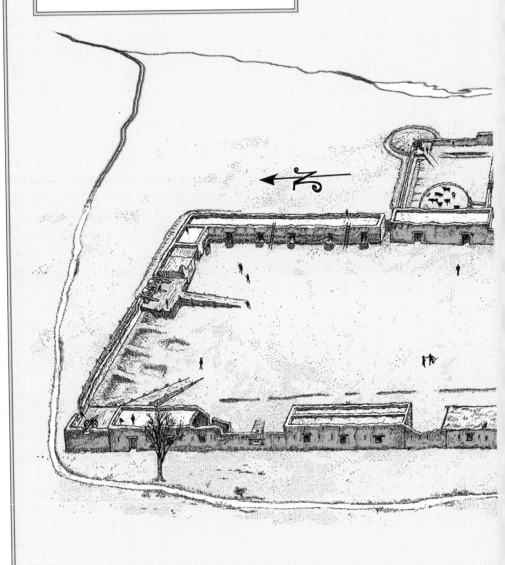

THE ALAMO
1836

JUL – 2013